NORTH–SOUTH AND SOU⌐

Also by Frances Stewart

ADJUSTMENT WITH A HUMAN FACE (*with Richard Jolly and G. A. Cornia*)
* ALTERNATIVE DEVELOPMENT STRATEGIES IN SUBSAHARAN AFRICA (*editor with Sanjaya Lall and Samuel Wangwe*)
ECONOMIC POLICIES AND AGRICULTURAL PERFORMANCE: The Case of Tanzania
EMPLOYMENT, INCOME DISTRIBUTION AND DEVELOPMENT (*editor*)
INTERNATIONAL COOPERATION: A Framework for Change (*with Arjun Sengupta*)
LINKAGES IN DEVELOPMENT: A Philippine Case Study (*with G. Ranis and E. Angeles-Reyes*)
MACRO-POLICIES FOR APPROPRIATE TECHNOLOGY (*editor*)
* PLANNING TO MEET BASIC NEEDS
* TECHNOLOGY AND UNDERDEVELOPMENT
THE ECONOMICS OF NEW TECHNOLOGY IN DEVELOPING COUNTRIES (*co-editor with Jeffrey James*)
THE OTHER POLICY: The Influence of Policies on Technology Choice and Small Business Development (*editor with H. Thomas and T. de Wilde*)
* THEORY AND REALITY IN DEVELOPMENT (*co-editor with Sanjaya Lall*)
* WORK, INCOME AND INEQUALITY: Payments Systems in the Third World (*editor*)

* *Also published by Macmillan*

North–South and South–South

Essays on International Economics

Frances Stewart

MACMILLAN

First published 1992

Published by
MACMILLAN ACADEMIC AND PROFESSIONAL LTD
Houndmills, Basingstoke, Hampshire RG21 2XS
and London
Companies and representatives
throughout the world

ISBN 0–333–49088–6 (hardcover)
ISBN 0–333–49089–4 (paperback)

A catalogue record for this book is available from the British Library

Printed in Hong Kong

To Kitty

Contents

PART IV   TECHNOLOGY TRANSFER

List of Figures

List of Tables

Acknowledgements

The author and publishers are grateful to the following journals/ publishers for permission to use (with some amendments) papers that were first published elsewhere:

Human Rights Quarterly (Chapter 3); Oxford University Press (Chapter 4); *Journal of International Studies* (Chapter 5); *World Development* (Chapters 6 and 11); *Third World Quarterly* (Chapter 9); *Trade and Development* (Chapter 10); *World Policy Journal* (Chapter 12); Westview Press (Chapter 13).

Chapter 8 was originally prepared for UNCTAD. The author would like to thank the United Nations for permission to reproduce it here.

Every effort has been made to contact all the copyright-holders, but if any have been inadvertently overlooked the publishers will be pleased to make the necessary arrangements at the earliest opportunity.

Part I
Relations Between
North and South

.

1 Introduction and Overview

INTRODUCTION

Underlying Themes

This book concerns the economic relations between North and South. The rules of the game and their interpretation, which govern North–South economic relations, have been developed almost exclusively by Northern decision-makers, from a Northern perspective. This is also true of the main corpus of economic theory which is advanced to justify these rules.

The main objective of these essays is to improve our understanding of both the rules and the underlying theory, taking a more balanced perspective with prime emphasis on Southern needs. The aim is to see what changes in the system might be justified from this perspective and, more practically, how such changes might be put into effect.

Although the essays cover a wide range of issues, there are some common threads: the first is the hypothesis that understanding decisions concerning international economic relations involves analysis of the interests and power of the main actors involved. Failure to comprehend these operational interests has been a prime factor responsible for lack of achievement in North–South negotiations, and for the ineffectiveness of Southern negotiating positions. Incorporating such interests into analysis leads to a different and more effective strategy for the South. This theme is expanded in Chapter 2; the ways in which interests influence North–South relations is developed in more detail in the specific context of debt in Chapter 11.

This approach to international economic relations is based on a 'political economy' view of decision-making at an international level, parallel to the type of political economy approach necessary for understanding national economic decisions.[1]

The second perspective adopted throughout the book is that a prime criterion for assessing international arrangements should be their impact on incomes and basic needs (BN) fulfilment of poor people. Other criteria, which are obviously important to the various actors – such as financial stability, economic growth, and adjustment – are for the most part regarded as *instrumental*, being generally necessary but rarely sufficient to achieve the BN objective.

A basic assumption of the essays is that *explicit consideration* of the impact of policy on the poor needs to be built into theory and policy design from the start. It cannot be assumed – as most theory and policy design tends to do – that benevolent governments will look after the poor by redistributional mechanisms, after the event. In most cases, the primary income distribution – i.e., that arising from the workings of the economic system, nationally and internationally – is not significantly changed by redistributive efforts at the secondary level. Consequently, the effects of any policies on the poor depend to a very large extent on their effects on primary income distribution.

Explicit focus on the needs of the poor is therefore necessary in the design of policy. While this alone will not ensure that such policies are undertaken, it is a necessary first stage. The next stage is to explore the political economy – internationally and domestically – of reorienting policies towards improvement of BN achievement.

The question of how the international system can contribute to improving BN performance is considered most explicitly in Chapter 3. The chapter assesses how far the international Human Rights Conventions, adopted under UN auspices, can contribute to increasing BN fulfilment.

Chapters on trade, finance, adjustment and technology also consider the implications of theories and policies for poverty and BN performance. They suggest that BN aspects have mostly been neglected in formation of theories and policies. While BN satisfaction progressed, nonetheless, in the 1960s and the 1970s, in the 1980s the neglect in conditionality and adjustment has had highly adverse effects. As a result of neglect of the human consequences of international economic decisions, rates of malnutrition, infant mortality and educational deficiencies have risen in many countries and in many others their long-term progress has been halted. Evidence for deterioration in BN achievements is provided by Cornia *et al.* (1987) and is briefly summarised in Chapter 12.

A third thread running through much of the book is the potential importance of South–South economic and political relations. Closer South–South ties, it is argued, are helpful both for improving the negotiating position of the South with the North, and for increasing welfare of the South, especially in relation to more appropriate products and technologies, and consequently better fulfilment of BN.

The South–South theme comes up in relation to the general nego-tiating stance of the South (Chapter 2); debt negotiations (Chapter 11); trading patterns (Chapter 4); mechanisms for achieving greater South–South cooperation in trade and finance (Chapters 9 and 10); and technology transfer (Chapters 13 and 14).

A Brief Summary of the Main Arguments

Part I is devoted to broad approaches to North–South relations.

Chapter 2 contains a general analysis of North–South relations. Despite an apparent consensus on the need for various reforms (e.g., more resource flows to the South, better access for trade), almost no progress has been made. Chapter 2 argues that this is because the appeal for reforms is justified with reference either to morality or to general mutual interests, neither of which are effective in bringing about action where there are conflicts with powerful particular interests. A clear example is provided by international trade: since decisions are made at a national level, subject to domestic pressures, the general and mutual interest in freer trade is often not translated into action. In contrast, on debt, where powerful banking interests are threatened, much more action has been taken.

Four strategies for the South are possible: first to continue to push for general reforms, but in the past this approach has achieved little. Secondly, in recognition of this the South could – as it did in the 1980s – reduce its demands to a more realistic level, but recent develop-ments suggest that the North will then seize the opportunity to improve its position (e.g., with demands for inclusion of services in the GATT). Thirdly, countries may focus on internal policies, trying to maximise gains from the existing rules and possibilities. This has been very successful for some countries (e.g., in East Asia). Fourthly, countries may develop the concept of *operational* interests in order to improve their bargaining power. For example, the South may use their power as buyers, as debtors, in relation to technology transfer. While the gains may be uneven, considerable potential exists for powerful bargaining among groups of countries. If the world moves further from openness and multilateralism, the poten-tial gains for Southern countries from using their bargaining power will become greater, as will the losses from not doing so.

The issue considered in Chapter 3 is how far the human rights approach – as recognised in the International Covenant on Economic and Social Rights of 1966 and the Declaration on the Right to

Development in 1986 – can be effective in promoting BN achievements. A preliminary requirement is for greater understanding,
among lawyers and officials trying to enforce these human rights, of
mechanisms necessary to improve BN achievements. In addition, for
such human rights to be upheld, much more effective monitoring and
enforcement mechanisms are needed. It is suggested that the international financial institutions – notably the IMF and the World Bank
– should use their leverage to help in both monitoring and enforcement.

The essays in Part II discuss trade issues. Each is concerned with
the validity of the orthodox position, and the legitimacy of alternative, more interventionist, policy stances.

Over the 1980s, a consensus has developed on optimal trade policy
for developing countries. The interventionist and protectionist policies widely introduced in earlier decades were rejected in favour of a
broadly non-interventionist policy stance, with at most mild and even
protection. From the path-breaking work of Little, Scitovsky and
Scott (1970) it has been argued that from a theoretical point of view a
free trade policy promises higher welfare, while in practice more
export-oriented policies have been associated with higher growth and
more rapid adjustment to vicissitudes.[2] The theoretical underpinning
of this position is the Heckscher–Ohlin (H–O) model of international
trade, showing that, under certain assumptions, welfare is maximised
with a free trade policy.

Chapter 4 reviews some 'recent' theories of international trade,
considering their implications for the South. The theories considered
each relax one or more of the assumptions made in the H–O theory.
Distinguishing features of Southern economies, which require special
analysis, are low *per capita* incomes; capital and (normally) skill
scarcity; relatively small size of market; limited industrial experience;
and technological laggardness, with most countries being (mainly)
importers not initiators of technological change. The 'recent' theories
emphasise the relevance of demand in determining trade patterns;
the importance of economies of scale and product differentiation;
and the importance of learning economies and technological change.
The theories do not downgrade the role of trade – indeed, rather the
reverse since economies of scale increase the productivity-raising
effects of international trade. For the South, the theories lend support from two points of view for efforts to promote South–South
trade. In the first place, such trade permits countries to exploit both
inter- and intra-industry economies of scale, while providing their

industries with some protection against Northern competition, which is necessary for industrial development given the significance of economies of scale and learning economies. Secondly, demand similarity among Southern countries should lead to trade in appropriate products and technology, permitting a more appropriate direction of technological change than that emanating from the North.

A major conclusion of Chapter 4 is that the 'recent' trade theories have considerable relevance for the South. This is in contradiction to the conclusions of Krugman and Srinivasan who argue that while the theories may justify a more interventionist policy stance in the North they do not do so for the South.[3] The difference partly stems from a difference in views about the capacity of Southern governments to make welfare-improving interventions. Moreover, Krugman and Srinivasan also analyse 'strategic' theories which are not discussed in Chapter 4. These 'new new theories', concerned with large companies playing strategic games, are reviewed in Chapter 5. The conclusions of Chapter 5 largely agree with those of Krugman and Srinivasan: for the most part, the developing countries are not large enough, nor technologically advanced enough, to have a comparative advantage in this type of industry. If they did promote such strategic industries, they would use substantial resources, probably without commensurate gains, and would also distort their choice of technique and product in an inappropriate direction. Nonetheless, strategic theories may be of some relevance to Third World countries in two respects: first, in understanding (and perhaps countering) the 'games' the advanced countries are playing, by tax and trade policy; and secondly, in promoting a few special products – e.g., motor cycles – where it may be appropriate that a developing country dominates world markets.

The existence of significant externalities is one important and well acknowledged reason for departure from non-interventionist industrial and trade policies. Chapter 6 is devoted to assessing the significance of externalities in developing countries and providing an analytic taxonomy, with some illustrative evidence on the magnitude of externalities. Assessment of the significance of externalities has gone in waves over the decades: such authors as Rosenstein-Rodan (1943) and Hirschman (1958) justified a big push, or imbalanced growth, to set off the development cycle, based on the assumption of very large pecuniary externalities. In contrast, some (e.g., Mishan, 1971; Newbery, 1980) have concluded that pecuniary externalities do not constitute genuine externalities, while others (e.g., Corden,

1974; Little and Mirrlees, 1974) have suggested that real externalities are insignificant. Moreover, Coase (1960) has argued that agents will deal with externalities by direct negotiations, without the need for government intervention. The review in Chapter 6 distinguishes between static and dynamic externalities, and argues that dynamic externalities – consisting of the non-market transmission of technological innovations from one agent to another – are of major significance. Moreover, these interact with pecuniary externalities to create a cumulative growth cycle. The examples of the development of semiconductors in the USA and of agroindustrial development in the Punjab provide empirical support for this view. Where many agents are involved, they cannot be expected to deal with externalities through direct negotiations, because of high transaction costs. Government intervention may consequently be called for in support of industries with high externalities. Such intervention, however, is not necessarily a question of trade policy – indeed, industrial policy is generally preferable, the most appropriate type of intervention depending on the situation and on the political possibilities.

Countertrade arrangements formed a major departure from non-interventionism, which was of growing importance in the late 1970s and early 1980s but has lessened somewhat in recent years. Chapter 7 reviews the role of countertrade. It is suggested that countertrade occurs only where there are imperfections in the international trade or monetary situation – e.g., quotas on exports or imports; lack of foreign currency for imports; etc. It is thus incorrect to assess countertrade as an alternative to a policy of free trade, as is normally done, because this is *not* the alternative. While a comparison with free trade policy usually shows countertrade to be inferior, comparisons with the actual *n*th-best alternative often indicates that countertrade performs a useful role. For example, countertrade can enable debt-ridden countries to enjoy higher levels of imports, exports and output, since they can trade between themselves without use of hard currency. Or, where countries do not wish to devalue across the board, countertrade can permit partial devaluation. The view that countertrade helps countries to make the best of a poor environment is supported by the fact that the extent of countertrade deals increased with the deflation and restrictions of the early 1980s. Nonetheless, countertrade has some important negative effects – it tends to be associated with defence contracts and with other large and capital-intensive items, and rarely covers BN items. A switch to countertrade is likely to lead to more inappropriate technology and products; because of the heavy government intervention involved, it also lends itself to corruption. Where the deals are North–South, the developing country partners may suffer poor terms of trade, compared with arm's-length transactions. Moreover, such planned bilateral deals may be less efficient than the market system in terms of resource allocation. However, a blanket condemnation, such as has been voiced by the IMF or the GATT, is not appropriate in an imperfect world.

In the current round of GATT negotiations, the developed countries have been leading an attack on Article XVIIIb, which permits the developing countries to impose quantitative restrictions on imports (QRS) to ensure adequate reserves for the implementation of development programmes. Article XVIIIb was introduced in 1957 in recognition of the structural and persistent nature of balance of payments (BoP) problems in developing countries. The case for and against abolition of Article XVIIIb is reviewed in Chapter 8. The developed countries have argued that changes in the international monetary system have eliminated the need for the Article; Chapter 8 argues that these changes have not reduced but rather increased the need for resources among LDCs, while their BoP problems remain as structural and persistent as before. Consequently, the need for special measures to protect the BoP of developing countries remains as acute as when Article XVIIIb was first introduced. While, in some circumstances, the BoP is best tackled by policies towards the macro-balance of the economy, not by trade measures, reliance solely on macro-measures can lead to deflation and falling incomes, as in many countries in the 1980s. The evidence shows that alternative trade measures – such as devaluation and tariffs – are often ineffective, especially in the short term. There remains, therefore, an important role for QRS as a short-term measure. However, more effective surveillance of Article XVIIIb is needed to prevent its over-use, especially over the medium term, when other measures (e.g., exchange rate changes) might be better.

The five chapters on trade in Part II suggest serious qualifications to the orthodox free trade non-interventionist position. Similar conclusions have been reached by others, examining different issues; e.g. Pack and Westphal's work on learning by doing, economies of scale and S. Korea's trade policies (1986), which provides a powerful case for infant-industry protection or promotion; Wade's evidence of effective trade and industrial intervention in both Taiwan and S. Korea (1988); and Rodrik's exposé of the weakness of the theoretical connection between free trade and dynamic efficiency (1988). Neither theoretical arguments nor empirical evidence (see Evans's, 1990, critique of the postulated empirical connection between free trade and growth)[4] give unqualified support to the dominant conventional view.

The essays in Part III cover issues of international finance and adjustment. Chapter 9 reviews the international monetary system from a Third World perspective, suggesting that most current arrangements have been designed on North–South lines, as the neo-colonial replacement of colonial monetary arrangements. It puts forward a case for new South–South monetary arrangements to promote South–South trade, to increase Southern control over monetary arrangements and to improve the Southern bargaining position in negotiations. New Southern arrangements are proposed in four areas: a Southern currency or payments union to facilitate South–South trade; the use of commodities as foreign exchange reserves, providing the South with more control over credit creation and strengthening commodity prices; developing a Southern IMF to provide mutual balance of payments support and 'Southern' conditionality within the Third World; and a South Bank to provide finance within the South for a variety of functions. While the new arrangements would not replace North–South arrangements, they would reduce dependence on the North, diversifying financial support for short- and medium-term needs, with positive effects in themselves and also for the workings of North–South arrangements (for example, the existence of alternative BoP financial support and policy dialogue would be likely to reduce the rigidity of IMF policy requirements). The major difficulty with most of the proposals is the generalised foreign exchange shortages in the South, with many countries needing support simultaneously. Whether such arrangements would be effective would largely depend on whether the stronger countries in the South (e.g., currently S. Korea and Taiwan) would be prepared to cooperate.

Chapter 10 explores one of the proposals in greater depth – the proposal for a Southern currency, termed Rocnabs. Chapter 10 argues that such a currency would permit higher levels of trade within the South, offering benefits both for countries seeking finance and countries seeking markets.

Chapter 11 considers the interests and bargaining positions – adopting the perspective put forward in Chapter 2 – associated with the debt problem. The emergence of a negative basic transfer, caused by reduced inflows of new money and higher interest rates, is critical to bargaining strategies. So long as the basic transfer is negative and can be expected to continue to be so (i.e., overall outflows exceed inflows of finance) countries are in a strong bargaining position, since default would improve their financial position. Solutions to the debt problem may be divided into three: default (i.e., unilateral action taken by borrowing countries, which may be overt or implicit); full or partial rescheduling, which is agreed by creditors (commercial banks and Northern governments); and debt reduction (also agreed). Of critical importance is whether schemes increase or reduce the net present value of the debt burden (NPVD), and whether they involve a negative or positive net basic transfer over the medium term. Satisfactory schemes from a Southern perspective will reduce the NPVD and lead to a positive transfer. Otherwise, they increase the debt burden, and maintain a borrowing country interest in default. From this perspective, rescheduling is unsatisfactory since it normally raises the NPVD, while leading only to a temporary improvement in the basic balance, followed by a reversal. Debt reduction could achieve a lasting solution to the debt crisis – (a) by reducing the NPVD; (b) leading to a positive transfer; (c) without intolerable cost in terms of growth of incomes. However, in practice, the net debt reduction schemes introduced have not been on a sufficient scale for the affected countries, nor have they extended to enough countries to constitute such a solution, so the debt crisis continues to be endemic.

Chapter 12 assesses the role of the IMF in recent years. The IMF has played a dominant role in macro-policy-making in the majority of developing countries in the 1980s. The Bretton Woods institutions were conceived as Keynesian – the international counterpart to the Keynesian domestic revolution – with the objective of sustaining world trade, output, and employment. But in practice in the 1980s, the IMF was anti-Keynesian: its focus on deficit countries and emphasis on deflation in a large number of developing countries imparted a major deflationary bias at a world level. For individual countries, IMF conditionality has usually been associated with falling *per capita* incomes and investment, deteriorating social services, and often rising rates of malnutrition and illiteracy and worsening health conditions. Undoubtedly, the world environment, including the debt situation and major economic imbalances, has been mainly responsible, but the IMF has not succeeded in protecting countries from such adverse developments. Chapter 12 concludes that there is a need for Keynesian alternatives both at a world and at a country level. At a world level, there is need for more emphasis on sustaining world output, with more focus on adjustment by surplus countries and on the adequacy of world liquidity and financial flows. At a country level, there is a need for adjustment with a human face – i.e., policies which combine adjustment, economic growth and protection of the vulnerable.[5]

One of the most important ways in which the North impinges on the South is through technology transfer (TT). Chapters 13 and 14 in Part IV deal with aspects of TT. Chapter 13 provides an overview of how TT affects development and of alternative policy options. The nature of technology is such that the market *cannot* give the correct signals, since technology has many of the characteristics of a public good, being costly to produce but, once produced, having very low marginal cost. Consequently, the state *has* to intervene to secure adequate R and D and technology development, either by direct financing, or by creating private monopolies, through the legal system of patents, etc.

Despite growing R and D in developing countries, in most industries the market for technology remains largely dominated by the North, often by a few large companies. Even where the technology is not transferred directly through multinational company (MNC) investment, but in a more arm's length way through joint ventures and licensing, the sources usually remain the same Northern companies. The dominance of TT by the North has consequences for the characteristics of the technology transferred, and for its cost. Technology change broadly follows the trajectory dictated by Northern conditions, and is as a consequence often inappropriate for the South.

The cost of TT is high: it is estimated that LDCs spend around $6–7 billion annually on TT. Effective TT requires active technological efforts on the part of the recipients. On balance it seems that MNC transfer is high cost and has limited learning effects. More arm's length transactions permit a more selective import of technology, lower costs of transfer and more positive local learning effects. Policies towards TT include direct regulations; policies to build up technological capability; and general policies to improve economic decision-making and choice of technology. Evidence shows that direct regulation can considerably improve the terms of TT without reducing the inflow. Policies to build up local technological capability are essential for improved and more efficient use of imported technologies. However, general policies towards competition, prices and credit are most important for determining the choice of technology and the direction of technology change.

Chapter 14 discusses the impact of technical change in the North on the South in more depth, considering policy options for the South. Theoretical discussion has tended to focus largely on issues of choice of technique rather than technical change. But the latter is more important since it often renders existing choices obsolete. To understand the impact of technology change (TC) it is essential to take a multidimensional view of the characteristics of a technology, including not only capital and labour requirements, but skills, scale of production, energy, raw material use and product attributes. TC may alter any or all of these characteristics. From a theoretical perspective, TC in the North may be expected to be often (but not always) output-raising in the South. But it can also have distorting effects because of the different socioeconomic circumstances in Northern economies, reducing labour requirements for a given capital expenditure, increasing scale, skill requirements and infrastructural needs, and changing product attributes in a direction which may hurt poor consumers. New technologies from the North are thus neither universally good for the South – as argued, for example, by Emmanuel (1982) – nor universally bad. A selective policy towards TT is therefore desirable, supported by policies promoting the development of domestic technology and the import of technology from other Third World countries with more appropriate characteristics.

SOME CONCLUSIONS

Many of those who comment upon and influence North–South relations share a common paradigm or understanding of the workings of the economic system, and consequently of desirable policies. The paradigm can broadly be described as neoclassical and monetarist: prime emphasis is placed on monetary aggregates for controlling the macro-economy, and on the unfettered price system for resource allocation. With minor qualifications, the view is adhered to by most Western economists, and by those determining the policies of the powerful international financial institutions – notably the IMF and the World Bank. The policies developing country governments are required to adopt in return for financial support are derived from this paradigm: they include strict monetary targets; price decontrol;

import liberalisation; devaluation; privatisation; and the encouragement of multinational investment. In general, government regulation
of any kind is disapproved of, partly because the paradigm suggests
that it leads to inferior resource allocation, and partly because
governments are not regarded as trustworthy – in general, it is
believed that they are likely to make matters worse, not better.

The expanding influence of the IMF and World Bank over policy-
making that occurred in the 1980s, as more and more countries
encountered financial difficulties and needed their support, has made
this paradigm increasingly powerful in determining policy.

The essays in this book have one feature in common: they each
question the universal validity of the paradigm; and find justification
for departures from the laissez-faire policy prescriptions currently so
widely advocated:

- on trade and industrial policy, the existence of economies of scale,
  learning economies and externalities is shown to justify an interventionist policy stance;
- on technology transfer, imperfections in the market for technology, the importance of the build up of development capability and
  the need for appropriate technology justifies regulation of the
  terms of TT, limits on the role of MNCs and the encouragement of
  local and South–South R and D efforts;
- on adjustment, the focus on macro-monetary aggregates has led to
  rising hardship for the most vulnerable, and cuts in human and
  physical capital undermining future growth potential; the paradig-
  matic packages of the Fund and Bank have also proved politically
  unsustainable;
- on debt, 'business as usual' has proved unworkable, and the
  country-by-country approach has postponed a debt-crunch at a
  heavy cost in terms of economic growth and human suffering,
  without producing a lasting solution.

The dominant paradigm has thus been shown to have severe
deficiencies, both theoretical and in terms of practical results. That it
nonetheless persists can be explained only with reference to the
powerful interests – mainly, but not exclusively, in the North – which
it continues to serve. If more benign alternatives are to be devised, it
is necessary to uncover the theoretical and practical defects of the
paradigm, to develop practical and efficient alternatives, and to
recognise and counter the political and economic motivation which

underlies the debate. What makes this task especially difficult – as is apparent from many of the essays – is that for the most part the paradigm should not be rejected wholesale: on most issues, there are elements of the paradigm and its policy conclusions which contain important and useful insights. A selective approach is needed – which requires more careful analysis and political skill than the more tempting options of 100 per cent acceptance or rejection.

NOTES

1. See e.g., Stewart (1987) for an example of application of this approach to domestic issues.
2. See Little, Scitovsky and Scott (1970); Balassa (1971 and 1975); Krueger (1978, 84); Bhagwati (1978); World Bank (1978 and *World Development Reports*, various years).
3. See Krugman (1989); Srinivasan (1989).
4. Singer and Gray (1988) also show that the relationship between growth and trade is complex and the direction of causality unclear.
5. See Cornia *et al.* (1987) for more in-depth discussion of this topic.

2 Alternative Approaches to North–South Negotiations*

Over the last forty years, growing attention has been paid to North–South issues. At a political level this was a natural development following many Third World countries' independence, and their increasing recognition of the gap in *per capita* incomes between North and South. While this gap may not have widened in relative terms, it has certainly widened in absolute terms over this period. The questions at issue relate to the 'rules' of the game – whether these are biased, how they might be reformed, and how best to operate within them. Despite much talk, there has been very little progress in terms of changing the rules. This essay is concerned to analyse why this is so, and within the perspective this analysis gives, to make suggestions for more fruitful approaches to North–South negotiations.

PROPOSALS FOR REFORM

There has been rather remarkable agreement on the content of proposals to reform the international economic system so as to improve the development prospects of the Third World. Thus the proposals for reform for the UN Development Decades were similar to those launched by the Group of 77 (G77) in their claims for a 'New International Economic Order' (NIEO). These proposals in turn contain the same main elements as those advocated by the two Reports of the Brandt Commission. Despite the consensus among those concerned with development at an international level, and despite the fact that most of the main proposals have been around now for quite a time, there has been almost no progress in realising the changes. The document on an International Development Strategy for the Third United Nations Development Decade began

---

* Revised version of a paper prepared for the Committee on Development Planning (December 1983); first published in Lall and Stewart (1986).

16

with the statement that, 'The goals and objectives of the International Development Strategy for the Second Decade remain largely unfulfilled' (para. 3).

The main elements of the reform proposed by the G77, the Brandt Commission and the United Nations for the Development Decades are:

1. A substantial increase in concessional resource flows from North to South towards (and beyond) the achievement of the 0.7 per cent target.
2. Enlarged flows of non-concessional (private) finance.
3. The restructuring of debt and some debt relief among poor countries.
4. Improved access for exports of LDCs to the markets of developed countries, including both manufactured and primary products.
5. The stabilisation of commodity prices through the Common Fund and the Integrated Programme for Commodities.
6. The reform of the International Financial System so as to increase the participation of LDCs in decision-making; to increase the role of SDRs; to reform IMF conditionality.
7. Improvements in the behaviour of multinational companies through a Code of Conduct.
8. Other proposals, including policies towards the development of energy; towards population; towards food security; and towards arms reduction.
9. Recent reports, notably the International Development Strategy for the Third Decade and the Brandt Commission, have stressed the mutual need for sustained growth – in the North to increase markets for Southern goods, and in the South to increase markets for Northern products.

These proposals have been justified in two ways. It has been argued that they are necessary to promote development in the Third World and therefore they have a *moral* justification for those concerned with development. However, this argument has been challenged from two points of view. First, it has been contended that some (at least) of the changes are not necessary to promote development and may indeed actually impede it. (See, for example, the debate about aid.) Secondly, it has been argued that development can only impose a moral obligation if the fruits of growth are going to the most deprived. Since many of the proposals would, at least in the first instance, help governments of LDCs, or middle-income groups, rather than the deprived, it is suggested that there can be no moral case for the proposed changes (see Lal, 1983, and Seers, 1983). The second way that the proposals have been justified is by appealing to mutual interests. It is argued that interdependence between North and South is such that both have *mutual interests* in the proposals. For example, free trade should increase incomes in both North and South as resources move to more efficient uses; commodity price stabilisation, it is suggested, will help consumers of commodities as well as producers; acceptance of the Code of Conduct for MNCs would increase the stability of the environment for MNCs and thus help both North and South; and so on.

The International Development Strategy for the Third Decade exemplified the two types of justification. On the one hand, it pointed out the moral obligation: 'The stark reality confronting mankind today is that close to 850 million people in the developing world are living at the margin of existence'. On the other, it points to mutual interests, arguing that 'in an interdependent world economy, these problems [i.e., slow growth, high inflation and high unemployment in the North, prolonged monetary instability, structural problems and maladjustment] cannot be solved without resolving the particular problems facing the developing countries . . . accelerated development of developing countries is of vital importance for the steady growth of the world economy and essential for peace and stability'.

Despite the two justifications, few of the proposed changes have been made. When the NIEO was launched it was believed that major changes were possible. Since then aid has remained stagnant, protectionist pressures in the North have accumulated, and there has been no relaxation in restrictions; almost negligible resources were contributed to the Common Fund. A little progress has been made in negotiating a Code of Conduct for MNCs, but it is on a voluntary basis and few believe it will have much impact. Every assessment that has been made of recent North–South negotiations comes to the same conclusion: 'In recent years, international fora have yielded little or uncertain results', while the world economy has presented an increasingly hostile environment for developing countries.[1] Given this failure, it is clear that the two justifications put forward for the reforms have not been sufficient to produce action. It has been apparent for a long time – since Adam, indeed – that moral reasons are often ineffective by themselves. Recognition of this was behind the appeal to mutual interests, to supplement the moral appeal, which was made in the 1970s. Appeal to interests ought to be more effective since the reason the impact of altruistic appeals on action is limited is that self-interest is the more effective engine of action. Despite this, the appeal to interests also proved ineffective. This can hardly be due to an upsurge of altruism, since if it were, the moral justification would have become operative. Rather it was due to a mistaken identification and analysis of interests. This mistaken identification and analysis of interests is, in my view, at the heart of the failure of past efforts for reform. Correct identification offers the potential for securing change more effectively.

The mutual interests identified in discussion of proposals for reform are at an *aggregate, general and international level*. But operational interests – that is interests which are sufficiently powerful to produce changes – tend to be *specific* and *national*.

In many of the areas of reform there is an apparent general interest in reform. But there are three reasons why this general interest does not lead to specific political action. First, the gainers are often rather diffuse and poorly organised, in political terms, while the losers are specific, well organised groups. Secondly, the gains may be potential and uncertain, while the losses are immediate and certain. Thirdly, the gains may be unevenly distributed among nations, with some nations suffering a disproportionate share of the losses while others gain disproportionately.

The case for freer trade in manufactures provides an example where each of these reasons apply. There is a strong case that can be made, at a general level, that both North and South would gain if the North allowed free access to their markets to Southern manufacturers. Consumers in the North would gain from the cheaper goods they could buy. Output in the North should increase as resources were more efficiently deployed producing goods in which the North has a comparative advantage. Since in aggregate the South buys more from the North than it sells to it, it is likely that any increase in total imports from the South would be more than offset by extra sales of exports. But this general interest is not reflected in specific and politically operational interests.

In the first place, the gainers from freer trade would be consumers, who generally have little influence over policy because they are poorly organised. In any case, the gains, for each individual consumer, are likely to be quite small and hardly worth defending. In contrast the producers who would lose are normally specific groups of owners, managers and workers who are well organised and present a powerful lobby. Physical capital, in which the owners of the firms involved have invested, will be rendered obsolete, as will the human capital of the workers. The workers may not find alternative occupations – especially where there is high unemployment. They may have to move or to retrain, or both. Hence the general interest of the consumers (which is normally weakly represented) will be powerfully opposed by the particular interest of the producers. While other groups of producer should gain – for example, sellers of machinery to the Third World – their gain is normally not sufficiently certain for them to provide an opposing lobby in favour of free trade. Moreover, since the gains are *potential*, many of those who would gain may not themselves be cognisant of the gains and not in a position to argue for them (for example, people who would be employed in new export industries).

Thus even if there were net gains to a particular nation in the North from freer trade, it might oppose it because of the losses of particular powerful groups. In addition, since the North is composed of a number of nations, although there may be net gains for the North as a whole, there may be net losses for particular countries, and these losses may be of decisive significance in decision-making. For example, suppose the UK liberalised its textile imports, this might increase sales of machinery to the South, but the bulk of orders for that machinery might not go to the UK but to such nations as West Germany and Japan. To the extent that decision-making takes place at the national level, the UK will consider the interests of its producers, not those of other Northern nations, and would therefore not approve trade liberalisation. Hence while there is an apparent mutual interest in free trade for North and South, the interest is at a general international level, and not one at the operational level.

Policy-making is thus normally most influenced by pressures from groups that are specific and national. There are occasional exceptions, when some type of general interest is given precedence over particular interests. But in these cases the gains to the general interest need to be very obvious and certain. With the internationalisation of some powerful interest groups (for example, MNCs, arms manufacturers, large retailers), international interest groups may become critical in determining national action. The internationalisation of decision-making – for example, in the EC – may also give more weight to international concerns, but even here national interests remain of major significance, and where they seem to be threatened nations normally retain the power to take action of their own. In the past, there have been occasions of major trade liberalisation and of apparently imaginative and generous financial reforms, which might seem to contradict this rather pessimistic diagnosis. But, on closer examination, it invariably turns out that the more grandiose schemes were in the interests of powerful and specific groups.

An example is British trade liberalisation in the nineteenth century, starting with the repeal of the Corn Laws. The intellectual justification for this repeal had been developed by Smith and then Ricardo, but its realisation had to wait until the interests of the manufacturers in cheap food dominated those of agricultural interests in protection, and the shifting power of different interest groups had acquired political expression, through the Reform Act. Free trade in manufactures was clearly in the interests of British manufacturers in the nineteenth century. Protection was introduced in the twentieth century when the British had lost their competitive lead. The next wave of trade liberalisation – after the Second World War – reflected the dominance of the USA politically and economically and the interests of major multinational firms in the free movement of goods and of capital. The Marshall Plan which financed trade and capital liberalisation was in the clear interest of US firms who were thereby provided with markets. In each of these cases, there was a coincidence between particular interests and the 'mutual' interest, which made reforms politically realistic. This coincidence is absent in most elements of the proposals in the IDS, Brandt Reports, etc. as a quick review of some of the proposals makes clear.

Aid provides an example. Apart from some specific commercial and political interests, which do normally produce aid flows, as shown by the heavy receipts of aid (especially military aid) in politically sensitive areas, the case for a greater general flow of aid rests on the argument that the North will benefit both economically and politically from a more prosperous South. It is evident that such gains are diffuse and uncertain – even more so than in the case of freer trade. Hence the 'aid lobby' is not powerful. Multilateral aid directed at poor countries shows least direct connection between aid flows and economic returns, and consequently IDA is the most vulnerable type of aid. Arms control provides another example. The general interest in arms control is very clear. But the groups who gain from selling arms are specific and very powerful, while the gainers from arms control are again diffuse. Moreover, national limitations on arms supplies will not necessarily produce results since other nations may well supply arms if some hold back, so that nations who hold back are guaranteed loss of markets, but may gain nothing.

Commodity price stabilisation is a case where the potential gainers among consumers – within the North – are both uncertain and diffuse, and therefore the proposals are not likely to gain much effective support.

It is not difficult, then, to see why little progress has been made in North-South negotiations. In a few areas, some progress has been recorded, notably in the field of banking and finance and in some specific country negotiations. In each case, change can be seen as the outcome of pressures from powerful interests for whom gains and/or losses are obvious, specific and large. At a general level, the most obvious example is provided by the debt crisis.

It is apparent, in the current debt and banking crisis, that default is not just an option for some countries, but unavoidable unless the debt servicing burden is reduced and new international finance is found. Moreover, it is an option that would hurt some major banks more than individual countries. Apart from the general economic implications of default in major countries, the effects on particular banks (especially in the USA) would be catastrophic. It has been estimated that if Brazilian, Mexican and Korean debts had had to be written off in 1982 when the debt crisis 'broke' the capital and reserves of several major US banks involved in international lending would have been wiped out. Since the Mexican crisis of August 1982, the banking crisis has met with substantial response from the international community:

1. The BIS provided large amounts of short-run bridging finance, as has the US Treasury.
2. The IMF reached agreement with the main countries more rapidly and on terms which are considerably less tough than those offered to less powerful debtors.
3. The Fund helped to organise continued lending by the private banking community, which recognises that 'It does not appear to me to fly in the fact of reason to suggest that new lending, often with a tinge of doubt attached to it, may on occasions be the best way of protecting the quality of existing lending and ensuring its ultimate soundness' (Peter Cooke, head of banking supervision at the Bank of England, *Financial Times* Conference on World Banking 1983, December 1983).

4. IMF quotas were increased by 47.5 per cent in 1983 and by 50 per cent in 1990, despite considerable opposition in the US congress because this was recognised as primarily aimed at helping the banks, rather than countries (gaining support from the US administration for similar reasons).
5. After the failure of the Baker scheme to elicit significant increases in new lending to debtor countries, there is now acceptance of the need for 'orderly' debt reduction and this is beginning to be translated into some modest reality in some cases – e.g., debt relief in Mexico and Costa Rica following the Brady initiative.

ALTERNATIVE STRATEGIES

Thus analysis of the changes that have not been achieved, the bulk of those contained in the IDS, and of those that have, provides the same lesson: for effective change there must be support from particular interests; arguments based on the 'general' interest are not sufficient. This lesson needs to be at the forefront in choosing future strategies. At this stage, four alternative strategies may be distinguished.

First, to continue in a similar way to the past, to identify international reforms that would promote development, and to use every opportunity to put them forward. This strategy may produce some results from time to time, when there is a particular conjuncture of events in which there is a coincidence between the distribution of gains from change and powerful interests, and it may get further with political changes in the North. But in general it seems certain that the changes will be rather minimal; the proposed agenda for reform by bodies such as the Committee for Development Planning, the Brandt Commission and the G77, and the UN Development Decade targets – being continually advocated and never fulfilled – will be taken less and less seriously. Where changes are made, it is likely that they would have occurred without the fanfare of international demands, through the pressure of interests.

A *second* strategy which seems to be being followed in part now (for example, by the non-aligned and the Commonwealth Secretariat Group) is to redefine the agenda for reform to a more modest level, concentrating on a few areas only. This strategy will reduce the gap between aspirations and achievements, mainly by reducing aspirations. It does not seem likely to increase achievements much. Broadly, this seems to have been the approach adopted in the 1980s, which saw much less strident demands by Third World countries than in the previous decade. However, possibly because of this, the decade also saw demands for changes in the system coming from the North – for example, for reforms of the GATT to incorporate services.

A *third* strategy would be to place less emphasis on the international dimension and more on national policies, with each country trying to maximise its performance through internal efforts, regarding the international environment as 'given'. The most successful countries have in fact followed this strategy very effectively. Japan and S. Korea, for example, managed to exploit the existing rules of the game very successfully and made little effort to get them changed.

However, this leaves some countries (e.g., those dependent on a single commodity whose terms of trade fluctuate) in a very difficult position. Moreover, it may be that the external environment is becoming more hostile. However, if negotiations on the international strategy continue to be fruitless, this may be the best strategy to follow.

Focusing on making the best of the prevailing international environment is clearly sensible for particular countries, and would be compatible with simultaneously trying to secure reform of the international system. But in practice it is uncommon for countries to pursue both strategies together. Countries that are most successful within the existing framework rarely make much effort to change it, while countries that are active in pursuit of international reform often neglect domestic changes that would help exploit the existing environment. This fact could be one reason for the comparative failure of North–South negotiations, since the countries with the strongest bargaining position will generally be those which have most been successful economically, while those that are not successful usually have little to bargain with. The debt situation has somewhat changed things, since countries that had been doing very well out of the system and were making few efforts to change it have suddenly become major potential losers, therefore putting their weight behind reform for the first time and strengthening the bargaining position of the South.

The *fourth* strategy is to make use of the concept of operational interest in devising and pursuing international reform. While the reforms identified in the NIEO claims or the Brandt Commission Reports give the broad dimensions in which changes might be sought, specific proposals need to be devised which involve politically operational interests. By bargaining, countries or groups of countries can produce a link between interests and change. The general or mutual interests may thereby be made specific and operational. For example, instead of relying on the general arguments for freer market access, LDCs may link access to their own markets with access for their goods in Northern markets. This type of negotiating strategy has been pursued by a few countries, in some cases with considerable success:

1. A British quota on Indonesian textile exports led the Indonesian Government to cancel orders for textile machinery and aircraft. The British Trade Minister, John Nott said, 'The Indonesians have no right to retaliate in this way . . . But they did and it hurts'. The textile quota was raised by 181 per cent (quoted by Seers, 1983).
2. Malaysia boycotted British goods, partly to gain better treatment for her students in Britain. Concessions were made, and the boycott lifted.
3. The Chinese substantially reduced their grain purchases from the USA because of restrictions on textile imports and were threatening to reduce them further. When the USA agreed that it would not impose further restrictions, the Chinese agreed to make up the shortfall in grain purchases.[2]
4. Mrs Gandhi threatened to withhold major contracts from the British unless the British supported the sixth IDA replenishment. The British supported the IDA replenishment.
5. The ASEAN pact countries threatened trade sanctions against Australia unless Australia supported a UN resolution condemning the presence of Vietnamese troops in Kampuchea.
6. Ten countries boycotted Nestlé because of the company's contribution to infant malnutrition in the Third World. After six and a half years, the company agreed to four major changes, involving changed labelling, the distribution of warning literature, the end of expensive gifts to doctors and limiting supplies to hospitals. The boycott was called off, but the boycotting countries agreed to continue to monitor the situation. The boycott was estimated to have cost Nestlé $40 million.[3]

Given the repeated failure of the previous negotiating strategy, it seems that there is not much point in continuing on that tack. The lessons, positive and negative, of the past twenty years suggest the two last alternatives would seem to offer most: to concentrate on internal reforms which enable countries to maximise their benefits from the given international environment and to negotiate changes by bargaining, through threats (or offers of gains) to specific interests in the North. The rest of this chapter will further examine the potential of the last strategy.

An obvious objection to the bargaining approach is that it is liable to introduce all sorts of 'distortions' into international trade and payments. Whereas the International Development Strategy and Brandt Commission approach involves general rules and multilateral negotiations, this approach is likely to lead to specific rules and exemptions, working through bilateral negotiations.

How seriously this objection should be taken depends on what one is comparing with what. To the extent that the present world is an nth best one, riddled with imperfections, and that reform is unlikely, the suggested approach need not make matters worse in this respect, and may even make them better. For example, in reaction to the foreign exchange crisis of the early 1980s, together with depressed markets for their exports, a number of countries negotiated barter deals (known as *countertrade*). Whereas in 1976 an estimated 2 per cent of world trade was countertrade, in 1982 it was estimated to account for about 30 per cent of world trade.[4] In a multilateral, full employment, free trade world, this would be likely in most circumstances, to reduce welfare. But in the early 1980s it permitted a higher level of trade, output and employment than otherwise possible.

A further objection is that the approach could lead to a series of beggar-thy-neighbour actions – a form of escalating economic war between North and South in which ultimately neither side gains. Whether this is so or not depends on the issues at stake, the negotiating stance adopted and the subsequent reactions from each side. The examples given above did not lead to that outcome, but rather an outcome in which most groups could reasonably be argued to have gained. Moreover, while the world may, in some sense, be a net loser,[5] some parties may gain. This would probably be a reasonable assessment of the OPEC action of the 1970s where despite the major losses for many parts of the world, the OPEC countries gained, and would presumably repeat their actions if given the opportunity.

The approach would be likely to enhance the gains of those countries with the strongest bargaining power, and this could be at the expense of the weaker countries. The debt situation provides an example. It is likely that use of the 'debt weapon' will lead to more generous financial treatment of the major debtors (e.g., more financial flows and/or reduced interest rates, and/or some debt write-down). But this may be associated with lesser flows of finance to the poorer but less indebted countries. This need not be the case; the more generous treatment of major debtors could, in principle, also lead to more generous treatment of the poor countries. The actual outcome will depend on whether the major debtor countries have serious concern for the poorer countries, and whether the developed countries wish, or the international agencies are able, to protect their interests.

The more *collective* action that is taken the less the likelihood of a negative outcome. If developing countries can negotiate together then the beggar-thy-neighbour danger will be less, and adverse effects on the poorest countries less likely. Moreover, collective negotiation is likely to be more effective, especially in some areas. For example, OPEC was only able to control the price of oil because the oil producers took joint action; the Andean Pact countries were effective in improving the terms on which they acquired foreign capital without suffering a major reduction in capital inflow, in large part because their action was collective. But collective action is much more difficult to organise than action by individual countries. However, it is clear from these examples that collective action need not involve the whole of the G77, but small sub-groups.

In devising the appropriate sub-groups for action, two considerations need to be borne in mind: first, that of the bargaining power of the sub-group, which will vary according to the issue under consideration; and secondly, the political possibility of decisive collective action. It seems that the second consideration would rule out most action at the level of the G77. Smallish regional groupings may best combine the possibility of collective action with negotiating strength. But this will vary from issue to issue. For example, where it is a matter of using producer power the major producers have to be included, which often means countries from all continents. On the other hand, in determining the conditions for tax and other treatment of multinational companies, intra-regional cooperation may be greatly superior to national action, and inter-regional cooperation may not be necessary. In some areas – and especially for large countries – national action can be very effective, as indicated in the examples already quoted.

International analysis of the various options, and subsequently international monitoring, might help in selecting issues and actions which ultimately result in a positive rather than a zero or negative sum game. Any of the three outcomes are possible with a bargaining approach. In contrast, it may be argued, the conventional multilateral approach suggested in the Brandt Commission Reports offers a positive sum game, but since the game is never actually played, this is not a major advantage.

AREAS FOR NEGOTIATION

Once a negotiating strategy is adopted and countries begin to explore the possibilities, a great number are likely to become apparent. But in a preliminary way, the following seem to be obvious potential sources of power offering possibilities of negotiating gains.[6]

1. *Buyer power* The Third World as a whole buys substantially more in total than it sells to the North, and the imbalance is particularly great in manufactures. The developed market economies sold $232 billion to developing market economies in 1985 while they bought $97 billion worth of manufactures from them. At times of international recession, when every country is seeking markets, developing countries can threaten to switch their purchases, unless their exports receive reasonable treatment. The threat may be made specific in industrial terms, thus activating specific interests in developed countries. For example, industrial economies export about $130 billion of machinery and transport equipment to developing countries. LDCs may pick out this item specifically. For use of buyer power, the action is likely to be more effective when conducted by single countries or smallish groups of countries in negotiation with particular Northern countries (or groups within the North), so that alternative sources of supply may be assured. But given the supply potential in many industries of the Comecon countries and the NICs, alternative sources should normally not be a serious problem.
2. *Seller power* This is less effective, especially in recession, because of the existence of stocks and of substitutes and the difficulty in controlling all sources of supply. OPEC's success caused overconcentration on this approach, given its limitations.
3. *Contracts* Large contracts offer potential power because they are related to very specific interests. Thus while any one contract is

likely to be very small in relation to the total income of Northern economies, it may be important for particular companies, which in turn may influence Northern government policy. In the case quoted above, Mrs Gandhi was able to relate big contracts to a major aid issue. A country or group of countries may refuse *all* contracts with another country unless certain changes are made; or they may negotiate over a particular contract, either on a general issue, or on the terms of the contract itself. (For example, Thailand recently threatened to withdraw a contract worth $622 million with a British and French consortium because of the strict credit guarantees demanded.)

4. *MNCs' Investment and technology transfer* To the extent that multinational firms are earning quasi-rents on their technology sales (which by the nature of the activity they normally are), these may be bargained away by seeking alternative sources of technology. Very often the technology is available in another company in the *same* developing country – and more often in other developing countries. Unitary taxation (or some variant) may ensure proper taxation of MNCs. Unnecessary tax incentives may be removed and codes of conduct may be imposed unilaterally. If these actions are taken on a regional basis, they are less likely to lead to a reduced flow of investment. Where countries already have substantial amounts of foreign investment, control over these assets presents a potential bargaining counter in discussion with the HQ government.

5. *Debtor power* Countries that have borrowed heavily from one (or several) banks, especially if these are all based in a single country, may have considerable leverage both over the banks themselves and their country of origin, because of the consequences for the banks and the country of origin if default occurs. Such leverage is likely to be greater the less the *net* flow of finance into the borrowing country (i.e., the smaller new bank lending less repayment of old debt and interest payments). When this net flow becomes negative, as it has in major Latin American countries such as Brazil (and in the Latin American region as a whole), the leverage becomes very strong. In this situation the borrowing countries are no longer net recipients from the banking system and would actually gain, in terms of foreign exchange, by default.[7]

In one way debtor power is enhanced by collective action (a borrowers' club), since collectively the debt of several countries will invariably amount to a larger share of any individual bank's lending; but it may also be weakened because the likelihood of forceful collective action may be less. In April 1984, Venezuela, Brazil and Colombia lent $100 million to Argentina. This has been interpreted as an example of regional co-operation. But in fact it seems to have been motivated by the desire by these countries to prevent an Argentinian default which might have had serious implications for lending to these countries. It is not an example of the collective use of debtor-power. So far debtor countries appear to have been more effective acting on their own rather than collectively.

However, while there has been no effective *formal* action, informally a number of countries have gained by each others' actions and negotiations. For example, one reporter commented, 'The Philippines . . . is likely to benefit from the recent trend towards bigger breaks for troubled debtors' (*Asian Wall Street Journal*, 13 March 1984). There are various areas where countries may gain by being in a similar situation and bargaining on similar matters, without the need for any formal agreement, which is difficult to secure.

Debtor power may be used (a) to secure a greater flow of resources (private and public); (b) to improve the terms of re-scheduling; (c) to secure reduced servicing obligations (for example, lower interest rates); (d) to improve the terms of IMF conditionality; and (e) to put pressure on Northern countries to relax trade restrictions, and take other action which will make it easier for the borrowing countries to repay their debts through greater export earnings.

6. *Political sensitivity* Some countries are – mainly for reasons of geography – in a politically critical position. Countries in such a position may exploit it by making political and military concessions dependent on improvements in aid/finance/trade. There are some parts of the world where this type of political role has brought about considerable flows of aid (for example, S. Korea and Taiwan in the 1950s; the Middle East; parts of Central America; Vietnam in the 1960s). Given the prevalence of disputes throughout the world, there are a large number of countries which fall into the 'politically sensitive' category and could use this position to exert economic leverage.

Issue Linkage

While the negotiating tactic may be concerned with one issue, for example trade, concessions may be sought elsewhere. The concession sought need not be confined to the particular country but could extend to general changes for Third World countries, as those of the NIEO. In the Indian example quoted, the threat against contracts was used to engender support for IDA. In the India case this made sense because of the large share India receives of IDA flows. In other countries such a stance might require an unlikely degree of Third World solidarity. However, if individual countries (or groups of countries) were prepared to negotiate on general Third World issues, it would be sensible for the G77 as a whole to prepare an agreed and co-ordinated agenda, so that countries were making similar demands on each occasion. These demands should not extend to all issues because, as is obvious, the Third World hasn't the power to enforce general and comprehensive demands. Hence priority needs to be given to one or two issues, which would be presented as a negotiating requirement by every Third World country whenever a suitable occasion arose. The problem here is to identify a single issue that is of real relevance to each Third World country – which is of course the reason why the demands of the NIEO were so wide-ranging. Debt relief, reduced interest rates and relaxed conditionality are issues that affect most countries. But even these affect different countries differently. If no single (or few) priority issues can be agreed upon, there could still be gains in groups of countries agreeing on one or two issues, as priorities for bargaining.

Problems of the Least Developed

The sort of negotiating strategy suggested here would seem to offer most to middle-income countries whose potential power is greatest in most areas. The least developed have small markets; although their debt may be large for them, it is small in relation to the commercial banks' lending. Moreover, their negotiating ability is often weak. The least developed undoubtedly will find less potential in this sort of strategy than other countries. Nonetheless, even for them it would be worth exploring and exploiting the power they have: for example, some of the least developed countries fall into the 'politically sensitive' area. Although their bargaining power is less, the magnitude of their demands is also generally less (for example, the cost of relieving them of some proportion of debt is much less than for some middle-income countries; the potential competitiveness of their exports is also lower). Small and low-income countries have more to gain from taking collective action. For example, any one African country is in a weak position to tax MNCs effectively, but if African countries negotiate together they would be in a much stronger position.

Strengthening the Negotiating Position

The strength of countries' negotiating position varies according to its circumstances. For example, countries with small markets are in a weak position to exercise buyer power; countries with little out-standing debt cannot exert debtor power. Also, the strength of any country's position depends on the possibilities and likelihood of retaliatory action by countries in the North. To some extent these are facts that are determined by history and outside the control of countries in their current actions. But there are ways in which their bargaining power, in the future, may be strengthened by current decisions. These include:

1. *Concentration*   The more concentrated a country's purchases are from a single source (country), the greater the potential loss of the selling country from switching sources. Thus concentration may increase potential buyer power of any given size of market. Another example lies in debt. The more concentrated the bor-rowing, in terms of lending institutions and country of origin, the greater the potential debtor power. But this concentration factor works both ways, also increasing the potential power of Northern countries. Consequently,

2. *Diversification of selling outlets for a country's exports*   This re-duces potential retaliatory action. Brazil provides an example: it has considerable debtor power arising from heavy past borrowing, the fact that this borrowing was concentrated on a few US banks, and the large *negative* financial flow (large current account sur-plus) that Brazil has to have at present to meet its debt obliga-tions, which is likely to continue over the next few years at least. These facts put Brazil in a very strong position to exert debtor power. But its exports are concentrated on a rather few commodi-ties and in the US market (notably for steel and orange juice) so that retaliatory action on trade could be very powerful. This

probably accounts for the fact that Brazil has not made much (if any) use of its debtor power.

3. *Reduced dependence on the external world*   The greater the potential for a country to do without any particular item (for example, capital inflow, technology inflow), the greater the bargaining power. In the past this has been interpreted as a reason for promoting import substituting industrialisation – to reduce dependence on imported industrial products, and consequently on export earnings in order to finance them. But in practice it turned out that import substituting industrialisation led to a new form of dependence that in some ways was greater than the one replaced, since countries that had industrialised in this way became dependent on imports of parts, technology, management, and capital for industrial activity. The countries that have successfully promoted export-oriented manufacturing (South Korea, Taiwan, etc.) turned out to be more independent than countries that had focused almost exclusively on import-substitution. This is because the import-substituting countries remained heavily dependent on traditional exports and on borrowing for essential finance. The export-oriented countries, on the other hand, acquired an ability to exploit the international environment (even when it is unfavourable), and to switch resources, if necessary, to adapt to new conditions, while being less dependent on traditional exports (where a hostile international environment is of greater significance) and, in the case of Taiwan at least, on borrowing for finance. Reduced dependence should not therefore be interpreted in a simple way as necessarily involving a withdrawal from the world economy. Rather it implies a greater ability to withstand external shocks. In some cases, this may be achieved by withdrawal – for example, China and India have been more insulated than many other LDCs against recent shocks. But for small countries especially, it is a matter of the nature of international relationships rather than their extent.

4. *Collective self-reliance*   Developing trade, capital and technology links among Southern countries may reduce dependence. Collective self-reliance is often suggested as an alternative to continued North–South negotiations. In fact it need not be an alternative but can be pursued simultaneously with greater collective self-reliance and unity strengthening the South's bargaining position. The need for South–South links and collective self-reliance has long been supported rhetorically by leaders of the South. But in fact few

links have been established, especially at the level of the South as a whole. Indeed, as a prospect, collective self-reliance seems as unreal as North–South cooperation. The reasons for the failure to realise South–South self-reliance are similar to those discussed above with respect to North– South relations. While there may be *general* interest in South–South cooperation, these do not operate at the level of particular interests. And, as with North–South relations, it is particular interests that are effective in bringing about action. Consequently, analysis of how countries of the South might effectively promote collective action requires the same sort of rethinking as in the arena of North– South action, taking into account particular interests of nations and of powerful groups, and exploring how these might be used to bring about effective cooperation. In practice, regional groupings develop where common interests are evident. The financial crisis has acted to create areas of action where common and particular interests meet: this has taken the form of expansion of countertrade (cited above), and of the early moves towards common markets in both Africa and Latin America. In addition, there have been a series of 'debtor' meetings in Latin America. Analysis of interests suggests that small groupings of countries are more likely to work than large ones; that countries may be able to cooperate effectively on some issues (for example, debt) but not others (for example, trade), and that the relevant groupings may vary according to the issues involved.

CONCLUSIONS

This essay has analysed reasons for the failure of proposals for changes in North–South relations over the past few decades. The main conclusion from the analysis is that the usual proposals for reform identify mutual interest for reform, but the mutual interests identified are at a very general level, and do not coincide with the interests of particular groups who effectively determine national action. Unless particular interests are identified and incorporated in analysis and proposals, reforms are unlikely to be realised. This conclusion applies to South–South as well as North–South relations. From this perspective, the chapter suggests various areas where the South could make more use of its bargaining power to bring about change; and also actions it might take to enhance this.

It is possible that exploitation of bargaining power to the full, without regard to the consequences for the distribution and efficiency of world resource use, or for retaliatory action, could lead to a situation where every country is ultimately worse off than in the current situation. Consequently, it only makes sense to follow this type of strategy in pursuit of changes that will improve the position of the countries concerned, when these considerations are taken into account. Areas need to be identified that are likely to produce positive sum (preferably) and zero sum (at worst) changes, while excluding negative sum gains. This also applies to the proposals for increasing negotiating strength. For example, reduced dependence is not worth pursuing if it involves a substantial loss in output and income. Increased South–South links seem likely to be an area where there are positive gains, as well as bargaining gains, but this is not invariably the case with every type of additional South–South link. The issues need to be analysed in depth before they can be categorised.

In general, analysis of interests suggests that, both for North–South and South–South relations, small flexible groupings of countries, negotiating on particular issues, are more likely to bring about reform than large global negotiations, of the type that have failed so often in the past.

NOTES

1. See the reports of the UN Committee for Development Planning.
2. *Financial Times* (13 January 1984).
3. *Financial Times* (27 January 1984).
4. See Chapter 7.
5. There are difficulties in defining gains and losses at a world level because their valuation depends on how one weights gains received by different groups in different countries. Where some lose and some gain, whether there are net gains or losses depends entirely on the weighting system. At a world level the 'compensation principle' makes no sense at all because of the absence of a mechanism to achieve redistribution of income. Even where every group gains (or loses), if relative as well as absolute levels of income matter, how distribution changes – and the value placed on various distributions of income – is relevant to the assessment of the change.
6. Paul Streeten (1976) categorised some of these sources of power.
7. See Chapter 11 for a more detailed analysis of the debt situation in a bargaining context.

3 Basic Needs Strategies, Human Rights, and the Right to Development*

INTRODUCTION

The failure of the economic and social system to achieve a basic minimum condition of life for hundreds of millions of people in the third world has led to widespread recognition of the need to give primacy to securing universal access to basic social and economic goods and services. This recognition has been shared by economists, philosophers, and advocates of international human rights, but each have proceeded separately to develop conceptual frameworks and policy mechanisms to achieve the same or similar goals. In the latter part of the 1970s, development economists adopted a 'basic needs' (BN) approach to development, largely as a response to the failure of economic growth to alleviate poverty in many developing countries. The objectives of the economists' basic needs approach were similar to the conclusion of John Rawls's philosophical system that everyone should have access to 'basic social goods'.[1] Simultaneously, in a parallel and complementary development, international human rights access to goods were recognised first in the International Covenant on Economic, Social and Cultural Rights (1966)[2] and subsequently as part of the Declaration on the Right to Development (1986).[3]

This essay sets out some of the interconnections between economists' approach to BN and international human rights, particularly to see how far the BN approach can help in defining and realising the international rights to BN which are encompassed in the Covenant and Declaration. The aim is to explore the nature of plans and policies needed to fulfil BN, especially domestically but also internationally, in order to assess how and to what extent human rights to

* *Human Rights Quarterly*, 11 (1989).

BN can be enforced, and to identify changes necessary to make the 1976 Covenant and the 1986 Declaration more than pious hopes.

The BN approach to development focuses on the need to ensure that everyone has access to enough basic goods and services to maintain a level of living above a basic minimum, as a prime objective of economic development.[4] This short statement about the BN approach leaves important aspects undefined, which have given rise to considerable controversy. First, there is the issue of whether the fulfilment of BN should be the sole objective of economic development, and if not what weight the objective should have. Allied to this issue is the question of timing (i.e., the urgency of meeting BN, and whether some trade-off can be accepted between incomplete fulfilment of BN in the short term for the sake of greater fulfilment later). While all who advocate the approach agree that it should be given more weight than in the growth-maximisation approach and that there is urgency about its achievement, few would argue that it be accepted as the sole objective and that in all cases everything should be sacrificed for immediate achievement.

Second, there has been some disagreement about precisely how to define BN goods, but there is general agreement about a 'core' which includes food, water, health, education, and shelter. Some have extended the list to include non-material aspects such as access to work and participation in decisions. Non-material aspects – including liberty – also form an important part of Rawls's 'primary social goods'.[5]

Third, there is a difficult issue of defining the basic minimum. Each of these issues has parallels in problems arising in interpreting human rights in this area.

The International Covenant on Economic, Social and Cultural Rights, entered into force in 1976, encompassed most of what would be generally described as BN goods, including the right to food, health, shelter, education, and work, as well as to other non-material aspects of life which many would include as 'basic' needs.[6] In addition, the General Assembly's recognition of the 'right to development' as 'an inalienable human right by virtue of which every human person and all peoples are entitled to participate in, contribute to and enjoy economic, social, cultural, and political development, in which all human rights and fundamental freedoms can be fully realised',[7] also clearly includes rights to fulfilment of BN as one intrinsic aspect of the right to development, a necessary part of the enjoyment of economic and social development.

However, in several ways the right to development goes beyond what most would define as fulfilment of BN. It extends to cultural and political development, which is typically not included in the BN approach. It also implies dynamic achievements (i.e., growth in levels of living over time), while the BN approach is primarily concerned with extending certain standards to everyone as soon as possible, and less concerned with growth over time. Moreover, economic development is an attribute of a society as a whole, while BN fulfilment and rights concern rights of individuals within society. These distinctions can be overdrawn, since a dynamic version of BN must include, as we shall see, improving standards over time, while there is interdependence between individuals' fulfilment of BN and what is happening to society as a whole. Nonetheless, it is aspects of the Covenant on Economic, Social and Cultural Rights – and in particular the rights to food, health, shelter, and education – which are most closely related to a BN approach to development. In what follows we shall describe achieving these rights as being the same as fulfilling BN. The main focus will be on these aspects of the 1976 Covenant.

Interpretation of the Covenant depends on the meaning of human rights, in particular, when recognised in an international covenant. In everyday language, concepts used to talk about human satisfactions include desires, wants, needs, and rights, ordered by the moral imperative attached to their satisfaction. At one extreme, desires are often regarded as immoral; wants are morally neutral, though sometimes regarded as greedy and somewhat reprehensible. There is a strong implication that needs ought to be fulfilled, while rights connote not only a stronger moral, but also some legal imperative. There is therefore an implicit moral and political agenda involved in categorising types of satisfaction associated with different goods, services, or activities. In practice, in many economic systems human satisfactions tend to be met in the opposite order from the moral ranking just elucidated. The market system in particular – which is currently making global strides – is premised on 'consumers' sovereignty' which means that first priority goes to meeting the desires and wants of those with purchasing power. Whether or not those wants that are thereby fulfilled include, in part or in full, the set of BN is a contingent matter. There is nothing in the system to ensure that they do. In practice, many millions of peoples' BN were unfulfilled, despite economic growth throughout most of the world, in the decades following the Second World War.

The BN approach to development therefore stressed needs rather than wants in an effort both to recognise different priorities than those produced by the wants-driven system, and to give these priorities the moral legitimacy associated with the language of needs. The institution of economic and social rights performed a similar function, using the language of rights, involving the strongest moral imperative. Both the BN and the human rights approaches can be seen as attempts to develop a moral and political agenda which would ensure fulfilment of BN and not leave the extent of fulfilment to contingent forces.

Needs are not the same as rights. Making BN into human rights adds two elements to the BN approach. It increases the moral weight of and political commitment to their fulfilment, and it gives BN fulfilment some international legal status, the extent and nature of which depends on the nature of the supervisory and enforcement mechanisms associated with the rights. Potentially, the legal status conferred on BN adds a very important additional instrument to ensure fulfilment of these needs. But whether it does in practice depends on a number of factors. First, it will be necessary to know what is meant by the rights conferred by the economic and social covenant – or what we here describe as fulfilment of BN[8] – not just vaguely but in precise enough terms to be able to say whether these needs are being fulfilled or not in a particular case. A similar precise definition of 'development' will be necessary to make a reality of the right to development. Second, it will be necessary to monitor fulfilment of BN and progress in realising 'development'. Third, effective enforcement mechanisms are necessary. These might include three types of mechanisms: (1) a system of international monitoring, reports, and recommendations; (2) enforcement by individuals or states through the legal system (national and international); and (3) the use of other international levers such as finance and trade to support enforcement.

The rest of this essay is devoted to seeing whether and how these requirements are or might be met. The next section deals with the problem of defining BN achievement and the right to development. The third section briefly describes alternative BN strategies. The fourth section is a review of the issues of monitoring and enforcement, considering the existing system of enforcement with respect to social and economic rights and how this system could be strengthened.

The subject is an extremely important one. First and most important, many millions of people suffer because their BN are not met, while universal satisfaction of these needs on at least a minimal level is feasible. Second, proliferation of internationally agreed human rights with little attempt to define them precisely, monitor, or enforce them is likely to debase the status of human rights. The legal authority of the concept may be undermined, since there is little point in making laws if no attempt is made to define what the laws mean or seriously to enforce them. The concept of human rights may also lose its moral and political force. Without serious enforcement, international human rights will come to be regarded as a fairly harmless way of occupying members of the UN General Assembly, international lawyers, and some academics. It is true that in an area as difficult and ambitious as this, complete success cannot be expected all at once, and stepwise progress – even with some retreats – may be necessary.[9] Nonetheless, there remains a real danger that social, economic, and cultural rights may come to have little real content or achievement. Major efforts are needed to sustain any stepwise progress.

DEFINING BN

There are fundamental issues at stake here. This section is not merely about use of words, but what it means for a society to meet basic needs of its people, and what it means for a society to fail in this. Fulfilment of BN implies that all members of the society are meeting their BN at some minimum level. At the extremes there are no problems: if everyone is healthy, educated, and enjoying levels of living well above standards that seem appropriate, BN are being met, and if significant numbers are dying of starvation then they are not. But most cases are less extreme and more difficult to solve: poor societies where people are malnourished but not starving and have some but very limited access to health and other essential services, or rich societies where there is no sign of actual malnutrition and everyone goes to elementary school but where sections of society are not meeting some of their needs at all (e.g., no work, no shelter) with other people's needs being met at standards which might be considered unacceptably low by the standards of that society.

The following issues are critical to the determination of definable and consequently enforceable standards.

1. Does fulfilment of BN mean providing some specific level of goods and services to everyone or does it mean achieving conditions which lead to a minimally defined satisfactory life which we shall call, for shorthand, the 'full life'? The full life would seem generally to be the objective that people wish to fulfil in a BN approach since other aspects are for the most part instrumental to the achievement of this full life rather than wanted in themselves. For example, what is wanted is health, not access to doctors; education, not access to schools; good nutrition, not access to certain quantities of food, while commodities are valued only insofar as particular levels of consumption are necessary for the achievement of the fundamental objective of improving human life. However, if for some reason certain goods were wanted in themselves and not only for their contribution to the full life, they would be objectives too. But in the interpretation of the full life adopted here, the BN goods are regarded as instrumental for the achievement of a full life. The instrumental goods and services are related to the ultimate objective in what I shall call the metaproduction function, as shown in the following expression:

$$FL = f(F, H, E, S, W \ldots)$$

FL is a measure of the achievement of a full life (e.g., life expectancy), while F, H, E, S, and W are measures of the availability of goods and services in various sectors – food, health, education, shelter, and water, respectively. This metaproduction function can apply at various levels of aggregation. For example, it can express the average achievements of a full life at the level of the entire nation by relating the output of different BN sectors to the population as a whole, or it can be regarded as a household metaproduction function, relating household size to household consumption of the goods and services that fulfil BN, or it could represent an individual's success in meeting his or her needs. The more aggregated the function, the more the relationship achieved will depend on the distribution of the goods and services among different parts of the population, as well as total availability. Even within the household, intrahousehold distribution is an important determinant of how quantities of BN goods relate to achievement of a full life.[10]

Sen has adopted a similar approach in his work on capabilities.[11]

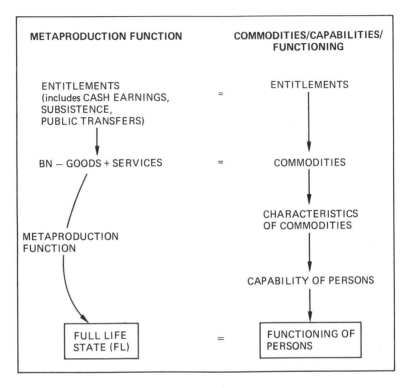

Figure 3.1 Metaproduction function and capabilities approaches

He regards the achievement of equal basic capabilities among people as the prime objective. Capabilities are an attribute of individuals and consist of a person's capacity or capability of functioning or performing in a particular way – for example, the capability of being well-nourished. The realisation of these capabilities generally requires commodities. For example, in the case of the capability of being well-nourished a person may require food, and also certain facilities of health and hygiene to avoid malnutrition caused by ill health. Consequently, commodities are instrumental. Figure 3.1 compares the two approaches.

In both approaches entitlements or full incomes – which include money incomes arising from employment and asset ownership, subsistence income (that is, products produced and consumed within the household) and public transfers, subsidies and public goods provided free of charge – form the pool of 'income' out of which households secure access to goods and services. In the metaproduction function approach, these goods and services relate to the achievement of a full life or fulfilment of BN via the causal relationship represented by the metaproduction function.

In Sen's approach there are two additional steps. First, the goods are converted into characteristics (e.g., the calories and proteins associated with food, or the health giving qualities of health services). This step could easily be incorporated into the metaproduction function but was avoided because of major empirical problems in identifying characteristics, while often it is difficult not only empirically but also logically to identify characteristics independently of their effects on a full life. From a pragmatic planning perspective, it is easier to work with goods, which can be observed and planned for, rather than with characteristics. But there can be cases where the addition of the characteristics step would be useful – for example, in deciding what type of cereals to produce, knowledge of calorie and protein content is valuable. Sen's 'functioning' describes people's performance with respect to health, nutrition, and so on.[12] It is therefore the same as the full life. But as noted, Sen places prime attention on capabilities – the capability of functioning – rather than functioning itself.[13] This is an important difference compared with the BN approach which is concerned with what actually happens to people rather than with their capabilities. The metaproduction approach omits the capability step altogether, while for Sen this is the prime objective.

The metaproduction function thus relates commodities directly to functioning, the commodities being represented on the right-hand side $(F, H, E, S, W, . . .)$ and Sen's functioning being the same as the achievement of a full life (health, nutrition, etc.). The intermediary steps of characteristics and capabilities could be incorporated. Whether it is desirable to do so depends on whether the enrichment this would represent would outweigh the additional complexity involved.

From the human rights perspective what is important is the conclusion – common to both approaches – that it is not the commodities which are the objective but their effects on human life – on full life, or on capabilities and functioning. Consequently, any review of achievement should not only look at the commodities to which people have access, but must also look at the effects these have on the achievement of a full life. It follows that it is important to know the properties of the metaproduction function.

The relationship described by the metaproduction function is an empirical one, which may vary according to culture, stage of development, or technical possibilities. For example, access to clean water – which is widely regarded as an important BN – has been found to be quite ineffective in improving health unless also accompanied by hygiene education. Access to small pox vaccination was essential for health until recently but is now unnecessary. However, economic and social planning necessarily relates to the instrumental goods and services rather than to the more amorphous 'full life', and most political agendas for meeting basic needs are described in terms of the goods and services – for example, water for all by the year 2000.

The human rights approach has encompassed both aspects, but in general international action has also been directed primarily at the instruments rather than the objective – such as vaccination for all children by 1990 and universal primary education. From the point of view of international planning and monitoring these specific targets are easier to handle than the vaguer concept of satisfactory life, but they can lead to serious mistakes. First, achievable objectives that nevertheless do not improve health, education, or nutrition can be pursued. When specific targets are chosen but not assigned a priority, massive resources can be (and actually are) spent on providing clean water, when a much more cost-effective approach would have been to increase education and access to larger supplies of 'dirty' water. Similarly, large expenditures are devoted to Western-style doctors to achieve the targets, while extension of primary health care and the introduction of barefoot doctors would do much more for health. Second, by focusing on quantities of goods and services, their distribution and effective use can be neglected. The doctors may be available but inadequately used: the country as a whole could have massive resources of water, but the poor may have limited access; the total supply of food to a family may be sufficient but the women may have too little, and the children may have food they cannot digest efficiently. A basic needs approach – and a human rights approach – should therefore focus on the objective, a full life as a test of BN fulfilment, and on goods and services as essential instruments.

2. How is a 'full life' to be defined, measured, and monitored? The first problem is to define the constituent elements. Health, nutrition, and education seem reasonable initial approximations of

material aspects of well-being, and they can be monitored fairly well (although somewhat controversially[14]) by measures of life expectancy, infant mortality rates, prevalence of different kinds of malnutrition, and levels of literacy. Some non-material elements are also fairly easy to define and measure – for example, access to work and leisure and democratic rights. Other elements are important but very difficult to define and measure – for example, adequate cultural life, participation, and communication. Economic and political strategies have to encompass all aspects. But for effective international supervision and enforcement of economic and social rights, especially among the poor, it would be desirable to focus on obvious and measurable aspects, such as nutrition, health, and education. Extension to other areas might follow once success has been achieved in these areas. However, many of the constituents are complementary, such that the achievement of non-material elements both depends on and itself partly determines the achievement of the basic material rights.[15] These interdependencies mean that a simple linear approach is not possible or desirable.

3. Are standards of BN fulfilment to be the same for all countries or relative to the level of development of each society? The ability to meet BN arises with the level of *per capita* income. Countries with higher incomes have more resources to invest on meeting BN that are provided by public expenditures (e.g., health, education, water) and generally have a greater availability of food *per capita* and high levels of exchange entitlements (i.e., cash incomes in relation to prices of basic goods) for the population including the lower income segments (see Table 3.1). These factors are reflected in higher levels of achievements in full life indicators – life expectancy, infant mortality rates, standards of nutrition, and literacy rates. If a universal set of standards were set, they would either be unrealistically high for some very poor countries or unrealistically low for others. Consequently, it would appear more useful to set standards relative to income levels. This could be achieved, for example, by relating the full life indicators to the level of *per capita* income across countries and then identifying poor achievers as those that fall below either average achievements or the achievements of the best few countries in that income group.[16]

The 1976 Covenant has been described as involving a principle of 'progressive realisation', as indicated by the fact that the rights in question are 'recognised' rather than 'declared' or 'ensured' and

Table 3.1 BN: goods, services and achievements, selected years

	BN: goods and services				BN: achievements			
	Population per doctor 1984	nurse 1984	% of population with access to safe water 1980–7	Per capita calory supply 1986	No. of females enrolled in primary school as % of age group 1986	No. enrolled in secondary school as % of age group 1986	Life expectancy at birth 1987	Adult literacy 1985–8
Low-income countries	5410	2150	46	2384	92	35	61	61
Middle-income countries	2390	980	75	2855	100	54	65	80
Industrial market economies[1]	450	130	100[2]	3390	102	93	76	96

Notes:
1. OECD countries
2. Not given, estimated.
Source: World Bank (1989); UNDP Tables from *Human Development Report* (New York: United Nations, 1990).

that Article 2(1) commits parties to 'take steps' towards the realisation of the rights recognised 'with a view to achieving progressively' the rights 'to the maximum of its available resources'.[17] The Covenant thereby recognises that achievements will take time and should be related to a country's resources. This means that monitors must look not only at actual achievements but at progress being made or steps taken and must also interpret the meaning of 'to the maximum of its available resources'. This interpretation presents problems. It does not seem plausible to expect a country to spend all its resources on BN goods. In any case, if it did so it might achieve immediate success in fulfilling BN but at the cost of imperilling future economic performance and future ability to meet BN. But once one no longer interprets 'to the maximum of its available resources' as requiring 100 per cent resource-use for BN, deciding what is maximum resource use becomes largely arbitrary.

The problem of setting standards for each country for human rights is the same as that with respect to BN. A similar approach would seem appropriate. As a first approximation, an attempt should be made to establish standards relative to levels of *per capita* income, by comparing achievements in countries with similar income levels.

It is not only a question of the level of achievement with respect to particular indicators, but which indicators are appropriate, which may change at different stages of development. For richer societies, some of the indicators suggested earlier may not be appropriate, since such societies can be expected to have eliminated malnutrition and achieved universal literacy and primary health care. It could also be argued that their people are entitled to higher levels of achievement, and consequently different measures would be appropriate (e.g., the very low proportion of young people in tertiary education in the UK could be regarded as a violation of human rights to education for a high-income country). However, the disadvantage of a relative approach as a legal standard or as an approach with operational significance for international agencies is obvious. There would be considerable scope for dispute about how the comparisons are arrived at and the justification for changing indicators. This is one reason why BN are harder to interpret as universal human rights than more traditional rights which are less costly in resources. With the latter, standards can be developed regardless of a country's stage of development, though evidence of the interconnection between social and economic rights and the ability to pursue non-material rights suggest that even the realisation of non-material rights may in reality be dependent on stage of development.[18]

Some full life indicators could appropriately generate universal standards. Universal literacy is achievable by all societies and so is access to basic primary health care, including mass immunisation[19] and the elimination of acute malnutrition. Such universal indicators might be the most appropriate ones to pursue initially.

However, it is important not to neglect richer societies in enforcement of social and economic rights and the right to development. More ambitious standards generally will have to be devised for these societies. Graduated standards varying with resources are also appropriate for some aspects of BN fulfilment in poorer societies – for example, availability of doctors and nurses per person and quality and proximity of water supplies. For all such areas the problem is to devise standards which vary according to the resources of the society, but which nonetheless have a sufficiently objective basis to be sensible and acceptable as international standards. Further work is needed in developing such standards.

4. Distribution of achievements among different groups within each society is critical. Information is needed that can be broken down into relevant detail, including race, region, income group, sex, and age. In many societies this type of information is not available currently, but in societies more concerned with protecting the most vulnerable, good disaggregated data are available. International monitoring of the rights to the fulfilment of BN depends on improvements in data availability as a first priority.[20]

5. Timing is sometimes suggested as a major issue. High achievement today can be, but need not be, in conflict with growth in achievement over time, as illustrated in Figure 3.2. Figure 3.2 assumes some trade-off between focusing on the immediate fulfilment of BN and maximising growth, with the result that eventually the growth approach overtakes the BN approach. Given this trade-off, the choice between strategies must depend on the length of time involved: if the crossover point (O_t) is more than fifty years, a BN approach would be more efficacious than the growth alternative. In the case of Sri Lanka, Sen estimated that it would take between 58 and 152 years for Sri Lanka to have achieved the same level of fulfilment of BN primarily through growth rather

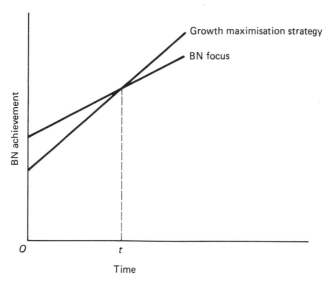

Figure 3.2   BN over time

than public action.[21] If, however, the crossover is much more short term, then there are difficult decisions to be made, as between immediate and medium-term fulfilment of BN. But the situation is more complex than Figure 3.2 depicts, since BN fulfilment is one important input into growth, as it determines the health, nutrition, and educational status of the workforce. Empirical investigation has found no systematic conflicts between growth and fulfilment of BN.[22] Moreover, failure to achieve growth eventually undermines a society's ability to meet BN, as illustrated in Ghana during the 1970s.[23] Consequently, the appropriate BN strategy is one that focuses on BN and growth, both of which are achievable as shown by some highly successful countries.[24]

6. The right to 'development' embodied in the 1986 Declaration raises even more difficult definitional problems. As noted earlier, development encompasses and goes beyond fulfilment of BN. A common perception of development is that it involves a pattern of sustained economic growth, the benefits of which extend to the whole society, including the most deprived, so that BN are met and poverty is eliminated. Consequently, the assessment of achievements with respect to the right to development should include a look at growth in *per capita* incomes, income distribu-

tion, measures of poverty, and fulfilment of BN, as well as the various political and cultural aspects which form part of the right to development, as defined in the Declaration. Since the right to development applies to a society as a whole, it points more strongly to the international conditions and obligations necessary to sustain this right than do BN rights in the Covenant, though these too have international implications.

When attempts are made to interpret and enforce rights under the Covenant and the Declaration, these definitional questions will have to be solved at an early stage. Some suggestions have been made above. What is needed is an international discussion and agreement on these questions, so that what it means to achieve or not to achieve these human rights is well-defined in a way that is widely acceptable.

BN STRATEGIES

To identify political and economic strategies likely to be effective in fulfilling BN it is necessary to clarify major elements involved in meeting these needs.[25] The actual achievement of satisfactory conditions of life is the outcome of a complex and lengthy chain of developments in the economic system. At the end of this chain is an interaction between a set of goods and services (the BN goods) and a person, leading to a certain condition of human life, which may be defined as satisfactory or unsatisfactory according to the agreed criteria of fulfilment of BN.

The chain of events leading to this outcome consists of all those aspects of the economic system which result in the availability of some level and quality of BN goods and all those events leading to household distribution of cash income, subsistence income, and access to public goods which together determine each household's full income, (or entitlements), which they may use to acquire basic needs goods.

The first category represents the supply aspects of a BN strategy, while the second represents the demand aspects. Both determine the level of household consumption of BN goods, and an inadequate provision of these goods may be due to failure of either. For example, availability of food is clearly an essential requirement for meeting household food needs – the supply side – but if a household lacks cash income with which to buy the food, then severe malnutrition is possible (and indeed often results) even though there is no supply deficiency.

Similar factors apply to the other BN goods. Even 'free' goods, like schools in some countries, have hidden cash costs – such as the cost of uniforms, books, transport, and lost earnings from child labour – so that using them also requires cash income. Sometimes access or entitlement to public goods also requires individuals to have some non-cash assets, such as education or position in society. In some societies non-cash characteristics are also of significance in determining access to marketed products. In countries where the private sector and the market are dominant, cash income is the major determinant of entitlement. In countries where the public sector is dominant and controls are prevalent, other factors may be more important in determining household access to BN goods.

The level of entitlements does not determine actual consumption of BN goods but rather determines households' potential access. Actual access depends on how far this potential is exercised. In other words it depends upon whether incomes are saved, how incomes are spent (on BN goods or other items) and, for public goods, what actual use is made of the goods available – for example, whether people go to the clinic or children attend school.

The supply and demand factors determine BN goods availability at the level of the household. But this is by no means the end of the story. Fulfilment of BN at the level of the individual depends on (1) how the goods are distributed within the household, and (2) how 'efficient' is the consumption of any quantity of goods. Since the rights to BN pertain to individuals, not households, it is essential also to investigate intra-household distribution of BN goods.

The efficiency of the metaproduction is the outcome of a number of factors, not all of which are fully understood. But three are clearly important. There are first the characteristics of the person involved. For example, calorie needs for any level of nutrition depend partly on the age, sex, and size of the person, the sort of activity the person does, and the person's state of health. Second, the metaproduction function also depends on the combination of BN goods available. Food may be more effective in producing nutrition if there are also abundant supplies of clean water which reduce diarrhoea; similarly, if diseases such as measles that cause loss of appetite are reduced, children will eat more from any available supply, so that if the population is vaccinated, extra food supplies will be more effective. Third, culture and education affect the efficiency of the function:

choice of diet, cooking methods, and levels of hygiene are obvious examples.

Successful BN strategies, therefore, involve achieving sufficient household entitlements and an adequate supply of BN goods chiefly through domestic production, since most BN goods are not internationally traded in large quantities with the exception of food in a few countries. But these are only necessary, not sufficient, conditions since households must exercise their entitlements to acquire enough BN goods, distribute the goods within the households to ensure adequate access to the various individuals who make up the households, and consume the goods efficiently to enjoy a full life. Better performance, in theory, may then be achieved without increasing total household entitlements by increasing the proportion spent on BN goods, changing intra-household income distribution, or improving efficiency of use of the goods. But while these are possibilities, in planning to secure adequate demand for BN it is necessary to assume actual patterns of consumption, intra-household distribution, and metaproduction efficiency to estimate the level of household entitlement necessary to achieve a full life. If potential instead of actual figures are used, a severe underestimate of the necessary level of entitlements may result.

Figures 3.3 and 3.4 provide a framework which illustrates the stages by which an economic system determines supply (Figure 3.3) and demand (Figure 3.4) for BN goods. Choices can be made at each level of the two diagrams, which will influence the extent to which society performs well or poorly in providing BN goods. This indicates the very many points at which important choices are made and consequently the wide variety of ways in which societies can succeed or fail in meeting BN. Moreover, it is also possible to compensate for poor performance at one level by improved performance at some other level. On the 'supply' side (Figure 3.3) a country may allocate relatively few resources to the BN sectors broadly defined, such as the health sector, but within the health sector the country may allocate a high proportion of resources to basic health services as against hospitals. Or, on the demand side, low national income *per capita* may make it difficult for a country to generate adequate incomes, but an egalitarian distribution of income can compensate for this in terms of income levels of the poor and their access to basic goods. Alternatively, a fairly unequal distribution generating inadequate incomes for meeting BN may be offset by income transfers by the state or by subsidies for BN goods. In addition, improvements

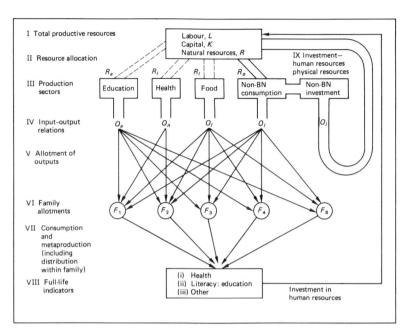

Source: Stewart (1985a)
Figure 3.3   A macroeconomic production framework

in intra-household distribution and the efficiency of the metaproduction function may compensate for poor supply and/or demand performance.

The multistage process by which BN are fulfilled means that there are a variety of ways in which good performance may be affected, and also a multitude of factors which may account for poor performance. Empirical analysis of country performance on material basic needs in 1979–87 shows that this is indeed the case in practice. Table 3.2 lists countries which did exceptionally well or poorly in providing for basic needs in 1979 and 1987. The criteria for success or failure used in Table 3.2 is the percentage deviation above or below that which would be predicted on the basis of *per capita* income alone, where a full life is defined in terms of life expectancy. Other indicators such as literacy rates and infant mortality, produced a very similar listing of countries.[26] Examination of the strategies pursued by those countries listed provides some indication of the different strategies likely to lead to success or failure in fulfilling BN.[27]

Among the successful countries, three types can be distinguished:

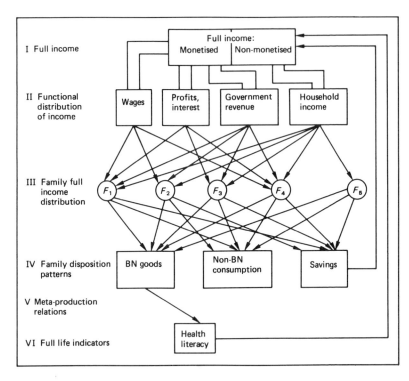

Source: Stewart (1985a)
Figure 3.4   Incomes and BN

Table 3.2   BN: Exceptional performers as measured by life expectancy, 1979 and 1987

	Good			Poor	
	1979[a]	1987[b]		1979[c]	1987[c]
			% of deviation from predicted level		
Sri Lanka	37.2	21.0	Saudi Arabia	–27.0	–14.2
China	30.9	22.7	Ivory Coast	–22.0	–13.5
Albania	20.3	n.a.	Libya	–21.8	–16.7
Burma	18.2	n.a.	Iraq	–21.5	n.a.
Bangladesh	16.4	2.6	Iran	–21.2	n.a.
Jamaica	14.2	18.3	Angola	–20.3	n.a.
Cuba	13.7	n.a.	Yemen Arab Republic	–19.8	–13.0
Thailand	12.5	6.5	Senegal	–18.0	–18.5
Philippines	12.3	8.5	Yemen PDR	–15.8	–8.9

Table 3.2   continued

	Good			Poor	
	1979[a]	*1987*[b]		*1979*[c]	*1987*[c]
		% of deviation from predicted level			
El Salvador	12.1	3.3	Mauritania	−14.7	−21.4
India	11.1	7.7	Cameroon	−14.0	−8.3
Panama	10.7	8.7	Algeria	−13.2	−6.1
Mongolia	9.5	n.a.	Niger	−12.6	−17.0
Syrian Arab Republic	8.1	1.7	Congo People's Republic	−12.4	−1.7
Malaysia	8.0	7.9	Central African Republic	−11.4	−8.2
Costa Rica	6.2	13.8	Afghanistan	−11.1	n.a.
Chile	7.5[d]	13.2	Guinea	−11.0	n.a.
Dominican Republic	7.5[d]	10.7	Ethiopia	−10.0	−3.0
Paraguay	7.5[d]	9.3	Burundi	−9.7	−6.9
Taiwan	12.8[e]	n.a.	Nigeria	−9.5	−7.4
Vietnam	35.6[e]	n.a.	Papua New Guinea	−8.9	−8.7
			Zambia	−8.8	1.1
			Sudan	−8.6	−8.2
			Bolivia	−8.3	−8.6
			Sierra Leone	n.a.	−30.5
			Oman	n.a.	−30.1
			Gabon	n.a.	−28.7
			Somalia	n.a.	−13.4
			Uganda	n.a.	−9.7
			Mali	n.a.	−9.2
			Rwanda	n.a.	−9.2
			Malawi	n.a.	−8.0

Notes:
a Good performers for 1979 were defined as those showing 8 per cent or more positive deviation in life expectancy on the basis of estimated relationship between life expectancy and *per capita* income. Three equations were adopted and the estimates shown are the average of the three, see Stewart (1985a).
b For 1987, good performers were defined as those showing 8 per cent or more positive deviation in life expectancy on the basis of estimated relationship between life expectancy and *per capita* income, where Life expectancy = $18.7 + 6.1 \log y$ ($r^2 = 0.74$).
c Poor performers for 1979 & 1987 were defined as showing 8 per cent or more negative deviation in life expectancy on the basis of the estimated relationship between life expectancy and *per capita* income for that year.
d Exceptions for 1987 only
e Estimates for 1979 *per capita* income.
n.a. Not available.
Source: World Bank (1989); Stewart (1985a).

1. The socialist strategy has been employed in countries such as China, Albania, and Cuba. Among these countries there were: (1) egalitarian income distribution as a consequence of the major reduction in privately owned assets, near full employment, and state mechanisms to support incomes of those whose incomes fell below some minimum; (2) non-market elements in the allocation and pricing of goods, which ensured relatively low prices for BN goods and fairly equal access; (3) a production system which gave explicit priority to BN goods; and (4) an especially high priority to education[28] (partly for political reasons) which helped improve the efficiency of the metaproduction function. Socialist systems are not invariably successful. There can be massive production and organisational failures such as occurred in Ethiopia and Mozambique and during the drought in China.

2. The capitalist market has been successful in Taiwan and Hong Kong, countries where the economic system has produced rapid, egalitarian and labour-using economic growth, so that the incomes of the poor rose sufficiently to enable them to acquire enough marketed BN goods, while the government ensured high levels of publicly provided BN goods, especially health services and education. The successful capitalist model produced high levels of income as well as BN. Consequently, Hong Kong, which has one of the highest life expectancies in the world (at 76 years) is not shown in Table 3.2 because the achieved life expectancy is not especially high in relation to the high *per capita* income. These capitalist successes are few in number because, more typically, a predominantly capitalist system produces inegalitarian patterns of growth so that incomes of the bottom sections of the population may be insufficient to meet BN, and often, in parallel, public BN goods are in short supply and badly distributed.

3. Welfare state, mixed economy successes have been achieved in countries such as Sri Lanka and Costa Rica. In these economies the government intervened to make sure BN were met by providing food subsidies, food rations, and other BN goods. This third category tends to be politically and economically vulnerable. In Sri Lanka economic difficulties and political change have led to a dismantling of much of the programme since 1977. Consequently, standards of nutrition and education have deteriorated. Costa Rica too has been forced to abandon some of its basic needs programmes as a result of the economic crisis of the 1980s and pressures led by the international financial institutions to cut

public expenditures. But Costa Rica broadly sustained BN performance. Despite the changing circumstances of the 1980s, Table 3.2 indicates a fair amount of consistency in performance over time. Most of the countries showing good performance in 1979 were also good in 1987, and similarly for poor performers.

This classification of successful approaches to fulfilling BN has focused on types of political economy, and not on achievements with respect to particular BN goods. A supplementary approach is to examine how performance with respect to these goods is related to success in fulfilling BN. A number of investigations have been conducted along these lines.[29] Briefly, these studies agree on the following conclusions:

1. Levels of education are highly correlated with indicators of the full life, in terms of life expectancy, with female primary education being the most important variable.
2. Income per person is of substantial significance.
3. The number of doctors per person usually but not always is positively related to life expectancy.
4. Other variables that one might expect to be important do not serve systematically to explain variance in life expectancy across countries. The variables that are *not* significant include proportion of expenditures devoted to the social sectors, availability of clean water, and average availability of calories per person.

The variety of ways in which BN may be met is both a strength and a problem in raising fulfilment of BN to the status of a human right. It is a strength because it means that very different types of societies can succeed without having to change fundamental features of political economy such as the ownership and organisation of production. It is a problem because it means that there are no simple ways of identifying whether a society is going about it in the 'right' way. For example, it is not possible to say that food subsidies are or are not essential to meeting BN. Fulfilment of these needs depends on the whole structure of the economic system, along with cultural and sociological factors, so that in some societies food subsidies are essential, while in others they are actually counterproductive. This is not an unexpected outcome since the earlier theoretical reasoning about the determinants of basic needs fulfilment, as summarised in Figures 3.3 and 3.4, leads to the same conclusion. Just as the theoretical discussion suggested that there could be a variety of ways of fulfilling BN, the empirical examples show that quite a few of the theoretical possibilities have been exemplified in practice. This adds significantly to the theoretical reasoning because it shows that some sub-sets of the total range of possibilities are realistic politically. In the initial framework no account was taken of issues of political economy, but these can be of overwhelming importance in determining actual possibilities, as economists are increasingly recognising.[30] Some suggested strategies that seem plausible, (for example, the redistribution-with-growth strategy proposed in the 1970s[31]) in fact turn out to be ineffective because of these factors.

This brief overview of BN strategies has suggested some important conclusions for the possibility of enforcing BN as human rights:

1. The objective is a state of life, not the instrumentalities by which this state is realised. Therefore, state-of-life indicators should be the measure of achievement or failure. The variables to be chosen must depend ultimately on international agreement, but variables that are strong candidates include life expectancy, infant mortality rates, rates of malnutrition, and rates of literacy.
2. The wide variation in achievement with respect to these variables, even between countries of the same income levels, shows that for most countries there is a possibility of improved achievement.
3. Instrumental variables, which represent access to BN goods, are less suitable as human rights because they are not the 'state-of-life' objective but instruments to achieve it. In addition, empirical investigation shows a lack of systematic relationship between many of the obvious candidates for inclusion and the ultimate objective. However, they might nonetheless qualify as rights on two grounds. First, if there is strong empirical support for the view that some instrumental variable is necessary for the achievement of the objective, then this variable could usefully acquire the status of a quasi-right (that is, a human right by virtue of its causal connection with fulfilment of BN). Such a right would be 'quasi' in the sense that were the causal relationship subsequently found to have changed, the commodity in question would lose its human rights status. This could not happen for the constituent elements of a full life, such as health and nutrition. Empirical investigation so far suggests that access to primary education might be supported as such a quasi-right.

Second, certain commodities might be regarded as necessary for a decent life even though they are not strictly related to living a full life. For example, even if it were established that food was no longer necessary for nutrition but could be replaced by pills, a society that met its people's BN through pills might reasonably be argued to have failed to meet its full obligations. Where this is the case – when it is the goods themselves that are regarded as necessary for the fulfilment of BN, irrespective of their consequences for the human state – then these too may be regarded as quasi-rights. They may lose their status if changes in attitudes mean they are no longer essential aspects of a decent existence.

MONITORING AND ENFORCEMENT

Will giving BN the status of human rights have any effect on actual fulfilment of these needs? It may do so in a variety of ways, ranging from being good public relations for BN to encouraging the use of financial leverage to promote needs fulfilment. At its weakest, the fact that BN are human rights may strengthen those in the political process both inside a country and outside it who are trying to improve achievement. In itself the announcement that BN are human rights may do something – but probably very little – in this direction. More should be achieved with comprehensive and regular monitoring and reporting. Use of financial leverage to encourage fulfilment of BN also requires effective monitoring. Consequently, monitoring is fundamental to any attempt to make the human rights approach useful. As Harris stated, 'a human rights guarantee is as good as its system of supervision'.[32]

Monitoring requires agreement on definitions and indicators as well as regular, comprehensive, disaggregated, well-disseminated, and well-publicised statistics on the agreed indicators. The disaggregation is necessary because average countrywide statistics can appear satisfactory while concealing major deficiencies in certain regions, classes, age groups, etc.

These requirements are obvious. What is less obvious except to anyone who has worked in this field is that for most countries they are in no way being met. Some countries have little idea of the size of their population, and even less of other aspects of the human condition. While most countries can provide details on trade totals, with industrial and country disaggregation, on money supply in all its arcane aspects, few countries have up-to-date or comprehensive information on nutrition or infant mortality. Consequently, before BN can become meaningful as rights, the first priority is to generate mechanisms for recording relevant aspects of human well-being. The information needs to be collected regularly and disseminated quickly because this is an area where devastating changes can occur, involving rapid rise in death rates or falls in nutrition levels with permanent effects, as in the case of famines, and also as a consequence of recession.[33]

International machinery has been established to assist in the process of monitoring and supervising compliance with the covenant. The initial efforts to enforce the 1976 covenant were not effective.[34] The main responsibility for supervision was a working group consisting of government representatives and, subsequently, government experts, which did little to establish norms and secure effective supervision.[35] However, this was replaced in 1986 by the Independent Committee of Experts on Economic, Social and Cultural Rights (ICESCR), which is intended to strengthen the process of monitoring and thus facilitate enforcement. To do so effectively requires that the committee develop norms by which to judge compliance or noncompliance and that provide for comprehensive, relevant, and regular reporting on country performance. In the short time since the committee was established, governments themselves have determined the type of reports they submit, which have then been subject to questioning by the committee.[36] More detailed guidance to governments on reporting requirements would produce more systematic, relevant, and comparative reports. The committee also needs to develop standards against which compliance can be defined. The early discussions of the committee have shown a tendency to focus on areas which are readily defined – e.g., social security law and unemployment rates – with less attention paid to areas where definition of standards and data collection are much more difficult, such as health and nutrition. There is also a problem arising from the fact that governments themselves compile their own reports, a situation which is likely to lead to weak coverage of major problem areas unless very detailed guidelines are provided about required coverage.

Reporting and identification of failures to comply with the Covenant are only the first steps in enforcement. It is then necessary to secure action in light of these findings. At present the reports are submitted to the UN Secretary-General and are then reviewed by the

specialised UN agencies, the United Nations Economic and Social
Council (ECOSOC), with the assistance of the Committee of Experts
and the Commission on Human Rights. The Commission on Human
Rights and ECOSOC can then make recommendations 'of a general
nature', while ECOSOC can suggest measures of technical assistance
required in light of the reports and reviews. The general nature of the
recommendations envisaged make it unlikely that enforcement will
be very effective. Moreover, there is no provision for interstate or
individual complaints for noncompliance. At present then, enforcement depends entirely on publicity associated with the reporting
system.[37]

A somewhat more rigorous system of enforcement was established
for the European Social Charter. Here, too, a committee of independent experts was established to monitor and report achievements
with respect to the social and economic rights conferred by the
Charter. The committee asks for regular reports from member
countries and comes to conclusions. The major difference compared
with the Covenant is that a Committee of Ministers is empowered to
make recommendations to countries in light of these conclusions. In
practice, the Committee of Ministers has not made any recommendations; nonetheless, there is evidence of some changes made in response to the Charter. However, overall, 16 per cent of the
obligations are not being met, while two states are in breach of over a
quarter of their obligations.[38]

International supervision and enforcement of the rights conferred
by the 1976 Covenant could be increased in a number of ways. One is
to permit specific recommendations by ECOSOC to individual states.
Another would be to establish a mechanism whereby states and/or
individuals could file complaints against governments for non-
compliance. In effect both these mechanisms would increase publicity
regarding human rights performance and particularly failures to
protect human rights, but they would not necessarily ensure compliance. ECOSOC might not make recommendations (as in the case
of the European Social Charter), or if it did they might not be
accepted by the governments. In addition, any complaints procedure
through an international body is very difficult for the deprived to use,
is likely to cover only a small proportion of cases of non-compliance,
and when used may not secure any action.[39]

Another enforcement mechanism would be to use the influence of
international financial institutions to secure compliance. The World
Bank and the International Monetary Fund already use leverage

to try to enforce economic reforms. Neither so far has extended this into the arena of BN. Indeed, until recently, they took no notice of the effects on BN of economic developments or of their own policies, both of which have had a negative effect in recent years.[40] Not only did their policy packages not deal with meeting BN, but their monitoring of country performance did not include any systematic review of poverty, income distribution, or BN, which is one reason why statistics in this area are so deficient.

However, there have been signs of change. In a 1986 speech, de Larosière, then managing director of the IMF, spoke of the importance of securing 'adjustment that pays attention to the health, nutrition, and educational requirements of vulnerable groups'. In 1987 the World Bank produced a paper on methods of avoiding the 'social costs of adjustment'.[41] The IMF has not extended its programmes or monitoring to these areas, however, and the World Bank has confined its social costs policies to offsetting the direct costs to vulnerable groups of the bank's structural adjustment loans. It has not yet considered redesigning the programmes as a whole, nor extending protection to all vulnerable groups whose BN are not being met, irrespective of the cause. There is therefore a long way to go before the World Bank and IMF use their influence to see that BN are met, although both institutions have clauses in their constitutions which make this a reasonable – possibly even a compelling – aspect of their duties. The potential here is great because the two institutions have dealings with almost all countries where BN are not being fulfilled. At a minimum the World Bank and the IMF could demand statistics on the human conditions for their appraisal of country performance, thus greatly increasing effective monitoring. They should also ensure that their own programmes do not actually interfere with fulfilment of BN.

So far there has been no connection between the legal process of human rights review and the system of economic appraisal conducted by the international financial institutions. If the review procedures of the legal system were strengthened, as suggested, so that individual states' performance on economic and social rights were comprehensively monitored, this review could be used in decisions affecting finance and aid. Where the ICESCR found gross violations of social and economic rights, the information should be fed to the financial institutions. Good performance with regard to rights would earn the country a 'certificate of approval' from the ICESCR which would merit especially generous treatment by aid donors and financiers.

The Covenant on Economic, Social and Cultural Rights and the Declaration on the Rights to Development impose obligations not only on those governments of the Third World that fail to meet such rights, but also on the international community generally and the richer countries in particular. These obligations require the promotion of a financial and trading system that supports development and fulfilment of BN. Much of the growing failures to meet BN in the 1980s can be directly attributed to the deteriorating international economic environment – to accumulating debt, high interest rates, dramatic fall in lending to developing countries, poor economic growth among industrialised countries, rising protectionism, and falling commodity prices.[42] The deteriorating situation undermines countries' ability to meet the basic needs of their people, and has led to economic stagnation and falling investment which has put a halt to development in much of Africa and Latin America.

So far reviews of achievements of human rights under the Covenant have made no reference to the international economic system. Yet, since this is the environment that constrains what individual countries can do, the enforcement mechanism should include an examination of the performance of the rich countries in forming this environment. This would require that the international financial and trading environment also be reviewed by the Committee of Experts and ECOSOC and recommendations be made to governments and to the international financial institutions. The right to development has even stronger implications in relation to international obligations than the basic needs rights in the covenant, since adverse international economic conditions can interfere with or even halt development.

Improved performance in meeting BN and providing a climate more conducive to development is likely to require the following sorts of changes internationally: (1) increased resource flows especially to the poorest countries, where the current financial strangulation is causing substantial damage to both growth and BN; (2) improved buffering mechanisms to protect poor countries from recession and primary commodity price fluctuations; (3) improved trade and price prospects for low-income countries; and (4) increased BN content of aid, with less spent on inappropriate goods and technologies and more on low-cost activities and technologies which may reach many more. In fact, since the 1976 Covenant, which implicitly recognised BN as a human right, performance in these areas has not improved but deteriorated.

CONCLUSION

If the purpose of establishing international human rights is that action should and will be taken to see that they are realised to the maximum extent possible, then General Assembly resolutions are just the beginning of the story. The recent establishment of the ICESCR indicates that serious action is intended. The basic needs analysis summarised above indicates areas where the ICESCR could make important contributions. First, the ICESCR could help secure international agreement regarding what these human rights mean more precisely in both rich and poor countries. Second, the ICESCR is well placed to provide systematic monitoring of the well-being of the most deprived, identifying areas of non-compliance and specifying where actions are needed, not only with respect to the individual governments, as currently envisaged, but also in the international economic system. The ICESCR would need to provide detailed guidelines to governments on reporting requirements and also provide for some independent reporting, for example, through the specialised agencies.

In addition, enforcement mechanisms need to be strengthened. ECOSOC and the Commission on Human Rights should be encouraged to make specific recommendations, not merely general ones. Individual and state complaints procedures could be introduced, and international financial leverage could be used to support protection of economic and social human rights.

It is clear from the analysis above that recognising BN as human rights requires a complex process of definition, monitoring, and enforcement, of which only the very first steps have been taken so far. A similarly complex process would be involved with respect to the right to development, although less has been said on the subject here. There is a danger that such complexity may mean that little is achieved, which could undermine the significance of international human rights in this area. Progress is therefore most important in making these economic, social, and cultural rights a reality. Such progress could make the international human rights system a significant mechanism for the achievement of BN and for the reduction of human deprivation.

NOTES

1. Rawls (1971) p. 62.
2. G. A. Res. 2200 A/21, UN Doc. A/63/6 (1966).
3. G. A. Res. 41/128 (1986).
4. For a description of the BN approach, see ILO (1976); Streeten *et al.* (1981) pp. 3–45; and Stewart (1985a) pp. 1–13.
5. Rawls (1971) p. 62.
6. See Trubeck (1984) pp. 205–71; Alston and Quinn (1987) pp. 156–222 for a description and analysis of the social and economic rights in the 1976 International Covenant on Economic, Social and Cultural Rights.
7. G. A. Res. 41/128, art. 1.
8. Defined as 'social welfare rights' in Trubeck (1984) pp. 228–30.
9. See Alston (1987b).
10. See Stewart (1985a) pp. 17–19, for further elaboration. The metaproduction function and the framework for planning to meet basic needs described in this paper were developed jointly with John Fei and Gustav Ranis.
11. Sen (1985) pp. 1–71.
12. Sen (1985) pp. 10–11.
13. Sen (1985) pp. 52–71.
14. One problem with all these measures is that they represent an average, and countries may do well on average despite very poor performance among some groups. Moreover, there is considerable controversy about some measures of the degree and incidence of malnutrition; see Suhatme (1982); Gopolan (1983).
15. See Jhabvala (1984) pp. 149–82.
16. This methodology is developed in Stewart (1985a) pp. 55–86.
17. Trubeck (1984) pp. 213–17. Also see the discussion in the Limburg Principles (1987) pp. 122–35.
18. Jhabvala (1984) pp. 149–82.
19. UNICEF has identified a set of low-cost health interventions that should be in the reach of every country. See UNICEF (1984) pp. 1–5; Cornia *et al.* (1987) pp. 218–23.
20. Data requirements for monitoring fulfilment of BN are similar to those identified as necessary for monitoring the situation of vulnerable groups during periods of economic recession and adjustment. These are analysed in Cornia *et al.* (1987) pp. 257–72.
21. Sen (1981) pp. 287–319. For further discussion of Sri Lanka, see Isenman (1980) pp. 237–58; Edirisinghe (1986).
22. Hicks (1979) pp. 985–94.
23. Cornia *et al.* (1987) pp. 93–125.
24. For a discussion of Taiwan see Ranis (1978) pp. 397–409; Hicks (1979) pp. 985–94.
25. These are described in more detail in Stewart (1985a) pp. 15–35; see also Van der Hoeven (1987).
26. Stewart (1985a) pp. 66–70.
27. Stewart (1985a) pp. 70–86.
28. Education has been found universally to be highly correlated with full

life indicators such as life expectancy and (negatively) infant mortality; Stewart (1985a) pp. 19–102.

29. Sheehan and Hopkins (1979); Hicks (1982); Berg (1981). The results are summarised in Stewart (1985a) pp. 99–102.
30. Krueger (1984); Bates (1983).
31. Chenery *et al.* (1974).
32. Harris (1984) p. 261.
33. Cornia *et al.* (1987) pp. 11–35 describe the negative impact of the recession of the 1980s on low-income groups.
34. Westerveen (1984) pp. 119–24; Alston (1987a) pp. 332–81.
35. Described in Alston (1987a) pp. 332–81.
36. This view is derived from the summary records of the First Session of the Independent Committee of Experts on Economic, Social and Cultural Rights, E/C/12/1987/SR.1–28 Add.1.
37. Alston (1987a) pp. 340–50.
38. Harris (1984) pp. 188–99.
39. Dhagamwar (1987).
40. See Cornia *et al.* (1987) pp. 48–72.
41. World Bank (1987a).
42. Analysed in Cornia *et al.* (1987) pp. 12–35.

Part II
Trade

4 Recent Theories of International Trade: Some Implications for the South*

INTRODUCTION

Over the last thirty years, a set of new theories has been put forward to complement (and/or substitute for) the simple Heckscher–Ohlin (H–O) model. The new theories were a response to two deficiencies in the H–O paradigm. First, the oversimplified and often patently unrealistic, assumptions behind H–O, especially in the simplest text-book versions: these include 'perfect competition, international identity of production functions and factors, non-reversibility of factor intensities and international similarity of preferences',[1] together with constant returns to scale, if the usual free trade, and specialisation in accordance with factor endowment, conclusions are to be derived. Second, the theory, at least superficially, seemed incapable of explaining certain significant empirical findings about the world economy. These included the Leontief paradox; the growth in trade between *similar* economies with near-identical factor endowment; the fact that a considerable portion of trade in manufacturers (and its growth) is intra-industry; and the fact that there appears to be a strong tendency for growth in trade to exceed growth in income.

The focus of the new theories, which aim to adopt a more realistic set of assumptions and to incorporate some or all of these awkward facts, has been on trade between advanced countries (i.e., North–North trade),[2] because it is between these economies that growth in trade has been greatest, while factor endowment theories are least applicable. Grubel and Lloyd (1975) have shown that intra-industry trade is greatest for North–North trade, much less significant for North–South and South–South trade; in addition, while trade growth has greatly exceeded income growth among advanced countries, this

* First published in Kierskowski (1984). I am grateful to other contributors and to Subra Ghatak and Gustav Ranis for comments.

69

has not been the case for poor countries.[3] Moreover, the Leontief paradox (with a capital abundant USA exporting labour-intensive commodities and importing capital-intensive ones), which can be 'explained' by incorporating skill into factor endowment,[4] does not apply to poor countries. In general North–South trade is in accordance with H–O theory, with the North exporting capital- and skill-intensive products and the South exporting (unskilled) labour-intensive goods.[5]

None the less, in one vitally important respect – that of eventual factor price equalisation – the Samuelson–Stolper development of H–O has not shown much sign of coming to fruition; and this respect, that of substantial and in absolute terms growing, income differences between North and South is the one that the Third World cares about most. In addition, the assumptions of H–O are in some respects even less realistic with respect to North–South than North–North (or South–South) trade – in particular with respect to the assumed identical production functions between countries (which involves equal knowledge about and access to technology) and similar preferences. Moreover, since the prime concern of developing countries is development (i.e., to *change* their factor endowment, their incomes, and their consumption patterns), they tend to find a theory, such as H–O, which assumes all these as given and unchanging, particularly unattractive.

Nonetheless despite some problems for the South about the H–O theories, the new theories have been directed in the main to North–North trade. The aim of this essay is to explore what relevance (if any) these theories have for the South, given this predominantly Northern focus, and the satisfaction of many observers with an H–O model for predicting trade patterns for the South.[6] Perhaps because of the Northern focus, the new theories in the main remain surprisingly undynamic, particularly with respect to the direction of technical change in products and processes. For the North this may not be of great significance since technical change being endogenous to them can be assumed to be broadly in line with factor availability and income levels, while for the South, where technical change is largely exogenous coming from the North, it can incorporate significant biases.

This essay therefore will try to add a dynamic dimension to the theories under discussion, especially with respect to technical change.

THE 'NEW' THEORIES

A very brief description of the main features of the various theories, 'old' and 'new', to be considered is helpful before exploring implications for the South:

1. Simple factor proportions theory, described as H–O, with two factors of production, capital and labour, in which, given the assumptions already described, trade flows in accordance with relative factor endowment of capital and labour (Heckscher and Ohlin, 1988; see Heckscher, 1919; Ohlin, 1933).
2. Factor proportions theory encompassing 'human capital' as a third factor of production. Again trade flows occurs according to endowment, including human capital (Leontief, 1953; Kenen, 1965; Keesing, 1966).
3. Scale economies with homogeneous products, where a large home market gives a cost advantage in products with significant economies of scale. Small countries with small markets would specialise in constant returns/diminishing returns products (Drèze, 1960).
4. Technological gap theory: countries which innovate gain an advantage and export to countries which are technologically lagging in particular lines. This trade is eliminated when the laggards catch up, but new innovations create new possibilities for trade (Posner, 1961; Hufbauer, 1966).
5. Product cycle theory: advanced countries develop and then export new products. Once the technology has been standardised (matured) it is transferred to low wage-cost countries and the product re-exported to the technological leaders (Vernon, 1966).
6. Preference similarity: differentiated products are developed for the home market in accordance with domestic preferences. These preferences depend in large part on income levels. The products are exported to markets with similar tastes (Linder, 1961).
7. Economies of scale through intra-industry specialisation, where specialisation is limited by the extent of the *international* market. International trade takes the form of intra-industry trade in intermediate products to exploit economies of specialisation (Ethier, 1979; Krugman, 1979a).
8. The significance of *intra-firm* trade. This has been shown to be of substantial and growing importance. Its existence suggests certain

advantages (which could consist of organisation, or market access or technology access, which accrues within firms as compared to trade between firms). The convenience of intra-firm trade may help overcome some of the disadvantage of geographic dispersion in trade in intermediate products and thus help explain its existence (i.e., theory 7) (Lall, 1973; Helleiner, 1981a).

In the absence of international firms, it seems likely that much trade in intermediate products would take place at the national level, since national sales are easier to organise than international. This possibility is illustrated by the large amount of national sub-contracting and national trade in intermediate products in Japan, in the absence of multinational firms, while in Europe many of the major multinationals deploy their production to exploit economies of scale in different countries (e.g., Ford producing bodies in one country and engines in another). However, marketing agencies can substitute for the organisational advantage of the multinationals, as in S. Korea. According to this view, the growing predominance of multinational intra-firm trade both explains and is explained by specialisation and consequent trade in intermediate products.

9. Economies of scale in differentiated products, with diversity of preference. Each economy produces a limited number of differentiated products and international trade widens potential choice (Lancaster, 1980; Krugman, 1980).

10. Economies of scale in differentiated products, in the presence of transport costs. In this case, the larger the home market, the greater the possibility of exploiting economies of scale so that there is a terms of trade advantage to the larger market (Krugman, 1980).

11. Product variety plus transport costs. Each country produces a limited variety of products. Because of transport costs, foreign products generally cost more than home products. As incomes rise, the propensity to import rises as consumers can satisfy their inherent desire for variety, while exports also rise in response to similar tendencies in other countries. The net result is that international trade rises faster than incomes (Barker, 1977).

N.B.

12. The implications of *learning* economies for international trade. Here increasing returns are related to the accumulation of experience, rather than scale alone. These learning economies may be internal to the firm, external to the firm but internal to an industry, or may accrue as a result of the accumulation of

manufacturing experience as a whole. Learning economies generate cumulative tendencies between countries, so that countries that acquire an initial advantage in any area where learning economies are significant enjoy an increasing advantage over time (Westphal, 1982; Stewart, 1982; Krugman, 1984).

13. Recent developments in trade theory have focussed on *strategic* games played by large firms in the international arena (e.g. Spencer and Brander, 1983). This set of theories is not discussed here, but considered in the next chapter.

It should be noted that none of these theories needs to be treated as an exclusive explanation of trading patterns. Indeed it is unlikely that any one of the theories would explain all trading patterns. This is a major deficiency of many empirical tests of different theories which tend to apply to all manufactured commodities (e.g., Hufbauer, 1970). In some cases, commodities may fit into just one of the categories – e.g., homogeneous goods produced under constant returns to scale, with capital and labour as the major elements in production costs, would fit the H–O model. For other types of trade, more than one of the theories may be applicable. For example, some intra-industry trade takes advantage of different factor costs in locating production of different elements of the productive process, and thus both exploits economies of specialisation and is located along H–O lines.

SPECIAL FEATURES OF SOUTHERN ECONOMIES

Certain features of Southern economies are of particular relevance to the applicability and implications of the various theories. These features all stem from lower levels of development. The first concerns patterns of demand: the remainder affect conditions of supply.

1. The substantial difference in *per capita* incomes between North and South has implications for consumer preferences, not only as between broad categories of goods (food and manufactures, for example) but also as between particular characteristics of goods. If, as a short cut, we assume that goods embody varying combinations of 'high-income' and 'low-income' characteristics (following Lancaster's approach to consumer demand), then one would expect low-income countries to have preferences more weighted

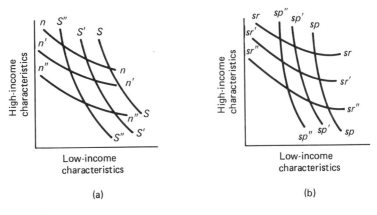

Figure 4.1   Country preference patterns

towards low-income characteristics, as shown in Figure 4.1. Actual preferences, as expressed through the market, depend on the
distribution of money income. Countries with highly skewed income distribution will exhibit demand for goods similar to those
demanded in the North, from their high-income groups. But they
will then have large numbers of consumers with very low incomes
and consequently with a greater preference for low-income
characteristics than in countries where incomes are more evenly
distributed. This is also shown in Figure 4.1.

2. In general, most Southern economies are capital scarce and
   skilled-labour scarce, and unskilled-labour abundant, as compared with Northern countries. (There are, however, exceptions:
   for example, the oil-rich countries tend to be capital rich, but
   skilled- and unskilled-labour scarce; some Asian countries have
   quite abundant supplies of particular types of educated–skilled
   labour.)

3. Southern economies have small domestic markets, relative to
   most Northern economies.

4. Industrial experience in general, and in particular types of production, is more limited (in terms of time and quantity) than in
   Northern countries.

5. For the most part, the South does not initiate technical change.
   Recently a few countries have shown some technical innovations
   but these are very small in magnitude compared with the innovations coming from the North. The fact that – in the main – the
   South is the recipient of technical change from the North means

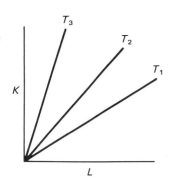

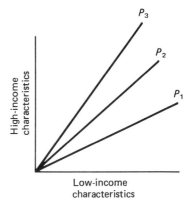

T_1-T_3 shows technical change over time, in relation to K/L

P_1-P_3 shows technical change over time in relation to product characteristics

Figure 4.2 New technologies and products from the North

that the characteristics of the technical change reflect the Northern environment. It therefore exhibits biases in terms of the Southern environment. These biases relate both to techniques of production and to product characteristics. More formally, Lancaster (1984) shows how, in equilibrium, in the presence of economies of scale and therefore with a finite number of firms, products actually produced will tend, relatively, to be in accordance with the tastes of the larger market. Since developed countries constitute the largest market, this theory, applied to North–South, would mean that the product space filled would be proportionately biased towards markets of the North. Similarly, Shaked and Sutton's analysis suggests that with vertical product differentiation, firms will tend to fill up the space at the higher-income end of the spectrum – which means that new products emanating from the North will tend to have increasingly high-income characteristics. (Shaked and Sutton (1984)).

New technologies from the North tend to be increasingly capital-intensive (higher K/L) and (often) skill-intensive, while the products tend to embody increasingly high-income character- istics, as illustrated by Figure 4.2.

6. Southern economies are characterised by very substantial el- ements of x-inefficiency – in terms of under-employment of some resources and poor productivity of resources in use.

7. For the most part of the organisation (and headquarters) of MNCs

is in the North, not the South. This is being gradually modified, but remains true for the vast bulk of MNCs – see Lall (1982b) and Lecraw (1977).

8. Owing to colonial and neocolonial experience the infrastructure (of trade, finance, administration, experience and contacts, transport) has a heavy North–North and North–South bias and is relatively highly deficient with respect to South–South trade.

As already noted, these generalisations do not apply uniformly to all countries, but they are of sufficient generality to permit some conclusions with respect to the implications of the various theories for the South. Among the three major directions of trade, North–North, North–South, South–South, it is helpful to distinguish two sub-groups, regional North–North and regional South–South. These regional groups are distinct in that organisational problems and transport costs are generally less than for non-regional trade.

SOME IMPLICATIONS OF THE THEORIES

As far as the South is concerned the criteria for assessing international trade are generally broader than in much 'gains from trade' literature. As well as the obvious gains from allocational efficiency, general development effects need to be considered. These include effects on the accumulation of capital, skills, learning (and hence on future 'endowment'), the terms of trade effects (including the terms of trade for technology acquisition), effects on x-inefficiency and on the employment of resources, since the 'full employment' assumption of much trade theory is singularly inappropriate, and effects on the distribution of income and of consumption. In addition, some would include 'independence' or 'self-reliance' as a significant consideration. 'Self-reliance' forms one of the major objectives of the Group of 77, but it is not included in the discussion of the theories below.

Most of the theories apply to trade in manufactures, not primarily products where climatic conditions play a significant role. The advantages and disadvantages for the South of trade in primary goods is normally mainly discussed in terms of trends and fluctuations in the terms of trade. Aspects of production and trade in primary products do fit into some of the theories, but in this essay we confine attention to manufactures.

Table 4.1 briefly summarises some implications of the theories outlined in the second section in the light of the special features of the South suggested on pp. 73–6. Here I will briefly discuss the main findings.

A. Theory 1: simple H–O. Given the substantial difference in factor availability between North and South, with the North capital abundant and labour scarce and the South labour abundant and capital scarce, the H–O theory explains North–South trade in terms of this difference, with the North exporting capital-intensive goods and importing labour-intensive goods from the South. The theory concludes that both parties gain from the exchange. With some minor qualifications, the theory leads to free trade policy conclusions. This is a strong conclusion with, for the most part, strong empirical backing in the form of evidence on the actual characteristics of trade in manufactures between North and South. The remaining eleven theories all suggest the need for some qualification to this theory both as descriptions of actual trade flows and in terms of policy prescriptions.

B. Theory 2: H–O plus human capital. The introduction of a third factor of production – human skills – as an explanation of trade flows involves a major change as far as the South is concerned. The theory suggests that the North will export both capital-intensive and skill-intensive products and import unskilled-labour-intensive products. The South specialises in unskilled-labour-intensive manufactures, as it is relatively short of human skills. But from a South point of view this is likely to involve adverse terms of trade, since human skills *N. B.* (and their products) command a higher price than unskilled labour. This indeed is one of the causes of Emmanuel's (1972) 'unequal exchange'. Because human skills can be created, the South may wish to subsidise the creation of human skills, and interfere with the workings of free trade in order to do so.

C. The technology gap–product cycle theories (5 and 6). The relevant special feature of the South in relation to these theories is that, for the most part, the South is a recipient and not an innovator of technical change. While Northern countries may both initiate and receive technological change, the South is in an asymmetrical position, receiving but not initiating new technologies. This has implications both for the terms of trade and for the direction of technological change.

Table 4.1 Summary of implications of trade theories for the South

	Theory	Special feature of South	Direction of trade	Nature of trade	Terms of trade	Technical change	Other factors	Policy implications
1.	Simple 2-factor H-O	Capital scarce, labour abundant	North→South	Mainly inter-industry	'Unequal' exchange as South specialises in low-wage activities	May undermine comparative advantage, e.g. garments tc: 'inappropriate'	South wishes to change endowment	'Free' trade; South may need to innovate to maintain comparative advantage
2.	H-O plus 'human capital'	South generally human-capital scarce but varies between countries	North ↔ South; some North ↔ North; some South ↔ South	Mainly inter-industry	'Unequal' exchange as skilled labour receives higher rewards	Changes skill requirements and comp. advantage	–	–
3.	Scale economies in homogeneous commodities	South small domestic markets	North → South; North ↔ North for scale econ. goods: South → North; South ↔ North, non-scale econ. goods	Mainly inter-industry	Tends to favour countries with scale econ. where imperfect competition may prevail	Tends to accentuate scale economies	–	–
4.	Technological gap	South generally technological laggards	North ↔ North; North → South	Inter- and intra-industry	North receives Schumpeterian profits as innovators	Direction of tc in products and techniques inappropriate for South	Tendency for tc to create dualistic development	South needs to create own innovatory capacity to enter this trade as technological leader

5.	Product cycle	South does not innovate in products	Initially North → South; subsequently South → North	Inter-industry	North receives quasi-rents as 4	Direction of tc inappropriate as 4; reverse trade may be undermined by innovations, as 1	As 4	South needs to promote own product innovations
6.	Preference similarity	South lower incomes per *capita* than North; does not innovate in products	North ↔ North; North → South for élite markets; South ↔ South, but limited by lack of South innovations	Inter- and intra-industry (final products)	–	Products likely to be for increasingly high-income markets	Potential for South–South trade if South innovates	South promote own product innovations
7.	Econ. of scale, intra-industry specialisation in intermediate products	South earlier stage of development; weaker trading infrastructure	Mainly North ↔ North; some South → North with H–O element; limited South ↔ South	Intra-industry	–	H–O element in such trade in South changed by tc	Potential for productivity gains for South from South–South trade	Improve South–South infrastructure, organisation; reduce South–South trade barriers
8.	Intra-firm trade	North dominate MNCs	North ↔ North; and North → South	Intra-industry	Major gains to countries which control MNCs	tc leads to relocation of industry via MNC	–	South may bargain; also promote own MNCs
9.	Intra-industry specialisation in differentiated final products	South markets and scale of production smaller	Primarily North ↔ North; potentially South ↔ South	Intra-industry	Equivalent for producers of differentiated products. May be against producers of homogeneous products	Element of product differentiation may increase	Being late-starter may be disadvantage where ec. of scale significant	Promotion policies to enter market. Potential for South–South

continued on page 80

Table 4.1 continued

	Theory	Special feature of South	Direction of trade	Nature of trade	Terms of trade	Technical change	Other factors	Policy implications
10.	As 8 with transport costs	South smaller markets	As 8	As 8	Larger market secures better terms of trade	–	–	–
11.	Product variety – dynamic	South lower *per capita* incomes	Primarily North ↔ North; tendency for North → South	Intra-industry	–	Product differentiation increases	As South incomes rise greater variety of products demanded	Need for policies to deal with demand for greater variety
12.	Learning economies	South at earlier stage of 'learning'	North → South where learning significant factor	Inter- and intra-industry	South produces less 'learning-intensive' products: probably lower returns	tc requires ability to adapt to new processes	Learning economies present disadvantage (and potential) for South	Justifies South protection against North

The South first imports the products of technological innovation from the North, then imports the technology and may re-export the product back to the North. But because of continuous innovation, countries in the South are permanently in a position of importing the products of later and later innovations and of having their own competitiveness in existing lines undermined unless they import recent technologies, or are able to introduce sufficient innovations in the technologies they are using to maintain competitiveness. The terms of trade tend to be adverse to the South because they pay a form of Schumpeterian profits to the innovators, in the form of high product prices, when a new innovation first occurs. In the initial phases of a new product, prices are high enough for the entrepreneur to reap 'abnormal' profits *and* to pay the high wages necessary in developed countries (DC). But as more producers enter the market, the price tends to fall so that eventually production is transferred to low wage countries. Thus when the South is *importing* the product, they pay the high prices which cover Schumpeterian profits and high DC wages; by the time they become producers and start to export the product the price has fallen, so that it is sufficient to cover the low LDC wages, but not the high DC wages. So long as firms in DCs maintain property rights over the technology, even when they are producers of a particular product, they will still pay the North for the use of the technology. Meanwhile, while the South begins to export the product whose price has fallen, new products will have been developed in the North, which they will sell to the South for prices high enough to cover their wages and to earn some Schumpeterian profits. Hence an intrinsic aspect of the product cycle process is that the technology-initiating high-wage economy enjoys high prices for its products relative to the technology-receiving low-wage economy. Krugman (1979b) has presented a formal model of aspects of this process.

The second implication of the asymmetry is that the South has to accept the direction of technological change emanating from the North. As described earlier this tends to be inappropriate in both process and product dimensions, with the techniques being yearly more capital-intensive and the products embodying more high-income characteristics (see Figure 4.2).

The technological gap explanation of trade as initially put forward was supposedly a two-way phenomenon between equally developed countries, so that the net terms of trade effect would be

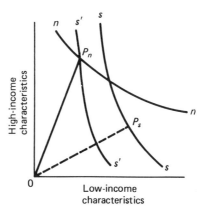

Figure 4.3   Southern trade and preferences

insignificant and the direction of technology change could be
assumed equally appropriate for each country. But this is not the
case between North and South. To benefit from such a process
and avoid the adverse consequences the South would need to
become innovators themselves.

D. The preference similarity theory (6) is primarily applicable to
North–North trade, since it explains trade between innovating
and similar economies. It is assumed, with some empirical justification, that products are first designed for the home market; they
are then exported to countries with similar tastes, where tastes are
assumed to be mainly determined by income level. Strictly, then,
the South – which generally does not innovate, especially in
products, and which has substantially lower-income levels, on
average, and consequently according to the theory, different
tastes from the North – would not participate in this form of
trade. In practice, as is well known, the South does import
consumer products from the North, despite the difference in
incomes. This may be explained by two factors: first, marked
inequality of incomes among some South economies means that
the incomes of the rich in these economies are similar to those in
the North – hence among these groups there is a market for
Northern products (as depicted earlier in Figure 4.1b). Second, in
the absence of alternative products, the South may consume
products from the North, as shown in Figure 4.3. While the South
has different tastes (represented by indifference curves *ss*), if
product OP_n is the only available product there is a market for it.

The main lesson for the South from this theory is that potentially the South could enjoy preference-similarity trade with other South economies but only if the South innovates and produces its own products. For example, if a South product OP_s, which cost the same as OP_n, were available it would be preferred to OP_n (Figure 4.3).

E. Theories of monopolistic competition and product differentiation (9 and 10) are fairly closely related to the preference similarity theory. The existence of economies of scale in the production of differentiated products means that each nation produces only a limited variety of the infinite possible combination of characteristics. International trade permits consumers to enjoy a wider range of choice.

Models of this type of trade have shown that the actual combination of characteristics of the products produced and traded will tend to be nearer to the tastes of the larger market (Lancaster, 1984), while, with transport costs, the terms of trade will tend to favour producers in the larger market (Krugman, 1980). With this type of trade, then, those in smaller markets will tend to get worse terms both as consumers (in terms of the availability and/or price of the combination of characteristics they prefer) and as producers. The South can be thought of as a smaller market, relative to the North, in this context. Given economies of scale and transport costs in the production of differentiated products, the South generally has a comparative disadvantage in the production of these goods which, for the most part, it produces only with heavy protection. International trade in these products permits Southern consumers a wide choice of products produced in the North, but these tend all to have high-income characteristics since it is among high-income consumers that the main market lies.

One major difference then, for this type of trade in differentiated products, for North–South trade, as compared with North–North for which the models have been primarily developed, lies in the different preferences of South consumers arising from different (lower) levels of income so that the combination of characteristics preferred in the North and embodied in most Northern products may differ from the preferred combination of the majority of South consumers, as depicted in Figure 4.3 in relation to the preference-similarity theory. This difference in preferences is not confined to consumer goods, but also applies to producer goods, where differences in conditions of production,

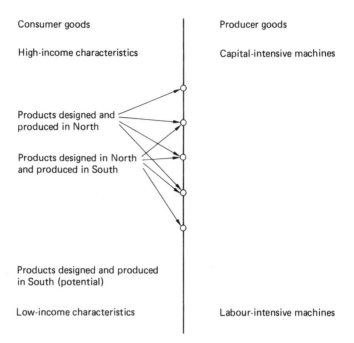

Consumer goods   Producer goods

High-income characteristics   Capital-intensive machines

Products designed and
produced in North

Products designed in North
and produced in South

Products designed and produced
in South (potential)

Low-income characteristics   Labour-intensive machines

Figure 4.4   Combinations of product characteristics

notably in factor availability and scale of market, make for
demand for different producer goods. However, as shown in
Figure 4.3, in the absence of any alternative the South may and
does consume Northern products (both consumer and producer)
but the combination of characteristics offered gives less welfare
than a specifically designed South product would. Though the
South may produce differentiated products, in general it does so
on the basis of Northern designs. Hence Southern production
does little to modify the range of characteristics available.

In Figure 4.4 we depict one dimension of possible combinations
of characteristics that might potentially be embodied in actual
products as being represented by a vertical line running from
high-income characteristics to low-income characteristics (for
consumer goods), and capital-intensive to labour-intensive (with
respect to producer goods), while the circles depict actual products. The upper portion of the line shows the type of products the
North would be likely to design and produce, while over time new
products would tend to move upwards along the line. So long as

the South does not design its products but uses Northern designs it will be confined to a similar range, although it may select the most appropriate (lowest) out of the range, and may, by minor modifications, shift the range further downwards. New products designed in and for the South would tend to be in the lower portion of the line.

Where the South produces differentiated consumer goods, it tends to do so on a small scale and hence fails to realise potential economies of scale. Lacking a natural comparative advantage in the production of these goods, especially in the initial stages of production when there are diseconomies of small scale and x-inefficiency is high due to lack of experience, most countries start production under heavy protective barriers, where the market is confined to the relatively small domestic market. In the pre-import substitution stage, consumers are able to import a variety of products made by different manufacturers. When it is decided to establish domestic production, governments often permit this variety to be reproduced locally, establishing (e.g., a Fiat plant, a VW plant, a Ford plant, etc.), thus ensuring that each plant will have a very limited market. For example, in Mexico in 1977, 57 different automobile models were being produced, with costs that were over 50 per cent higher than country of origin costs. In contrast, in Brazil, a much smaller number of car producers had been allowed and Volkswagen had captured nearly 90 per cent of the domestic market with the 'beetle', producing on a scale that reduced costs to internationally competitive levels, so that a substantial export market was built up.[7] The two cases illustrate a dilemma for LDC governments in relation to the production of differentiated consumer goods, subject to economies of scale. If local production is to be established on a sufficient scale to realise economies of scale, then normally very few varieties can be justified, given the small scale of the domestic market. Hence there appears to be a trade-off between efficiency and variety, unless international trade can perform the role of permitting specialisation, economies of scale and variety to be exploited, as occurs within the North. But in the South, in the initial stages at least, free trade would normally eliminate local production. Here trade within the South, with one country specialising on one type of car, and others on others, could provide a means of combining infant industry protection (against the North), exploitation of economies of scale and economies of specialisation and variety.

This conclusion may be especially relevant to the pressures that arise over time, as the demand for variety increases with incomes.
F. The Barker theory of product variety plus economic growth (11) is a dynamic development of theories which explain trade by preferences for product characteristics. In this theory, as incomes rise the variety of products consumed tends to rise, as people are able to afford to buy goods more nearly representing their preferred combination of characteristics. Because of economies of scale, each nation produces only a limited variety of goods and additional variety is achieved by spending an increasing proportion of income on imported goods. For the North, the increase in proportion of income imported can be expected to be paralleled by an increase in the proportion of differentiated products exported, since rising incomes abroad also cause a rise in the variety of goods consumed and imported. But the position is rather different for the South. In general it seems correct to argue that for the South too a rise in incomes will be accompanied by a demand for increasing variety of products consumed. It is helpful to interpret this 'demand for increasing variety' rather more broadly than simply a question of more variants of a rather narrowly defined product (e.g., demand for Fiats as well as Minis), as in the original article. The demand for additional variety also encompasses demands for goods which were not consumed when incomes were lower (e.g., at very low levels of income a move away from spending most income on food and housing towards also spending on textiles and shoes; at higher incomes a move towards a variety of consumer durables).

A consumer survey in Brazil in 1972 illustrates how consumer demand alters with income level (Table 4.2). As incomes rise, each income group will tend to demand different products and a greater variety within any product group. If there were no restrictions on trade, this change in preferences associated with rising incomes could be expected to lead to increasing (proportionate) expenditure on imports. But for the South this leads to a major difficulty because the South produces only a limited number of differentiated products of the type for which demand is increasing. While most countries will produce some of the goods demanded at the lower- and middle-income ranges, the new demands that arise among the upper-income groups, as incomes rise, will generally not be satisfiable by local production, or by imports from other South economies except at very high cost. With

Table 4.2 *Brazil*: % of households in each decile of the household income distribution owning consumer durable goods, 1972

	0–10	10–20	20–30	30–40	40–50	50–60	60–70	70–80	80–90	90–100	Average for all households
Gas and electric stoves	10	14	24	33	56	56	77	82	88	92	53
Electric iron	7	10	18	26	45	45	69	75	84	95	47
Table radio	19	24	32	36	43	43	48	49	49	43	39
Portable radio	10	13	18	21	29	29	37	42	49	67	31
Refrigerator	3	3	6	10	16	24	41	53	68	87	31
Television	3	3	6	10	17	27	45	57	70	85	32
Liquefier	2	3	5	8	16	16	36	46	60	81	27
Floor-polisher	1	1	2	3	7	7	19	28	41	65	17
Bicycle	5	7	11	13	18	18	21	23	24	26	17
Gramophone	1	1	2	3	5	7	13	19	27	50	13
Motor car	0.4	0.6	0.9	1.6	2.4	4.2	8.2	14.8	24.9	59.7	11.7
Fan	1	1	1	1	5	5	11	15	22	38	10
Washing-machine	0	0	0	1	1	2	3	6	12	33	6
Cake-mixer	0	0	0	1	1	1	4	7	13	36	6
Vacuum-cleaner	0	0	0	0	0	1	1	3	6	25	4
Air-conditioner	0	0	0	0	0	0	0	0	1	7	1
Motor-cycle	0	0	0	0	0	0	1	1	1	1	0
Average annual household income (US $)	128	254	400	506	686	934	1305	1819	2636	8663	1726

Source: Wells (1977) p. 260.

unrestricted trade then there will be a strong tendency for imports of differentiated products to rise, but no parallel tendency (in contrast to North economies) for exports to rise. There will therefore be a tendency for the North–South trade balance to deteriorate, as a result of changes in preferences with rising incomes.

The tendency for preferences for imports of differentiated products to rise as incomes rise is liable to occur irrespective of the initial income distribution. Even with egalitarian income distribution, the incomes of those at the top of the scale will rise as incomes rise, unless income distribution becomes more egalitarian over time to such an extent that the incomes of the rich are stabilised over time. For income distribution to become steadily more equal over time is very unusual. In the typical case, as Kuznets (1955) first noted, incomes tend to become more unequal with development.

The tendency for demand for increasing variety of differentiated consumer goods as incomes rise has long been apparent to governments of LDCs, and they have dealt with it in a number of different ways. On the one hand, governments in some rather inegalitarian states have tried to keep domestic production in line with domestic demands, leading to the production domestically of a wide proliferation of consumer goods. This has tended to mean rather inefficient production because of the small scale of the domestic market, and involved capital-intensive production with a heavy reliance on imports of machinery and technology and parts. Some of the Latin American patterns of development, for example in Brazil and Mexico, have been on these lines. At the other extreme, radical governments have tried to repress these demands by prohibiting imports and local production of certain luxury items. But this leads to pent-up demand, black markets, and political protests. In India colour television provides an example. Until recently, colour television was not available in India. But after considerable pressure, it was decided to permit local production of a limited number of colour sets: 'So starved are the comparatively few rich Indians of entertainment that there is a ready market for these sets even at the price (£2,470).[8] The production of these sets involved a heavy foreign exchange cost initially. Only countries with no balance of payments constraints are able to 'solve' the problem by permitting unlimited imports. The problem is compounded by the increasing number of goods available, at a world level, as technical change in the developed countries generates new consumer goods.

This problem is the dynamic version of the general problem noted above of production of differentiated products, subject to economies of scale, in small and highly protected markets. South–South trade could, as suggested above, contribute to a solution by permitting specialisation on particular differentiated products within LDCs and exchange between them. In this way some of the demand for variety may be met without leading to a deteriorating trade balance.

South–South trade is unlikely to present a total solution to the problem, especially in relation to the élite demand for the latest products, but it would make a major contribution compared with the existing country-by-country solution.

If one set of countries specialises in differentiated products (the North) while another (the South) specialises in homogeneous products, this is liable to mean poor terms of trade for the non-differentiated producers, since some rent is normally associated with brand-name differentiated product production, as shown by the high price that companies can charge for permission to use the brand name.

G. Intra-industry trade in intermediate products and intra-firm trade (theories 7 and 8). According to Ethier, the size of the international market is the limiting factor in determining specialisation and economies of scale, and geographic location becomes almost irrelevant. Yet clearly geographic proximity is an advantage in providing intermediate products. However, the MNC may use its organisational facilities to substitute for geographic proximity. There is therefore a close association between intra-industry trade of this type and intra-firm trade. Even so geographic proximity remains an advantage and there have to be strong cost advantages for it to be worth locating production of different parts in a very dispersed way. Much of the North–North trade of this type is concentrated geographically if not nationally – e.g., within Europe. As far as production in the South is concerned, where some parts of the productive process are very labour-intensive, such trade may be justified despite the transport and communication costs involved. Hence for South–North trade, this tends to be a special variant of H–O trade, normally organised by an MNC (see Helleiner, 1973).

North–South trade of this type is very vulnerable to technical progress, which can eliminate the labour-intensive parts of the productive process, as seems to be happening in electronics, for example. Moreover, because the trade is mostly organised by Northern MNCs, the gains for the South tend to be confined to the employment generated and wage payments, while the profits are located in the North. While then this type of traders offers some advantages to those economies who participate, it is unlikely to form the basis for sustained development.

As far as South–South trade is concerned, the (limited) available evidence suggests that such intra-industry specialisation and trade within the South is rather small. Yet this type of trade within the South is potentially of enormous development value. As Adam Smith pointed out with his famous pin example, division of labour and specialisation in the production of a single product enables huge growth in productivity; not only does it enable productivity to rise through repetition of simple processes and through learning and new methods which evolve as a result of that repetition, but it also gives rise to mechanisation of processes that would not be justified with lesser specialisation because of indivisibilities in machinery. A large proportion of the growth in productivity that has occurred with and since the industrial revolution has been associated with increasing specialisation and division of labour within industries. But as Adam Smith noted, such specialisation is limited by the extent of the market; the size of the market determines how much division of labour and mechanisation is justified. International trade extends the market and hence the scope for specialisation. This could be of great significance for LDC economies, whose markets are small. This type of trade within and across regions could increase the size of the market and hence give rise to increased specialisation and productivity.

South–South trade of this type is limited by two factors – institutional deficiencies and trade barriers. In the North the rapid growth of this trade occurred when trade barriers were being dismantled, especially with the European Economic Community, while the institutional vehicle for much of the trade was the MNC. As well as a dismantling of trade barriers, the South needs institutions to facilitate this type of trade. Specialisation and trade within an industry across national frontiers is difficult to organise without institutions which operate easily across nations. South-based MNCs offer one possibility: there is evidence that these are developing quite fast in certain areas (see Lecraw, 1977; Lall,

1982b; Wells, 1983). Other institutional possibilities are trading agencies such as those in Japan and S. Korea.

A number of common markets and regional trading agreements have tried to provide the required trading infrastructure and to reduce trade restrictions within the South. But for this purpose many of the arrangements have been somewhat misconceived, in that they have been designed for *inter*-industry, rather than *intra*-industry trade. For example, industries are sometimes 'allocated' to countries. Both for the Adam Smith trade being considered here, and for trade in differentiated consumer products discussed above, what is required is rather different since the major trade expansion is likely to be within industries. An industry allocation exercise becomes irrelevant; it is likely that the specialisation will most readily evolve within a liberal trading environment, with the actual 'allocation' occurring as a result of market forces. Where generalised relaxation of trade restrictions has occurred within the South, there is evidence that intra-industry trade has expanded rapidly (see Willmore, 1972, on the Central American experience).

While then in fact, in the past, expansion of trade in intermediate products has been greatest between Northern economies, its *N.B.* greatest potential today for promoting growth and development may well be within the South.

H. Learning and international trade (theory 12): a major deficiency of the H–O theory for the South is the assumption that each country faces identical production functions. In fact, as is well known, the South normally operates the 'same' technology at much less efficiency than the North. Moreover, the degree of lesser productivity varies across technologies. The exact explanation of these differences (in general and as between different technologies) is not known, but learning seems to play some role. The efficiency with which a technology is operated varies with the time over which it has been operated. In most countries, productivity with any given technology tends to rise over time. In those industries where learning economies are known to be substantial, the South may appear at a disadvantage in the short run despite a potential advantage in the long run. This forms the classic infant industry case for protection. It may be confined to a single industry or extend to the whole of manufacturing sector depending on the nature of the learning process.

The learning justification for protection may have different implications according to the direction of trade: while the South may justify general protection of their manufacturing industry against the North because of the earlier stage of development and lesser accumulation of learning, the justification is much smaller (or non-existent) in relation to trade with other countries at a similar level of development and of accumulated learning.

SUMMARY OF IMPLICATIONS

As stated at the outset, most of these new theories have been specifically designed to explain North–North trade, while there tends to be a certain widespread complacency that H–O can deal with North–South trade, since the country groups exhibit the required difference in factor endowments. This brief sketch of a great number of theories has, however, suggested that they do contain a large number of insights for trading patterns and policies for the South. The most general conclusion is that while the theories explain North–North trade, South–South trade would offer a potential way for the South to gain from the types of trade being considered – in products for countries with similar preferences, in differentiated products and in intermediate products. This South–South trade is mainly *potential* rather than actual, and is likely to remain so without significant changes. Yet, the gains for the South from making the trade actual are likely to be great. These gains stem from:

1. extending the choice of product for South consumers, through South countries specialising in differentiated products and exchanging them without running into a chronic tendency for balance of payments problems, which tends to arise if product variety comes from importing differentiated products from the North;
2. extending the gains from specialisation, increasing division of labour and economies of scale through trade in intermediate goods and trade in differentiated consumer goods within the South.

   Both 1 and 2 represent classic gains from specialisation through trade, but on a South–South basis.
3. permitting a more appropriate direction of technology change in products and processes;
4. making the terms of trade more 'equal' than for North–South trade.

Points 1 and 2 have been elaborated sufficiently above, but it is worth saying more here about points 3 and 4.

1. *Trends in technology*   As indicated earlier (Figure 4.2) there is a tendency for technology in products and processes, emanating from DCs to be increasingly inappropriate for South countries although, of course, in some respects new technologies offer substantial productivity gains and product improvements, which represent gains for the South as well as the North. Let me illustrate this point with respect to printing inks.[9]

Initially printing inks used simple (inexpensive) machinery and raw materials that were widely available (mainly vegetable material). But over time, the industry has moved towards the (near-exclusive) use of petrochemical products, which most South countries have to import. Even where vegetable matter is retained, modern processes require such standards that most countries have to import the processed materials from DCs. The machinery has become much more expensive, more automated, and less labour-using. The quality of the end product has also improved substantially – with printing of highly defined quality, robust (e.g., won't wash off, withstands low temperatures for freezing, and is capable of adhering to a wide variety of surfaces). Technical change in this industry follows neatly the presentation in Figure 4.2, in terms of changes in both product and technique characteristics – in both cases the tendency has been for a move away from characteristics which would best suit the South. Moreover, there has also been a close link between choice of technique and choice of product. If a recent product is chosen then the corresponding technique also has to be selected, and conversely.

It is illuminating to consider how an actual case of technical change relates to the various theories considered above. If LDCs aim to trade with the North, in labour-intensive commodities along H–O lines, they would have very little choice in printing ink technology but to follow many of the latest technological developments because consumers in the North require advanced standards in the print they receive (in terms, for example, of colour fastness in textiles, packaging with printing of high definition and durability, etc.). A focus on trade with the North tends to lock countries into the trends in technological change in the North. Trade with other South countries might potentially permit the use of more appropriate technology producing more appropriate

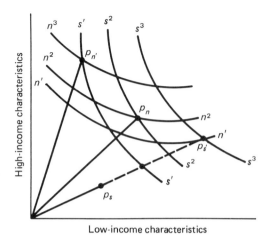

Figure 4.5 Inferiority of Southern products

products.[10] But here, too, countries face competition from the high-quality North products, which they find it difficult to withstand for two reasons: first, in countries with unequal income distribution, actual monetary preferences may be on Northern lines, as illustrated in Figure 4.1. Second, lack of R and D into products for the South may mean that they are of poor quality and the technology is of low productivity so that, although more appropriate, they remain inferior to Northern products. This is illustrated in Figure 4.5. Some improvement in the quality of the South products P_s, towards $P_{s'}$ is necessary before it will be freely chosen in the South.

P_n shows the combination of characteristics obtainable initially with a North product; after technical change a new combination, $P_{n'}$ (assumed to use the same amount of resources) is obtainable; P_s shows the combination possible for the same resource expenditure with South technology. Assume the South preferences are given by the ss set of indifference curves, and the North by nn. With North preferences the new product, $P_{n'}$ is unambiguously preferred. With South preferences, the old North product is preferred. The South product is inferior offering less of both characteristics than the North. If a South country trades with the North, it may need to move to the North-preferred product, $P_{n'}$. If it trades with the South, it would be able to succeed producing the old North product, P_n. If South products were to become competitive they would need to be improved so that they are on a preferred indifference curve (e.g., as at $P_{s'}$). Even with this technical change the new South product would not be chosen by Northern consumers. The range of product choice itself affects welfare, as indicated. But in addition, each technology corresponds to a different production technology, with the more recent products from the North being generally more capital-intensive[11] than earlier techniques.

Kaplinsky's study of sugar technology developments[12] provides an example of the developments illustrated in Figure 4.5. The open-pan sulphitation techniques (OPS) have long been advocated as more appropriate for developing countries. But their productivity was so low that they were not competitive, without subsidies, with conventional large-scale techniques (see Forsyth, 1977; Tribe, 1979). But recent developments in the technology have greatly improved it, pushing it out from P_s, to $P_{s'}$, so that now the technology offers potential for South–South trade.

In terms of the technology gap–product cycle theories, taking into account the direction as well as the existence of technical change means that if the South participates in this trade, as technological followers, they will be tied into the technology trends of the North, while their advantage in 'mature' products may be temporary, to be displaced by new technological developments.

Figure 4.5 illustrates how preference-similarity works in international trade. Among similar countries where each country innovates, each can be expected to develop products similar to $P_{n'}$ and to exchange them – hence trade in differentiated final products. But the South, with different preferences, and little innovation, cannot participate in this type of trade. While it can potentially participate in such trade among South countries, this will occur only if it innovates sufficiently to make these products competitive with advanced products from the North.

While South–North trade much restricts the possibilities for generation and use of more appropriate technologies, South–South trade provides an environment in which such technical change is likely to be encouraged.[13]

2. *Terms of trade* Much of the literature of North–South terms of trade has concentrated on the terms of trade between primary products and manufacturers, while industrialisation was advocated as a means by which the South might avoid the supposed worsening in the terms of trade for primary products as against

manufactured goods. But as the South moves into manufactured exports, it is relevant to look also at the likely terms of trade within manufactures. In general, as illustrated in Table 4.1, there is a tendency for the terms of trade to favour the North because the North tends to export technology-intensive and product-differentiated products while the South exports 'mature', standardised, and homogeneous products. In various ways, the North is able to levy a rent (which may take a number of actual forms – e.g., over-invoicing technology payments, payments for use of brand names, and so on) for its products, while the products the South exports face a much more competitive environment. South–South trade offers a way in which these rents may be more equally distributed among South countries.

CONCLUSIONS

The discussion has suggested that the South could benefit from the types of trade described in the new theories by developing trade ties on a regional and South–South basis. To do so effectively would require three types of policy change: (1) improved South trading infrastructure, including transport, payments systems,[14] financial services; (2) liberalisation of trade restrictions within the South; (3) organisational ties which would make it easier to exploit the economies of specialisation in intra-industry trade; and (4) the creation of an effective innovatory capacity for the development of more efficient products and techniques suitable to South conditions and preferences.

One important question is whether South–South trade can add to and complement North–South trade in manufactures, or whether it is a substitute for it. If it is a question of substitution, then more consideration of the various costs and benefits is required. While there are undoubted advantages for the South of trading within the South, these may not outweigh the gains from trade with the North, including the large markets and access to goods and technology not available within the South.

As far as intra-industry specialisation and exchange is concerned, it is solely a matter of more efficient deployment of resources within the South, and should raise productivity and not divert resources. In other words, this is a form of trade creation, not diversion. Other types of trade under consideration will also fit the 'trade creation' categorisation. For example, if countries in the South specialised in particular differentiated final products and then exchanged them (as in the exchange of Minis for Fiats, for example) each country should be able to use its resources more efficiently, raising output without diverting resources.

In other cases – e.g., where the South specialises in the production of appropriate consumer and producer goods which it exchanges within the South – there may be some reorientation away from trade with the North. Whether this makes much difference to trade with the North will depend on the major constraint on manufacturing output. For many products, it appears that the size of the *market* provides the major constraint. Where this is so, South–South trade may be additional to North–South trade. Market constraints appear particularly critical during world depression, where depressed markets everywhere, but especially in the North, and growing protectionism, threaten Southern exports. Lewis (1980) has argued that in such a conjuncture Northern markets can no longer act as the 'engine of growth', and that this is a sufficient reason for the promotion of South–South trade.

The new theories considered in this essay provide powerful support for the conclusion: specialisation and the division of labour within the South can raise productivity in the production of producer goods, intermediate goods and consumer goods; similarity of environment means that technology development and trade within the South could create the conditions for the development of efficient, dynamic, and appropriate technologies.

NOTES

1. H. G. Johnson, in Vernon (1970) p. 11.
2. In the rest of this essay North–North trade refers to trade between advanced nations; North–South to trade between rich and poor nations. We recognise the obvious non-homogeneity within both North and South but maintain the fiction, for the most part, that they represent two distinct and relatively homogeneous groups.
3. Barker (1977) shows the following growth rates:

	1950–70 *% growth GDP* *p.a.*	*Imports*
Developed	4.5	7.9
Developing	4.9	5.0

4. See Kenen (1965); Roskamp and McMeekin (1968); and Keesing (1966).
5. See Rahman (1973), also Hubauer (1970). The fact that trade in manufactures between North–South is in accordance with H–O predictions does not mean that it is explained by H–O since the facts are also in accordance with other theories (see Hufbauer). But it does mean that there is no awkward inconsistency between theory and facts for North–South trade, as there is for North–North.
6. Little, Scitovsky, and Scott (1970); Bhagwati (1978); Krueger (1978); for example.
7. Example from SRI International (1980) Appendix B.
8. *Financial Times* (18 July 1982).
9. Example based on an interview with Mr S. Tingley of Coates Brothers.
10. The definition of 'appropriate' products–techniques has been subject to much discussion. Very broadly, appropriate techniques are techniques in line with resource availability and productive environment, while appropriate products are products whose characteristics correspond to the needs and incomes of the majority of consumers. But see also, e.g., Morawetz (1974); Stewart (1983); and Singh (1981). In this essay the many difficulties involved in the definition are ignored.
11. Technique's characteristics vary in many dimensions of which capital intensity is one, other relevant ones include scale of product nature of inputs and skills.
12. See Kaplinsky (1984b).
13. See also Kaplinsky (1984a), who develops this argument for South–South trade and illustrates the argument with reference to the implications of the electronics revolution for North–South trade and technology choice.
14. For one possible financial mechanism for promoting South–South trade see Chapter 10 in this volume.

5 A Note on 'Strategic' Trade Theory and the South*

INTRODUCTION

During the 1980s, trade theorists have advanced a new case for government intervention based on supporting the 'strategic' rôle of key firms in oligopolistic industries.[1] It is assumed that firms in these industries so dominate the international market (either actually or potentially) that their actions influence the actions of other players in other countries. Government support for such firms may increase their credibility to such an extent that it alters foreign firms' reactions in a way that is advantageous to the home country.

The 'strategic' or games-playing justification for government intervention in trade differs from the theories discussed in Chapter 4. Although many of these theories incorporated economies of scale and learning, the justification for government intervention derived from these theories in no way depended on *interaction* between firms in the international market.

This essay considers how far the *strategic* justification for trade intervention extends to Third World governments. Three sets of reasons are advanced for suggesting that the strategic theories are of much less relevance to developing countries than many of the theories considered in Chapter 4. First, limitations of the policy conclusions for *any* country, developed or developing, because the assumptions on which the policy conclusions are based do not (or may not) apply; secondly, the economic and technological conditions in developing countries make it particularly unlikely that they will have comparative advantage (actual or potential) in suitable strategic industries; and thirdly, because policies favouring strategic industries are likely to lead to distortions in the domestic economy. However, despite these reasons, there are certain conditions in which Third World countries could benefit from policies justified by strategic trade theories.

* *Journal of International Development*, 1991

Before considering these arguments in depth, the next section briefly reviews elements of strategic theories.

STRATEGIC TRADE THEORY

Assume an industry subject to very large economies of scale (which may be internal to the firm or external, and may consist of static economies or dynamic learning economies). Assume just two firms (one domestic, one foreign) in this industry, because of the economies of scale. The optimal output level of each firm will depend on what the firm assumes about the actions of the other firm. The situation is thus a 'game-playing' one, often used to describe oligopolistic industrial structures within an economy, but here played out in an international arena.

As is well known, the outcome of such a situation depends on the game being played. Assuming Cournot behaviour (i.e., each firm assumes a given output level from the other firm and then sets its own output to maximise profits), the Cournot equilibrium occurs where the reaction curves of the home and foreign firm intersect, as in Figure 5.1. In Figure 5.1 *rdrd* describes the profit-maximising output levels chosen by the home firm, assuming different levels of foreign output, while *rfrf* is the foreign reaction curve. Each reaction curve joins the set of maximum points of domestic iso-profit curves, since this indicates the maximum domestic profits consistent with any given level of foreign output. The Cournot equilibrium is given at C, the intersection of the two reaction curves.

Government policy can increase the profits of the domestic curve (and thereby national welfare) if it can shift the equilibrium position to a higher profit position. The maximum profit consistent with the assumed foreign reaction is where an iso-profit curve is tangential to the foreign reaction curve, at *Cm*. To make this an equilibrium, the domestic reaction curve must be shifted to *rd'rd'* where it intersects with the foreign reaction curve at the position which maximises domestic profits, *Cm*. The domestic firm then becomes a Stackleberg leader. Government policy can shift the domestic reaction curve to *rd'rd'* by subsidies of various sorts (e.g., R and D subsidy; output subsidy; tax relief). In the Spencer and Brander (1983) case, the subsidy analysed was an R and D subsidy. Real life examples of government intervention of this kind can be found, for example, in

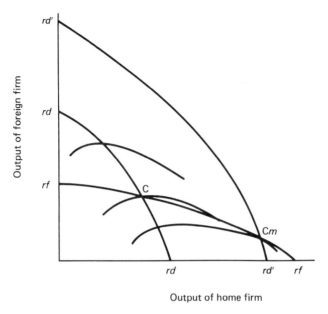

Figure 5.1   Cournot equilibrium in output

the development of supersonic commercial aircraft in the 1970s, when Anglo–French support led to the development of Concorde, and Boeing's retreat from that market. Similar game-playing, with government support for domestic players, has occurred in the semi-conductor industry,[2] and also in competition between Air-Bus, Boeing and McDonnell Douglas in production of a 150 sector jet plane, which Air-Bus, supported by a consortium of European governments, seems to have won, with production starting in 1985, while McDonnell Douglas ceased production of a potential competitor plane.[3]

ROBUSTNESS OF THE THEORY FOR APPLICATION IN THE REAL WORLD

There are a large number of reasons why caution is required before using this type of theory to justify government intervention in any economy, developed or developing.[4]

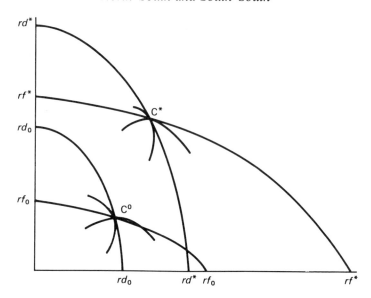

Figure 5.2   Equilibrium with governments' intervention

Is the Game Worth the Candle?

Like any other policy intervention, the gains must exceed the costs –
the critical Mills–Bastable test. While the intervention permits a
higher level of output and domestic profits, the subsidy removes
resources from other potentially profitable uses. This requirement is
particularly difficult to establish in the real world where most potential strategic industries involve high levels of R and D and where total
costs and eventual pay off are therefore uncertain.[5] In the case of
Concorde, for example, it turned out that the costs of over £6 billion
were not justified.[6] This does not, of course, mean that such costs
could never be justified, but rather that it may be easy for vested
interests to exaggerate the usually uncertain gains.

Which Governments are Playing Games?

On p. 100 it was assumed that only one government was supporting
its domestic industry. But if both governments support their industries, *both* may end up in a *worse* position than with no intervention.
This is illustrated in Figure 5.2. In Figure 5.2, if both governments

intervene, equilibrium will eventually occur at C^*, where the reaction curve of the foreign and domestic firm is tangential to their own firms' iso-profits curve. Output of both firms is higher than in the initial position but each firm is showing *lower* profits than in the initial position.

What Game is Being Played?

The outcome of firms' reactions and government policy critically depend on which game is being played. On p. 100 it was assumed that a Cournot game was being played (each player taking the output level of the other player as a given and adapting its own output level): an alternative is a Bertrand-type game, where each firm sets its own price and assumes certain price-setting behaviour by the other firm. With this type of game, collusive price behaviour maximises firms' profits. To make this behaviour credible, a *tax* on output may be necessary and desirable. In the context of a Bertrand-type game, a subsidy on output would actually worsen the outcome for the domestic firm.[7]

The Nature of the Domestic Industry

The model on p. 100 assumes only one firm in each country. But if there are a number of domestic firms, or only one but no barriers to entry and a number of potential entrants, the subsidy could encourage excessive capacity creation domestically, so that domestic average costs do not fall. In this context, too, an export tax, not a subsidy, would be appropriate for improving the terms of trade.[8]

Market Segmentation

Various models have shown that the effects of alternative policy instruments depend not only on whether there is fixed or free entry, but on the combination of conditions of entry and market segmentation or integration. For example, in a model which assumes linear demand curves, constant marginal costs and Cournot behaviour, Markusen and Venables (1988) show that an import tariff raises domestic welfare when markets are integrated and there is fixed entry, but that an export tax raises welfare with integrated markets and free entry.[9]

Market Creation

The model assumes a given level of demand (or a given growth in demand over time). The sort of industries to which the model applies involve high levels of R and D and have high rates of product innovation. The size of the market is not only usually unknown, but may itself change as result of production decisions. For example, the market for commercial supersonic travel is likely to increase the greater the number of producers, because the advertising effort will be greater and governments more supportive (e.g., with respect to restrictions on speed over land), while competitive R and D will increase the speed and improve the quality of innovations, thus producing a lower-cost and higher-quality end-product. It thus seems certain that if Boeing had remained in the supersonic aircraft business, the total market today would be much greater than it is for Concorde alone, possibly more than twice as great. For this reason, a more sensible strategy for the producers of Concorde might well have been to go ahead only if Boeing went ahead, the reverse of the actual loss-making strategy adopted.

In summary, the optimal policy intervention depends critically on the validity of alternative assumptions with respect to the game firms play, the conditions of entry and market segmentation or integration and demand levels. The sensitivity of optimum policy to varying some of the assumptions is illustrated in Table 5.1. This means that the policy conclusion put forward by Spencer and Brander in their path-breaking article (1983) is not very robust.

ECONOMIC AND TECHNOLOGICAL CONDITIONS
IN THIRD WORLD COUNTRIES

The last section showed how the sensitivity of the policy conclusions to the validity of alternative assumptions made it difficult to identify the correct strategic policies for *any* economy. This section considers the special conditions of Third World economies which make it particularly unlikely that the strategic theory will be widely applicable in most Third World economies.

For the theory to be applicable, industries must be identified which have enormous economies of scale relative to the size of world markets, such that an oligopolistic (or even monopolistic) industrial structure is inevitable for technological reasons. Economies of scale

Table 5.1 Models of strategic trade policy

Source	No. of firms	Game conjecture	Markets	Optimal policy
1. Spencer and Brander (1983)	Fixed: no entry	Cournot	—	R and D subsidy
2. Brander and Spencer (1985)	Fixed: no entry	Cournot	—	Output subsidy
3. Eaton and Grossman (1986)	Fixed: no entry	Bertrand	—	Export tax
4. Krugman (1984)	Fixed: no entry	Cournot	—	Import tariff or output subsidy
5. Grossman (1986); Dixit (1984)	Variable: free entry	Cournot	—	Export tax
6. Venables (1985)	Variable: free entry	Cournot	Segmented	Import tariff or export subsidy
7. Horstmann and Markusen (1986)	Variable: free entry	Cournot	Integrated	Free trade
8. Markusen and Venables (1988)	Fixed	Cournot	Integrated	Import tariff
	Free	Cournot	Integrated	Export tax
	Fixed	Cournot	Segmented	Import tariff
	Free	Cournot	Segmented	Import tariff

Table 5.2   Manufacturing value-added, 1987, selected countries

	$m	As % US MVA
Ethiopia	576	0.06
Kenya	762	0.08
Bangladesh	1232	0.10
Nigeria	1951	0.20
Philippines	8645	1.00
Thailand	11,568	1.30
Turkey	15,813	1.80
Mexico	35,485	3.90
Korea Republic of	36,393	4.00
India	44,166	4.90
Brazil	83,784	9.30
China	99,749	11.10
UK	143,935	16.00
W. Germany	368,867	41.00
Japan	689,162	76.60
USA	899,444	100.00

Source: World Bank (1989).

may derive from huge production economies or from very large R and D costs, which may or may not be associated with very large production scale economies.

There are two reasons why developing economies are unlikely to have a comparative advantage in these industries – market considerations and resource considerations.

The *market* size of Third World economies is almost always very small in relation to developed countries (see Table 5.2). Only three countries – Brazil, China and India – approach the total market size, as measured by manufacturing value-added, of even the smaller developed countries, and among developed countries cooperation is often necessary in these strategic industries, if production is to be justified. In a completely integrated world economy, the size of the domestic market might be thought to be relatively insignificant, as a domestic firm has access to the world economy. But a sizeable home market gives an advantage to a home firm – because of the close contact with and knowledge about consumers and because government support is often provided for domestic consumption of locally produced products. The advantage of a large home market is specially marked for *new* products, where the market is not yet established, but the product has to be designed to suit consumers, market outlets have to be created, etc.[10] The relatively small total market size of most developing countries consequently presents a major obstacle to potential production of products with very large economies of scale. Moreover, the scale of the domestic market for the products in question is even smaller, relative to developed countries, than their total market size, because these products are mostly 'frontier' products with high-income characteristics (e.g., airplanes), while the markets of developing countries are mainly for fairly standardised products, like processed foods, clothes, building materials.

Market size considerations thus suggest that for the most part developing countries will not have a comparative advantage in 'strategic' industries. There may, however, be some exceptions: (1) in some 'niche'-type products, production by one firm may be large in relation to the world market without being very large in total (e.g., specialised types of vehicle); (2) the main markets for some products may be in developing countries – e.g., water pumps; rugged vehicles; and (3) the larger markets among Third World countries may then form a sizeable proportion of world production (e.g., bicycles). Thus while in general market conditions in Third World countries are not likely to favour production of 'strategic'-type products, in those products where consumption is concentrated in the Third World, Third World firms could be in a position to play strategic games.

Resource or technological conditions provide the second reason why Third World countries are usually at a disadvantage in operating in strategic industries. The major source of economies of scale in strategic industries is most often high levels of R and D which have to be spread over very large production runs to be worthwhile. Most developing countries do relatively little R and D and have relatively few scientists and technologists per head of population (see Table 5.3) and are therefore not in a position to undertake R and D-intensive activities successfully. The normal pattern is for most new technologies to be developed in advanced countries and for R and D and technological efforts in developing countries to be focussed on making modifications to these technologies so that they work well in a different environment. Again, there are exceptions: as is well known, Mexico successfully developed a new steel-making process; Brazilian firms developed a new commuter aircraft; and India has pioneered new products or processes (for example, in heavy electrical equipment and rugged tractors). But these innovations are exceptional and are virtually confined to a few large economies. It would be mistaken to base an industrial and trade policy on an assumed

Table 5.3   R and D, selected countries

	Scientists and engineers per million people	R and D expenditure[a]
Congo	431	0.08
Costa Rica	158	2
Burundi	67	3
Sudan	165	8
Pakistan	53	30
Egypt	398	34
Turkey	51	145
Venezuela	250	316
Indonesia	145	389
S. Korea	763	828
Brazil	230	1206
India	117[b]	1989
UK	1346	9510
W. Germany	1888	16,102
Japan	4350	30,557
USA	2989	80,205[c]

Notes:
a Converted from local currency at 1982 exchange rate.
b Includes technicians.
c Current expenditure only.
Source: *UN Statistical Yearbook 1985/1986* (New York: United Nations, 1986).

comparative advantage in R and D-intensive activities.

Nonetheless, despite the general presumption (based on both market and resource considerations) that developing countries are not in a position to enter 'strategic' trade, there are some cases where it appears this is incorrect, as shown by actual developments. Two examples illuminate how and why these exceptions occur.

Example 1:   Commuter Aircraft Produced by Brazil[11]
A Brazilian firm has succeeded in designing, producing and selling a 30–40-seater commuter aircraft, taking approximately 20 per cent of the world market, with the remainder being equally shared by a Canadian and a Swedish firm.

The industry has classic 'strategic' features, being subject to high R and D costs (estimated to be $270 million), while there are learning economies of around 20 per cent of initial production costs. It is estimated that there is 'room' for only three firms worldwide. The market is dominated by the USA, with Europe as a secondary market. Of the three producers, only the Canadian firm benefits from a sizeable domestic market, which it virtually monopolises. Each of the three firms has received heavy government backing.[12]

The justification of government support in this industry can be made in terms of a strategic model of competition, as summarised on p. 100 and/or in terms of learning-by-doing-infant industry-spillover considerations.

From a strategic perspective, the Brazilian policy can be regarded as fairly successful, in the sense that the Brazilian firm has succeeded in gaining a sizeable market share. However, it appears that the costs exceed the benefits – according to Baldwin the project resulted in net losses to the Brazilian economy of $183 million (over $100,100 per worker), without considering spillover benefits. Spillovers and learning effects seem unlikely to justify the extent of this loss. However, it is wrong to view this project in isolation. The Brazilians have built up a considerable capacity to design and sell small civil and military aircraft. The aggregate costs and benefits of these efforts would need to be assessed before a final judgement could be made, since experience with each individual plane contributes to the total capacity in the industry.

The example shows that a large and high-income developing country *can* have sufficient presence in a strategic industry to play strategic games: in the Brazilian case this occurred *without* a large domestic market. But this was made possible by a long history of building up technological capability in the industry, which was mainly due to a large domestic market for military aircraft, leading to government support for the industry which made early development in the industry feasible.

Example 2: The Korean Semiconductor Industry[13]
The semiconductor industry also has 'strategic' characteristics with very high fixed set-up costs and significant learning economies. This is indicated by sharply falling prices over time: for example, the price of the 64K RAM, which was $150 in 1978 had fallen to just over $1 by 1987. Each generation of chip is replaced by larger memory chips in a 3–4-year cycle. The market for 16K chips had disappeared by 1986 and 64K chips were being displaced, with peak world production in 1984. Large-scale commitment to the production of high density

chips by some Korean firms began in the early 1980s. Despite the competitive nature of the market, disadvantages stemming from lack of experience, and the relative insignificance (10–15 per cent) of labour costs in total costs, the Koreans have been very successful: their world market share of 64K chips had risen to over 20 per cent in 1988 while their market share of 1 million K chips was 6 per cent.

With respect to the highly competitive 64K market, Yoon explains this achievement by successful playing of an 'exit' game.

The 64K production was dominated by 5 US and 6 Japanese firms who had entered the market in the early 1980s. The Korean firm, Samsung, was the latest entrant. Abnormal profits were being earned until 1985, when the effective price of the next generation chip (256K) fell below the 64K chip. Leading US firms left the market in 1985; the more efficient Japanese firms left in 1987. The Korean firm stayed in the market, thereby increasing market share; as the other firms left, the price of 64K chips recovered so that the Korean firms were covering some fixed as well as variable costs.

Allowing for learning-by-doing benefits in production and marketing, the Korean decision to survive the exit game appears to have been justified.

The Korean example shows that late entry firms can break into high-technology industry successfully. Moreover, in this case they did so without any obvious government support, so that this case does not fully fit the model described in our second section.[14] In this case the very large economies of scale originated not from these R and D costs, but from indivisibilities in fixed investment. The Koreans did not do their own R and D but bought technology from the USA.

These two examples show that middle-income developing countries which have already built up high levels of technological capability can enter the types of industry subject to strategic games, even in the absence of a large domestic market. But in the high R and D case (Brazilian aircraft), the domestic market for military aircraft had facilitated the build-up of this industry, while in the Korean case high local R and D was not necessary. Both countries had adopted long-term industrial strategies which had resulted in unusually strong technological capability: even so, the Brazilian aircraft was almost certainly a loss-maker in private and social terms, while the benefits from Korean 64K chip production depended on spillovers into future production lines. Since the Koreans came into a type of production that was in the process of being outmoded, product success in this particular line had to be temporary, justified only if it enabled Korean firms to move forward into future generations of chip manufacture.

THE EFFECT ON CHOICE OF TECHNIQUE
AND DISTRIBUTION OF INCOME

A strategic trade or industrial policy involves favouring selected 'strategic' industries relative to the rest of the economy. The characteristics necessarily associated with 'strategic' industries mean that the policies will favour industries with high R and D and capital-intensive technologies, producing high-income 'frontier' products. The direct beneficiaries will be the entrepreneurs (where the firms are in the private sector), managers and workers in the strategic industries and consumers of the promoted products. Because of the nature of the technology, the workers affected will be mainly highly skilled, while consumers of promoted products tend to be relatively high-income because of the product characteristics. Support for strategic industries will thus push both choice of technique and product in a direction which is inappropriate for most low- or middle-income countries, and will favour relatively well-off groups, thereby leading to a more inegalitarian income distribution.

The effects, it should be noted, are present even in developed countries where the strategic industries are R and D and skill-intensive, and tend to produce frontier products relative to other production. For example, UK and French government support for *Concorde* has benefitted very high-income travellers and relatively well-off workers in R and D and on the production line. However, movement in the direction of raising R and D, capital and skill intensity and product quality is a natural, and often desirable, part of the growth process in advanced countries. In developing countries, however, where the capital and skill availability and average income levels are much lower, and the poverty of unskilled workers (those in the informal and agricultural sector) much worse, the inegalitarian distributional effects of tilting choice in this direction is much greater.

Moreover, not only are domestic producers and consumers usually relatively high-income, but both production and consumption involve a high element of foreign participation. Thus, typically, there is a relatively high proportion of imported technology and capital inputs (because the technology is a frontier one), and also the domestic market accounts for a small proportion of the total market (i.e., many of the beneficiaries will be outside the country, more so than in the typical advanced country). It should be noted also that developed country subsidies of strategic products, which also partly benefit foreign consumers, will tend to go to higher-income consumers, located mainly in other developed countries.

Evidence on the characteristics of strategic industries supports the view that they have inappropriate characteristics for production in most developing countries. Industries which are appropriate candidates for strategic trade policy must have characteristics which make them an oligopolistic industry on a world basis. They must therefore be subject to large 'indivisibilities' – either because there are very heavy R and D costs or because of very substantial production economies of scale in relation to the size of the world market. Industries which have been listed as potentially strategic include semiconductors, aircraft, telecommunications, steel and automobiles (Branson and Klevorick, 1986).

Data for the USA

Table 5.4 provides some data for the USA on these industries. Each has high value-added per person, high pay per person, and large scale of establishment (as indicated by the number of employees and value-added per establishment), compared with the average values for US manufacturing as a whole, and more markedly as compared with apparel, the relatively labour-intensive industry. The date on value-added and pay per person indicate that these industries are relatively capital-intensive, with respect both to physical and human capital.

Data on individual industries show large economies of scale in these industries, due to high R and D costs, and big production indivisibilities (Tables 5.5 and 5.6)

Aircraft Industry
In aircraft there are two sources of indivisibility: first, huge development costs (see above) which exceed the total national R and D budget in most developing countries. Secondly, learning economies associated with the increased production of any model are substantial (costs may fall by 20 per cent or more after the initial production).

Automobiles
In automobiles, indivisibilities are due both to very large R and D costs and to economies of scale in production.

It is widely agreed that for full realisation of economies of scale, 2 million cars need to be produced annually.[15] A CPRS review concluded that firms producing less than 750,000 cars a year 'will find it difficult if not impossible to compete in volume car markets'

Table 5.4 Data on 'strategic' industries in the USA, selected years

	Value-added per person (1986) ($)	Pay per person (1986) ($)	No. of employees per establishment (1982)	Value-added per establishment (1982) ($m)	% of shipments by 4 largest companies (1982)
Motor vehicles and equipment	81,560	32,002	159	8.87	{92[a] 61[b]
Aircraft and parts	66,123	33,877	366	19.99	64[c]
Communications equipment	63,179	29,578	221	10.40	76[d]
Blast furnaces and basic steel	63,703	31,028	343	13.78	42[e]
Apparel	27,975	12,263	49	1.07	n.a.
All manufacturing	56,366	24,538	53	2.30	n.a.

Notes:
a Motor vehicles and bodies.
b Motor vehicle parts and accessories.
c Aircraft.
d Telephones, telegraph apparatus.
e Blast furnaces and steel mills.
n.a. Not available.
Source: Statistical Abstract of the US 1989 (Washington, D.C.: Dept of Commerce), 1989.

Table 5.5   Development costs of aircraft

Type	R and D costs ($billion)	Source
150 seater	1–2	Baldwin (1988)
30–40 seater	0.22	*Financial Times*
Boeing, wide body	4.0	(19 January 1990)
New jet engine	1.2–2	*Financial Times*
'Adapted' engine	0.6	*Financial Times*
Concorde	5–7.1[a]	Henderson (1977)

Note:
a Total development costs, 1988 prices; lower limit assumes $4\frac{1}{2}$ per cent discount rate; upper limit 10 per cent.

Table 5.6   Investment costs in automobiles, selected years

	Capital investment (1968–77)	($billion) (1977)	R and D costs (1978)
General Motors	22.2	3.6	1.6
Ford	11.8	1.8	–
Chrysler	4.7	0.7	–

Source: Schnapp *et al.* (1979).

(CPRS, 1975). A survey of the world motor industry concluded: 'Almost without exception the technological gap and diseconomy of scale make it impossible for a developing country to enter the world market with a unique vehicle which has been developed, designed, manufactured and marketed by its nationals' (Maxcy, 1981).

Microelectronic Chips
'Semiconductor manufacturing is probably the most complex mass production process ever attempted'.[16] Indivisibilities are due both to heavy R and D and massive economies of scale in production. 'Entry costs rose dramatically over the 1980s, as escalating research and production costs increased the minimum efficient scale of production.[17] By 1985, the 'state of the art production line' was estimated to cost $150 million.[18] US companies spent 9 per cent of sales

revenue on R and D in the 1980s. While developing and installing 64K capacity, Japanese firms' annual investment was $2.6 billion and US firms' $2.7 billion (Yoon, 1988). It is estimated that a single production facility for the 64M chip being developed in the early 1990s will cost in the region of $ 1.2billion. Costs of production of the new chips appear too high (or risky) even for the mega-firms based in developed countries, so that IBM and Siemens have agreed to develop the 64M chip jointly (*Financial Times*, 26 January 1990). Agreements for joint developments have also been concluded between Texas Instruments and Hitachi, Intel and NMB conductors and AT and T and Mitsubishi (*Financial Times*, 16 February 90).

SOME CONCLUSIONS

This chapter has argued that the new strategic trade theory is of limited relevance to Third World trade policy. This is partly because of the limitations of some of the policy conclusions for *any* economy, arising from the inapplicability of the assumptions necessary if a subsidy of the sort recommended by Spencer and Brander is to be justified, and partly because the conditions required for generation of a comparative advantage in strategic industries are especially unlikely to hold in developing countries. Moreover, support for strategic industries will tend to distort choice of technology in an undesirable direction and distribute the benefits of the policy in an inegalitarian way. Where the policy proves to involve net costs, not benefits, as in the Brazilian aircraft case, beneficiaries of govenment subsidies will be among the better-off, but the costs are likely to be borne by tax payers as a whole.[19]

The two examples given, where a developing country managed to produce and market products in an industry subject to strategic games, show that there can be exceptions. But in each case the countries had already built up a strong technological capability. Other exceptions could occur in products where the Third World dominated the world market. But in general strategic trade theory does not present an important reason for trade intervention in developing countries.

It must be strongly emphasised that this conclusion applies only to the strategic trade theories and not to other recent theories emphasising learning, economies of scale, product differentiation and externalities which can provide a strong justification for some industrial promotion, and (in this author's view) for especial promotion of South–South trade.[20]

Thus the arguments above do not support the *more general* conclusions of Krugman referring to *all* recent trade theories: 'Import substituting looks even worse in the new theory than in the standard theory'.[21] However, the case for intervention relates much more to the theories concerning economies of scale, learning by doing, technological change, product differentiation and externalities than to the strategic theory considered in this chapter.

NOTES

1. Spencer and Brander (1983) initiated this approach. Since then numerous papers have elaborated or qualified the theory, including Brander and Spencer (1985); Dixit and Grossman (1986); Venables (1985); Markusen and Venables (1988). A good overview is provided in Krugman (1986).

2. In this case, in the USA, government procurement was the main intervention (see Chapter 6) while in Japan the six largest electronics firms adopted an implicit 'buy Japanese' policy (Baldwin, 1988).

3. The R and D expenditure on developing such a plane is $1–$2 billion, while a steep learning curve gives rise to large dynamic production economies. The world market is at most large enough to justify only two producers, who would be likely to earn super-normal profits, thus justifying government support – see Baldwin (1988). The industry thus has classic 'strategic' industry features.

4. Many of these criticisms are summarised in Grossman in Krugman (1986).

5. In the case of Concorde, the agreement to go ahead occurred in 1962, thirteen years before the first plane went into service (Henderson, 1977).

6. Development and production costs at 1988 prices, using a 10 per cent discount rate, derived from Henderson (1977). Using data up to 1975–6, Henderson estimated that the internal costs of R and D, production and operation of Concorde exceeded benefits by £5.0 billion at current prices (4½ per cent discount rate). External costs and benefits were estimated to be relatively small, but negative on balance. Henderson concurred with Sir Alan Cottrell, Chief Scientific Adviser to the British government, 1970–4, in concluding that the programme represented a 'tragic waste of resources'.

7. See Eaton and Grossman (1986).

8. The argument is developed in Horstmann and Markusen (1986).

9. See also Horstmann and Markusen (1986); Venables (1985).

10. Linder (1961) pointed to the fact that products are usually developed first

for the home market while Drèze (1960) argued that small economies would have a comparative advantage in products not subject to significant economies of scale.

11. This example is entirely drawn from Baldwin (1988).

12. In the Brazilian case the government-owned firm has received periodic subventions from the government since its inception in 1949; in Canada, in addition to subsidies, restriction on market access ensure that the firm has nearly 100 per cent of the Canadian market; the Swedish firm has received a large loan of indefinite duration.

13. This example is taken from Yoon (1988).

14. To some extent government support was made unnecessary by the internationalisation of externalities achieved in Korea by the close links between firms: 'Spillover effects are easily internalised through their affiliated companies in such diverse fields ranging from consumer electronics and communication equipments to optics, synthetics fibre and robotics' (Yoon, 1988, p. 3).

15. See Maxcy (1981); Altschuler *et al.* (1984).

16. Finan and Lamond (1985) p. 149.

17. Finan and Lamond (1985) p. 160.

18. Finan and Lamond (1985).

19. The effects on income distribution then depend on the distributional effects of the tax system, which differ from society to society but are rarely strongly progressive, or by those who bear the burden of inflation, which is usually thought to have regressive consequences.

20. See Pack and Westphal (1986); and chapter 4 in this volume.

21. Krugman (1989); Srinivasan (1989) comes to identical conclusions.

6 How Significant are Externalities for Development?*
with Ejaz Ghani

> If one man starts a new idea, it is taken up by others and combined with suggestions of their own; and thus it becomes the source of further new ideas. And presently subsidiary trades grow up in the neighbourhood, supplying it with implements and materials (Marshall, 1920, p. 225).

> Here is not just another exception to the doctrine of free trade. What is involved is the problem of a structural change in the pattern of specialisation which may be all too important in the early stages of economic development (Bardhan, 1978, p. 455)

INTRODUCTION AND PRELIMINARY DEFINITIONS

Externalities occur where market priced transactions do not fully incorporate all the benefits and costs associated with transactions between economic agents. Externalities thus constitute market failures. Their presence means that the unregulated price system does not result in a social optimum, and consequently provides a *prima facie* reason for government intervention.[1]

Pigou defined an externality as occurring in a situation where

> one person, A, in the course of rendering some service, for which payment is made, to a second person B, incidentally also renders services or disservices to other persons (not producers of like services) of such a sort that payment cannot be exacted from the

* This paper was originally written for a World Institute for Development Economic Research (WIDER) project. We are grateful to WIDER for permission to publish it here. We have greatly benefited from comments on earlier versions of this paper from Paul Anand, G. K. Helleiner and participants at the WIDER meeting on 'New Trade Theories and Industrialisation in Developing Countries' (August 1988). The paper appeared in *World Development* 1991.

benefitted parties or compensation enforced on behalf of the injured parties (Pigou, 1938, Chapter 9, p. 183).

Linkages describe *all* transactions between economic agents, whether through the market or outside it, fully or partially priced. Consequently, externalities are a subset of linkages. The linkage approach, however, provides useful insights: the conceptualisation of linkages, and in particular the breakdown into different *types* of linkage, suggests a similar classification of externalities, while the empirical work on linkages, although evidently capturing a much larger range of transactions than externalities alone, points to the areas where externalities may be found, since the existence of linkages is generally a precondition for the existence of externalities.[2] *Spillovers* is a rather loosely defined concept, which is sometimes used to mean the same as linkages, sometimes as externalities. We will not be using the term.

The significance attributed to externalities in development thinking has gone in waves. Initially, it seemed that the type of externalities typically referred to in the economic literature – for example, bees and orchards or laundries and smoke-creating factories – were relatively unimportant in the context of development, and could be ignored without much damage. But this view was challenged by Rosenstein-Rodan (1943) and Hirschman (1958), who emphasised the significance of linkages between industries in creating a dynamic growth path: these linkages, it was argued, justified investments which on their own would not be worth undertaking. Scitovsky's analysis of the importance of pecuniary externalities was essentially an elaboration of this position. The Myrdalian view of cumulative causation contained similar reasoning: the whole was substantially greater in development impact than the parts, as would be expected in the presence of significant externalities.

However, the series of cost-benefit methodologies put forward in the early 1970s paid little attention to externalities. Little and Mirrlees's methodology assumed that at the margin international trade rather than domestic resource use was affected by tradable production, thus ruling out domestic linkages and pecuniary externalities. They stated that externalities were unimportant empirically, citing the empty field they had observed:

One of us when visiting a vast new industrial project, which had been operating for more than two years, pointed to an adjoining empty area apparently reserved for some industrial use, and asked what it was for. He was told that it was reserved for the industries which would grow up to supply the project (Little and Mirrlees, 1969, p. 217).

The market philosophy which has pervaded much development thinking in the 1980s also downgraded the significance of deviations between social and private costs, which might justify government interventions, including externalities (see, e.g., Little, 1982; Lal, 1983; and World Bank, *World Development Reports*, various years).

This essay reviews the question of the significance of externalities, by providing an analytic typology of externalities, making reference to empirical work to help elucidate the nature and significance of various types of externality (in the second Section). The third and fourth sections present two case studies where externalities have played a major role in securing rapid growth – the development of the electronics industry in California, and agro-industrial development in the Punjab. The fifth section briefly considers some problems in measuring externalities, and the sixth section concludes with an analysis of some implications for industrial and trade policies.

A TYPOLOGY OF EXTERNALITIES

Let us start with a more formal version of the definition: externalities exist where the utility function of a consumer or the production function of a producer are affected not only by their market activities but also by the activities of other economic agents (producers or consumers).

Formally if u_i represents the utility function of the ith consumer, and $x_1, x_2, x_3 \ldots$ purchases of goods and services by this consumer,

$$u_i = f(x_1, x_2, x_3 \ldots z_1, z_2 \ldots) \tag{6.1}$$

where z_1, z_2 are the activities of others (consumers and producers) which directly affect consumer welfare. These may take the form of non-market effects (e.g., consumer satisfaction depending on the behaviour of the Jones's), or of effects mediated through the market, where the behaviour of other units affects the conditions (price, availability, qualities) of their own consumption bundle.

In parallel, the profits function of the ith producer, p_i, may be a function both of its own purchases of inputs and expenditures on factors, $y_1, y_2, y_3 \ldots$ and of the activities of other economic agents, $z_1, z_2 \ldots$, i.e.

$$p_i = f(y_1, y_2, y_3 \ldots z_1, z_2 \ldots) \tag{6.2}$$

As in the case of consumption, the externalities, $z_1, z_2 \ldots$ take the form both of non-market effects (e.g., smoke nuisance for laundries) and market effects.

Externalities can be categorised in a number of (cross-cutting) ways, which are useful for understanding their origin, estimating their significance, and (more generally) for designing policy. The following categorisations will be considered:

1. Externalities categorised by the nature of the interacting agents.
2. Externalities categorised by the numbers of agents involved.
3. Externalities characterised by 'salience'.
4. Externalities characterised by the economic status of those affected.[3]
5. Externalities categorised by location of recipient.
6. Externalities categorised into 'real' and 'pecuniary'.

The Nature of the Interacting Agents

The major distinction here is between producers (p) and consumers (c). External effects may in principle go in four ways (Scitovsky, 1954):

$p - p$, from producers to other producers
$p - c$, from producers to consumers
$c - c$, from consumers to other consumers
$c - p$, from consumers to producers.

It is easy to devise examples of each of the first three types and, as we shall see, each is very relevant to trade policies. The last category is less easy to fill with examples,[4] although consumer groups which exercise non-market influence over producers are an example of this type of interaction; another would be the influence of local behaviour (as consumers) on tourism. In the discussion below we shall focus on producer externalities. Consumer externalities – which are of considerable importance, and are frequently neglected, raise rather different issues, and are better treated separately.

The Number of Interacting Agents

Externalities caused by any one agent may affect one other agent, a few others, or many others. Equally, one agent may be affected by externalities caused by one other, a few others or many other agents (see Table 6.1).

The externalities caused by one agent may be of very minor significance for any one other agent (so minor as to be negligible), but the aggregate effects on a number of agents may be significant. One agent may be affected to an insignificant extent by externalities associated with any one other agent, but the added-up external effects of large numbers of other agents may again be significant.

We shall define the different types of interaction as shown in Table 6.1. The distinction between the various types is of importance in determining the type of policy approach relevant. For example, one–one interactions might be expected to be dealt with by individual negotiations between the agents (see Coase, 1960) but this is less likely as the numbers involved increase, whether on a one–many or many–many basis. Large one–one interactions may lead to integration of the agents into a single unit.

Salience of Externalities

Some externalities are very obvious – e.g., a nose – while others are much less obvious (e.g., air pollution). The distinction partly depends on the nature of the externality, and partly on how many agents are affected and how significant the externality is for each individual agent. The distinction is important, because where the externality is very obvious action is much more likely than where it is hidden. Categorisation of particular externalities in this respect may change as information is improved and publicised: for example, the negative *c–c* externality caused by smoking was first completely unknown, subsequently it was known to a few; but now in developed countries it is widely known, and as a result action (both private and governmental) is being taken. Because of lower levels of literacy, a weaker scientific base and fewer channels of communication, externalities are more likely to remain hidden in developing countries.

Table 6.1 Types of agent interaction

Externalities: defined as	Definition	Example
One–one[a] (or one–few)	The externalities of one agent significantly affects one other agent, or a few other agents	Factory smoke – laundry/laundries.
One–many individually	The externalities caused by one agent significantly affects each of many other agents	Bhopal, Chernobyl
One–many collectively	The externalities caused by one agent significantly affects many other agents, when the effects are added up	Radiation effects of nuclear power stations
Many individually–many individually	The externalities caused by many agents individually have significant effects on the activities of many agents, individually	Same as one–one, but multiplied up, by number of agents
Many individually–many collectively	The externalities caused by many individual agents have significant effects on the activities of many agents, collectively	Same as one–many collectively, but multiplied up by number of agents.
Many collectively–many individually	The externalities of many agents collectively have significant effects on many individual agents	Farming-desertification. Ozone destruction
Many collectively–many collectively	The externalities of many agents added together have significant effects on many other agents when added together	Car pollution. Training

Note:
a No distinction is made here between one and a few agents. For completeness these, types could be distinguished but the important distinction, for policy purposes, is between one (or a few) and many.

Economic Status of Those Affected

Some externalities affect one class of people more than another – large producers or small; rich people or poor; urban or rural. The category affected is important from the point of view of evaluation of the externality, and also of whether action is likely to follow. Evaluation of costs and benefits often depends on the income of those affected, since 'ability to pay' is an important element in much evaluation. In general, externalities affecting the poor are likely to be valued less than externalities affecting the rich. Economic status will also affect the likelihood of private negotiated solutions, since poor and less educated people are less likely to bring about negotiated solutions, while there is also less likelihood of political solutions (because of differences in articulateness and political power).

Location of Agents

The *location* of agents here includes *spatial* location and *industrial* location. Space can be divided up in a variety of ways – by nation, by region, urban or rural, etc. Externalities may occur among agents within the same sub-division, or across divisions: externalities may occur between agents close together in the same place (as with smoke and laundries), and they can also occur across the various sub-divisions (from rural to urban), or across national boundaries. The spatial dimension of the externalities is relevant because policies are normally focussed on a spatial sub-division – e.g., concern may be with regional development, or rural development, or national development, but is rarely with 'world' development where the spatial dimension can be ignored. The only relevant externalities are those that occur between agents in the sub-division of space which is the concern of policy. As far as international trade is concerned, this means that the relevant externalities are domestic, and externalities that occur across national boundaries can generally be ignored, except in so far as a nation represents a sufficiently important market, so that domestic consumption affects foreign externalities.[5] We therefore need to add a spatial dimension to the initial definition, including only z_1^d, z_2^d . . . (equations (6.1) and (6.2)) and excluding z_1^f, z_2^f, where superscript d represents externalities between domestic agents, and superscript f refers to externalities that affect foreign agents.

The spatial dimension of externalities is also relevant to the formulation of appropriate policies. For example, if externalities occur mainly between agents in the same area policies to subsidise production in that area (e.g., favourable tax treatment, or provision of infrastructure) can be used to help realise the externalities. This is not possible where the agents affected by the externalities are spatially dispersed.

Another dimension is *industrial* location. Externalities can occur within an industry or between industries. In the latter case they can be clustered among a few industries or widely distributed across all industries. Where externalities are confined to a single industry (or a cluster of a few well defined industries), selective industrial promotion may be justified, whereas if the externalities are distributed across many industries the promotion would be required across all these industries.

Pecuniary–Real Externalities

The distinction between technological and pecuniary externalities was first drawn by Viner (1931), and developed by Meade (1952) and Scitovsky (1954).

The definition of externalities adopted earlier includes both real and pecuniary externalities. Real (or technological) externalities affect a firm's production function (or a consumer's utility function) while pecuniary externalities affect the price vector.[6]

Scitovsky and others (e.g., Corden, 1974) have suggested that real externalities are – with the important exception of human skill formation – *relatively insignificant* in developing countries, with the implication that they can and should be ignored. In contrast, Scitovsky, Rosenstein-Rodan and others argued that pecuniary externalities are of significant magnitude, justifying economic planning and other interventions. However, before making any judgement on this issue, and to get a more precise idea of what we are looking for in empirical work, we need further to unpackage the two types of externality.

Real Externalities

Real externalities involve changes in the environment affecting the firm, resulting from the activities of other firms. Meade (1952) defined such externalities as being a property of the production function, and as occurring whenever the output of a firm, 'depends not only on the factors of production utilised by this firm but also on the output and factor use of another firm or firms'. The examples given by Meade and others of real externalities are of a one–one (or one–few), p–p, and static nature. This is the case both in the laundry factory and the bee-keeper–orchard example. Other examples could be found, but it seems reasonable to agree with Meade and Scitovsky that these are not likely to be of widespread significance.

However, departing from the one–one, p–p, static type, greatly extends the prevalence of real externalities.

Environmental externalities   One class of externalities which is being given increasing attention is that coming under the broad heading of 'environmental' effects (see James, 1981, and Bruntland Report, 1987, for many examples and references). These environmental externalities generally involve unpriced (negative) effects of producers' decisions, and may lead to enormous environmental degradation (e.g., desertification), and even to changes in the world's climate (e.g., destruction of the rain forest). In other cases, their effects are confined to localised health hazards (increasing cancers or bronchial problems) of a chronic or prolonged nature, or sudden local disasters to the environment and health (Bhopal, Chernobyl, the 1984 Mexican oil disaster). No-one can claim that these effects are insignificant. In some cases, the effects are due to the activities of a great number of agents, with the effects being spread among a great number of producers or consumers (e.g., those resulting from farming practices in the Sahel, or car pollution). These are p–c, p–p-type externalities, of the one–many, many–many variety. These real externalities are difficult to handle because they are often difficult to identify, measure and evaluate. The most appropriate policy interventions are normally specific to the particular case, though some general principles can be drawn up. These environmental externalities will not be considered further here.

Dynamic externalities   Another class of real externality are those related to economic growth: there are three types – changing attitudes and motivation, skill formation, and changing knowledge about technologies and markets. Because these are all of fundamental importance to sustained economic growth, we describe them as *dynamic* externalities.

1. *Attitudes and motivation*   One of the fundamental changes that

occurs in the transition to modern growth is the change in attitudes from one of following well established traditions in technologies and markets to one of accumulation, continuous technological change and extension of markets. All sorts of factors are responsible for this change, including education and cultural change, as well as various 'push' factors (e.g., the impossibility of surviving without change because of population pressure). The spread of modern ideas, modern technologies and modern products through trade and improved communication is a major influence on attitudes. These influences are a form of externality – that is, for any agent they depend on developments resulting from the actions of many *other* agents, in adopting new technologies, selling new products, etc. Work on agriculture–industrial linkages has shown that the growth of nearby industry has positive effects on agricultural productivity, which is in part a result of these demonstration-type effects on attitudes (see Nicholls, 1969; Tang, 1974; Katzman, 1974; and the summary in Ranis, Stewart and Angeles-Reyes, 1990).

These attitudinal changes have been looked at most closely for the agriculture–industry linkage, but they can also be expected to apply within industry. These externalities are of a p–p, p–c, and c–c type and mostly many collectively–many collectively.

2. *Human capital formation* This is the one area which is generally acknowledged to be an important source of real externality (see Scitovsky, 1954; Corden, 1974).

Human capital formation is not only a matter of formal training, but also of informal learning on the job, and consists of both acquisition of a body of knowledge and know-how and also of attitudes to work. Where the human capital transfer relates to technological change, it is discussed further in the following section.

For the most part this externality is of a p–p, many collectively–many individually type – that is, the training activities of large numbers of agents collectively materially affect the production conditions of large numbers of agents individually. Some aspects of this human capital formation are industry-wide (i.e., apply to all industries) and some are industry-specific (the skills being helpful only in a particular industry).

Policy prescriptions derived from this well acknowledged market failure include special training subsidies, and generalised support for industrialisation.

3. *Technology change and technology transfer* Many aspects of

technology transfer leading to technological upgrading occur through interactions between firms that are partially or wholly outside the market. Such interactions occur in the following forms:

(a) Movement of labour from one firm to another bringing knowledge of new or improved technologies/products. Bell (1986, p. 109) records the significance of labour movement as a source of technological upgrading:

> Hiring more-or-less ready made resources for change seems to have been significant in the accumulation of technological capability reported in some plant studies.

One example was the Ducilo Rayon plant where technical change was associated with peaks in expenditure on technicians and engineering staff (Katz, 1978). Hiring was also found to be an important source of technological change for several machinery producers in Brazil and Argentina (Da Cruz, 1980; Da Cruz and Da Silva, 1981; Castana, Katz and Navajas, 1981).

A study of a capital goods firm in S. Korea identified a jump in technological capabilities associated with the joining of a new individual to the firm with a higher calibre technical capability. Similar evidence was found in all twenty firms in S. Korea shown to have made a technical transition, where those who played a central role in up-grading technology 'gained experience of producing related but more sophisticated products elsewhere' (Kim, 1981).

Diffusion of knowledge through labour mobility is not confined to high-technology industries. Bagachwa (1988) found that 35 per cent of the proprietors of small maize mills in Tanzania had previously served on apprenticeships in other milling firms.

The externality associated with movement of labour could be classified under the 'human capital' label. It is distinguished here because it relates to technological change, and because it is not so much due to formal training as to on-the-job experience with more advanced technologies, and therefore cannot be appropriately dealt with by providing training subsidies.

This type of externality is of greatest significance *within* an industry. It may be one–one, one–many or many–many.

(b) Technology transfer through trade journals, meetings, etc.

Technology diffusion among firms within an industry has been shown to occur through trade journals and meetings of people from different firms. This has been most thoroughly documented by Saxonhouse (1971) in connection with the early history of the Japanese textile industry, where there was a well developed system for exchange of information, including both local and foreign technology.

The pages of the monthly trade journal were filled with discussions of attempted innovations on the part of Japanese firms, reports from correspondents on practices in foreign industries, discussions on the appropriateness of the practices for Japan (p. 46; see also Cooper and Sercovich, 1970, with some documentation on this form of technology transfer between countries).

There is well known disagreement about how to treat technology change in economic theory, and precisely how to measure its contribution to growth (Solow, 1970; Denison, 1967; Kaldor, 1957; Scott, 1986; Balogh and Streeten, 1963). But all are agreed that technology change has accounted for the bulk of growth of productivity among the now developed countries. Similar conclusions apply to contemporary developing countries, although here it is to a greater extent a question of importing new or improved methods from abroad, adapting them to local conditions, diffusing them, learning to operate them more efficiently and upgrading them over time (see Fransman and King, 1984; Katz, 1984; Lall, 1987b; Dahlman and Westphal, 1982; Pack and Westphal, 1986). Some of these developments occur within a single firm, and some through market transactions, but many result from non-market interactions between firms (i.e., constitute externalities). These externalities occur within and between industries. Interactions leading to diffusion of best practice techniques and upgrading of existing technologies may occur largely within an industry. But induced innovations also occur as a result of interactions between suppliers and users across industries, although these are frequently not industry-wide but are concentrated in clusters. It seems that the existence of quite a large number of independent firms (suppliers and producers) is likely to be specially conducive to such technology change, because it increases the range of experience and contacts, and also the degree of competition which is likely to encourage such change.

(c) Technology innovation induced by interaction between innovations and requirements in complementary activities.

Interactions between suppliers of inputs (capital goods and materials and parts) and purchasers have been shown to be a very important source of innovation and diffusion in the nineteenth-century experience in Europe, the USA, Japan and in some contemporary developing countries (see Rosenberg, 1976; Landes, 1969; Saxonhouse, 1971; Ranis and Saxonhouse, 1987; and Bell, 1986)

After examining American technological development in the nineteenth century, Rosenberg (1982) concludes that

> Inventions hardly ever happen in isolation. Time and again in the history of American technology, it has happened that the productivity of a given invention has turned on the question of the availability of complementary technologies . . . technologies depend upon one another and interact with one another in ways that are not apparent to the casual observer, and often not the specialist . . . The growing productivity of industrial economies is the complex outcome of large numbers of interlocking, mutually reinforcing technologies, the individual components of which *are of very limited consequences in themselves* (p. 56; 57; 58; 59; my italics).

Some of these interactions are captured *within* an industry, but many are captured in industries other than where the innovation is made. Rosenberg (1982) gives examples in electricity and aluminium, the development of commercial fertilisers and chemicals (see also Landes, 1969, on textiles).

In his review of technical change in infant industries, Bell (1986) finds that

> technical change will often involve detailed interaction between product-centred change and cost-reducing change . . . not only within firms but also between them. Hence *technical change may generate significant external economies; while productivity growth may depend on external costs* – those involved in the technical change efforts of other firms (p. 29, my italics).

These externalities take the form of interactions between machine users and producers, and between suppliers of other inputs and producers (Bell, 1986, p. 92). In the latter case sub-contracting from large to small firms has often involved a significant element of technology transfer (see Watanabe, 1978 and Paine, 1971 on Japan and Taiwan; Lall, 1980 on India). Machinery user – producer interaction leading to improved technologies has been documented for textiles in Japan and India (Ranis, 1973; Saxonhouse, 1971) and nineteenth-century Britain (Rosenberg, 1976), as well as for agricultural tools in the Punjab (see p. 143). Component suppliers have been shown to be an important source of technological transfer in Argentinean machinery production (Cortez, 1978), and machine tools in Japan and Taiwan (Fransman, 1986b). For Korea, interaction between purchasers of exports and suppliers led to technology upgrading (Westphal, Rhee and Pursell, 1981).

The rate of technical change appears to be strongly related to these technology interactions between firms. Since they are externalities, they are not automatically generated in sufficient quantities by the market mechanism. It is argued (e.g., Bell, 1986) that they may be rather limited in some developing countries: as for example in Thailand's modern industry, according to Bell and Scott-Kemmis (1987); Amsden (1977) notes non-diffusion in Taiwan from the modern sector, using foreign technology, to local machine-tool firms.

Interaction leading to technology change is likely to be greater

(i)   the greater are *local* linkages – i.e., if foreign firms supply capital goods and parts *local* technological externalities will be limited;

(ii) the greater is firm specialisation – 'specialised producers typically provide a substantial push behind the process of change. Their efforts to market their goods and services induce change in other firms' (Bell, 1986, p. 92). This specialisation is in turn related to the size of the market. It is a form of pecuniary externality arising with growth which leads to a real externality.

The technology change interaction type of externality occurs both within and across industries. It occurs among *clusters* of technologies which may be located in different industries but are all *linked* to the production of related products. As with the labour mobility type it may be one–one, one–many or many–many.

Dynamic externalities are likely to be more pervasive in industries subject to considerable technical change as in the two cases described below. Industries with broadly stable or slowly changing technologies will not experience the same level of externalities. The extent of technical change in an industry, and consequently the potential dynamic externalities, may differ according to the stage of development of the country – i.e., more industrialised countries may have reached the stable plateau (or slowly changing technology) while in other countries the industry is experiencing rapid technical change as it catches up the frontier country.

Summary of findings on 'real' externalities   In contrast to the conventional view that real externalities are relatively insignificant except for manpower training, this review has suggested they are widely prevalent and potentially of substantial magnitude in two broad areas: the first is environmental effects, where the externalities are generally negative in direction. The second is that of dynamic externalities relating to technology change, where the externalities are mostly positive.

Pecuniary Externalities
Pecuniary externalities occur where the activities of one firm affect the *terms of trade* of other firms (i.e., the price or characteristics of their inputs, or the markets for their output): i.e., they occur where

$$|p| = f(y^1, y_2, \ldots z_1, z_2) \tag{6.3}$$

where p is the firm's price vector.

However, the activities of some agents affect the prices faced by others all the time in the normal working of a competitive economy, and appear to be satisfactorily mediated through the market, without calling for government intervention (e.g., with changes of tastes). For this reason Mishan (1971) and others suggested that the concept of pecuniary externalities was misplaced. This conclusion is correct where there is perfect competition and no indivisibilities throughout the economy. But where there are imperfections in the market due to imperfect information or incomplete markets Greenwald and Stiglitz (1986) have shown that government intervention to offset pecuniary externalities may be Pareto-improving. Two cases provide examples of how in the presence of indivisibilities pecuniary externalities can give rise to market failures which may justify government interventions.

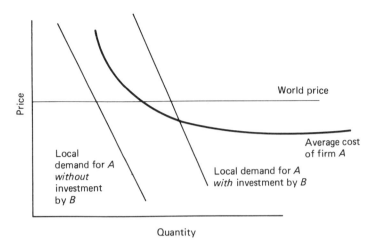

Figure 6.1 Demand and pecuniary externalities

1. Suppose two firms are linked (i.e., each supplies inputs to the other), both are large enough for their prices to influence the market price, and both are subject to economies of scale. Then it might be that investments in both firms would be profitable (privately and socially) but in one alone would not be. Consequently, some intervention would be justified. This one–one case is illustrated in figure 6.1.[7]
2. Suppose a competitive industry is linked to some other industry subject to indivisibilities (internal or external). Expansion of the first industry increases the market of the second, whose costs fall because of indivisibilities thereby improving the terms of trade of the first industry, justifying the initial expansion. Consequently, expansion of the competitive industry is both privately and socially justified. This could be a many–many or one–many example.

In both cases, firm collusion (or integration) would ensure exploitation of the externalities. This may not happen, however, where the costs of negotiation are large, or where the agents are ignorant of the potential economies of scale (i.e., where there are incomplete markets or imperfect information). In such situations, the Mishan–Newbery conclusion that the market can and does deal satisfactorily with all cases of pecuniary externality is incorrect.

However, in each case of pecuniary externality, policy intervention is justified only in the presence of some other departure from perfect markets. From a policy perspective, it is normally efficient and sufficient to deal with these cases of market failure directly.[8] Where the factors that create pecuniary externalities are themselves aspects of bad domestic policy – as, for example, may be the case with trade barriers – the first best policy is clearly to correct the underlying policy choice. The policy prescriptions to be discussed on pp. 153–61 will be concerned primarily with real externalities. However, the interaction of real and pecuniary externalities can be very important in causing (or preventing) a dynamic growth path, as is shown in the two case studies below. It is therefore of relevance to identify the type of conditions which give rise to pecuniary externalities.

Since pecuniary externalities occur where firms' activities influence the relevant prices of inputs or outputs, they can occur only if local prices (and/or product characteristics) are affected by local activities and would not exist if world prices ruled locally. In practice, barriers to trade, both natural (transport costs and other transaction costs) and artificial (trade restrictions) lead to divergencies between local and world prices. The high level of such barriers in most developing countries creates the potential for pecuniary externalities. As these barriers are reduced, with falling transaction costs and reduced trade restrictions, pecuniary externalities will diminish in importance, which is one reason why pecuniary externalities can be expected to be greater in developing contries than at later stages of development. Formally, if world prices are given

$$l_i \geq w_i + t_i + b_i \tag{6.4}$$

where l_i represents local prices of the ith commodity, t_i transaction costs, and b_i the monetary value of trade barriers. Then the potential size of pecuniary externalities are $t_i + b_i$.[9] Reducing trade barriers therefore reduces the potential size of pecuniary externalities.

It is worth stressing that the size of indivisibilities necessary to create such externalities is relative to the size of the market. The smaller the market the greater the likelihood of such externalities. Pecuniary externalities, therefore, may be particularly relevant to less developed economies with small markets, and to regional planning.

Pecuniary externalities may involve a change in the characteristics of goods available, related to local needs. Adaptation of product characteristics requires sufficient local demand to justify the over-head expenses of research, development and adaptation – and, of course, will not occur at all with no local production. Examples of local adaption of product characteristics are given in Ranis (1973); van Ginneken and Baron (1984); Stewart (1977) and James and Stewart (1981).

Pecuniary externalities may occur through reorganisation of production and increased firm specialisation. The division of labour is limited by the extent of the market: as the market expands, and new specialisation develops, this often takes the form of specialist firms emerging to perform functions that were previously performed in-house. The capital goods industry developed in this way, as did firms specialising on particular types of capital goods (Landes, 1969; Rosenberg, 1976). New types of specialist firms are continuously emerging in a growing economy. This tendency is reinforced by (and also reinforces) technical change. In modern economies specialist firms abound – e.g., for specialised legal services, computer services, repair and maintenance, etc. At an early stage of development, developing countries have few such firms and have to rely on in-house capabilities or imported services, which are generally subject to long delays and have inadequate knowledge of local circumstances. Some specialist services may emerge in response to a general expansion of the production base; other more specialised services depend on the emergence of a *particular* industry.

Pecuniary externalities can interact with real externalities: pecuniary externalities may thus lead to increased production, which in turn results in learning, increased technological capability and technological adaption, all of which are strongly associated with real externalities.

The next two sections present examples of dynamic developments in two very different areas, in each of which there is strong indication that externalities have played a very important role. The examples illustrate the different categories of externality defined in the discussion above. However, the studies do not attempt to provide any precise quantitative of externalities in the two cases. The difficulties of arriving at precise measures of externalities are discussed on pp. 150–3.

EXAMPLE: SEMI-CONDUCTOR INDUSTRY IN THE UNITED STATES

The Silicon valley in the Santa Clara county, where the semiconductor industry is based, was a 'peaceful agricultural valley' in the 1940s (Saxenian, 1985). In the 1950s a few firms moved to the county to take advantage of the science park set up by Stanford University. By 1970 the region had gained international fame, with the highest concentration of high technology enterprises in the USA.

The history of Silicon valley presents an example of an industry whose development depended on, and which in turn generated, substantial and significant externalities both within the industry and with the rest of the economy. The clustering of firms in the Silicon valley was induced by the diffusion of research and development knowledge that stemmed from the university and independent research institutes in the region. The rapid development of the semiconductor industry induced substantial growth in a large number of related industries, including telecommunications equipment, computer products, consumer products, industrial process control equipment, scientific instruments, and defence systems. The expansion of related industries in turn generated additional demand for semiconductor devices. A dynamic process developed, resulting in successive rounds of innovations and applications in both semiconductor and related industries. As a consequence many new industries have emerged, ranging from the software industry, data processing, robotics to videograms.

Government support was vital in nurturing the nascent silicon industry in the early 1960s. Prior to the Second World War, the American electronics industry was less developed than the British or the German; but today Europe lags behind America in this industry. This development has been attributed to the catalytic role of the government in the USA (Malerba, 1985; Saxenian, 1985). American defence and space programmes provided the market and the funds for the industry.

The main areas where public policies played an important role were public procurement and R and D. Public procurement provided a market in the early 1960s, when a commercial market for semiconductor products did not exist. In 1962, government procurement constituted 100 per cent of the total value of US integrated circuit sales. This share fell gradually to 10 per cent of the market by 1978, while the share of the industrial and computer market had increased to 75 per cent, as the industry matured.

Public procurement was important in the initial phases because it stimulated innovations in the industry by reducing the market uncertainty associated with the introduction of innovative products and R and D efforts. Secondly, it helped firms to acquire the volume on which scale and learning economies depend.

The history of the industry indicates very substantial externalities. In the first place, the presence of considerable amounts of highly trained manpower from universities and government research laboratories provided the human capital essential for this high-technology industry. Rapid technology change in the industry both led to and was partly caused by technology transfer between firms in the industry, often mediated outside the market (e.g., by transfer of people; and through the products themselves). Technological change in one product frequently induced technology change elsewhere (via the cumulative process) – a process which took place both within firms and also between them.

The very high rate of technology change, and the greatly increased volume of production, led to rapidly falling costs. This cost reduction formed a pecuniary externality for user-industries, which also benefited from the changing products available and were in turn stimulated to change their own processes and products in response. Thus we observe the dynamic process shown in Figure 6.2.

Dynamic real externalities

(a) *Human capital* Silicon valley benefited from a large supply of scientific and engineering manpower coming out of the universities, and research laboratories in the area. Table 6.2 shows the number of doctoral degrees awarded in electrical engineering between 1950 and 1974.

   The supply of engineers made it easier for small firms in the area to recruit, whereas large firms (e.g., IBM) could recruit nationally and internationally.

(b) *Mobility of skilled labour* An important characteristic was the very high mobility of skilled engineers and scientists (Markusen *et al.*, 1986), which formed a major source of real externalities. A large number of highly skilled engineers and scientists trained and paid by government research centres set up their own firms. Defence spending accounted for 48 per cent of aeronautical engineers, 23 per cent of physicists, 21 per cent of electrical engineers and 19 per cent of all mathematicians. Although many of the projects they worked on were 'classified', the scientific processes they used were not. Research concepts, originating in publicly financed research institutions, landed up in private commercial firms.

   The existence of publicly funded research programmes in the

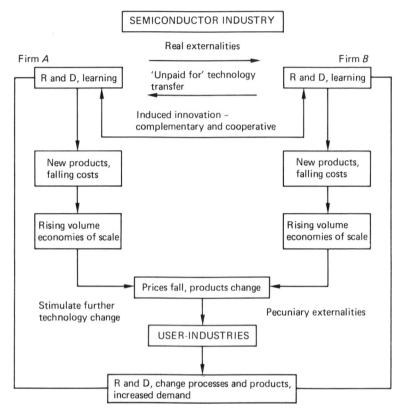

Figure 6.2 Dynamic growth in semiconductors

Silicon valley also attracted a number of new firms which benefited from the intellectual external economies and could recruit from the available pool of experienced and skilled labour.

'Spin-offs' were a more enterprising form of mobility, where skilled people left their initial employer, both public and private, to set up their own firms. W. Shockley, one of the three original inventors of the transistor, left Bell Laboratories to establish the first semiconductor firm. In 1957, eight of Shockley's scientists in turn broke off to start their own firms. Intel, which introduced the first microprocessor in 1971, was a spin-off of skilled personnel from Fairchild. Many of the thirty new firms that emerged in the semiconductor industry in the period 1966–72 were a direct

Table 6.2 Doctoral degrees awarded in electrical engineering,
selected years

	Stanford University	University of California (Berkeley)
1950–4	67	19
1960–4	185	72
1970–4	242	202

Source: Saxenian (1985).

consequence of spin-off of skilled engineers who had worked at Bell Laboratories and Fairchild Semiconductors.

(c) *'Networks' of technology diffusion* In a high-technology industry, a new product does not embody the entirety of a new technology. Understanding how the technology was developed, the know-how, its uses, and the potential for further modifications extends beyond the market into the 'network or community of people who developed the technology and who help to apply it' (Borrus *et al.*, 1987, p. 93).

The substantial degree of connectedness between firms, due to the Stanford science park, and complementary facilities, including university research, encouraged the diffusion of technological information among firms. The flow of information between firms, the firms and Stanford University, and the research institutions was, in turn, important in the further technological development in the semiconductor industry. As noted by one commentator:

there was an unusually high degree of interaction between employees of rival firms in the Santa Clara county . . . much information, brainstorming and gossip were exchanged . . . at the local 'watering holes'. Stanford's education and seminar programmes . . . further encouraged this interchange (Saxenian, 1985, p. 30).

The presence of patents and licensing internalises some potential externalities. However, given the shortness of the product cycle in the semiconductor industry, patents were circumvented with ease through 'inventing around' (Taylor and Silberston, 1973; Levin, 1982). Two special historical circumstances, Bell's liberal patent-licensing for the transistor, and Fairchild's and Texas Instruments' claims on integrated circuit patents, led to wide availability of key patents and subsequent patents did not effectively protect inventions (Malerba, 1985).

(d) *Interaction with other industries*   The semiconductor industry has linkages in both input industries (backward linkages) and user industries (forward linkages). In each, innovations have fed on each other, creating a cumulative cycle of innovation, extended markets and falling prices. The importance of linkages to local industrial development has sometimes been questioned on the grounds of low transportation costs, especially given that silicon chips are relatively light and can be easily transported. However, in a survey the majority of the firms emphasised the importance of local input linkages (Oakey, 1985). Given rapid technical change, it is important that input suppliers can respond rapidly to meet new requirements.

(i) *Backward linkages*   A variety of local input firms established themselves to produce the photomasks, testing jigs, chemical, silicon and special production equipment essential to manufacturing semiconductors. Providing all these inputs and services in-house would have been relatively expensive for small firms. Even the larger firms benefited from taking advantage of the lower costs due to learning economies and economies of scale in producing inputs and services for a large number of firms.

The software industry was a direct offshoot of the semiconductor industry. The industry's sales were $20 billion in the 1970s, increasing substantially in the 1980s. It is estimated that nearly 4000 to 4500 firms exist in the software industry (Hall *et al.*, 1985, p. 45). The majority of the software products and services come from small firms, many of which are spin-offs from other firms.

(ii) *Forward linkages*   Over the past forty years, the rise of the semiconductor industry has been associated with very major changes in a number of other industries. Semiconductor devices are used by a wide range of final markets: industrial, military, commercial and consumer. The production of integrated circuits totalled $7269 million in 1982. Table 6.3 shows the end-use distribution of integrated circuits in the USA in 1982.

The transistor, the integrated circuit and the microprocessor constitute the basic components of most electronics final products. Innovations in the semiconductor industry thus led to innovations in electronics final products. Since electronic final

Table 6.3 End-use distribution of integrated circuits in the USA, 1982

	%
Industrial	72
Computer	40
Communications	21
Office automation equipment	5
Other industrial	6
Consumer	11
Government/military	17
Total in $US million	7269

Source: OECD (1985b).

products have also become important inputs in many other sectors, product and process innovations in the semiconductor industry set in motion waves of innovations.

The wide range of end-users benefited both from real externalities in the form of new products and technology transfer, and also pecuniary externalities, arising from the rapid fall in prices associated with the high rate of learning in the industry, and economies of scale as volumes increased.

Prices and pecuniary externalities It is impossible to distinguish and quantify the relative impact of learning economies, economies of scale and technological development in contributing to the fall in semiconductor prices. There is evidence to suggest that all three played an important role industry (Finan and Lamond, 1985).

The net effect was a rapid fall in prices (see Table 6.4). For example, in the case of linear integrated circuits the price fell from $30 in 1964 to $1.08 in 1972. The decline in the costs of semiconductor devices created a multitude of openings for applications, and profitable investments in many sectors, playing a crucial role in stimulating demand for semiconductor products by end-users. The extent of pecuniary externalities which arose from falling prices is indicated by the increase in usage of semiconductor products by other industries. Pecuniary externalities mostly occurred across industries.

The semiconductor case: conclusion This brief survey of the dramatic developments in the Silicon valley indicates very substantial externalities, within the industry and between industries. Strong US

Table 6.4   Average price per unit of transistors and integrated circuits, 1960–72, current US dollars

Year	Transistors		Integrated circuits	
	Geranium	Silicon	Digital	Linear
1960	1.70	11.27	–	–
1961	1.14	7.48	–	–
1962	0.82	4.39	–	–
1963	0.69	2.65	–	–
1964	0.57	1.46	17.35	30.00
1965	0.50	0.86	7.28	28.83
1966	0.45	0.64	4.34	13.39
1967	0.43	0.58	2.98	6.18
1968	0.41	0.44	2.17	3.35
1969	0.37	0.37	1.58	2.22
1970	0.41	0.38	1.42	1.86
1971	0.46	0.33	1.22	1.48
1972	0.52	0.27	1.01	1.08

Source: OECD (1985b); *Electronic Market Data Book* pp. 106–7.

government support for the industry through government procurement, training and government R and D laboratories permitted the realisation of these externalities. Although some of these externalities occurred between industries, support for the semiconductor industry alone was sufficient for their realisation. However, it is not possible to say whether government intervention in this case was 'optimal'. Much more information would be required on many areas – some intrinsically 'unknowable', including the potential of other nationally supported industries, what would have happened with more (or less) government support in this industry, and the effects of alternative forms of industry support.

EXTERNALITIES IN AGRICULTURE AND INDUSTRY IN THE PUNJAB

In the Indian Punjab rapid growth in agriculture has been accompanied by even faster growth in industry. At first the industrial growth was agriculture-led, induced by the growth in agriculture, but subsequently the industries so created gained sufficient comparative advantage to find markets in the rest of India and also overseas.

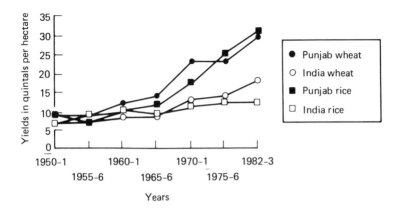

Source: Chadha (1986b)
Figure 6.3   Wheat and rice yields in the Punjab

Strong externalities are to be found both within agriculture and industry and through inter-sectoral linkages. Realisation of these linkages permitted the growth observed.

**Agricultural Growth and Agricultural
Externalities**

In the 1950s, the growth in agricultural production and productivity in Punjab was relatively low but since the 1960s, it has consistently exceeded the national average (see Figure 6.3). From 1965–6 to 1978–9 cereal production in the Punjab grew by 10.7 per cent p.a. compared with 5 per cent for the whole of India. The adoption of new technology, for wheat in the mid-1960s and rice in the early 1970s, was the main reason for this change in performance. This innovation was not induced by the market alone, because of the presence of externalities and undeveloped markets.

Five areas generated substantial externalities in agriculture in Punjab: technology development; irrigation; credit; informational markets; and human capital. In each case, government policies acted to offset market weaknesses.

1. *Research and development*   The public good properties of technology development in small-scale agriculture meant that public funding was essential for the development of new technologies and their adaptation to local conditions. Funding for the new

technologies came first from international efforts (through CGIAR) and subsequently from nationally funded R and D which adapted the international development to local conditions.

2. *Irrigation*   For success the new technology package requires irrigation. The nature of agricultural property rights limited the spread of private irrigation; privately owned tubewells were not economically feasible where land holdings were fragmented, and family plots non-contiguous. Even where it was economically feasible to use a privately owned tubewell, the ability to appropriate water could be adversely affected if the neighbouring farmer used deeper tubewells. Proper drainage of water requires the cooperation of farmers, which is difficult where there are a large number of farmers, and some farmers have an incentive to free ride on others. There is a tendency, therefore, to under-invest in the construction and maintenance of water control facilities.

   In the Punjab, policies to overcome these difficulties included public canal irrigation, and changes in property rights. Land consolidation was encouraged. Irrigation in the Punjab far exceeded that of the whole of India. In 1965–6, it was 59 per cent for Punjab and 19 per cent for India. Government canals accounted for 57 per cent of the net area irrigated in Punjab, with 37 per cent for India as a whole. While public canals dominated irrigation in the Punjab in the early phase, with the completion of land consolidation and rising agricultural incomes, the demand for tubewells increased, and the proportion of public canal irrigation fell to 40 per cent (Chadha, 1986b).

3. *Incomplete and imperfect credit markets*   The rural areas in developing countries are notorious for imperfections in credit markets limiting farmers' ability to purchase essential inputs. An important reason for the success of the green revolution in Punjab was the well developed network of agricultural cooperative credit societies, at the village level. These made it possible for large numbers of farmers to adopt modern practices. Geographical proximity and cooperative arrangements lessened the problem of imperfect information faced by the credit societies, limiting the problems of adverse selection and moral hazard.[10]

   The agricultural credit societies have lent greatly increasing amounts to farmers in Punjab since the mid-1960s, while the loans disbursed per hectare of cropped area has been far greater in Punjab than the rest of India. In 1983–4 the credit available to

Table 6.5 Expansion of areas under HYV seeds in Punjab, HYV area as % of cropped area

Crop	1967–58	1970–1	1973–4	1976–7	1981–2	1983–4
Wheat	34.8	69.1	84.3	90.3	99.0	99.5
Paddy	5.4	33.3	83.3	88.3	94.9	95.0
Maize	6.1	8.8	4.6	20.2	35.9	43.3
Bajra	24.4	60.9	4.1	33.8	63.3	66.7

Source: Chadha (1986b).

farmers in Punjab was nearly four times greater than the rest of India.

4. *Informational externalities*   The new technology requires a specific combination of inputs which depend on soil conditions. An individual farmer wanting to adopt the new technology would have to incur the cost of acquiring information on input requirements, yet the farmer is not in a position fully to appropriate the benefits since neighbouring farmers, with similar soil conditions, may observe the information on input mix. The presence of such informational externalities hinders the adoption of new technology. The agricultural extension services, funded by the government, provided information on input mix and soil conditions, thereby permitting the realisation of these externalities.

The application of inputs improved considerably through the agricultural extension services (Chadha, 1986b, p. 118). Taking fertiliser use as an indicator of the effectiveness of extension services, its success was remarkable. Fertiliser consumption in the Punjab increased from 1.1 kg per hectare (1960–1) to 142.0 per hectare (1983–4).

5. *Demonstration effect*   The adoption of new technology by one farmer encouraged its adoption by another, and in one district by others. Consequently there was a dramatic increase in the new areas adopting HYV in Punjab as shown in Table 6.5. The demonstration effect, at the district level in Punjab, can be captured by measuring the inter-district disparity in agricultural performance. Figure 6.4 shows the change in coefficient of variation of wheat yields for the period 1950–83. The inter-district disparity was low in 1950–1, as all the districts in Punjab used traditional farming. With the introduction of the new wheat technology

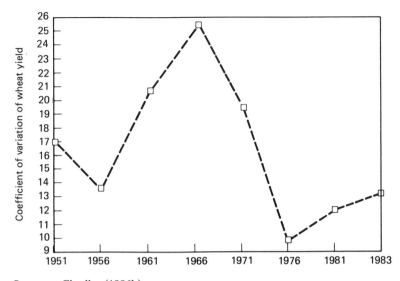

Source: Chadha (1986b)
Figure 6.4   Variation in wheat yields

(HYV) in 1965–6, the disparity increased as some districts adopted the new technology quicker than others. As the other districts adopted the HYV, the regional variation fell.

Linkages Between Agriculture and Industry

Industrial Growth
Strong agricultural performance in the Punjab was accompanied by strong industrial performance. Growth of the manufacturing sector has exceeded agricultural growth since the 1970s (Table 6.6). The contribution of the secondary sector to the net state domestic product increased from 17.5 per cent in 1965–6 to 21.1 per cent by 1980–1, while that of the primary sector fell from 50.8 per cent to 44.5 per cent.

In the early stages, much of the industrial growth was due to pecuniary externalities – i.e., improved markets for industrial products arising from linkages with agriculture. This launched a cumulative growth process in industry in the region, which benefited from learning economies and real externalities within the sector, so that the sector acquired national and even international comparative advantage, extending its markets well beyond the 'home' market of the Punjab.

Table 6.6 Sectoral distribution of net state domestic product in Punjab

Sector	Annual (compound) growth rate (%)			
	60.1–65.6	65.6–70.1	70.1–75.10	75.76–80.81
Primary	2.4 (54.0)	7.1 (50.8)	2.6 (48.1)	4.5 (44.5)
Agriculture	1.1	6.9	1.9	3.6
Livestock	10.2	8.0	5.2	6.0
Secondary	5.8 (15.8)	5.6 (17.5)	6.6 (18.7)	8.7 (21.1)
Registered manufacturing	9.5	4.8	7.8	10.3
Unregistered manufacturing	3.5	6.7	6.0	9.4
Electricity, gas and water supply	11.32	9.2	7.5	14.5
Tertiary	4.6 (30.4)	6.6 (31.6)	5.3 (33.2)	6.9 (34.4)
Transport, communication and storage	1.0	8.3	5.7	8.2
Trade, hotels and restaurants	5.0	7.2	5.6	7.0
Banking and insurance	6.1	6.51	4.5	10.9
Total	3.7	6.8	4.2	6.1
Per capita income	1.6	4.61	2.2	3.2

Note: Figures in parentheses are percentages of total net state domestic product at the end of the period indicated.
Source: Chadha (1986a).

Linkages
The existence of linkages between agriculture and industry in Punjab is well recognised. 'The chain of forward and backward linkages between agriculture and all levels of industry still remains the identifying characteristic of the Punjab economy even though the industrial structure of the state has become steadily diversified'.[11]

(a) *Backward linkages from agriculture to industry* The adoption of new technology created sharply rising demand for industrial inputs. Purchased inputs rose from 30 per cent to 87 per cent of

Table 6.7   Capital accumulation in Punjab agriculture

Item	1951	1956	1961	1966	1972	1977	1981
No. of cane crushers							
– power operated	476	547	1566	3 223	9 500	16 599	–
Tube-wells							
– diesel engines (no.)	1285	3972	6983	25 670	249 687	304 000	310 000
– electric motors (no.)	300	6355	6565	20 233	78 763	196 579	307 392
Tractors (no.)	1418	2909	4935	10 636	41 185	64 307	117 627

Source: Chadha (1986b).

total inputs from 1960 to 1980. There were huge increases in the use of cane crushers, tubewells and tractor production over the period 1951–81 (Table 6.7). Mohali tractors, Khanna–Gobindgarh steel tubes and spares, pipes and fittings, and other tubewell accessories manufactured in Punjab have a market not only within the state, but in the rest of India as well. The growing market for industrial inputs in agriculture attracted local investment. Though some of the demand was met by imports, most was locally satisfied by small-scale and medium sized industries.

(b) *Forward linkages from agriculture to industry*   Local food processing industries were expanded with the growth in agricultural production; for example, many rice-husking mills were established. Food products, beverages and cotton textiles are examples of forward linkage industries which relied on agriculture for their inputs.

(c) *Consumption linkages*   It is well established that consumption linkages are quantitatively the most important type of local linkage (see, e.g., Ranis, Stewart and Angeles-Reyes, 1990). These are industries and services which develop to cater for rising consumption demand associated with rising agricultural production and incomes. Nearly half of industrial employment in the Punjab is in consumption linkage industries. A further substantial element consists of services, which accounted for over a third of the net domestic product in 1980–1 (see Table 6.6).

It can be seen that linkage industries dominated industrial development in the Punjab. The strong linkages present can be seen in the geographical spread of industries which closely corresponded to the agricultural development of the state.

(d) *Industry–agriculture linkages*   Industrial developments in the

Punjab were not only stimulated via linkages with agriculture, but also in turn helped agricultural growth in a form of reverse externality, consisting of both real and pecuniary externalities. The pecuniary externalities were probably dominant, with industrial development improving the terms on which agriculture received its inputs (as producers and consumers), by reducing price and/or improving the speed of service or delivery compared with importing the goods from outside the region; the speed factor was particularly important for repair services. The industrial sector also provided a better market (higher prices) for agricultural products.

Real externalities took the form of technologies better adapted to local farmers' needs, better diffusion of information on inputs, and the visible presence of consumer goods and of investment opportunities which raised the incentive to maximise production in agriculture.

Locally produced technologies were adapted to local conditions. This was helped by the close proximity of the industrial firms to the farmers, which facilitated exchange of information on technological elements. Considerable modification of imported technology, and the local adaptation of tubewell technology has been noted for Pakistani Punjab (Child and Kaneda, 1975, p. 256).

The linkages between industry and agriculture, and between urban and rural areas, were feasible due to the even distribution of towns and villages in Punjab, connected by a well developed road network. The towns serve as centres for marketing and trade in agricultural and agro-industrial products. The rural–urban proximity led to regular contact with urban marketing and industrial centres, encouraging a greater flow of information.

Intra-sectoral Externalities in Industry

Industrial sector development was also subject to externalities: the initial success of a few local firms was copied by others, technologies were rapidly diffused by copying, sometimes aided by the transfer of labour from one firm to another.

A survey of firms producing industrial inputs for agriculture in Pakistan Punjab showed that all workers were trained outside the government system by small firms. Operators of 70 per cent of the firms in the sample reported that they had learned the business in other firms before establishing their own independent enterprises (Child and Kaneda, 1975). The growth of the industrial base increased the scope of specialisation. Rather than one firm producing the entire range of products and services (e.g., tube-wells, electric and diesel motor engines, spare parts, metal casting, threshers, cane crushers and repair services), firms specialising in few products emerged, leading to a more efficient local division of labour.

The Punjab: Conclusions

This case study has shown that there were numerous sources of externalities in agriculture and industry in the Punjab. Policy interventions in agriculture were essential as markets were not in a position to internalise the externalities because the externalities were of the many–many type, so that the transaction costs of bargaining and coordinating were high. Property rights were also not conducive to voluntary correction of the externalities.

External economies resulting from linkages between agriculture and industry mutually reinforced the growth in the two sectors. The lower-priced industrial goods made agriculture more profitable. As a result, new farm lands were brought under HYV seeds, and growth in agriculture further increased the demand for industrial inputs. The increasing size of the market meant that the firms could take advantage of economies of scale and learning.

In summary, developments in the Punjab constituted a 'microcosm of the development process: mobilisation of skills, diffusion of technology, and generation of income and employment . . . [with] mutually reinforcing growth of industry and agriculture' (Child and Kaneda, 1975, p. 271, writing about Pakistan Punjab).

The interaction of real and pecuniary externalities within and between agriculture and industry gave rise to this cumulative growth process.

MEASUREMENT OF EXTERNALITIES

If policy interventions are to be justified on the basis of externalities it is necessary to have some idea of potential orders of magnitude involved, in principle, *ex ante* (i.e., before decisions are made). A subsidy or tariff should not exceed the value of the externalities, if it is directed solely to correcting the market failure caused by the existence of externalities.

By their nature externalities do not have a direct market value (since by definition they are not priced and traded). Therefore, unavoidably, they are difficult to measure, and can be estimated only by indirect means.

The discussion that follows focusses on the measurement of dynamic production externalties, dividing them into the three categories put forward on pp. 126–8: attitudes and motivation, human capital formation and technology transfer.

1. The first – attitudes and motivation – tends to be a discontinuous change that occurs in the early stage of industrialisation. It can have a very large effect on rates of capital accumulation and productivity change. A switch in capital accumulation from 5 per cent to 10–15 per cent of national income is not uncommon, with a doubling or more in rates of productivity growth. Once these rates have been achieved – as in most contemporary LDCs – this type of externality loses significance, except in isolated areas.

2. The value of human capital formation is approximated by the change in earnings associated with different levels of education/training.[12] Numerous estimates have been made of the returns to formal education (see summary in Schultz, 1989); although less attention has been paid to the returns to training, estimates for skill differentials should indicate the value placed on training, assuming equilibrium in non-segmented labour markets. Differentials in wages between skilled and unskilled of two or more are typical in developing countries (see, e.g., Chowdhury and Bhuiyan, 1985, for some evidence for Bangladesh). To the extent that individuals receive additional earnings for training, they have an incentive to pay for this training themselves, but where wages are at subsistence there is no scope for this. Imperfect foresight and imperfect capital markets prevent workers borrowing to finance their training.

3. Technology change and technology transfer is the most important source of dynamic externalities and also the most difficult to estimate. As shown in our second section, it is composed of a variety of elements, including movement of labour transferring technology from one firm to another, technology transfer through networking of various kinds and technology innovation induced by interaction between firms.

   The labour transfer–technology transfer element could be measured by the additional wages firms are prepared to pay for workers moving from one firm to another. Figures for 'transfer' wages, or more generally for how wages change as particular industrial experience accumulates would provide an estimate of the value of technology transferred in this way, aggregated (and discounted) over the remaining working life of the worker (see Baldwin, 1988). There is no obvious way of making a direct estimate of the value of technology transfer through networking (magazines, useful meetings and so on). However, the potential maximum value of such transfer is suggested by the difference in total factor productivity of the best practice technology in an industry and the average. The dispersion represents how much technology a firm might acquire by efficient networking – i.e., the maximum value of the externalities to be acquired. This measure would also include the technology which might be acquired by human transfer, so this estimate should not be added to the previous estimate to avoid double counting. Another measure of the externality potential would be given by profit differences between the most profitable and average firms. However, in both cases there may be other reasons for the differences in productivity or profitability so such estimates may exaggerate the extent of potential externalities. An estimate of difference in productivity among farms in the Punjab is shown in Figure 6.4.

This illustrates the large potential externalities which existed when the new technologies were first introduced – the coefficient of variation of yields rose from about 13 in 1966 to nearly 26 in 1972. The thorough exploitation of externalities in this case is shown by the fall in the coefficient of variation to under 10 in 1976. Much information has been collected or disparities in productivity within industries (see Mahmood, 1989, for a survey). In most cases, unlike the case of agriculture in the Punjab, these productivity differences persist over time, suggesting either that the potential externalities are not realised, and/or that they are realised but that the leading firms are improving their own performance over time, and thus opening up new opportunities for the exploitation of externalities. The former explanation is more likely in industries whose productivity is changing little over time, the latter in industries exhibiting rapid productivity gains. In the latter type of industry, the potential size of externalities, accumulated over time, tends to be much greater than in the more static industries.

The third type of dynamic externality – induced technical change caused by interactions between input- and user-industries – is most difficult to measure. A necessary but not sufficient condition for it to occur is the existence of significant linkages between industries. It is easy to find examples where this type of interaction has occurred (see, e.g., Rosenberg 1976; and the semiconductor study above), but difficult to estimate the extent to which technological change is due to the change in the linked industry as against innovative activity in the industry itself, which would have occurred anyway. Possible indicators of the existence of interactive technology change include (a) a high degree of linked activities, (b) technology change in each of the two or more linked industries, (c) a large element of *product* change (as against process change) in the linked industries. Where all three occur, the existence of such externalities is indicated, but this does not provide an estimate of their value. An upper estimate would be given by an estimate of the increase in the factor productivity (weighting for product changes) associated with technical changes that qualify under the three indicators. This would represent an upper estimate because other changes – not related to these externalities – may also have contributed to the technical changes.

To conclude, identifying and estimating individual elements does not permit precise estimation of externalities, but it does allow broad indications of the range of externalities in particular industries.

CONCLUSIONS AND IMPLICATIONS FOR POLICY

The existence of externalities of significant magnitude creates a *prima facie* case for departures from non-interventionist industrial or trade policies, since without intervention it seems likely that the externalities will not be taken into account in resource allocation. Consequently, there would be a tendency for under-investment in areas subject to a high degree of external economies relative to those with less external economies. Developing countries may have a dynamic comparative advantage in an industry subject to dynamic externalities – but be uncompetitive according to static comparative advantage. Consequently government intervention (by subsidy, tariff, quota or other means) would appear to be justified to enable dynamic comparative advantage to be realised, as in Figure 6.4. Protection (or subsidy) could be temporary if private costs eventually fall below international costs, or permanent if private costs still exceed world prices, although social costs fall below them. If the home market is too small (as OH'), protection may not permit production at internationally competitive prices. For small economies therefore an alternative is regional trade groupings to extend the market to OS, or a production subsidy to permit export markets to exploit economies of scale.

While this simple depiction applies most directly to real externalities, it also extends to cases of pecuniary externalities where these interact with economies of scale, learning economies, or real externalities so that industrial expansion causes social costs to fall, as occurred in both the US semiconductor industry and agro-industrial development in the Punjab. However, in the policy analysis that follows we shall focus on real externalities, since pecuniary externalities can normally be dealt with as an aspect of policies towards economies of scale, learning economies or real externalities.

Current recommendations on trade–industrial policy fall broadly into three categories: first, a free trade approach, according to which a country's investment, production and trade patterns should be left to market forces, which are assumed to reflect its current comparative advantage. The second category is recommendations of policies intended to give *mild* support for industrialisation. The version favoured by most economic advisers is to provide a small general subsidy to industrialisation (e.g., 5 per cent), together with some government expenditure on industrial infrastructure. An alternative is to provide the same generalised support for import substitution, by the use of a low uniform tariff (see, e.g., Corden, 1974; Balassa, 1975; Little, 1982). The third category has been described as the 'strategists'' approach (by Pack and Westphal, 1986), involving a strong *selective* support for particular industries. Again the promotion may take the form of subsidies to production or exports, or of import restrictions (or both). The practice is intended to be temporary.

One of the main differences in hypotheses between the proponents of the different approaches concerns the existence, size and nature of externalities, since it is the extent and nature of market failures (of which externalities are an important, but not the only, component) which justifies departure from the free trade position and which suggests the most appropriate design for policy interventions. However, the precise implications of the existence of externalities for industrial and/or trade policies depends on the nature of the externalities, and of the economy in which they occur.

The first issue is the pervasiveness of industries subject to exter-

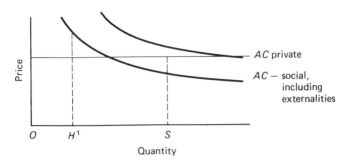

Figure 6.5   Costs with externalities

nalities: if every part of the economy were subject to similar external economies, there would be no case for special support of any sector, since one cannot protect everything. However, although externalities of some sort are pervasive, they are likely to be much stronger in some industries/sectors than others, because of the nature of dynamic externalities. As shown earlier, the prime source of real dynamic externalities – which are the most important beneficial externality – lies in technological change and the (unpriced) ways in which this technical change is transmitted from one firm to another, both within and between industries. Such externalities are likely to be greater in industries subject to rapid technological change.

From a policy perspective, special support would be justified for those industries going through a dynamic phase. While an industry is undergoing rapid learning (usually at an early stage), then special support would be justified.

The second issue concerns the spatial location of externalities: if external economies created by an industry were transmitted worldwide, then each industry could benefit from externalities created by any other industry, irrespective of where the industry was located. There would therefore be no case for special promotion of home industries. The evidence suggests that some externalities do cross boundaries, through general communications and international trade; these provide a justification for a pro-trade set of policies. But the majority of dynamic externalities described earlier are nation-specific, and some of them are specific to a particular region (e.g., the Punjab case, the Silicon valley). Krugman has argued that even where the externalities are nation-specific no intervention is justified where factor prices are unaffected and where the externalities are industry-specific (see Krugman, 1986 and Helpman and Krugman,

1985). But Krugman's model is a full employment model where real wages are determined in the constant-returns sector which is shared by both trading partners. In this model, a rise in productivity throughout the economy can only happen if either (1) a nation specialises entirely on external economy industries; or (2) the external economies arising from one industry benefit the whole economy, raising productivity everywhere. In contrast, developing countries which succeed in raising productivity in the externality creating sector may increase the size of the modern sector (through absorbing surplus labour) and thereby raise real incomes for the economy as a whole. The recent efforts of Taiwan, S. Korea and Singapore in their post-labour surplus phase can be seen as a gradual effort to shift the whole economy into technologically dynamic increasing return sectors (i.e., to fulfil condition (1)) though the policy has to start with one industry at a time.

The third question is the industrial location of externalities: as noted earlier, externalities can be concentrated industrially as to source and also as to beneficiary, but they may be dispersed in either or both senses. Assume they are all nation-specific, where they are concentrated as to source; there is a case for selective promotion of the source industry, irrespective of whether it is also the beneficiary or the sole beneficiary, as with the semiconductor industry. Where other industries are the main beneficiaries it is the recipient industries which may acquire international competitiveness as a result of the policy, not the promoted industry. (Examples would be the competitiveness acquired by user-industries in the US as a result of the development of the semiconductor industry, or competitiveness or other advantages, such as appropriate technology, that user-industries might gain as a result of promotion of capital goods industries.) In all cases where linked industries are the main beneficiaries care is needed to establish that the externalities are nation-specific and could not equally (or better) be acquired by importing. An example of the latter might be India's protection of its capital goods industry, which has probably led to lower technology transfers to user-industries than those they would have received through imported capital goods (as well as involving them in worse terms of trade).

Where the externalities are concentrated as to source, and nation-specific as to beneficiary, then selective industrial promotion is justified. But if the source of externalities is spread widely among industries, but not outside industry, then the type of intervention justified is non-discriminatory industrial promotion.

In practice, the industrial location of externalities depends upon their nature. Some, like engendering work habits and learning some management techniques, are likely to be pervasive. These may be particularly common in the early stages of industrialisation. Others, like the dynamic externalities associated with technical change, are likely to be focussed on particular types of technology and industry, where the rate of frontier technology is changing fast. These externalities will generally be concentrated on a single industry or a few closely linked industries.

A popular criticism of selective policies is that it is difficult (some say impossible) to 'pick winners' – indeed this is used as a decisive criticism of the approach in much discussion by orthodox economists (e.g., Krugman, 1983; Schultz, 1983; Council of Economic Advisors, 1984). The empirical counter argument is the undoubted success of Japan and later S. Korea apparently in doing precisely that (Pack and Westphal, 1986; Chung, 1988; Enos and Park, 1988).

But the phrase 'pick winners' is incorrect: what is at stake is *not* for the most part picking winners, but *creating winners*. Assume that *every* industry is subject to the same significant external economies, real and pecuniary, static and dynamic. Assume that with a 'non-intervention' policy, very limited industrialisation would occur and these externalities would not be realised. Neither an across-the-board import substitution policy of the type commonly adopted, nor a generalised low subsidy to industrialisation of the type commonly recommended, might be sufficient in this situation to realise enough of the external economies to secure socially competitive production. Sufficient externalities would be realised only if some industries were heavily promoted while the rest were not. With this model, where it is assumed that all industries are subject to the same externalities, there is no question of picking winners – any industry could be a winner: it is a matter of choosing a *few* industries (and *not* promoting all industries), and then creating winners.[13]

In practice, it may not be true that such externalities are likely to be equal irrespective of industry – and, more importantly, a country's comparative advantage (static and dynamic) after allowing for externalities, learning effects, etc. is likely to differ between industries, according to its own history and stage of development. Consequently, it is not realistic to argue that it does not matter what you pick as long as you pick something (as with Aesop's donkey). In reality, the situation is somewhere between picking winners and creating winners. But given industry-specific dynamic economies (internal as well as external), the policy of low generalised support for industry (or across-the-board import substitution) could prove to be worse than a random policy of selective promotion.

To summarise, the *prima facie* case for intervention in the presence of externalities in a developing country has justification where the externalities are nation-specific, and are concentrated on particular parts of the economy. The externalities must be sufficient to ensure eventual competitiveness in the industry in question or in user-industries, and the eventual gains must be sufficient to outweigh the temporary costs (the Mills–Bastable test). Selective promotion is justified where the source of externalities is concentrated on one or a few industries. The evidence of rapid and uneven technical change suggests that these conditions are quite often met – but empirical investigation is needed to ensure they are, or losses can ensue. As shown earlier, even *ex post* empirical evidence is problematic. It is even more difficult to estimate the significance of externalities before the industrial development occurs, but some orders of magnitude are needed to take well-founded decisions on industrial promotion.

Type of Intervention

Suppose a case for intervention has been established; this leaves open the question of the type of intervention – or indeed whether the market will not bring about its own solution without government intervention.

Much of the literature on externalities has been concerned with this issue. Three categories of solution have been proposed: (1) Integration; (2) negotiations and bargaining between the agents leading to voluntary coordination and/or the creation of property rights; (3) government interventions.

Integration
This solution may occur where the externalities are large in relation to other costs, and where they are of a one–one type. Some pecuniary externalities fit this model. But this solution is not suitable for one–many or many–many-type externalities, since too many agents are involved for integration. As noted earlier, many of the dynamic externalities are of the many–many type (e.g., those associated with

mobility of skilled workers; technology diffusion, etc.). All the externalities in the Punjab case, and most in the semiconductor case, were many–many types.

Bargaining and the Creation of Property Rights
Coase (1960) – who saw defects in the 'tradition' solution of taxes–subsidies – suggested that negotiated solutions might be brought about by the agents themselves, without outside interventions. The potential gains (losses) would induce those benefiting (suffering) from the externalities to bribe those imposing them to generate–limit the externalities, thereby creating property rights, or a market, in the externalities. However, this will happen only if the benefits exceed the transaction costs. Where this occurs the externalities are effectively internalised. A similar solution is voluntary coordination among agents. Direct bargaining (or coordination) is likely to occur only where there are very few agents and/or very large benefits–costs to each agent, because of the increasing transaction costs arising with greater numbers.

In the many–many case, too, many agents are involved and the gains for each individually are likely to be too small to warrant the transactions costs. There can also be enforcement problems where many agents are involved. For dynamic externalities there is the further problem that the potential gains may not be known and/or uncertain – not a promising scene for bargaining and property rights (e.g., where they involve stimulation of technical change).

Property rights could be extended to cover some aspects of real externalities of the many–many type, with legal changes. For example, if firms 'owned' workers and sold them to other firms (like footballers or baseball players), this would internalise the training–learning externality. But there could be objections to this on grounds of civil liberties! In Japan internalisation has been achieved by the system of lifelong employment. The patent system could be extended (again on the Japanese model of 'utility' patents) to extend markets over technology transfer. But this has enforcement costs, limits the diffusion of technology, and will never fully 'marketise' all the ways in which technology is diffused.

Government Intervention
It thus appears that, for a large proportion of the dynamic externalities described in this essay, the market cannot provide an adequate solution on its own, and that direct government intervention

is needed.[14] This applies to most dynamic externalities, where many agents are involved. Government interventions can take a variety of forms. These include facilitating and perhaps partially financing coordination among agents (e.g., the MITI in Japan organised joint research among major companies); providing subsidies in various forms (e.g., investment subsidies or tax relief; support for R and D, education, hiring); government procurement (which was the most powerful policy used in the US semiconductor industry); and trade measures, including tariffs, quotas and export subsidies.

In this area, as in others, the more directly the intervention deals with the situation which justifies it, the better. This means that subsidies to the externality-creating source (e.g., for R and D) are preferable to more indirect measures. In view of this, direct trade measures are rather clumsy compared with many other policy instruments. However, in a second best world, where there are limited funds for subsidies, protection may be appropriate. The protection should be directed to those industries experiencing an actual (or potential) phase of high externalities. In this phase, high levels of protection could be justified on a temporary basis; it should be temporary, not only because the realisation of externalities and economies of scale should normally make protection unnecessary after a specified time, but also because the industry will be denied externalities coming from abroad during protection. Moreover, protection for the industry as a whole will not necessarily induce externality-creating activity, since individual firms will still not retain the full benefits of such activities (e.g., of R and D or learning) (see Baldwin, 1969). Where protection may be beneficial is if pre-learning costs of production exceed international prices, but post-learning costs do not. Protection may then induce domestic production, and along with that cost-reducing learning. This situation may result from a combination of internal and external economies, both static and dynamic.

CONCLUSION

In conclusion, this essay has argued that externalities are of major significance to development – not the static type described by Pigou and Meade, but the dynamic externalities associated with technological change, as indicated in the two case studies. These externalities are not mainly the pecuniary externalities pointed to by Hirschman, Rosenstein-Rodan and Scitovsky, but real dynamic externalities, although interaction with pecuniary externalities increases their biting power in terms of generating dynamic development. Because they are mainly many–many, they will not be negotiated away through private transactions. Government intervention is needed. The best type of intervention is likely to vary according to circumstances and will require empirical investigation, not only as to the economic conditions but also as to the political constraints.

NOTES

1. There are of course other reasons why the market system may not lead to a social optimum (e.g., unsatisfactory income distribution).
2. However, negative externalities could be present where there are *no* linkages, since the negative effect might be to eliminate (for example) local supplies of inputs. Also, the linkage literature itself is not comprehensive and may therefore have missed some externalities.
3. I am grateful to Paul Anand for suggesting categories 3 and 4.
4. Scitovsky used the example of the influence of an inventor on producers, but we would interpret this as a p–p type.
5. See Dasgupta and Stiglitz (1988), who argue that in certain circumstances a subsidy on imports may be justified to encourage foreign learning.
6. Technological externalities are here termed 'real' because of the many other uses of 'technological'.
7. This is the type of case noted by Scitovsky and Rosenstein-Rodan, both of whom believed it had wide empirical application.
8. See for example, Pack and Westphal (1986) on policies towards learning economics and economies of scale.
9. The same approach can be used to identify pecuniary externalities within a particular region, but in this case W_i should be interpreted as prices in the economic centre of the country, t_i the transactions costs of trade with the centre, while b_i would usually be zero.
10. Policy intervention to correct market failures associated with imperfect information which limits credit distribution has been criticised on the grounds that the government itself would also be subject to imperfect knowledge (see Stiglitz, 1987).
11. Chadha (1986a) p. 168.
12. To the extent that private returns to education reflect screening or credentialism, these will exaggerate the social returns.
13. Suppose a student asks advice on whether she would be better advised to be a doctor or a lawyer. Assume, in fact, she would be equally good at either, if she undertakes the required training. Should the adviser recommend doing a little training for both, because it is difficult to pick a winner?
14. See also Greenwald and Stiglitz (1986), who come to this conclusion and codify alternative policies.

7 Do Third World Countries Benefit From Countertrade?*
with Harsha V. Singh

INTRODUCTION

In recent years there has been a rapid expansion of unorthodox methods of arranging and financing trade, especially in trade with or between Third World countries. The phenomenon is known as *countertrade* and includes all exchanges of goods and services between nations, which do not consist of a straightforward sale of goods for internationally convertible money, but involve an exchange of goods for goods, or goods for a combination of goods and money, or other unorthodox methods of payment. Traditionally, of course, the socialist countries have accounted for a major share of bilateral deals in world trade. The new phenomenon is the extension of countertrade to the rest of the world. During the late 1970s and early 1980s, for example, it became pervasive in the oil market, as well as in arms deals. In recent years, a number of developing countries – including Nigeria, Malaysia, Pakistan and Indonesia – have explicitly adopted countertrade as an important element in their trading strategies.

The aim of this essay is to analyse major costs and benefits of countertrade, as a Third World trading strategy. To do so we first provide a brief description of the phenomenon, considering the type of deals included (the 'modalities'), a review of the quantitative debate, and of the direction of flows and the nature of goods and services involved in recent deals. Identification of the phenomenon at a rather detailed and concrete level is important because some of the arguments about benefits and costs at a general level miss important elements necessary for any assessment. In the third section, we

* This essay was first published in Dell (ed.) (1988). Harsha V. Singh is a member of the GATT secretariat. This chapter contains our personal views and does not necessarily represent those of the GATT or of Richard Blackhurst, to whom we are grateful for comments on an earlier draft.

162

consider dominating major motives which have led to the growth of countertrade in deals concerning Third World countries. With this essential background we discuss costs and benefits in the fourth section; a final section presents our conclusions.

A DESCRIPTION OF COUNTERTRADE

'Modalities'

Countertrade covers a considerable range of deals – a range which is rapidly evolving. There is no general definition of countertrade except that there is an element of reciprocity. The reciprocal component may consist of an immediate transaction or exchange over a protracted period of time, may involve two or more partners, may cover only a small proportion of the transaction as countertrade or may require this component to exceed the value of the initial trade deal. Countertrade is not synonymous with pure barter and usually involves some cash financing (see Jones, 1984).

Countertrade deals have been categorised in a variety of (not always consistent) ways.[1] Sometimes it is difficult to decide when a deal qualifies as countertrade. For example, sometimes there is no contractual agreement involving countertrade, but there may be an understanding that one of the partners will make 'best efforts' to sell the products manufactured by the other partner.

The countertrade categories described here are those that have been commonly distinguished in the literature. A single countertrade deal may span more than one of these categories.

1. *Barter* is exchange of goods and services for goods and services. Though third parties can be involved, they do not sign the barter agreement. Barter deals are not very common because of their . limited flexibility (see, for example, Jones, 1984, p. 20): 'In practice, supply of principal exports is often held up until sufficient revenue has been earned from selling the bartered goods'.[2]
2. *Counterpurchase* appears to be the 'most common form of countertrade'.[3] Two separate contracts are signed for this and each contract has its own financial arrangement. The agreement may vary from a declaration of intent for 'best efforts' to binding commitment which involves a penalty if unfulfilled. These deals usually have a short time frame (i.e., up to three to five years).

3. *Advance purchase* eliminates risk of non-payment. In this situation, the receipts from the sales of one of the partners are placed in an escrow or evidence account, to be used later for counter-purchase.

4. *Offsets* involve the condition that the exporter incorporate inputs from the importing country into its final products. This form of countertrade has been long established in trade in defence systems and aircraft. Now it is becoming a component of deals in other sectors also. Offset deals may or may not involve direct use of the products linked to the initial transaction. Direct offset includes coproduction, licensed production, sub-contractor production, overseas investment or technology transfer. Indirect offsets are like counterpurchase and may be part of a wider 'offset package'.

5. In *buyback*, the supplier of capital plant or equipment agrees to take the future product as part or full payment. These deals involve a much longer time period (e.g., five to fifteen years) compared with counterpurchase. A looser form of this type of an agreement is encompassed in *framework agreements* or long-term protocols or agreements (see OECD, 1981).

6. *Bilateral agreements*, which use clearing accounts, bind all or some part of the trade between two countries. Normally, the goods must be from a pre-specified list. The value of goods is denominated in artificial accounting units, such as clearing dollars or rupees. Though trade is supposed to balance in a given time period, usually a maximum trade imbalance is specified. Large imbalances in these accounts could lead to *switch trading*, which involves swapping documents and destination of goods and may involve complex deals amongst several buyers, sellers and brokers across different markets.

The Extent of Countertrade

There are very wide variations in estimates of the extent of counter-trade in world trading, ranging from less than 5 per cent to 40 per cent.[4] While some official estimates suggest that countertrade constitutes only 8 per cent of world trade, the US Department of Commerce has suggested that one-quarter of all world trade involves some form of barter. These variations derive from differences in definition, differential access to statistics on countertrade, which are in any case dubious because of the secrecy involved in many deals, the fact that some deals represent only a portion of a larger deal and guesstimates are therefore needed, and the inclusion of deals in process of negotiation in some estimates, while a number of deals are initiated but break down before completion.

The very low estimates certainly understate the true extent (for example, the IMF put forward an estimate of 1 per cent of world trade in 1983) but figures of 30 per cent or 40 per cent certainly exaggerate its current significance. The true figure is probably between 10 per cent and 20 per cent of world trade, with the proportion depending on the definition adopted. This can be seen by estimating countertrade separately by region.[5] Table 7.1 shows estimates of countertrade based on two assumptions about the significance of countertrade in the trade of different regions with different parts of the world. The upper estimates (*A*) are, we believe, unrealistically high. They indicate that, at most, countertrade amounts to 25 per cent of world trade. The lower estimates (*B*) represent a more realistic figure. This suggests that countertrade may account for around 15 per cent of world trade.

Despite disagreement about absolute quantities, there is general agreement that countertrade grew rapidly in the 1980s, especially in the trade of developing countries. According to one estimate, the number of deals increased by 50 per cent in 1981, by over 60 per cent in 1982 and over by 100 per cent in 1983.[6] In the early 1980s, 88 countries either had formal countertrade regulations or had initiated deals, compared with about 12 countries in the early 1970s, according to a survey of US industrial companies conducted by the National Foreign Trade Council. The increase has been especially marked in deals involving Third World countries as at least one of the partners. A number of countries now include countertrade as an acknowledged and important element in their trade strategy; this extends beyond the socialist countries and the major oil exporters to such countries as Brazil, Pakistan, Malaysia, Colombia, Argentina and Turkey.

The fall in the oil price in 1986, together with the collapse of several major companies involved in countertrade, is likely to have led to a slowdown in the growth of countertrade, but the phenomenon remains a persistent element in trading options of Third World countries.

Table 7.2 lists countries[7] reported to have conducted countertrade deals with other non-ETA countries since 1983 and shows the broad products countertraded. This shows that a large number of countries, both developed and developing, have resorted to countertrade in the recent past. The list includes all the large debtors except Morocco, all

Table 7.1   Total trade (exports plus imports) and countertrade amongst
regions as a share of global trade under different hypothetical assumptions

Trading regions	Share of world trade in 1984 %	Two sets of assumptions about share of countertrade in total trade[a]		Share of countertrade in total trade under the two assumptions	
		A	B	A	B
1. Amongst Eastern Trading Area[b]	6	90	90	5.4	5.4
2. Eastern Trading Area and industrial countries	6	20	15	1.2	1
3. Developing countries and Eastern Trading Area	3	100	50	3	1.5
4. South and Central America and world (ex-ETA)	9	50	20	4.5	1.8
5. South and East Asia and world (ex-ETA)	15	10	3	1.5	0.45
6. Other developing countries and world (ex-ETA)	12	50	20	6	2.4
7. Rest (mainly between industrialised market economies)	49	6	2	3	1.5
Total	100			24.6	14.1

Notes:
a Estimates based on Barovick (1986) for USA; OECD (1985a) for developing countries; OECD (1981) for Eastern Europe; Agarwala (1984) for Indonesia; Sherwell (1985) for the Philippines; Dodwell (1986) for China and Eastern Europe; Richter (1982) for Eastern Europe.
b Eastern Trading Area (non-market economies): Albania, Bulgaria, Czechoslovakia, German Democratic Republic, Hungary, Poland, Romania, USSR, China, Mongolia, N. Korea and Viet Nam.
Source: UNSO COMTRADE Data Base.

Table 7.2 Reported countertrade by different market economy countries, 1982–5

Country	Number of countertrading partners		Type of commodity countertraded	
	Developed	Developing	Exports	Imports
Developing countries				
Algeria	1	1	OM	PM
Angola		1	O	PMC
Egypt	2	2	PM	MC
Ethiopia		1	P	M
Ghana	1	1	P	P
Kenya	1	1	P	P
Mozambique		1	N	N
Nigeria	3	3	OPM	OPM
Sierra Leone		1	P	N
Somalia		1	M	M
Sudan		1	P	N
Tanzania		4	PM	MC
Togo	1		O	C
Tunisia	1		N	N
Burkina Faso		1	P	P
Zambia		1	N	N
Zimbabwe		2	P	N
Bangladesh		3	PM	P
Burma		2	P	PM
India	4	6	PMC	OPM
Indonesia	6	4	PM	PMC
South Korea	2	9	DMC	OPM
Malaysia	4	10	OPC	PDMC
Nepal		1	N	N
Pakistan	2	3	PM	OPM
Philippines		4	PM	PM
Singapore		1	M	C
Sri Lanka		2	P	OP
Taiwan		1	DMC	O
Thailand		8	P	OPMC
Abu Dhabi	1		O	M
Libya	3	2	O	PC
Iran	6	8	O	PDMC
Iraq	5	8	OP	PDMC
Jordan	2	4	PMC	OPMC
Qatar	3	2	O	PMC
Saudi Arabia	2		O	DMC
Syria		1	C	O

continued on page 168

Table 7.2 *continued*

Country	Number of countertrading partners		Type of commodity countertraded	
	Developed	*Developing*	*Exports*	*Imports*
Argentina	1	1	OP	OC
Brazil	1	14	OPDMC	OPMC
Chile	1		N	N
Colombia	3	1	P	MN
Costa Rica	1	3	PM	PM
Dominican Republic	1	1	P	M
Ecuador	1	4	PMC	OPM
El Salvador		1	N	N
Guatemala	2	1	P	O
Guyana		2	P	OP
Jamaica	1	1	P	PM
Mexico	3	5	OPM	OPMC
Nicaragua		4	PM	OM
Panama		1	P	P
Paraguay	1		P	M
Peru	1	1	OPM	PMC
Trinidad and Tobago		2	OM	PM
Uruguay	1	3	P	OMC
Venezuela	2	3	OM	OPMC
China	4	14	OPMC	PMC
Developed countries				
Australia	1	2	P	M
Austria	1	1	N	O
Belgium	1	1	M	N
Canada	2	3	MC	OPM
Finland		1	M	PM
France		11	DMC	OPM
West Germany		3	MC	O
Greece		2	PC	O
Israel	1	5	M	OP
Italy		4	M	OP
Japan	1	9	PMC	OPM
New Zealand	1	1	P	OM
Turkey	1	2	C	O
Spain	1	1	N	N
Sweden		2	M	P
Switzerland	1	2	C	D
UK	1	4	DM	OPN
USA	7	18	OPDM	OPMC

O = Oil and oil products
P = Other primary products
D = Defence equipment
M = Other manufactures
C = Other; includes civil engineering and construction, services, technology transfer and miscellaneous
N = Not known

Source: Helmut Ferenz, *Special Transactions in Third World Trade* (August 1984), reported in Avramovic (1985); OECD (1985a) and several newspapers and periodicals for the period 1984 onwards.

the major members of OPEC except Kuwait and Dubai, and members of OECD. It is also clear that countries using countertrade included developing countries which do not suffer from immediate foreign exchange problems (It should be noted that this list is not exhaustive.)

Countries with a large number of countertrade partners are to be found among both developed and developing countries in the deals reported in Table 7.2. Countries in both categories exported primary commodities as well as manufactured products, although oil was exported in countertrade deals only by developing countries.[8] Most developing countries and five developed countries exported primary products. The trading pattern associated with countertrade broadly follows overall trading patterns. Of the 52 developing countries listed in Table 7.2 for which there is information on commodities exchanged, over 90 per cent of the countries included primary products (including oil) in their countertrade exports, while just over half the countries exported only primary products.

Manufactures, technology, etc. formed the exclusive export of just five countries (Somalia, Singapore, Taiwan, Syria and S. Korea) and a part of the countertrade exports in another 20 countries. The import composition was balanced between primary commodities and manufactures, with about one-fifth of the developing countries importing only primary products, one-fifth only manufactures and three-fifths both. The manufactured exports of developing countries were in relatively less sophisticated products.

Among developing countries, two countries out of the 16 for which there is information exported only primary products (New Zealand and Australia); nine only manufactures, civil engineering, etc. and five both. 87 per cent of developed countries' imports included some primary products (44 per cent were only primary products), and two out of 16 countries imported only manufactures (including defence).

Defence products were exported by three developed countries – France, UK and the USA – via countertrade. But these countries accounted for 45 per cent of the developed–developing country trading partners. In the case of the USA, it has been reported that defence-related offsets accounted for $US5.8 billion out of $US7.1 billion worth of US countertrade in 1984.[9] Defence products were also exported by the Republic of Korea, Taiwan Province and Brazil but it must be noted that defence deals are probably under-reported as they generally are surrounded by secrecy.

The Reality of Countertrade

The following examples of recent deals give a more concrete idea of the phenomenon of countertrade:

1. Brazil–Nigeria came to a $US1 billion agreement, with Nigeria exporting crude oil in exchange for raw materials, spare parts and manufactures.
2. Brazil–Iran: Iran exported oil in exchange for chickens from Brazil.
3. Brazil–West Germany: iron ore for submarines.
4. Israel–Guatemala: arms for Guatemalan goods using an escrow account.
5. Turkey–USA: purchase of F-16 fighters from General Dynamics for investment in agro-business in Turkey.
6. Malaysia–S. Korea: oil, rubber and timber products for electrical goods and patrol boats.
7. France–Middle Eastern countries: Mirages for oil.
8. USA–Saudi Arabia: oil for 747s from Boeing worth $US1 billion.
9. Soviet Union–Peru: Peru supplied gold, silver and manufactures to the Soviet Union as an offset to debt obligations.
10. Soviet Union–Finland: 25 per cent of Finland's trade is tied up on countertrade deals with the Soviet Union.
11. Greece has plans to acquire military construction equipment from Japan, Czechoslovakia and the Soviet Union in exchange for Greek goods.

These examples show that countertrade can be used for various kinds of trade. A large amount is among socialist countries and between socialist and other countries. This is not a new phenomenon but has always been the socialist countries' dominant method of trade. The new phenomenon is the North–South and South–South trade financed in this way. In the deals reported in Table 7.2, about 50 per cent are between developing countries, 45 per cent between North and South, and only 5 per cent among developed countries.[10] Not all countertrade is government to government. In the case of Boeing and General Dynamics, large private firms used countertrade methods. For the most part, Northern partners consist of large companies, while in the South governments predominate in organising deals. For the purpose of analysis, the deals may be divided into the following types:

Type 1 Military goods exchanged for other goods (mainly raw materials). These deals, though large in amount, have so far been concentrated in the exports of three developed and three developing countries.

Type 2 Raw materials exchanged for (non-military) manufactures, technology, construction, etc. This is a typical pattern for exchange between more industrialised and less industrialised countries and occurs both in North–South and South–South deals.

Type 3 Manufactures exchanged for non-manufactures: this has occurred on a small scale in some South–South deals.

Type 4 Primary products for primary products. This is a common feature of many South–South deals.

Hybrid deals also occur with some primary products and some manufactures being exported by one or both partners.

Table 7.3 shows an analysis of all South–South deals in 1982–3.

Table 7.3 Number of South–South deals, 1982–3

Type 1:	Military for other	2
Type 2:	Raw materials for manufacturers, etc.	28
Type 3:	Manufactures, etc. for manufactures, etc.	4
Type 4:	Primary for primary	18

Source: Helmut Ferenz, *Special Transactions in Third World Trade* (August 1984) quoted in Avramovic (1985).

MOTIVES FOR COUNTERTRADE

The motives for countertrade are numerous and varied. To complete a deal both parties must consider that there is some advantage to be gained as compared with normal trade. Since transaction costs are usually greater for countertrade, the perceived advantage must be significant. The perceived advantage may consist of improved access to markets, improved terms of trade, reduced hard currency requirements, improved payment prospects or increased certainty with respect to market access or payments.

Northern Motives

1. For companies in the North, the prime motivation is to secure *sales*. Unless they enter countertrade deals, companies may not be able to sell their products at all to countries with limited hard currency, strict import restrictions and a policy of countertrade deals. It is likely, then, that countertrade will be pushed more, when markets are depressed (i.e., during recession). But, even in the absence of recession, large companies are always seeking to protect and increase their share of the world market, and countertrade represents one way of achieving this. However, companies will accept higher costs (lower effective prices) for countertrade deals when markets are scarce because of recession. Countertrade offers companies the possibility of hidden and discriminatory price-cutting.
2. A second motivation of companies in the North is to ensure some *payment* for their sales, or some form of repatriation of profits from countries in payment difficulties. Countertrade is therefore likely to be more prevalent the greater the financial problems of Third World countries.
3. *Political* motivation may support some countertrade deals; for example, an industrialised country may want to secure especially good terms of trade for a country for political reasons (e.g., Cuba), or may want to promote military sales for political reasons, and countertrade may be the preferred way of doing so (this might underly some US military countertrade deals with, for example, Turkey). The use of economic power to support political aims is also facilitated by countertrade since countertrade deals involve specific decisions, which may be used as a political instrument more readily than normal market transactions.

Southern Motives

1. Primary producers may use countertrade as a means of *circumventing agreements* on price and quality. This was a prime motive of many of the oil deals in the early 1980s. Countertrade permitted avoidance of OPEC regulations, and may indeed have contributed to the near-collapse of the OPEC arrangement in 1986. There may have been a similar motive behind some of the deals involving tin. All the primary commodities which have price-setting agreements or collusive agreements among sellers have been countertraded.

2. *Improved terms of trade* (and/or increased certainty) has been a motive in other deals involving primary products, such as Cuban sugar exports to the USSR and some bauxite deals between Caribbean countries and the USA and the USSR. The absence of a free market in some major primary commodities – including sugar and bauxite – has meant that countries may get market access at all or on good terms only if they negotiate deals (for which the recipients may have political as well as economic motivation).

3. The *financial crisis* for many Third World countries has meant, paradoxically, that they may prefer to receive goods rather than hard currency for their exports, because hard currency receipts are likely to be pre-empted for payment of arrears and would not be available for imports. This seems to have been an important motive in countries trying to bypass the IMF, including Nigeria, Brazil and Tanzania, for example.[11] In some cases, countertrade lessens dependence on trade credit and thus may strengthen bargaining power in debt negotiations.[12]

4. For deals involving exports of manufactured or semi-manufactured products from developing countries, a prime motive for Third World countries has been to secure *greater and more certain market access* for their exports in circumstances where there are restrictions on imports of manufactures. There is also a motive for companies in advanced countries seeking sales in Third World or ETA markets. For trade with advanced countries, this possibility is more remote, but may arise because of the restrictions on imports of manufactures from developing countries in Northern countries, which may be avoided by countertrade. This is especially likely to apply to trade subject to non-tariff barriers, although gains made by one developing country may be at the expense of another. For trade with other developing countries also in financial difficulties, countertrade may be the only way of

securing market access, given the lack of convertible currencies to finance imports. Brazil has extended its export markets in Third World countries by use of countertrade deals.

5. Countertrade in manufactures may also permit developing countries to secure markets despite non-competitiveness of their manufactured exports because of low quality and/or high price. Straightforward price competition may be ruled out by the exchange rate policy being pursued by the country, while countertrade permits hidden price discounts (a form of *selective devaluation*).

6. In a world of rapid changes in environment – including changes in trade restrictions as well as economic factors – countertrade may be believed to *offer more certainty*, which may be desired by countries trying to plan their industrialisation, trade and payments in a coordinated way. Countertrade deals may be planned in advance and sales will be less dependent on the vagaries of the market. This seems to have been a prime motivation in Pakistan's decision to greatly expand the role of countertrade.

While these motives are varied, they have one important feature in common. They all arise from 'imperfections' in the world trade and payments system, i.e., from the fact that the free trade – perfect competition – fully employed model of the world economy, often assumed in trade theory, does *not* exist in the real world. For developed countries, the imperfections consist in the existence of oligopolistic companies seeking to increase their market share, and the depressed markets arising from recession and payments problems. For the developing countries, distortions and restrictions in the primary product market (some largely created by the developing countries themselves – e.g., in oil), some by the developed countries (the carve-up, for example, of the markets for bananas, sugar and bauxite), and restrictions on access to markets in manufactures in both developed and developing countries are a major underlying factor; the manifold restrictions on financial payments and exchange rates are a further important element. And for all countries lack of certainty lies behind many deals.

The fact that these deals arise from imperfections is very important to the assessment of countertrade, because it means it is quite wrong to take a free trade – full employment world as a model against which countertrade should be judged. Yet this is the assumed 'counter factual' in many assessments of countertrade.

COSTS AND BENEFITS

The major trade and financial institutions have taken a firm stand against countertrade. A report from the Fund,[13] for example, states that

> The Fund is generally concerned with their [countertrade deals] proliferation because they may be seen as undermining the objective of the multilateral trading system, the promotion of which was a basic objective for the setting up of the Fund, and also because they share many of the micro-economic disadvantages that are common in bilateral payments arrangements.

It has been reported by senior officials in a number of developing countries that the single most important factor constraining countertrade deals for government procurement and parastatals is the fear that this would jeopardise their IMF packages (see Kopinski, 1985). Clearly, this perspective is not fully accepted by many decision-makers – as indicated by the growing prevalence of countertrade. In most deals involving industrialised countries, the decision-makers are private companies, so that the existence of countertrade indicates private advantage, but does not necessarily reflect government perceptions of the social value of these deals. However, the Chairperson of the US International Trade Commission, summarising their study on countertrade, stated that it

> helped to maintain or increase existing levels of employment and plant capacity due to new business generated by such sales agreements . . . other benefits from countertrade include larger and more efficient production runs, lower unit costs, increased capital formation and the development of new technology (Ericson, 1985).

In Third World countries, there is near universal government involvement in countertrade deals. It therefore appears that many Third World governments believe the gains may extend beyond the private beneficiaries to the society at large.

From a Third World government perspective, the case *for* countertrade is that it permits a greater level of activity and a higher level of income in the short term than would be possible without it. It is also (implicitly) assumed that these apparent short-term benefits would not be offset by medium-term costs, although for countries in crisis a certain level of medium-term costs might be judged worth incurring for the sake of short-term gains.

In order to assess the costs and benefits of countertrade, it is necessary to consider therefore:

1. Short-term consequences for levels of income.
2. Medium-term consequences for levels of income.
3. Effects on organisation and use of resources.

The assessment is complicated: first, the variety of deals and motives makes generalisation difficult; what follows will tend to be selective, both in discussion and conclusions. Secondly, a single Third World country might gain (either in the short or medium term) although Third World countries taken collectively may not. Thirdly, as noted already, any assessment depends critically on the assumed alternatives. In the short run, this is less problematic since the alternatives are more or less known, but the issue is more complicated and controversial in assessing medium-term costs and benefits, since the framework of trade and payments will itself be affected by decisions made on current trading strategies.

Short-term Effects

If more or less perfect competition and free or open trade prevailed in the world, there would be a general presumption that countertrade deals would involve losses for one or other partner, except in very special and unlikely circumstances where both gain a terms of trade advantage over the rest of the world as a result of the deal because, as a result of the countertrade deal, there is a shortfall of the commodity and a rise in price in trade with the rest of the world (see Caves, 1974).

In the normal case, prices are likely to diverge from market prices in such a way that one of the partners will gain at the other's expense, in terms of trade, by changing terms of trade compared with the free market price. In general, developing countries are not likely to be the gainers in such transactions when trading with developed countries – being normally in a weaker bargaining position and less skilled negotiators – so that if the terms of trade do change they are likely to be adverse to the Third World partner. There is some empirical evidence confirming this: for example, Jones states that 'the usual practice is for the countertraded export from a developing country to be sold at a discount', quoting one study which found an average discount of 12 per cent. However, another study showed that India improved its terms of trade in a deal with the USSR (Outters-Jaeger, 1979), but paid a higher price for imports in a deal encompassing Australia, Czechoslovakia and East Germany (*Financial Times*, 4 October 1984). Moreover, political circumstances can lead to improved terms of trade for the developing country, as with Cuban sugar. The likelihood of an adverse movement in the terms of trade has led a number of countries to exclude some hard currency exports from countertrade (e.g., Colombia with respect to coffee, Peru with respect to minerals and fish).

Within the South, the bargaining power may not be as unbalanced, but inequality in bargaining strength and negotiating ability may lead to a relative loss in terms of trade for the weaker partner. In addition, there may be heavier transaction costs than with normal trade. This clearly occurs when one partner does not want the items acquired and has to dispose of them subsequently in third markets. These extra transaction costs may be borne by one or other partner, or shared. Again it seems probable that the weaker developing country would bear disproportionate costs because of weak bargaining power. In one respect, developing countries may gain in terms of trade – that is, it may not pay as much interest costs on trade finance – but it is probable that such gains will be offset by other costs in the deal.

It has been suggested that export earnings would be more *stable* with countertrade than market transactions, which could offset any loss in terms of trade. However, empirical investigation of trade in Egypt, Ghana, India, Sri Lanka and Tunisia in the 1970s showed that stability was significantly greater with barter-like trade than multilateral trade only in the case of Sri Lanka (see Outters-Jaeger, 1979). But this evidence mainly concerns Eastern bloc trade and not the more recent developments in countertrade.[14]

For most deals, then, the terms of trade are likely to be worse for the weaker (often Southern) partner than with market transactions. If markets were perfect, and a country could sell any quantity at the existing price, countertrade deals would usually not make much sense, the one major exception being where any market-generated foreign exchange would be immediately pre-empted for payment of arrears and debt servicing. But in all other circumstances, market transactions would be preferable. However, most countertrade deals occur precisely because market transactions at prevailing market prices are *not* an option, because of import restrictions, market-sharing arrangements, etc. In that context, deterioration in terms of trade may be accepted or even sought as a means of enlarging markets and/or of providing immediate import finance. The 'bottom line' as to the short-run effects of the deals on levels of income and activity is whether they increase or decrease the volume of imports to which a country has access. The generation of import capacity through countertrade depends on three elements – price, quantity sold and proportion of earnings available to finance imports. Ignoring the last factor, the issue is whether the terms of trade loss is compensated by more than proportionate increase in market size.

To analyse this, it is necessary to distinguish between primary products and manufactures.

Some primary product markets come near to fulfilling the perfect competition model: there are world markets to which any producer has access, and neither price nor quantity is likely to be significantly improved by countertrade deals as compared with market transactions. Countertrade deals may permit more retained earnings for exports, but otherwise will not have major advantages. But there are many other primary product markets where the world market is dominated by cartels – of producers or processing and marketing companies – or where industrialised country governments play a dominant role in determining price and quantity. In these 'dominated' markets, countries may gain a temporary or even permanent advantage by countertrade deals. Very many primary commodities fall into this category to a greater or lesser extent – sugar, bananas, bauxite, tin, oil, plutonium, wheat, are all examples where some governments' decisions (or those of a few companies) may significantly alter the market. In all 'dominated' markets, individual countries may have much to gain by countertrade. But collectively, Third World countries gain much less because to some extent increased market share by one country will be at the expense of reduced share of others, while if all Third World countries try to gain market share by accepting reduced prices, total foreign exchange earnings may fall. (The estimates of elasticities by Stern *et al.*, 1976, Cline *et al.*, 1978, and Godfrey, 1985, show that many primary commodities have inelastic demand.) Where Third World market share exceeds the price elasticity of demand, output restriction and price appreciation would offer higher levels of foreign exchange in the short or medium term. Developing countries could avoid the fall in their overall earnings by coordinating production and sales. But problems of individual countries may overrule these collective considerations. This is especially likely with depressed demand or excess supply for exports i.e., the conditions which encourage countertrade.

If Third World countries – or a relevant sub-set of countries – wish to collaborate to counter some of these effects, they should draw up a list of commodities where such a situation is believed to prevail and develop guidelines for policies towards quantities, prices, exchange rate and countertrade deals, which would be in the medium-term interest of countries individually as well as collectively.

While such considerations apply to many major primary commodities, there is still some room for manoeuvre in most commodities on aggregate market size, in 'dominated' markets. For example, the US strategic stockpiles may increase or reduce the size of world markets significantly; decisions on protection and production may influence the size of the Third World market for other items also produced by industrialised countries (sugar is the most obvious example); and in the planned economies the size of the market may be greatly changed by policy decisions. These exceptions – all occurring where pure market forces do not prevail – create room for countertrade deals which increase Third World earning capacity.

Although primary commodity markets appear to offer less potential for gains for countertrade than manufactures, market transactions (accompanied by much intervention, especially from industrialised countries) have been rather largely unfavourable to primary producers. Prebisch's thesis of tendencies to deteriorating terms of trade for primary producers has gained support from recent developments. A more interventionist approach by the Third World – of which coordinated countertrade could play a role – might therefore be worth pursuing.

For manufactures, where markets are evidently not perfect, worsening in terms of trade is an acknowledged means of increasing market share. Devaluation represents the most straightforward way of achieving this terms of trade deterioration. An over-valued exchange rate generally leads to both static and dynamic inefficiencies in the economy. In that context, the use of countertrade as a device for avoiding or postponing desirable devaluation may offer short-run benefits compared with maintaining the over-valued exchange rate and having no countertrade, but serious costs compared with correcting the exchange rate. However, there are circumstances when across-the-board devaluation of a magnitude sufficient to correct the disequilibrium is either undesirable or even impossible to achieve. For example, countries whose exports are composed to a large extent of certain commodities (e.g., oil, copper) may not want to change the exchange rate for these commodities, but may want to change the manufacturing exchange rate. Countries may wish to avoid the inflationary effects of major devaluations – which can be so large that the real exchange rate actually appreciates, following nominal devaluation.[15] In these circumstances, real devaluation of the magnitude desired may not be possible. In the early 1980s, countries in sub-Saharan Africa recorded substantial and accelerating appreciation in their real exchange rate, despite a large number of nominal devaluations (World Bank, 1986).

Countertrade offers a way of introducing selective devaluation, in circumstances where a real change in the exchange rate across the board is not desired, for reasons such as these. In some circumstances, it can be a short-run device to permit gradual elimination of major disequilibrium, through successive exchange rate changes. However, if countertrade is used as a substitute for needed correction across the board in the exchange rate, it could result in resource misallocations and prolonged disequilibria.

Countertrade may be equivalent to a highly *selective* devaluation (being selective with respect to commodity, country and transaction). In addition, countertrade deals may bypass non-tariff import restrictions, such as quotas, especially in developing countries, where devaluation would not, and may also help in the export of low-quality products. Consequently, countertrade can be a valuable instrument for promoting manufactured exports, especially where there are problems with across-the-board devaluation, or there are non-tariff import restrictions, or if other competitors offer the inducement of countertrade in their trade deals.

These conditions are especially likely to apply to trade between Third World countries. The majority of developing countries have been facing foreign exchange difficulties in the 1980s and most countries have imposed tight import restrictions. Many also have adopted austerity measures to restrain imports. In Latin America GDP *per capita* fell by 1.0 per cent p.a. from 1980 to 1985; in Africa it fell by 2.6 per cent p.a. In Latin America imports (in current prices) fell by nearly 40 per cent from 1980 to 1985, and by nearly 20 per cent in Sub-Saharan Africa.[16] Substantial levels of industrial excess capacity have emerged. Rates of capacity utilisation of 50 per cent or less are quite common.[17] In these circumstances, shortage of foreign exchange is holding back imports, investment and output. Counter-trade agreements may permit higher levels of output, employment and investment for both partners; in these circumstances the alternative is often not a market transaction *but no transaction at all.*

The analysis of the short-run effects has suggested that counter-trade deals are likely to lead to terms of trade deterioration compared with market transactions for Third World countries trading with the North. Where this generates more import finance because it leads to a more than proportionate market expansion (trade creation), it is likely to be worthwhile. This may occur for a few exporters in some primary product markets which are already heavily 'distorted' by cartels and government interventions. For primary products, however, the effects on terms of trade should be carefully assessed before going ahead with the deals.

Deals involving manufactured exports from Third World countries are more likely to be advantageous than those involving primary products, offering higher levels of capacity utilisation, incomes and employment in manufacturing. It should be noted, however, that the majority of Third World countertrade deals do not consist of manufactured exports (see Table 7.2).

Medium-term Effects

On the whole, it may be assumed that most deals are perceived to offer short-term gains to both partners, or they would not be accepted. But is this at the cost of medium-term losses?

The medium-term losses result from reduced competitive pressures to trade on lines of comparative advantage, and to improve export efficiency over time. In this respect, the considerations are very similar to those often discussed with reference to import protection, except that countertrade does involve exports, and therefore generates more external pressures to increase efficiency than pure import protection. Some dynamic losses would be faced in countertrade – with respect both to allocational and export efficiency – compared with free trade. But against this there could be dynamic advantages of greater certainty and of learning generated by experience. In addition, the higher short-run levels of imports should permit higher levels of investment, sustaining medium-term growth. In both sub-Saharan Africa and Latin America, there have been sharp declines in investment in the 1980s: if these were reversed, this could do more for growth over the medium term than the possible negative allocational or efficiency effects. To the extent that free trade is not the real alternative, but rather no trade and import protection, the dynamic effects of countertrade in promoting efficiency are likely to be positive.

From a broader perspective, much depends on what happens to the world finance and trading system as a whole. Some see the growth of countertrade deals as leading to the break-up of the multilateral trading system, with substantial losses for all countries. Others would see countertrade as a constructive and trade-creating response to a very restrictive trading environment. Multilateralising countertrade (for example, by payments arrangements among Third World countries) would then offer advantages of both trade and protection, with greater trade links between Third World countries, combined with protection against others (for some advantages of Third World trade, see Stewart, 1984, Chapter 4 in this volume). The recent emergence of agencies providing information to facilitate multilateral countertrade is a first step in multilateralising countertrade and shows the potential for such a move.

But again the relative merits of these alternatives depend on broader developments. If the industrialised countries resumed rapid growth and fairly open economies on the lines of the 1960s, the advantages of an open trading environment for Third World countries would become very strong. But if the circumstances of the 1980s were to become prolonged, options which limited Southern dependence on the North and increased Southern links in trade and finance would have major advantages. Countertrade offers one way of promoting South–South trading links; discriminating tariff or payments arrangements are other (possibly preferable) alternatives.

In practice, countries do not have to make once-and-for-all choices, but can and do switch as events develop (see Kopinski, 1985; Outters-Jaeger, 1979). Consequently, while the medium-term effects could be seriously disadvantageous in some circumstances, countries should be able to opt back into a freer market environment if they wish. Probably of more consequence than the medium-term effects on growth, however, are the effects on internal organisation and use of resources, to be considered below.

Organisation and Use of Resources

The recent history of countertrade deals suggests tendencies in relation to organisation and use of resources.

(a) *Organisation* Countertrade deals tend to be associated with large companies (public or private). In the North, almost all transactions concern very large companies. In the Third World, the government (or government-appointed agent) acts as an intermediary, so the suppliers or consumers may be small companies. But, as with all administrative decisions, there are major economies of scale in dealing with a few large units as against many small ones. For the same reason, high-value products may be preferred to low-value ones. Institutional arrangements can be devised to offset the bias towards bigness. Where countertrade is intended to cover a large proportion of a country's manufactured exports (as in Pakistan), a conscious effort will be needed to devise institutional mechanisms so that small producers can participate as fully as large ones.

The large role of administration in countertrade also makes such deals susceptible to corruption. This was an explicit criticism of Nigerian deals that led to a committee of enquiry in Nigeria which reported 'that former government officials and some private individuals have exploited the deals for their own financial gain'.[18] This is not a unique feature of countertrade but is a tendency associated with any administrative decisions involving large sums of money, especially where large companies stand to gain or lose a lot from the deal. What countertrade does is to extend the area of corruption-prone decisions, so that special care is needed in this area.

(b) *Use of resources* There is a definite pattern of resource use associated with countertrade – a pattern which may be a consequence of the bias in favour of large companies and high-value products noted above. In manufactures from the North, high-technology items, and especially military sales, dominate. The ITC survey of 500 US corporations found that military-related offsets accounted for over 80 per cent of all sales agreements involving countertrade. Non-military items included computers, aerospace products, communications and electronics. Examination of all countertrade deals where the specific products were described in the *Financial Times* over a two-year period (1983–5) showed *no* BN-type products in any deal involving Northern manufactures.

Countertrade between North and South therefore tends to involve use of imports for military and high-technology uses and

not for basic needs. To the extent that resources are fungible, this
may not alter the actual pattern of resource use, but at times of
great foreign exchange scarcity, and where countertrade accounts
for a considerable portion of a country's trade, the countertrade
pattern could seriously affect resource allocation in a direction
which may be undesirable.

This feature of countertrade is less marked with deals involving
Southern manufacturers, where consumer products and simple
producer products often feature. For instance, jute textiles have
been exported in countertrade by Bangladesh and simple textiles
by Mozambique, as well as in a number of other cases. A detailed
study of earlier deals (Jones, 1984) showed the main manufactured products exported by developing countries to be textiles,
plastics and some wood products.[19] Processed foods are also a
frequent component. In principle, and to some extent in practice,
South–South countertrade could involve appropriate products
(with BN goods, like hand-pumps, basic foods and small-scale
machinery). But the potential bias in favour of large companies
and high-value products would need to be offset.

CONCLUSIONS

Countertrade as an instrument of trade policy – covering a significant
proportion of trade – is undoubtedly here to stay. The analysis in this
essay has suggested that it may offer Third World countries significant gains. But it can also be associated with significant losses. Thus
neither blanket condemnation, such as that of the IMF, nor blanket
approval, is appropriate. Rather, countries should exercise careful
surveillance over countertrade deals to ensure maximum benefits. To
do so requires:

(a) Surveillance of the terms of trade implications of any deal, but
    especially deals involving primary products in those cases where
    hard currency markets are an option. The probable terms of
    trade loss – allowing for higher cost imports as well as effects on
    the price of exports – must be offset by identified gains which the
    country considers outweigh these losses.
(b) For primary products where the Third World supplies a signifi-
    cant proportion of total exports, policies should be coordinated
    among Third World countries. This requires calculations of price

elasticities and consequent effects on Third World earnings resulting from price reductions and increased supply. Appropriate policies need to be devised for these commodities, including but by no means confined to countertrade. Countertrade must be incorporated in Third World commodity arrangements because otherwise it may provide a serious obstacle to their success.

(c) Manufactured imports need to be scrutinised not only for cost but also for type of product, making sure that the deals do not divert resource use in an undesired way towards military and high-technology items.

(d) The greatest potential benefits from countertrade arise where the deals involve manufactured exports from Third World countries. For these cases implicit selective devaluation can be a useful way of promoting exports, and countertrade may also bypass non-tariff barriers. Here too, countries should keep a check on the terms of trade. But, in addition, a conscious effort is necessary to ensure that the big-company bias is avoided and that the exports generated broadly follow dynamic comparative advantage. Otherwise the exports could involve negative value-added for the country concerned.

(e) South–South countertrade in manufactures is most likely to be trade-creating, permitting higher levels of output, employment and investment than would otherwise be possible in current circumstances. In the medium term, regionalising or multilateralising these arrangements by payments arrangements among Third World countries may economise on scarce convertible currencies and permit specialisation and competition between these Third World countries. This is especially important for small countries where bilateral countertrade deals could lead to high costs and inefficiency.

Countertrade politicises trade, in part replacing the market by administrative mechanisms. This has potential costs, which include the biases arising from administrative decisions, the tendency towards corrupt practices, and the danger of becoming specialised in non-dynamic high-cost areas of production. But where the market offers poor terms and has failed – and promises to continue to fail – to allow countries to make full use of their resources, capacities and potential, the costs are often outweighed by the benefits. To maximise these gains, Third World governments need to be selective in countertrade, making use of it only where there are clear gains, and instituting mechanisms to help minimise distorting effects. The interest-groups involved – especially as countertrade grows in importance – may make this a difficult task.

NOTES

1. See Banks (1983); Department of Trade and Industry (1985); External Affairs Canada (1985); OECD (1981; 1985a); Outters-Jaeger (1979); Tschoegl (1985); Verzariu (1984).
2. Department of Trade and Industry (1985) p. 5.
3. External Affairs Canada (1985) p. 1; also see Jones (1984) p. 20.
4. See OECD (1985a); Banks (1983); Cooper (1984); Grieves (1984); Eisenbrand (1985).
5. Barovick (1986) showed that 5.6 per cent of US firms' exports and less than 1 per cent of their imports involved countertrade. OECD (1985a) estimates 10 per cent of trade between developing countries and 30 per cent of their trade with Eastern Europe was countertrade. OECD (1981) estimated that, at maximum, 20 per cent of Eastern European trade with OECD countries was countertrade. Agarwala (1986), estimated only 2 per cent of Indonesia's imports (mid-1982 to January 1984) were countertrade financed. Dodwell (1986) estimated that one-third of China's trade was countertrade.
6. *Business International* (23 December 1983).
7. Including China and excluding other Eastern Trading Area countries (i.e., Albania, Bulgaria, Czechoslovakia, German Democratic Republic, Hungary, Poland, Romania, USSR, Mongolia, N. Korea and Vietnam).
8. The deals reported in Table 7.2 exclude the ETA. The Soviet Union has exported oil in countertrade deals.
9. International Trade Commission Report (reported in the *Financial Times*, 11 February 1986).
10. Turkey has been categorised as a developed country in Table 7.2.
11. See, e.g., Waldmeir in the *Financial Times* (5 June 1985). This will hold if the country has agreed to set aside a certain percentage of its hard currency foreign exchange earnings for payments of arrears.
12. See Griffith-Jones (1986).
13. IMF, *1983 Annual Report on Exchange Arrangements and Exchange Restrictions*.
14. The effects on overall export earnings' stability depend not only on the countertrade deals but also on what happens to the rest of exports. In principle, larger variations in countertrade deals earnings could be offset by an inverse movement in market transactions, thus leading overall to greater (relative) stability of export earnings. Outters-Jaeger (1979) provides some evidence for this stability effect.
15. See Godfrey (1985) who shows cases where devaluation in Africa led to revaluation in real terms as a result of the consequent inflation.

16. Data from UN Statistical Office, IMF *World Economic Outlook* (April 1986).
17. For example, in Tanzania, rates of capacity utilisation in manufacturing were estimated to be between 20 per cent and 30 per cent in 1981 (see ILO/JASPA, 1982). See also Bautista *et al.* (1981) and Phan-Thuy *et al.* (1981).
18. *Financial Times* (11 February 1986).
19. See also Agarwala (1986).

8 Are Quantitative Restrictions Outdated? An Assessment of Article XVIIIb of the GATT*

INTRODUCTION

This essay examines the role of Article XVIIIb of the GATT, with special reference to proposals for review of the article put forward by the US and other delegations to the GATT.

The first main section describes Article XVIII as a whole and briefly reviews the justification put forward for this Article when it was introduced. The second section summarises the reasons delegations are proposing a review. These reasons fall into three categories: those relating to changes in the world economic system since 1957, which might undermine the original justification for the Article; those which question whether there is ever any case for quantitative restrictions on imports, implicitly challenging the original decision to introduce the Article; and those which suggest that there has in practice been some abuse of the Article, and that therefore some changes are needed. The third, fourth and fifth sections respectively consider each of these categories of argument, and a final section presents some conclusions.

ARTICLE XVIII

Nature of the Provisions

While Article XI imposes a general prohibition on quantitative restrictions on imports (QRs), Articles XII and XVIII lay down the conditions under which QRs may be justified under the GATT.

* This paper was originally written for UNCTAD. I am grateful to Solomon Soquar for research assistance and to Mr B. L. Das and Mr Purie for comments on a previous draft.

Article XII, which applies to all countries, permits QRs for balance of payments (BoP) reasons, when reserves are 'very low'. It has fairly stringent surveillance procedures, and is increasingly rarely invoked. In 1979, the Tokyo Declaration committed developed countries to avoid using trade measures for BoP reasons to the 'maximum extent possible'.

Article XVIII was introduced in 1957 to make special provisions for the use of QRs by developing countries. It allows LDCs to introduce QRs 'to ensure a level of reserves adequate for implementation of their programmes of economic development' (XVIIIb). The Article states that no contracting party shall be required to withdraw or modify restrictions on the grounds that a change in development policy would render the restrictions unnecessary.

Article XVIIIc permitted the introduction of restrictions 'to promote the establishment of a particular industry'; this was widened in 1979 beyond protection for a particular industry to allow for measures which were intended to develop, modify or extend production structures generally, in accordance with the priorities of economic development.

If QRs are justified under Article XVIIIb (or XII for developed countries), countries adversely affected are not permitted to impose counter-measures, as they would be under GATT provisions, in cases that fall outside these Articles.

Surveillance

Multilateral surveillance was introduced to ensure that QRs imposed under these Articles do in fact qualify under their provisions.

For Article XVIIIb surveillance is exercised by the contracting parties through consultations in the Committee on Balance of Payments Restrictions (the BoP Committee). The IMF provides assistance at the Committee. Developing countries are expected to consult in the Committee every two years; these consultations may take the form of 'full consultations' or simplified procedures, which were introduced in 1972. In general, no retaliation is permitted for XVIIIb QRs.

For Article XVIIIc, multilateral consultations take place only if contracting parties decide, and then a Working Party is established specifically for the purpose. Those adversely affected may unilaterally retaliate, unless they have agreed to the restrictions.

In practice, probably because of the difference in surveillance procedures and possibilities of retaliation, section c of Article XVIII has rarely been invoked.

Origin of the Articles

The idea of permitting QRs in the post-war economic system was strongly defended by Keynes, who saw this as essential, if convertibility of currencies were to be maintained:

> I feel the gravest doubts whether we can accept convertibility if we are entirely cut off from using at our own discretion non-discriminatory quantitative regulation . . . To try and create an international system which excludes quantitative regulation is out of date and, I should have thought, impracticable (Keynes in Moggeridge, 1980, pp. 325–6).

A fundamental purpose of the Bretton Woods institutions was to restore currency convertibility, while avoiding the competitive exchange rate devaluation that had occurred in the 1930s. Given these dual aims, it appeared that QRs might be necessary in BoP crises if recourse to restrictions on convertibility or to frequent devaluations were to be avoided. Thus the general justification for Article XII arose in the post-war context where currency convertibility was limited and fragile, in a system of near-fixed exchange rates. This justification applied mainly to the developed countries.

However, a special need for QRs for developing countries came to be recognised, which had little to do with this general case. The recognition of the special needs of developing countries led to the 1957 introduction of Article XVIIIb.

As stated in the introductory section of Article XVIII, LDCs might need to take 'protective or other measures affecting imports' in order to implement 'programmes and policies of economic development designed to raise the general standard of living of their people'. The BoP problems of LDCs were recognised to be 'structural and persistent' (in contrast to those of developed countries which were thought to be cyclical and temporary), arising from 'efforts to expand their internal markets as well as from the instability in their terms of trade'. In other words, the justification for Article XVIII, whose provisions apply only to LDCs, were twofold: first, the needs arising from development efforts and, secondly, external instability as exhibited by instability in the terms of trade.

PROPOSALS FOR REVIEW OF ARTICLE XVIII

Three types of reason have been put forward as justifying review:

(a) changes in the international monetary system;
(b) changing philosophy about the role of QRs;
(c) 'abuse' of the procedures.

Changes in the International Monetary System

Commentators and delegations to the GATT have pointed to changes in the international monetary system since the 1950s which reduce the need and justification for using QRs for BoP purposes. These changes include the creation of SDRs, the switch to floating exchange rates, and the existence of IMF short- and medium-term programmes to support countries' BoP adjustment.

Changing Philosophy

In the thirty years since the introduction of Article XVIII, there has been a marked shift in the dominant beliefs concerning economic development, with greatly increased emphasis on the need for efficient allocation of resources, on the role of markets and the price system, and reduced confidence in planning and controls.

Whereas in 1943, Keynes could state that: 'You must have some way of switching off imports which you cannot afford. Of the various alternatives quantitative regulation is at the same time the most effective and much the most in tune with the modern world', (Moggeridge, 1980, pp. 325–6, quoted in Roessler 1987), today many economists in developed countries believe that trade measures are an inefficient (and often inappropriate) means of securing BoP equilibrium.

This new market philosophy is a major factor behind the call for review of Article XVIII.

'Abuse' of the Procedures

The following 'abuses' have been noted:

1. The use of Article XVIIIb for protection, rather than for BoP reasons, where Article XVIIIc or XVIIId would be more appropriate.

2. GATT provisions require that countries progressively relax restrictions as conditions improve, but many countries appear to
maintain them on a near-permanent basis.
3. Deficient surveillance procedures: many countries fail to notify
their restrictions, and are not subject to surveillance; there is an
absence of follow-up procedures for the findings of the BoP
Committee; there are increased time-lags between consultations;
'simplified' consultations have become a formality and do not
provide the information necessary to evaluate the BoP situation
and the evolution of the trade regimes of consulting countries.
There has been little guidance from the BoP Committee on
alternative measures to restore equilibrium or on the resource cost
effects of protection. External circumstances are not taken into
account systematically in the deliberations of the Committee (see
e.g. Anjaria, 1987; Eglin, 1987).

The next sections of this essay will consider the validity of each of
these sets of reasons for a review of Article XVIII.

HAVE CHANGES IN THE WORLD ECONOMY REMOVED THE JUSTIFICATION FOR ARTICLE XVIIIb?

The main change cited as justifying a review of the role of QRs is the
switch from fixed to floating exchange rates that occurred in the early
1970s. In addition, the greatly increased role of the IMF in developing countries, with the provision of short-term finance, is argued to
have reduced the need for short-term emergency measures such as
QRs.

The irony is that while both these changes have occurred, which in
principle might have been expected to have reduced the need for
emergency BoP measures, the underlying BoP position of most
LDCs has undoubtedly *worsened* during the 1980s; the existence of
'structural and persistent' BoP problems has, if anything, become
more evident; and external causes for these deficits (including, but
not solely, terms of trade instability) have become more significant.
Thus it appears, as will be explained in more detail below, that the
initial justification of Article XVIIIb, which was phrased in terms of
structural and persistent BoP problems arising from the combination
of development needs and external instability, has been *reinforced
and not weakened* by changes in the world economy.

Fixed to Floating Rates

In the first decades of the Bretton Woods institutions the exchange rate was rarely used as an equilibrating instrument. As noted above, a major justification of Article XII was to give countries some short-term means of improving their BoP in this context. The move from fixed to floating exchange rates would then seem to remove a good deal of this justification for the use of QRs.

However, as far as the original justification of the GATT articles permitting QRs is concerned, this argument applies to Article XII and not XVIIIb, unless it can be established that the move to floating exchange rates has succeeded in eliminating the structural and persistent nature of LDC problems. (It should be noted in passing that the move to floating rates has not been effective in reducing imbalances among *developed* countries: witness the huge and persistent US deficit, and the similarly persistent surpluses of Japan and W. Germany. But this is of relevance to Article XII, not Article XVIIIb.)

Developing countries were free to change their exchange rates even in the pre-1970 era, and frequently did so (see, e.g., Cooper, 1971). In this respect they have been very differently affected, as compared with the developed countries, by the move to flexible exchange rates. While for developed countries, the change has increased the instruments available to them for controlling the BoP, for developing countries the change has increased external sources of instability and the difficulties of managing their economies. Since the advent of flexible exchange rates, changes in the exchange rates among developed countries has been a major source of fluctuation and uncertainty for LDCs (see Helleiner, 1981b).

On balance, the move to flexible rates has made it more difficult for LDCs to manage their own exchange rates and has increased their need for reserves, because of the greatly increased uncertainty. Since LDCs generally have weak or non-existent forward markets, they are unable to guarantee their traders against exchange rate risk. Most LDCs have pegged their currencies to a single major currency or a basket of currencies; exchange rate changes among developed countries have consequently caused unplanned changes (appreciation or depreciation) in the exchange rates of LDCs. Reserve needs have risen because most LDCs lack access to short-term money markets, which permit developed countries to finance temporary imbalances by borrowing.

The costs to LDCs of the move to flexible exchange rates would have been easily offset had the change led to reduced imbalances among developed countries, a steady and more rapid expansion in their economies, reduced fluctuations in commodity prices, and relaxations of trade restrictions faced by LDCs. In fact, none of these developments occurred, so that the structural and persistent nature of their BoP problems was not reduced, and may have been enhanced, by the change to floating rates.

Other Changes in the World Economy

The international environment facing LDCs has deteriorated sharply in the last decade, and is now unquestionably worse than it was in the late 1950s when Article XVIIIb was introduced. The deterioration has consisted in a slowdown in the growth of the world economy; deteriorating terms of trade; increasing developed country protectionism; arising debt service burden; stagnant aid flows and a collapse of private capital flows. These changes will each be documented briefly.

1. *World economic growth*   Growth of world output was 4.1 per cent p.a. in 1970–9, and slowed to 2.8 per cent p.a. in 1980–9.[1]
2. *Terms of trade*   Terms of trade of non-fuel exporters among developing countries, fell both in the 1970s (by 1.1 per cent p.a.) and in the 1980s (1.2 per cent p.a.). The terms of trade of all developing countries (including fuel exporters) improved in the 1970s (by 4.6 per cent p.a.) and deteriorated in the 1980s (by 0.5 per cent p.a.).
3. *Protectionist measures*   Measures taken by developed countries showed a definite increase from the early 1970s, with some further acceleration in the 1980s. These took the form of non-tariff barriers, which are often difficult to identify and quantify. Sheila Page sums up a careful review of the evidence as follows:

> Until the 1960s, most types of barrier were diminishing . . . By the early 1980s, protection was unambiguously growing with only minor offsets towards the middle of the decade. This was most pronounced in industrialised countries' trade with developing countries; there was some deliberate freeing of developing countries' trade and they were less able to form commodity cartels. (Page, 1987, p. 49)

4. *The debt service burden* The burden for indebted LDCs increased sharply in the 1980s as a result of the high level of borrowing in the 1970s, and the marked rise in interest rates that occurred in the early 1980s. Despite some fluctuations, real interest rates remain high, well above historically normal levels. *Outstanding debt* of developing countries was 24.4 per cent of GDP in 1980 and had risen to 35.6 per cent in 1988. *Debt service payments* were 21.6 per cent of exports in 1980, rising to 26.8 per cent in 1988. The ratio of interest and amortisation to exports was 40.3 per cent for the Western Hemisphere in 1988 and 26.1 per cent for Africa, the two worst affected areas.

5. *Net capital flows* The crisis ushered in by the Mexican near-default in August 1982 resulted in an almost complete cessation of voluntary private capital flows. Net external borrowing from the private sector was estimated to be only $7.2 billion in 1988 compared with $73.4 billion in 1980. Other types of capital flow (private direct investment and official transfers and loans) held up much better, but did not compensate for this sharp fall. Overall net external borrowing fell from $101 billion in 1980 to $36 billion in 1988.

To sum up, the external environment facing developing countries in the 1980s was without question much more *hostile* than in any of the previous three decades. There has been a double squeeze – on the trade account and on the capital account. On the trade account countries experienced the combined effects of deteriorating terms of trade, slower growth in markets and increased restrictions, while on the capital account they faced a combination of increased debt servicing obligations and much reduced capital inflows. Moreover, both accounts showed marked fluctuations over the period (see Figure 8.1).

The reference in Article XVIIIb to 'instability in their terms of trade' has *not* been invalidated by recent events – indeed there is good reason to extend the phrase to include adverse trends as well as fluctuations, not only in terms of trade strictly defined, but also in market access in the capital account. As noted above, exchange rate fluctuations have also added to sources of external instability. Empirical work has shown the increased instability faced by developing countries, and that external developments account for much of this increased instability (see Brodsky, Helleiner and Sampson, 1981). There would be a strong case for replacing the phrase 'instability in

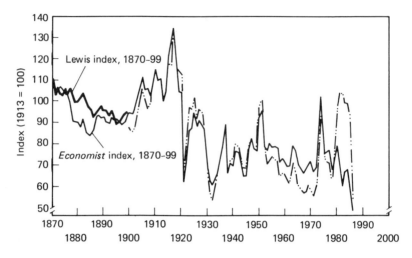

Source: Grilli and Chang Yeng (1988)
Figure 8.1   Primary product prices, 1870–1986

their terms of trade' in Article XVIIIb by 'instability and adverse trends in their external environment'.

The Role of the IMF

A further change in the international environment has been the increased role of the IMF. In principle, the availability of short-term emergency finance from the IMF should reduce the need for other quick-acting emergency measures such as QRs. However, there are two reasons why this is not a convincing reason to remove the possibility of using QRs: first, the inadequacy of financial support; secondly, the needs of those countries which do not want to adopt IMF programmes.

The inadequacy of IMF finance can be illustrated both at an aggregate and a country level (see Table 8.1).

As can be seen from Table 8.1, IMF net credit financed only a fraction of the current account deficits in the 1980s. Taking the years 1980–7 together, IMF net credits financed 9.3 per cent of the cumulative deficit of all developing countries on current account. After the heavy lending in the early 1980s, repayments began to exceed new finance, so that the IMF made a negative contribution to deficit finance from 1986.

Table 8.1 IMF finance for LDCs, 1980–8

Year	LDC balance current account ($ billion)	IMF net flows ($ billion)
1980	+30.6	+2.8
1981	−49.1	+6.5
1982	−77.1	+6.9
1983	−57.8	+11.0
1984	−27.6	+4.7
1985	−21.9	−
1986	−41.4	−2.7
1987	+2.5	−5.9
1988	−13.2	−5.0
1989	−13.8	−2.4

Source: IMF *World Economic Outlook* (April 1989; May 1990).

Moreover, the aggregate figures overstate the true proportionate contribution in two respects: first, the aggregate deficit on current account, shown above, includes surplus as well as deficit countries. Taking deficit countries alone (which are the countries needing short-term finance) would significantly increase the size of the deficit. For example, the cumulative deficits of capital importing countries over 1980–7 was £382 billion compared with $261 billion for developing countries as a whole, and the IMF contribution amounted to only 6.4 per cent of this deficit. Secondly, the size of the current account deficit over this period was constrained by inadequate finance, so that the actual deficits show the size of the deficits after various emergency action had been taken, including cuts in incomes and trade interventions. Without these emergency measures the deficits would have been very much greater and the proportionate contribution of the Fund even smaller. It is an indication of the inadequacy of short-term finance, including IMF finance, that such emergency measures were, and remain, necessary.

The second way in which the adequacy of Fund finance can be assessed is with reference to the experience of particular countries. Detailed case studies of Tanzania and Zambia, for example, have shown that the short-term finance available was inadequate to permit these countries to restore their productive structures and to resume growth, and even to permit expansion of production of exports (see ILO, 1982; Stewart, 1986; Gulhati, 1988; Lancaster and Williamson, 1986).

It is thus apparent that the availability of IMF finance for short-term balance of payments support has not been enough to obviate the need for countries to take emergency measures to protect their BoP.

The second reason why the existence of IMF programmes does not eliminate the need for alternative measures is that quite a number of countries do not wish to (or are politically unable to) come to agreements with the Fund. This arises for a variety of reasons, all having to do with the rather rigid and narrow set of policies that are associated with Fund finance (see Spraos, 1986; Stewart, 1987; Killick, 1982). Countries with different philosophical beliefs find it difficult to accept the programmes (see, for example, Tanzania under Nyerere, and Nigeria and Peru in recent years). Other countries do introduce Fund programmes, but then find they have to withdraw them because of the political opposition engendered, which threatens to bring down the government (see, for example, Zambia's recent history).

Both sets of countries are debarred from IMF finance, and usually also many other sources, including World Bank structural adjustment loans, finance from some bilateral donors and commercial banks, as well as rescheduling of both public and private debts. For these groups of countries, alternative emergency measures to protect their BoP and reserves remain essential.

The Nature of Developing Countries' BoP Problems in the 1980s

As indicated above, the 1980s witnessed unparalleled BoP problems for LDCs, requiring them to have increased recourse the IMF, to undertake drastic stabilisation programmes, involving cuts in GDP *per capita*, investment and government expenditure, and also to reschedule both their public and private debt at frequent intervals.

Table 8.2 indicates that there was some reduction in the aggregate size of the current account deficit over the 1980s, especially as compared with the worst years of 1982 and 1983, in part a response to lack of finance. But the experience of these years shows that the deficits experienced, especially among the capital importing group of countries and the primary producers were, without question, *persistent*.

BoP problems go beyond actual deficits, since they include undesirable measures which have been forced on countries because of the BoP and financial constraint. In the 1980s this took the form of cuts in GDP per head, especially focussed on investment (see Figure 8.2), which was necessary to bring about the required reduction in im-

Table 8.2 BoP deficit on current account, selected years, $ billion

		1980	1982	1984	1986	1988	1989
	All LDCs	+30.6	−77.1	−27.5	−41.3	−7.3	−16.3
	of which:						
I	Africa	−2.1	−21.6	−8.0	−10.4	−9.4	−8.3
	Asia	−14.4	−16.6	−4.2	+3.8	12.3	4.3
	Europe	−15.6	−2.9	−0.3	−1.3	7.0	5.1
	Middle East	+92.5	+4.8	−13.8	−17.1	−8.3	0.6
	W. Hemisphere	−29.8	−40.8	−1.3	−16.2	−10.7	−9.0
II	Primary product exporters	−37.0	−19.0	−13.5	−11.6	−14.5	−13.6
	Exporters of manufactures	−22.4	−22.3	+2.3	+4.5	28.6	18.3

Source: IMF *World Economic Outlook* (October 1989).

ports. From 1980 to 1988, GDP *per capita* fell by 9 per cent in Africa, and by 7 per cent in the Western Hemisphere. The investment ratio fell from 25.6 per cent of GDP in 1980 to 17.6 per cent in 1989 in Africa, and from 23.4 per cent to 17.5 per cent in Latin America. The volume of imports fell by over 20 per cent in Africa from 1980 to 1989, and by 25 per cent in Latin America.

The 1980s have thus undoubtedly shown the BoP problems of LDCs to be persistent. Have they also been shown to be *structural*?

'Structural' problems are those which arise from the basic structure of the economy, and cannot easily or quickly be overcome by domestic policy changes. The very fact of the persistence of LDC BoP problems is one indication of their structural character, especially in view of the quite radical policy changes taken by LDCs over the 1980s. There has, for example, been a very large change in real exchange rates (see Figure 8.3), and other significant moves towards liberalisation, both internally and externally. Yet the BoP problems have persisted.

This persistence stems largely from the adverse developments in LDCs' external environment which were described earlier. But the reason these developments have had such a major effect stems largely from the structural characteristics of LDCs. The most significant of these characteristics is the heavy dependence on primary products for export earnings for many countries. In 1988, primary products accounted for 73 per cent of the exports of low-income LDCs excluding

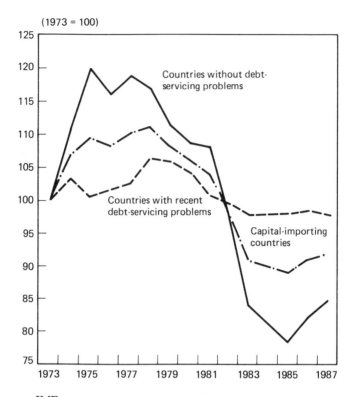

Source: IMF
Figure 8.2 Capital-importing developing countries: investment rates,
1973–87

China and India. For lower-middle-income countries the proportion
was 54 per cent, and it was 31 per cent for upper-middle-income
countries.[2] While these proportions are smaller than in 1965, when it
was 90 per cent for low-income countries (excluding China and
India), 85 per cent for lower-middle-income countries, and 78 per
cent for upper-middle-income countries, the very high proportion
still leaves many LDCs very vulnerable to fluctuations in primary
product prices; it makes it very difficult for them to diversify into
alternative exports (or even the production of import substitutes) on
any scale in a short time period and without major investments.

Moreover, a substantial proportion of the diversification that has
taken place over the last twenty years was into processing of raw
materials (leaving countries almost as vulnerable as before to price

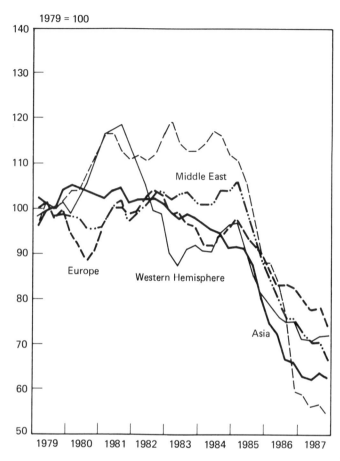

Source: IMF
Figure 8.3   Developing countries: real effective exchange rates, by region, 1979–87

fluctuations and changes in market access) and into textiles, which are subject to non-tariff barriers in developed country markets.

The handicap imposed on adjustment by heavy reliance on primary products is illustrated by the current account figures shown in Table 8.2. Countries classified as exporters of manufactures succeeded in transforming a current account deficit of $22.4 billion in 1980 into a surplus of $28.6 billion in 1988, whereas primary product exporters have had persistent deficits. Moreover, the exporters of manufactures (largely in Asia) managed to achieve this with quite high growth rates, while the primary producers had very low or negative growth in *per capita* income.

The accumulation of debt has constituted another structural constraint on debt-burdened countries. The debt was accumulated in the 1970s partly as a deliberate (and, as it turned out, misguided) policy stance, and partly because of the difficulties of adjusting to the high oil prices by economies with limited flexibility. The accumulation of debt was thus in part itself a product of structural characteristics of the borrowing countries. But in turn it itself now represents an important structural feature of LDC BoP problems. Many countries have to run substantial trade surpluses in order to meet their debt service obligations; moreover, because of limited finance they have to achieve this turnround very fast. Given the limited flexibility in their economies, the only way they can achieve this is through deflation and import cuts. For countries which have largely eliminated imports of consumer goods through import substitution, this means cuts in investment. As noted, these cuts in investment occurred, but then a vicious circle ensued: the cuts in investment precluded the adjustment into manufactured exports for which investment is often a precondition, so that the exigencies of the debt situation made long-term adjustment with growth a near impossibility. Similarly, cuts in government expenditure on health and education are reducing future human capital, and therefore growth potential, as well as leading to great human suffering (see Cornia *et al.* 1987).

Finally, a third 'structural' characteristic which limits short-term adjustment is represented by the political economy of policy change. Forces of political economy often limit the willingness (and ability) of governments to introduce, and then stick to, the type of policy change which would be necessary for rapid adjustment. Ranis and Fei (1988) have argued that this is particularly likely in countries which are heavily dependent on primary products, and subject to sharp terms of trade fluctuations. In practice, there are very few examples of steady and sustained moves towards liberalisation of the type considered by the World Bank and the IMF as necessary for adjustment although substantial policy changes have occurred both in Africa and Latin America (see Wolf, 1986; Helleiner, 1989; and Williamson, 1990). Some governments refuse to initiate an IMF programme, while others do so for only a temporary period and then withdraw them (e.g., in recent years in Zambia, Brazil and Nigeria). Cooper (1971) noted the high potential political costs of devaluation in research covering the 1960s, where devaluation was found to be frequently followed by the downfall of the Finance Minister responsible, or even the government itself. Even greater short-term political costs are associated with the adjustment packages now on offer associated with cuts in government expenditure on social services, the elimination of food subsidies, privatisation, reduced employment, as well as devaluation.

These political costs cannot be ignored: in the first place, they often prevent the policies being put into effect; in the second, they can lead to riots, and even deaths; third, they can cause the withdrawal of the programmes; fourth, they can cause the fall of the government and even a slide into political chaos.

BoP problems of LDCs thus remain not only persistent but also structural in character for the majority of Third World countries. The countries most affected by structural problems are those countries still heavily dependent on primary product exports, and those with a very large accumulation of debt. Within these categories, the 'soft' states (to use Myrdal's term) are most likely to be affected by political economy constraints of a structural nature.

IS THERE A CASE FOR QRs?

An important source of criticism of Article XVIIIb arises from the view that QRs are *intrinsically undesirable under any* (or almost any) *circumstances*. This argument has little to do with changes in the world economy since the Article was first introduced, but rather questions the underlying justification for having the Article at all. This view has been summed up by Maurice Scott (writing about Britain, but clearly intending much wider application):

> there is a mutual benefit from trade . . . Once this has been properly understood, it becomes a puzzle to see why import restrictions on trade should be thought to provide a remedy for Britain's, *or any other country's*, economic ills. . . . Let us hope then that Britain does not look for salvation through import restrictions. If the country does, it will be like a man who has failed to hold down a succession of jobs and finally in desperation, takes to the bottle (Scott, Corden and Little, 1980, pp. 75; 79; my emphasis).

This view contrasts strongly with that of Keynes:

You must have some way of cutting off imports which you cannot afford. Of the various alternatives quantitative regulation is at the same time *much the most effective and the most in tune with the modern world* (Moggeridge, 1980, pp. 325–6; my emphasis).

The argument against QRs can be summarised in a number of steps:

1. First, 'that trade measures are in general an inefficient means to restore BoP equilibrium' (GATT contracting parties, 1979) because BoP problems reflect problems of *macro-balance*, and these should be tackled directly.
2. Secondly, where trade measures are regarded as appropriate, QRs are inferior to devaluation.
3. Thirdly, if devaluations are ruled out, tariffs are preferable to QRs.

I shall consider each of these arguments in turn.

Macro-balance

It is argued that trade deficits on the BoP are due to macro-imbalances, caused by excessive domestic expenditure, which leads to high levels of imports and reduced exports as potential exports are switched to domestic markets to meet domestic demand. If excess expenditure is the basic cause of the trade deficit then the appropriate policy would be a cut in that expenditure, brought about by cutting government expenditure or raising taxes, and not by any trade measures.

Both the absorption and the monetary approach to the BoP suggest that BoP problems are the outcome of macro-imbalances. In the absorption approach which I shall primarily focus on here, a BoP deficit is a reflection of excess domestic expenditure over domestic savings, which has to be offset by foreign savings, where foreign savings are equivalent to the excess of imports over exports. BoP problems arise in these circumstances when the excess of imports over exports is greater than the long-term capital inflow.[3] The excess of domestic expenditure over domestic savings, it is believed, generally has its origin in the government account (excess of government expenditure over revenue), although it can also originate from an excess of private domestic investment over private domestic savings, i.e.

$$M - E = (G - T) + (I - S) \tag{8.1}$$

where M is the value of imports, X the value of exports, G government expenditure, T tax revenue, I private investment and S domestic savings.

According to this approach, then, the way to cure the BoP problem is to tackle the basic expenditure–savings imbalance at the macro-level. For most LDCs this is interpreted as requiring a reduction in the budget deficit, through reducing expenditure or increasing taxation.

In a context of macro-imbalance, it is argued, QRs would be likely to be ineffective because any excess expenditure that was diverted from imports by QRs would go towards other uncontrolled imports, or exportables, leaving the basic imbalance unchanged. This view was summarised in GATT's 1982–3 report on *International Trade*:

A change in trade barriers will alter the pattern of consumer spending, but there is not direct impact on the level of consumption: similarly, commercial policy can affect the pattern of investment, but it has no necessary impact on its level since trade restrictions can favour some domestic industries only at the expense of others . . . As far as the current account balance is concerned, however, changes in trade restrictions have no durable impact, even in the absence of retaliation (GATT, 1983, p. 16).

However, this conclusion depends on assumptions which are often incorrect in LDCs. Further analysis leads to two conclusions which contradict the simple macro-balance conclusion just presented. First, it can be shown that there are circumstances where QRs (or other trade policies) can by themselves *improve the BoP, or permit higher domestic incomes for any given BoP imbalance*. Secondly, it is almost always necessary to accompany any correction of macro-imbalances by *trade measures* to avoid unnecessary falls in incomes.

Implicit in the adoption of a macro-balance approach to the BoP is that there is full use of resources in the country concerned, so that any additional expenditure is invariably reflected in a worsened trade balance and not in increased use of domestic resources. In the absence of full capacity utilisation, QRs (or other trade measures) can *increase* capacity utilisation and thereby increase domestic supply without proportionately reducing exports or increasing other imports. An example of this occurred in Nigeria when import controls on food imports led to increased domestic supply of food.

In terms of the basic equation, (8.1), if domestic production rises while expenditure levels remain the same, domestic savings rise. In effect the unused capacity represents latent savings. It is unlikely that this would often occur in LDCs in a pure form because while there are high levels of unused capacity, the unused capacity is often not of a type that can substitute for imports, and additional domestic production frequently has a high import content. Nonetheless QRs usually result in some additional savings of this type, given the considerable degree of excess capacity prevalent in most countries.

In addition, the trade measures themselves affect the macro-balance of the economy, through a direct and an indirect effect. The direct effect works when import controls directly prevent expenditures, and thus contribute to savings. For example, import controls on items essential for some expenditures may lead to a reduction in investment or government expenditure. The indirect effect works via prices. Tariffs, QRs or devaluation can each cause prices of the items affected to rise, thus reducing purchasing power, at least in the short term (in the longer term there may be inflation, which counteracts this effect). Consequently, in the short term, trade measures themselves contribute to an improvement in the macro-balance, although this may not be sufficient to correct the imbalance.

QRs, or other trade measures, can thus sometimes be sufficient to correct a BoP problem, especially in the short term and where there is a high degree of excess capacity. A much stronger case, however, can be made for the view that while some correction of the macro-balance is often necessary, through reducing the budget deficit, operating *only* on the macro-balance usually leads to an unnecessary sacrifice of incomes and investment.

If deflationary mechanisms (e.g., cuts in government expenditure) are the sole means of improving the BoP, they will work, in the sense that imports will fall and the current account will improve. But they will do so at an unnecessarily high cost, because not only will imports fall but so also will expenditure on domestically produced goods and services, so that BoP equilibrium is attained at the cost of reduced output, incomes and investment – which has been precisely the experience of many countries in the 1980s, as described earlier. Suppose imports form one-quarter of all expenditure at the margin, then a fall of expenditure of $100 will be necessary to achieve an improvement in the trade balance of $25, and unused domestic capacity will increase by $75.

The case is illustrated in Figure 8.4. It is assumed that in the initial

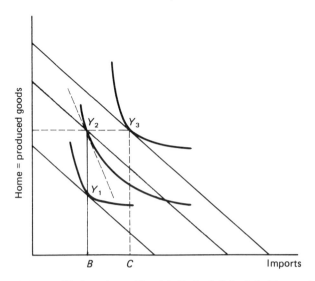

Note: Initial equilibrium is at Y_3 with BoP deficit BC. To cut back on imports by BC with no trade measures leads to a drop in income to Y_1, and a fall in home-produced goods of Y_2Y_1. Effective import controls would change equilibrium to Y_2, reducing imports by BC and maintaining production of home-produced goods. In practice, such completely successful QRs (or other trade measures) are not feasible normally, and some intermediate position would be achieved.

Figure 8.4 Alternative measures for BoP improvement

position, Y_3, there is full use of domestic capacity. Consequently, trade measures alone would not be sufficient to improve the balance of trade. Assume an improvement BC is necessary in the balance of trade. To attain this by deflation alone, income has to fall by Y_3Y_1, leading to unused domestic capacity of Y_2Y_1, whereas if trade measures are taken in conjunction with deflationary measures, income needs to fall only to Y_2, leaving domestic production at the same level as in the initial position. Some economists believe that relative prices will automatically adjust to restore 'full employment', so that there is no need to take special measures to attain the Y_2 position because market forces will react. But the evidence of rising unemployment and falling capacity utilisation suggests that this does not happen in the short to medium term, because of inflexibility of prices and low substitutability between different uses of resources.

Consequently, to avoid heavy costs of reliance on the macro-balance alone, it is essential to accompany any deflationary measures by *switching* policies, to encourage resources to move into exports and import substitutes and to reduce expenditure on imports. Thus while it is true that trade measures *alone* are rarely sufficient to improve the BoP, it is also true that macro-balance measures alone impose heavy costs unless accompanied by effective trade measures.

While this argument has been presented in terms of the absorption approach, similar arguments and conclusions apply to the monetary approach to the BoP: LDC price systems lack the short-term flexibility, and resources the required mobility, for policies with respect to monetary aggregates alone to achieve costless adjustment in the short to medium term.

A study of Colombia provides an example of some of the issues just discussed (Ocampo, 1988). In the 1970s and 1980s, the government switched policies as between heavy reliance on QRs as a mechanism of BoP adjustment and import liberalisation with restrictive demand policies (and sometimes depreciating exchange rates). Economic growth was generally higher during the import control regimes than with liberalisation. There was sharp contraction in industrial production during the liberalisation period of the early 1980s, and recovery with the reimposition of controls in 1983. Ocampo developed a model of the economy to show what would have happened with alternative policy instruments. He concluded that without the acceleration of import liberalisation 'economic growth between 1980 and 1983 would have been. 2.4 per cent a year instead of 1.5 per cent'. With the reversal of liberalisation and the imposition of drastic import controls between 1983 and 1986, growth accelerated. The contribution of controls to the economic recovery in 1983–6 was estimated to be close to 5 per cent of GDP.

In summary, there is often a need for macro-measures (reduced expenditure, increased taxation), but such policies usually need to be accompanied by trade measures.

QRs and Devaluation

Accepting the need for some trade measures as well as macro-measures it is argued that 'Exchange rate adjustments supported by appropriate macro-economic policies are generally considered as the "first-best" policy package to deal with lasting balance of payment deterioration' (Anjaria, 1987, p. 682).

Devaluation is argued to be preferable to QRs as a switching device on the following grounds:

1. it affects the competitiveness of both exports and import substitutes;
2. it is neutral between exports and import substitutes and within and between different categories of goods, and is therefore likely to be more efficient from an allocational point of view;
3. the automatic and across-the-board nature of devaluation make it less subject to pressure groups and corrupt practices than QRs;
4. in contrast, QRs are argued to affect only imports, not exports, frequently discriminate between categories of goods and can encourage corrupt practices.

The advantages of QRs compared with devaluation are argued to be:

1. that devaluation is often ineffective as a means of improving the BoP;
2. that devaluation can involve a terms of trade loss;
3. that devaluation leads to inflation;
4. that QRs are selective, and therefore help ensure that priorities are met;
5. that QRs act more quickly and with greater certainty than devaluation.

There is no question that in some circumstances the first set of arguments is decisive and that devaluation is the appropriate policy. Evidence has accumulated that countries adopting excessive and prolonged import substitution policies have grown less rapidly than those with more balanced policies towards exports and imports (see, e.g., Krueger, 1984; Balassa, 1970). The heavily protectionist countries have also, it appears, been on balance, less successful 'adjusters' (see World Bank, 1987b). But the evidence for these propositions has been exaggerated in presentation, while the direction of causality is not altogether clear (see Pack, 1988; Singer and Gray, 1988). To some extent, at least, the rapid growth in output and productivity brought about by high rates of capital accumulation and high levels of investment in human capital was responsible for the success in export growth, rather than the other way round. Moreover, those countries which eventually became very successful exporters of manufactures started with an import substitution stage. Even when they became manufactured exporters they frequently retained significant levels of protection, which included QRs as well as tariffs.

Nonetheless, experience as well as economic theory suggests that it does not make sense for countries with a strong manufacturing base to have a significant bias against manufactured exports, of a type that arises when all trade measures are focussed on imports and the exchange rate is not used as a switching instrument. For primary producing countries, a highly over-valued exchange rate can lead to a sizeable parallel market with a much lower exchange rate involving smuggling and large illicit gains for a few; can create severe financial problems for agencies marketing the primary products; and can lead to inadequate prices for primary product producers. From this perspective, it is definitely not desirable that QRs should substitute for a change in the exchange rate where a depreciation of the exchange rate would be appropriate for medium-term development needs. For countries with both a significant manufacturing base and primary producers, it is important to have an exchange rate which gives broadly the correct signals to producers for medium-term resource allocation.[4]

The argument for Article XVIIIb restrictions would thus be misconceived if it were thought that they could be a substitute for devaluation in all circumstances. However, while devaluation is appropriate in many situations, there are often limits to its effectiveness as a way of bringing about BoP equilibrium in the short term. These limits, which have been shown both by theoretical reasoning and empirical evidence, will be elaborated on below. In such contexts QRs are sometimes the more effective and appropriate instrument, or devaluation and QRs may be used as complementary measures, with devaluation designed to encourage the necessary medium-term resource allocation, while QRs can rapidly alleviate the short-term BoP situation and avoid the need for drastic cuts in incomes and employment.

The first problem about devaluation is whether it can be made effective (i.e., whether nominal changes in the exchange rate in fact translate into real changes). One reason that a nominal exchange rate does not lead to a proportionate real change is that it is often accompanied by reduced import restrictions (reduced QRs and tariffs). This is typically the case for IMF-engineered devaluations. But a more important reason why only a proportion of a nominal exchange rate change is reflected in a real change is that groups within the country secure a compensatory rise in prices–incomes. In general, in countries with well organised workers, wage-earners succeed in recouping at least part of the rise in the cost of living in improved wages, thus bringing about an inflationary spiral which offsets, at least partially, the devaluation. In countries with widespread indexation (for example, Brazil and Israel in earlier years), devaluation can be completely negated in real terms.

When devaluation does bring about a real rate exchange depreciation, it does not necessarily bring about an improvement in the balance of trade. It is necessary to distinguish between those cases where the foreign exchange prices of imports and exports are unaffected by the devaluation, and those cases where they are affected. In the first case, often described as the 'small country case' (and typical of many LDCs, especially primary producing countries), a devaluation does not affect foreign demand or the external terms of trade, and its effects depend on how the internal terms of trade are affected and the response of export supply, of import demand, and of supply of import substitutes to the change in prices.

In countries where the main effect is on the internal terms of trade and where domestic demand and supply elasticities are low, only a small improvement in the BoP will occur. This is likely to be the case for primary producers, especially in the short term. Primary production normally requires time and investment before it can be significantly increased (e.g., coffee bushes take 5–10 years to mature). Price elasticities of imports tend to be very low in countries with a small manufacturing base, where imports are largely composed of parts for manufacturing industry, capital goods and fuel for which there are no domestic substitutes. In these circumstances devaluation is likely to bring about at most only a small improvement in the BoP. Because of the small response expected, where a large improvement is needed countries are often recommended to make very large changes in the exchange rate. But the effect on the BoP does not multiply with the size of the exchange rate change, since there are absolute limits to how far supply can respond in the short run. Large changes tend to increase the inflationary impact of the devaluation, so that the real appreciation is small, or even negative.[5]

Where a number of primary producers devalue simultaneously and all increase the incentives to supply primary products, when a supply response does occur there may be a significant increase in world production and a consequent reduction in world prices. The late 1980s slump in world cocoa prices has been attributed to oversupply resulting from simultaneous exchange rate changes and improved producer incentives by most of the major cocoa producers (see *Financial Times*, 6 September 1988). Where world demand elasticity is less than 1, total earnings from exports will fall as production rises. It has been estimated that this is the case for 60 per cent of the primary product exports in sub-Saharan Africa (Godfrey, 1985).

Therefore in primary producing countries devaluation is likely to produce at best only a small response in the short term, and may actually have negative effects on foreign exchange earnings for some crops in the medium term, if adopted simultaneously by a number of countries producing the same product. Devaluation may still be important in primary producing countries to enable them to get their producer prices broadly right from a medium-term perspective, and to contribute to the financial viability of the marketing agencies; but it is not likely to be effective as a short-run emergency BoP measure.

In countries with a sizeable manufacturing and capital goods sector, devaluation might be expected to have more positive effects. There the switch to exports and import substitutes is likely to be much more easily achieved, and with smaller time lags because existing capital can be used. In these countries there can be a negative terms of trade effect (because export prices are likely to fall expressed in dollars), but given demand elasticity greater than 1, the net effect on the BoP should be positive. However, where the exports face QRs themselves in their foreign markets (as with textiles), the devaluation could produce a terms of trade loss without a corresponding gain in quantity sold. QRs, in contrast, do not produce a terms of trade loss, and in rare cases where the country imports a large proportion of world imports can cause a terms of trade gain; but this is an unlikely case and might produce retaliation.

The 'neutrality' of devaluation, which has been presented as an advantage, can be a disadvantage for countries during an emergency. On the import side, the fact that devaluation is across-the-board and neutral means that it does not differentiate in favour of more important imports. Where markets are already highly distorted, and incomes and wealth very unfairly distributed, the price mechanism alone will not allocate goods and services in a way that is desirable from the perspective of growth or equity. Priority allocation is especially important at times of cutbacks, since otherwise significant and unnecessary damage can be inflicted on vulnerable groups and on growth objectives. Devaluation on its own is too clumsy an instrument to achieve import allocation according to social and economic priorities. It needs to be supplemented by other means to ensure that priorities are met. (see the discussion of meso-policies in Cornia *et al.* 1987). An example has been provided by Zambia where the auctioning of foreign exchange led to most foreign exchange going to large-scale urban enterprises. Small scale enterprises and the agricultural sector got a disproportionately small portion of the allocation (see Ncube *et al.*, 1987). In the Sudan, household electricity generators were imported following import liberalisation because lack of imports for fuel and spare parts had caused major problems for the public electricity supply (Hussain and Thirlwall, 1984); a much more rational allocation of imports would have been to allocate them to the public electricity system. In general import controls are much more effective than devaluation as a way of ensuring that priority imports are obtained and lower priorities excluded.

The across-the-board nature of devaluation can also be undesirable for exports. There can be a case for differentiated exchange rates, or exchange rates combined with tariffs or controls, where one dominant sector (e.g., oil) is holding the exchange rate at a level that discourages other types of production and export. For non-oil primary producers, it is usually desirable to give special promotion to manufacturing production and to non-traditional exports. However, these are longer-term arguments for differentiation, and not related to the BoP aspect covered by Article XVIIIb.

Inflation
Harrod described devaluation as 'the most potent known instrument of domestic price inflation which has such sorry effects on human misery' (Harrod, quoted in Thirlwall, 1983). It has been argued that import controls are just as inflationary as devaluation, since the reduced quantities of imports available will tend to lead to price rises (Blackhurst, 1981). But the inflation produced by QRs is different from that set off by devaluation. This is because (1) QRs may be selective and not fall on essential commodities, while devaluation is across-the-board; (2) QRs may be accompanied by price controls on essential commodities; (3) where prices are cost-determined, QRs are less inflationary than devaluation (see Ocampo, 1987; 1988); finally (4) if QRs do raise prices this does not eliminate their effectiveness, at least on the import side. On balance, then, it seems that QRs are likely to be less inflationary than devaluation.

Empirical Evidence
On balance, this shows that devaluation has *not* been an effective instrument for improving the trade balance, especially for primary producing countries.

As noted earlier, the existence of floating exchange rates did not succeed in eliminating world trading imbalances in the 1980s, when there were major changes in exchange rates both among developed countries and developing countries. Trade imbalances persisted among developed countries in the 1960s and 1970s, despite exchange rate changes. It has been shown that changes in the exchange rate and changes in competitiveness frequently move in opposite directions (i.e., the depreciating countries have lost competitiveness and the appreciating countries have gained it – Kaldor, 1978). This does not prove any causality; the most obvious explanation would be that the countries with relatively rapid productivity growth have continuously increased their competitiveness and that this has required periodic exchange rate appreciation. Yet the exchange rate appreciation (and, conversely, the depreciation of those countries losing competitiveness) has not succeeded in reversing these trends.

An early study of the effects of devaluation in the 1960s (Cooper, 1971) showed that in 15 out of 24 cases the trade balance improved in the year following devaluation. The countries covered included several developed or near-developed countries (Canada, Iceland, Greece and Spain). The remainder were middle-income developing countries, apart from Pakistan. The devaluations were not on the whole accompanied by a significant change in the terms of trade. Cooper found that prices and wages rose following devaluation, but not enough to prevent some real devaluation. Bhagwati and Onitsuka (1974), also investigating the 1960s, found three things: (1) In most cases imports continued to grow after devaluation, mainly at a faster rate than in the pre-devaluation period. The faster growth of imports was attributed to the liberalisation which accompanied the devaluation, and to the expansion of exports, which led to additional imports. These expansionary forces outweighed effects of devaluation in reducing imports, indicating low elasticities of demand for imports. (2) Expansion in exports occurred in less than half the cases. These were countries which were relatively more advanced, experienced a high degree of real devaluation and had more effective supporting policies. (3) In general, primary producers did not experience a significant rise in exports. This was attributed to a low rate of effective devaluation because competing producers also devalued, small effects on producer prices, and non-price influences on production. Krueger (1978) also found that imports rose with devaluation, and that exports rose only after a time-lag, with no consistent pattern of response of the current account of the BoP.

The most sophisticated and systematic analysis of the effects of devaluation in the 1960s was carried out by Miles (1979). Using multiple regression, he looked at the impact of other variables as well as the exchange rate. He also extended the analysis over a longer time period than the one year studied by Cooper. He covered 16 devaluations in 14 countries, of which only five were developing countries. His results showed an improvement in the trade balance in the year following devaluation, but this improvement was small compared with the deterioration in the trade balance in the year of the devaluation, and in succeeding years. However, the BoP showed definite improvement because of improvement on the capital account.

Evidence for eight major (developed) countries in the 1970s 'indicates that the response of the trade balances to such real exchange rate changes has been hardly significant, manifest if at all only over periods of such length that the relationship is highly tenuous, many other changes having intervened in the meantime' (Blackhurst and Tumlir, 1980, p. 4).

The multi-country studies noted above for the most part cover industrialised and middle-income developing countries, which would be expected to have greater response to devaluation than low-income primary producing countries. Hussain and Thirlwall (1984) have conducted an in-depth assessment of the effects of the 1978 devaluation in the Sudan, a low-income primary producing country. They argued that this represented a test case of the 'supply-side' argument for devaluation, which views devaluation as a mechanism for increasing the profitability (and hence the supply) of exports. They found that the devaluation made little difference to the profitability of exports, and production of exportables in fact declined after 1978. The reason it made little difference was that domestic input prices rose with devaluation, wages rose in response to rising domestic prices, and prices of inputs rose further in response to rising wages. Consequently, it was estimated that input costs for export crops rose by 75 per cent of the rate of devaluation. All price increases accelerated following the devaluation, supporting the view that devaluation contributes to inflation, but the price acceleration was much greater for import prices and domestic prices than for prices of the main export crops. Comparisons showed that actual export production lagged behind the performance predicted pre-devaluation. Factors behind the poor production of export crops were identified as shortages of labour during picking seasons, of fertilisers, and of fuel and spare parts for transport; the devaluation did not make any contribution to any of these areas. They concluded that to ensure adequate supplies of consumption goods to the rural areas and foreign exchange for inputs 'tight import controls are required – not liberalisation'.

In many contexts, therefore, devaluation alone is not effective as a means of improving the BoP in the short term. The position is summed up in an IMF report 'it is clear that there is no simple relationship between developments in real exchange rates and in current account balances' (IMF, *World Economic Outlook*, April 1988, p. 73).

The exchange rate should be regarded more as an instrument of medium term resource allocation than for the short-term BoP. Given the ineffectiveness of devaluation as a short term device for improving the BoP for many countries, it remains essential that they have access to other methods of securing quick improvement in the BoP in the short term.

QRs and Tariffs

Article XVIIIb, strictly speaking, permits QRs not tariffs, although in practice it has been interpreted as also permitting emergency tariffs (Vincke, 1972). The prevailing view (e.g., of the IMF and World Bank) is that tariffs are preferable to QRs.

A great deal has been written in the theoretical literature on the differences between QRs and tariffs. In a competitive environment where information is perfect, there exists an 'equivalent' tariff which has exactly the same effects as QRs in terms of resource allocation and prices (see Figure 8.5).

Using a welfare theoretic approach, it has been shown that QRs are *not* equivalent to tariffs in the following circumstances:

(a) where there are monopolies (Bhagwati, 1965);
(b) where there is retaliation (Rodriguez, 1974; Tower, 1975);
(c) with uncertainty (Fishelson and Flatters, 1975; Driscoll and Ford, 1983);
(d) with 'non-economic' objectives (Pelcovitz, 1976);
(e) in the path of dynamic adjustment (Blejer and Hillman, 1982).

The welfare conclusions from a comparison between tariffs and quotas in these circumstances are not unambiguous. In (a) and (b) tariffs are argued to be superior to quotas, but in (c) and (d) quotas can, in some situations, be superior to tariffs.

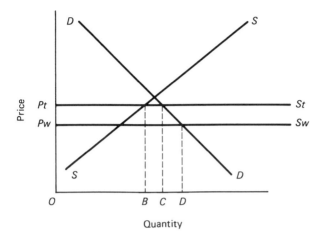

DD   domestic demand
SS   domestic supply
PwSw   foreign supply at world prices
PtSt   foreign supply at world prices and tariff
Cutback in imports due to tariff is equivalent to import controls with quota *BC*. Domestic production is *OB*.
Figure 8.5   Tariffs and QRs

A more 'real world' comparison between tariffs and quotas suggests the following differences, which are not allowed for in the theoretical models:

1. *Certainty* The effects of quotas on quantities imported are known in advance, whereas the effects of tariffs depend on estimates of elasticities.
2. *Prices* Tariffs raise prices. As discussed earlier, quotas may result in prices increases if (a) they are auctioned or (b) there are competitive markets; but they need not if (c) there is cost-plus pricing or (d) effective price control, as in Australia or the UK in the Second World War.
3. *Administration and speed of reaction* Quotas may be easier to introduce quickly. Several authors have noted that quotas act more quickly than devaluation or tariffs (see, e.g., Balassa *et al.*, 1971).

    Scott *et al* (1980, p. 16) note that 'general and ruthless import controls have [a] larger, and quicker, shock effect on imports than a fall in the exchange rate of the magnitude that might be desirable'.

In the longer term there are probably few differences in administrative problems.

4. *Priority allocation of imports*   Both tariffs and quotas can be differentiated by product, but quotas can be differentiated by *end-use* as well, whereas tariffs cannot (i.e., as between investment and consumption, or use by different categories of consumer, or by region, Bhagwati, 1978). Quotas are consequently much better instruments for ensuring that priorities are met.

5. *Effects on competitiveness and x-efficiency*   If allocated to existing firms, and not auctioned, quotas are more likely than tariffs to represent a barrier to new entrants. They also form an absolute cut-off from foreign competition, whereas tariffs handicap foreign competitors but do not debar them altogether. Consequently, quotas are likely to have both the disadvantages of reduced competition (less incentive to improve productivity) and the advantages (encouragement to large-scale investment and innovation in a secure environment). The latter effect was a major reason why the Cambridge Economic Policy Group advocated import controls for Britain: 'the greater security offered to British industry would safeguard productivity by avoiding the collapse of investment and increased restrictive practices' (CEPR, 1975, 1900 pp. 15–16). These are medium rather than short-run effects. On balance, it is likely that the disadvantages outweigh the advantages, and that quotas are associated with more x-inefficiency than tariffs.

6. *Creation of monopoly profits*   Quotas can create monopoly profits for recipients unless they are auctioned by the government, whereas tariffs create revenue for the government. But quota profits can be prevented by taxation or complementary tariffs, or by strict price control.

7. *Corruption and rent-seeking*   One important difference lies in income distribution. In the case of tariffs, the revenue goes to the government. With tariffs the licensees benefit if the licences are allocated by rationing, and the government benefits if the licences are allocated by auction. The existence of gains for licensees can lead to 'rent-seeking' behaviour of potential licensees who may use all sorts of means (including bribes) to secure the licences. But tariffs also can lead to rent-seeking behaviour by groups seeking to get tariffs established, or abolished.

Taking the effects together it seems that in the short-run quotas may be preferable to tariffs because they are more certain, quicker acting and administratively simpler to introduce, and can ensure that import use is in line with priorities. But in the longer term the adverse effects on competitiveness and efficiency, and the greater potential for corruption, may outweigh these effects.

'ABUSES' OF THE PROCEDURES

There have been criticisms made of the way Article XVIIIb has been applied, as noted above (p. 191). It has been argued that surveillance procedures were generally rather weak with respect to Article XVIIIb, and that many countries maintained the restrictions on a near permanent basis, despite a GATT commitment to progressive relaxation of restrictions as conditions improve.

Many countries seem to have applied the restrictions on a continuing basis: of the 18 countries invoking section b in September 1987, 16 had done so for over ten years (Roessler, 1987). In the period 1974–81, only four of the 21 countries that invoked the restrictions removed them (Eglin, 1987). These figures support the view that there has not been effective action to secure progressive relaxation of the restrictions permitted under the Article. However, there has been a significant move towards trade liberalisation among LDCs taken as a whole in recent years, partly under pressure from the IMF and World Bank, whose programmes and finance have often required such liberalisation, but also independently. This move is acknowledged by the IMF (see *World Economic Outlook* April 1988, p. 94) and contrasted with the opposite tendency towards increasing trade restrictions being adopted by developed countries. Consequently, it would not seem that the GATT procedures have been responsible for rising restrictions.

Earlier sections of this essay have argued that developing countries should retain the right to introduce QRs for BoP reasons, and that neither changes in the world economy, nor new thinking about development, justifies a shift from the position adopted in 1957. But there is a case for some review of procedures.

Areas which merit consideration are:

(a) The frequency of full consultations as against simplified procedures (from 1974–1985 a number of countries underwent only simplified procedures throughout the whole period – e.g., Sri Lanka, Egypt and Bangladesh).
(b) The development of more well-defined Guidelines for the BoP

Committee. These could include a review of the economic policies of the country, and some consideration of costs of prolonged
use of QRs; an assessment of how far growth in incomes and
investment would be constrained for BoP reasons in the absence
of restrictions; and some review of the contribution of external
instability to BoP problems.

Some commentators have suggested that the IMF should be integrated into GATT procedures more closely (e.g., Eglin, 1987). Any
increased use of full procedures would automatically bring this about
to some extent, since the IMF attends the full consultations. However, this is as far as it is desirable that integration should go. The
voting procedures in the GATT and the IMF are quite different; for
the former each member of the UN is equally represented, whereas
the IMF has a weighed voting system representing financial power.
Fuller integration would consequently shift power away from the
poorer countries. Moreover, and perhaps related to this difference,
the IMF has a very rigidly defined philosophy, according to which
(among other beliefs) there is no case for QRs. Integration would
then be likely to lead to an excessive bias against QRs.

CONCLUSIONS

This essay has considered the arguments put forward for a review of
Article XVIIIb of the GATT, which permits developing countries to
introduce import restrictions for BoP reasons.

It has argued that the justification for use of QRs remains as strong
as it was in 1957, when the clause was first introduced. In the first
place, changes in the world economy have not altered the persistent
and structural character of LDC BoP problems: indeed, if anything,
the changes since the 1950s have increased LDC needs for emergency
measures to defend their reserves, as well as making even more clear
the potential constraint imposed by the BoP on development programmes. Considerable instability as well as adverse trends have
characterised the external environment of LDCs, especially over the
1980s, forcing many countries to cut back on incomes and investment
for BoP reasons.

Secondly, the essay considered the view that trade measures in
general, and import quotas in particular, were an inefficient way of
dealing with BoP problems. It argued that trade measures were a
necessary supplement to action towards the macro-balance of an

economy, if the large costs of lost income, investment and growth potential were to be avoided. While some of the arguments for preferring devaluation are valid, it is from the perspective of medium-term resource allocation. On theoretical grounds, devaluation would be expected to be a poor instrument to improve the BoP of low-income countries because of rigidities and low elasticities. Empirical evidence bears out this expectation and shows, moreover, that devaluation has not even been effective for more developed countries to bring about short-run BoP equilibrium. Developing countries cannot consequently rely on devaluation alone as a short-term measure of BoP adjustment. QRs are much more effective, and have the additional advantage of selectivity, so that priority uses can be given preference. QRs have some short-term advantages compared with tariffs, but in the longer run tariffs may be preferable from the perspective of efficiency and corruption.

The previous section considered arguments that Article XVIIIb has been subject to abuse, in the sense that its use has extended beyond the BoP protection aspect to normal protection; that in many cases consultations were almost non-existent; than there was little follow-up to consultations; and than countries made very prolonged use of the quotas. There are areas where some review of procedures may be called for.

In conclusion, developing countries still need the right to impose QRs for BoP purposes. Developments since 1957, both in the external environment and in our knowledge about economic behaviour, reinforce rather than reduce this need. However, there is a case for review of some of the procedures used in applying Article XVIIIb.

NOTES

1. Figures are from IMF, *World Economic Outlook* (April 1988 and October 1989), unless otherwise stated.
2. Figures and classification of countries from World Bank (1990).
3. This simplified exposition ignores the service account – notably payments for debt servicing, remittances, etc.
4. It is of course very difficult to interpret what this means precisely in a particular case, though it is normally fairly easy to identify the direction of change considered appropriate. The correct exchange rate has more to do with medium-term resource allocation than with short-term BoP.
5. Godfrey (1985) gives some examples of cases where nominal depreciation has been accompanied by real appreciation of the exchange rate.

Part III
The International
Monetary System

9 Money and South–South Cooperation*

Monetary arrangements may sound technical and of subsidiary significance. The production and distribution of goods and services are what matter for the pattern of development. From this perspective it would appear that the important international arrangements are those that regulate flows of goods and services and of investment, technology and labour: trade agreements, and rules or codes of conduct concerning investment, technology and labour would appear to take precedence over monetary arrangements. The experience and achievements of South–South agreements seem to exemplify this view: there have been more, and more effective, agreements on trade and investment than on money, and where monetary arrangements have been undertaken they have, typically, been introduced as a supplement to trade arrangements.

But a brief look at the world today shows how fundamentally mistaken this view of priorities is: money dominates economic affairs. The debt crisis – which is basically a monetary matter, being concerned with flows of finance and their repayment – is of over-riding importance to most countries in Latin America and Africa and some in Asia. The International Monetary Fund (IMF) – the nearest we have to a world central bank – is now the central policy-maker in two thirds of the countries of Africa and Latin America. Exchange rate changes between the dollar and the yen threaten to bring about a trade war between the USA and Japan, and threaten financial disintegration. These events have a dramatic impact on countries in the Third World – in many cases far greater than that of their domestic plans and their own monetary policies. Yet in such areas they are virtually powerless – victims of decisions taken elsewhere, in which their interests are ignored completely or given very little weight. Decisions on the exchange rates of the major currencies are taken without regard to their effects on the Third World. Despite much pleading, the country-by-country approach to the debt crisis has been devised to rescue the major Western banks, with little concern for the Third World. Developing countries, which are overwhelmingly those

* *Third World Quarterly*, 9 (4) (October 1987).

most affected by IMF decisions, have a voice but no power over its decisions.

Monetary constraints and possibilities are also of decisive influence on South–South trade and investment, setting the limits to the effectiveness of trade agreements. This itself represents a powerful argument for Third World countries to support collective monetary arrangements. But there is more at stake than this. Third World countries need to take a more active role in monetary arrangements so that they can cease to be passive recipients (typically victims) of decisions taken elsewhere, and can instead begin to control events in their own interests. In the fifty years since Bretton Woods – years in which the majority of Third World countries acquired political independence – there have been a number of attempts to develop South–South monetary arrangements on a regional basis. On the whole these have been successful in relation to their aims. But while this progress has been important, it has hardly impinged on the broader issues of control. Northern domination remains as strong as ever in monetary matters, and this domination reinforces Northern power over policy-making in Third World countries, over trade and investment, and even over politics.

South monetary arrangements, then, can be viewed at two distinct levels: in terms of their impact on trade and development within the region they encompass; and in terms of their effects in countering Northern domination. The two are by no means unrelated, but it is helpful to start by considering them separately. The aim of this essay is to review the achievements of South–South cooperation at both levels: to consider the potential and past achievements in promoting Southern development through South–South flows of trade and investment; and to discuss how the South might develop monetary cooperation as a means of securing greater independence from Northern domination. The essay concludes by suggesting specific institutional arrangements which would help greater realisation of the potential in the area of monetary cooperation.

To start with, it will be helpful to review some of the major functions of international monetary arrangements, and how these have developed over recent decades.

FUNCTIONS OF INTERNATIONAL MONETARY ARRANGEMENTS

International monetary arrangements can be viewed as institutions which reproduce internationally the functions that are performed domestically by national currencies, commercial banks and government authorities, through the activities of the central bank.

Generally, within each country there is a single currency that is accepted as a means of payment for all transactions. In addition, commercial banks provide credit which facilitates transactions, and the central bank supports the commercial sector, being prepared to be 'lender-of-last-resort'. The central bank thereby prevents catastrophic bank failures, and it can also ensure adequate liquidity in the economy through its power of creating money. The system facilitates production and trade. There is no problem of currency inconvertibility, as there can be between countries, since there is only one currency. Similarly, problems of exchange rate fluctuations and uncertainty, which may also inhibit trade, are automatically ruled out. Assuming adequate but not excessive credit creation, the national monetary system provides the conditions for specialisation, production and exchange, and hence for growth and development.

International currency areas – generally associated with empires (both of the colonial and neocolonial variety) and their aftermath – have much the same conditions as national currency systems, with a single currency (or if more than one, fixed exchange rates and full convertibility) and credit creation controlled by the imperial central bank. While this system has some of the virtues of a national system, it has disadvantages which have led most countries (other than those in the franc zone) to reject it soon after gaining political independence. First, it means that only the imperial centre controls credit creation, and the other countries have to accept whatever is decided there. Secondly, the exchange rate of each country *vis-à-vis* the rest of the world outside the currency area is determined by the imperial exchange rate. Thirdly, there can be no change in the exchange rate of a country with respect to the rest of the currency area. Each of these factors can severely inhibit development. In a national system, there may be other policies to compensate weaker members (e.g., tax and investment policies). In an imperial-type system, this is less likely, and if it does apply, control tends to be with the centre. Probably, the decisive objection to the system, however, is symbolic: it is obvious that independence in such a system is only nominal. For most countries, the trappings of independence include separate currencies, national central banks, and independently determined exchange rates. Yet once these are instituted, there immediately follows a need for international monetary arrangements, because without such arrangements trade may be highly restricted except within national boundaries. Lack of currency convertibility between countries, the absence of credit to facilitate trade across boundaries, and exchange rate uncertainties all inhibit and may even prevent international trade flows.

For many Third World countries a complete interruption of international trade could be near-disastrous – more so than for most industrialised countries – for two reasons. In the first place, the very small size of most Third World economies (to be analysed more fully below) makes autarky very expensive. Secondly, their economies – partly as a consequence of the colonial experience with its single currency area and near-free trade policies – were highly specialised when they became independent. Apart from food for self-subsistence, the production of many countries was concentrated on one or two primary products, for which the domestic market was almost non-existent. To diversify and industrialise, imports were essential. To make use of their inherited specialisation, and to earn foreign exchange to pay for the imports, they needed to export. Consequently, international monetary arrangements were necessary to permit trade and payments across countries.

The functions of international monetary arrangements, then, are to ease international trade and payments, given the existence of national currencies and national exchange rates. Broadly they may be categorised as (1) securing currency convertibility and/or providing an internationally acceptable means of payment. This function provides for the international counterpart of a national currency; (2) providing international liquidity. Provision of liquidity to countries in foreign exchange difficulties can promote a greater degree of exchange rate stability, and prevent drastic trade-restricting action in response to temporary problems. Liquidity creation is also needed to ensure adequate levels of international liquidity and to prevent liquidity shortages from depressing economic expansion and trade. The liquidity function represents the international aspect of the credit creation and lender-of-last-resort functions of national central banks; and (3) providing international credit to help to finance international transactions. This is the function that is normally performed domestically by commercial banks.

Formal mechanisms are not always necessary to generate the arrangements or institutions which perform these functions. Over the last fifty years, a host of mechanisms have developed – some formal, the majority informal – to meet the international needs created by the change from imperial currency areas to domestic currency systems among Third World countries. Formal institutions include the

IMF, which provides international liquidity in the form of access to quotas and the creation of Special Drawing Rights (SDRs), and official export credit agencies in developed countries, which provide trade credit. There have also been regional monetary arrangements including those between Third World countries, to be discussed later. Informal mechanisms include the use of the dollar as a trading currency, and using dollars, other industrialised countries' currencies and gold as a source of foreign exchange reserves and international liquidity; as well as credit extended by commercial banks and companies to finance international trade and investment.

In one way or another, each of the three functions of international monetary arrangements has been fulfilled to some degree. But there have been major problems with the way in which they have been fulfilled. First, important functions have not been satisfactorily performed. This is especially true of the liquidity function, where levels of international liquidity have been very inadequate,[1] leading to a strongly deflationary bias in the world economy; and the lender-of-last-resort function has not been performed at all, thus putting the whole financial system at risk during the debt crisis.[2] The South has suffered from the excessive deflation, and the cautious view taken towards the debt situation, which has resulted from these deficiencies in international monetary arrangements. However, the second set of problems with the way in which international monetary arrangements have evolved is of even greater relevance to the discussion here. All the mechanisms have been directed towards North–South transactions, not South–South, and at the same time each mechanism has been dominated by the North which has retained much the same power as it had in the colonial system. This will become clearer with a more detailed discussion of how the three functions are performed.

Third World trade, for the most part, is denominated in dollars or some other industrialised country's currency, whether the trade is with the North or with other Third World countries. In general, payments for the sale of goods or for purchases are also made in such a currency, again whoever the trade is with. The only exception to this near universal rule is where there are specific regional payment arrangements, or countertrade arrangements (where the goods may be paid for with goods). The international means of payment are thus Northern currencies.

The international liquidity function is performed formally by the IMF. Voting power in the IMF is determined mainly in relation to size of national quotas. This means that the USA alone has 19.3 per cent of the voting power. The USA, European countries and Japan together have more than half the voting power. One-third of the votes are needed to veto a decision (i.e., an alliance of the USA and three European countries is sufficient). Informal liquidity creation is a function of US monetary policy, as long as dollars are accepted as means of payment and international reserves. Both formal and informal mechanisms for international liquidity creation are therefore controlled in the North. The irony is that this is true even where it is South–South trade and payments for which the liquidity is needed.

Credit for trade and investment is provided by Northern export credit agencies (which are often subsidised by their governments) and commercial banks whose headquarters, regulatory procedures and owners are located in the North. The main exception here – apart from some regional arrangements – is the growth of international banks based in, or financed by, the Middle East. But these are of minor magnitude compared with the activities of Northern banks. Again, besides trade with the North which forms the bulk of their business, Northern banks also finance much of the trade within and between Third World countries – trade which, aside from the financing, has nothing to do with the North, but which can be stopped or promoted by decisions made by Northern banks.

The dominance of Northern institutions in monetary arrangements reinforces trading links between North and South, and gives no encouragement to the development of intra-South trading links. The biases in the international monetary system as it has evolved, with the institutional dependency which reinforces and creates other forms of dependency, themselves provide a very strong case for promoting Southern financial arrangements. But there is also a more positive case: monetary arrangements within the South could promote a dynamic, efficient and independent pattern of development.

ADVANTAGES OF SOUTH–SOUTH TRADE

The historic – and current – biases which have favoured North–South trade and have discriminated against South–South trade justify corrective action. These biases are not only monetary, as described above, but include almost every element which facilitates trade – transport, insurance, technology, communications and culture. More positively, trade between Third World countries permits small and underdeveloped economies to exploit economies of scale, specialisation and learning, while maintaining some protection against competition from advanced economies which – if there were free trade – would limit or prevent any form of industrialisation for some countries.

The very small size of many Third World countries needs to be emphasised. It is not only a question of small populations – though this is true for many countries. 55 countries have populations of below 1 million, and another 29 have populations of between 1 and 5 million. But low *per capita* incomes, with a low proportion of those incomes spent on manufactured products, mean that the domestic market for manufacturing output is typically a fraction of the size of that of developed countries. This fact, together with the early stage of development, leads to very small manufacturing sectors in many countries. This is illustrated in Table 9.1, which excludes countries with population below 1 million. 26 countries have manufacturing sections which are less than US $0.5 billion in value-added or less than 0.06 per cent of the US manufacturing sector (less that 0.4 per cent of the UK manufacturing sector). This small size makes it impossible for countries to exploit economies of scale and specialisation. A study in 1969 estimated that only eight of 38 manufacturing industries would be efficient at a scale of production of 1 per cent of the UK market or below, while half the industries would be efficient only with more than half the UK market.[3] Economies of scale tend to increase with technological change over time, so it is likely that efficient size has grown since then. Some industries may be efficiently produced in small developing economies, but only if there is just one firm and one plant. This means there is a lack of competition, which is liable to result in inefficiency, and also that consumers can enjoy only a single type of product.

One of Adam Smith's most important statements was that 'Specialisation is limited by the extent of the market'. And the reverse is also true: the market depends on specialisation, because specialisation produces increasing productivity through economies of scale and learning. Small and under-developed economies are thus trapped in a vicious circle. Because of their small size, they cannot raise productivity through increased specialisation. Moreover, they also lack industrial experience which is another important aid to improved productivity. Consequently, they cannot compete in international markets. Protection is therefore introduced to offset these disadvantages and permit industrialisation. But protection confines

Table 9.1   Size of manufacturing sector of Third World countries, 1986,
$ million gross value-added

% of UK sector		
Over 50	China	91 463
	Brazil	69 406
25–50	India	38 311
	Mexico	31 968
	Republic of Korea	29 397
10–25	Argentina	21 496
	Venezuela	14 072
	Turkey	13 340
5–10	Indonesia	10 592
	Thailand	9 700
	Hong Kong	7 978
	Philippines	7 584
	Saudi Arabia	7 173
	Peru	6 746
1–5	Colombia	5 817
	Malaysia	5 563*
	Nigeria	5 196
	Pakistan	5 073
	Singapore	4 678
	Chile	4 150*
	Morocco	2 582
	Ecuador	2 230
	Kuwait	1 902
	Zimbabwe	1 444
	Cameroon	1 321
	Bangladesh	1 249
	Libya	1 222*
	Ivory Coast	1 191

% of UK sector		
0.5–1	Tunisia	1 161
	Sri Lanka	888
	Dom. Republic	841
	Nicaragua	759
	Kenya	709
	Ghana	639
	Senegal	626
	El Salvador	612
0.1–0.5	Paraguay	572
	Jamaica	553
	Burma	552*

Bolivia	529
Ethiopia	518
Jordan	508
Yemen AR	491
Honduras	482
Zambia	461
Panama	422
Mauritius	284
Congo Republic	177

Note:
* 1984.
Source: World Bank (1989).

the economy to the size of its own market and therefore prevents specialisation and economies of scale.

Countries in the early stages of industrialisation need to extend their markets without having their industrial sectors totally undermined by competition from the industrialised countries. Trade between Third World economies achieves this: it extends the market, and therefore the scope for specialisation, without destroying it. It permits countries to combine variety in their consumption, with specialisation in their production. It generates intra-industry trade – with different plants specialising in the production of different parts of a product – which is the quintessential feature of specialisation, and formed the core of the massive expansion in trade that occurred in Europe after the Second World War. It is also conducive to the development and adoption of more appropriate technology, since Third World markets offer potential for appropriate products designed for low-income consumers, and appropriate techniques are thus less likely to be rendered obsolete because they fail to produce the sort of sophisticated products demanded among high-income consumers in advanced countries.

Some Third World countries have overcome the disadvantages of very small size – nine countries have markets which are 5 per cent or more of the UK market, five of which are more than 20 per cent of the UK market. Most of these countries compete successfully in world markets, and do not face the dilemmas just described. But these economies today face other problems, for which trade with the South may offer a solution. First, the consequences of slowdown in growth in the North require a search for a new 'engine of growth'. For a variety of reasons – some to do with sociological and technological factors, and some related to society's objectives and policies –

the 'old' industrialised countries are likely to grow more slowly than the 'new' industrialised countries would like to – and could, given fast-growing trading partners. These countries would find it easier to realise their growth objectives and potential through focusing on trade with each other. This is the argument put forward by Sir Arthur Lewis[4] in favour of South–South trade. Secondly, and not unrelated to this, most of the countries in this group (in fact two-thirds) are in severe financial difficulties, largely because of debt-servicing problems. These countries are unable to buy imports essential for growth because they lack foreign exchange, are unable to sell their goods to earn foreign exchange in the North because of sluggish and protected markets, and are unable to sell their goods in the South because most Southern countries are also suffering from foreign exchange difficulties. The result is slow (or negative) growth. Trade with each other would permit faster growth for all.

SOUTH–SOUTH MONETARY ARRANGEMENTS

The functions of international monetary arrangements were described earlier. In summary, the main purpose is to facilitate trade. A large number of South–South monetary arrangements have been established on a regional basis, over the past quarter of a century. While the historic biases against South–South trade and the obstacles to its expansion extend well beyond monetary matters, monetary arrangements are a powerful and essential support for trading agreements.[5]

Three types of monetary arrangement have been instituted: clearing arrangements (typically also involving some credit), multilateral credit arrangements for balance of payments support, and monetary unions. Complete monetary integration – which is rare, but there are two instances in Africa – performs both functions. Multilateral clearing arrangements aim to encourage trade within the area by multilateralising payments, making greater use of local currencies in trade between members, economising on 'hard' currencies, and extending credit among members. For example, before the establishment of the West African Clearing House the 'principal channel for effecting settlements [was] through the region's commercial banks. They in turn settle[d] in convertible currencies through correspondent banks in the major financial centres of Western Europe, and the United States'.[6] By replacing this system, the Clearing House reduced the use of foreign exchange for transactions within the region, and also the transaction costs incurred by Western commercial banks. The second type of arrangement provides mutual support for temporary disequilibria in countries' balance of payments. Some of these arrangements involve formal pooling of part of countries' foreign exchange reserves. These schemes are not directed at intra-regional trade, but at mutual support, performing like a mini-IMF, with the resources of the associated countries.

Multilateral Clearing Arrangements

1. *The Central American Clearing House* (1961)   This is a mechanism for multilateral clearing and reciprocal credits established by the central banks of Costa Rica, El Salvador, Guatemala, Honduras and Nicaragua. The purpose is to expedite monetary transfers within the region and to support the Central American Common Market (CACM).
2. *Reciprocal Payment and Credit System of the Latin American Free Trade Association* (LAFTA) (1965)   This agreement is between Argentina, Brazil, Bolivia, Colombia, Chile, Ecuador, Mexico, Paraguay, Peru, the Dominican Republic, Uruguay and Venezuela, with the aim of achieving the orderly settlement of balances, and the extension of some credit between members.
3. *The West African Clearing House* (1975)   The agreement includes the members of the West African Monetary Union together with Cape Verde, Gambia, Ghana, Guinea, Guinea–Bissau, Liberia, Mali, Mauritania, Niger, Nigeria, and Sierra Leone. There is a common unit of account for trade between members and transactions between members are debited/credited in the centralised clearing system, with the outstanding balances settled periodically. Additional credit, above that arising between settlement dates, is not provided. The system is intended to encourage use of local currencies for intra-regional trade, thereby economising on hard currencies and encouraging intra-regional trade.
4. *The Asian Clearing Union* (1974)   This provides multilateral clearing for commodities traded between Bangladesh, Burma, India, Iran, Nepal, Pakistan and Sri Lanka. National currencies can be used so that members economise on foreign exchange reserves.
5. *The Multilateral Clearing Facility of the Caribbean Community* (CARICOM) (1977)   This covers Barbados, Belize, ECCA,

Guyana, Jamaica, and Trinidad and Tobago, and as with the others involves multilateral clearing facilities and the use of national currencies for approved transactions. It is intended to support the CARICOM trade arrangements.

6. *The Central Africa Clearing House* (1979)   Between Zaire and the Central African States, this provides for multilateral clearing.

7. *The Monetary Arrangement of the Economic Community of the Great Lakes* (1978)   This has clearing arrangements supporting the Economic Community of the Great Lakes covering Burundi, Rwanda and Zaire.

Multilateral Balance of Payments Support Arrangements

1. *The Central African Monetary Stabilisation Fund* (1969)   Established among five central African states to provide financial assistance to correct temporary disequilibria in the balance of payments of member countries.

2. *The Multilateral Mutual Assistance Agreement to Correct Temporary Deficiencies of Liquidity* (1969)   Established for mutual assistance among LAFTA members.

3. *The Central American Stabilisation Fund* (1969).

4. *The Arab Monetary Fund* (1976)   With 21 members, this aims to coordinate monetary systems with the objective of greater monetary and economic integration, as well as providing balance of payments assistance among members.

5. *The Association of South-East Asian Nations* (ASEAN)   *Swap Agreement* (1977)   This includes Indonesia, Malaysia, Philippines, Singapore, Thailand and Brunei.

6. *The Andean Reserve Fund* (1976)   Established among the five members of the Cartagena Agreement.

Monetary Unions

1. *The West African Monetary Union* (1962)   Covering six countries – Benin, Burkina Faso, Ivory Coast, Niger, Senegal and Togo. These countries have formed an integrated monetary area, with a freely circulating common currency which is pegged to the franc, and a common central bank, which holds the foreign exchanges of members in a common pool.

2. *The Central African Monetary Union* (1972)   Comprising Chad, Cameroon, Central African Republic, Congo and Gabon, which

operates on similar principles to the West African Monetary Union.

ASSESSMENT

It is apparent from this brief review that there has been considerable progress in instituting monetary arrangements among Third World countries. Over half the countries in the South have been affected in one way or other. Each of the three major functions delineated above has been performed in one or other arrangement (i.e., means of international payment, liquidity creation, and credit for international transactions). The Clearing House Mechanism had been most extensive – this performs the means of payment function and typically involves some credit, but not normally a great deal. The mutual balance of payments support schemes effectively add to countries' liquidity.

It is not possible to make a definitive assessment of the schemes because (1) they have typically been associated with other attempts to promote intra-regional trade, particularly agreements on tariff liberalisation; indeed their major function is to support such measures; and (2) in recent years, there has been a marked deterioration in the financial and trading environment for many countries. That being said, it seems the schemes were fairly successful while times were 'normal' in the 1960s and 1970s, but do not seem to have been able to counter the effects of the crisis of the 1980s. There were two aspects to their success in the 1960s and 1970s: first, the various schemes accumulated functions and members over time and were not limited or disbanded. In this respect they differed from trade agreements, which in some cases had a more chequered history, with some retreat and occasional complete breakdown. Secondly, South–South trade in general expanded fast over this period, and particularly intra-regional trade to which these schemes (together with trading agreements) have been directed.

South–South trade grew rapidly over the 1960s and 1970s, with the share of manufactures in the total growing from about 5 per cent of all South–South exports in the early 1960s to 30 per cent by 1980 (see Tables 9.2 and 9.3).

From 1973 to 1980, South–South trade in manufactures grew faster than any other category of trade, growing at a rate of 20.7 per cent per annum, compared with 10.2 per cent (South–North), 10.1 per

Table 9.2   Growth in export volume, selected years, % p.a.

	1962–73	1973–80	1980–7
All exports			
South–South	9.0	4.3	3.2
South–North	11.0	−1.4	−1.4
North–South	7.1	10.2	−0.4
North–North	11.1	3.6	6.1*
Manufactures			
South–South	17.6	20.7	7.3
South–North	21.2	10.2	16.5
North–South	6.9	10.1	0.7*
North–North	12.4	3.9	7.8*

Note:
* *Increase* in value of exports.
Source: Newson and Wall (1985); Hulagalle (1990); GATT (1988).

Table 9.3   % of total exports going to developing countries, 1965 and 1986

From	1965	1986
Low-income (excluding		
China and India)	37	22
China and India	32	53
Lower middle-income	36	37
Upper middle-income	31	30

Source: World Bank (1988).

cent (North–South) and 4.1 per cent (North–North). But in the 1980s, the cutbacks in imports into Third World countries necessitated by the crisis have hit South–South trade more heavily than other forms of trade, and South–South trade has fallen as a percentage of world trade and as a percentage of Southern exports.[7]

South–South trade is concentrated within regions. For example, one quarter of Latin America's exports went to other developing countries in 1980; of those exports going to developing countries, four-fifths went to other Latin American countries, and one-fifth to Asia and Africa. Similar ratios apply to Asia. Africa has a much lower proportion of exports going to developing countries (7 per cent in 1980), and a lower share of these are intra-regional (under 30 per cent). However, the rate of expansion in South–South trade in manufactures from 1965 to 1980 was roughly the same for intra and inter-regional exports. This was presumably the outcome of two opposing tendencies: on the one hand, rising income within OPEC countries led to growth in inter-regional trade; on the other, the various monetary and trade arrangements promoted intra-regional trade.

Evidence on the combined effect of specific monetary and trade agreements shows that, in general, intra-regional trade rose as a proportion of the total trade of the region in areas with agreements.[8] For example, among LAFTA countries, trade among members grew sixfold and in manufactures twentyfold between 1961 and 1974. The Andean Pact liberalisation efforts were found to have increased intra-regional trade, especially in non-traditional exports. The rate of increase of trade among countries of the Central American Common Market rose by over half following its establishment, with an increasing share taken by manufactures. Positive effects on intra-regional trade have also been found for the CARICOM countries, the Economic Community of West African States (ECOWAS) and the Central African Customs and Economic Union.

Each of the cases which have succeeded in increasing intra-regional trade has combined monetary and trade arrangements. This is what one would expect, since monetary arrangements will have little effect unless accompanied by tariff and non-tariff liberalisation. Their prime role – from the perspective of increasing intra-regional trade – is to permit such liberalisation to take place at less risk of causing monetary problems. In addition, such arrangements permit economy in foreign exchange reserves which should have a generally beneficial effect on levels of income among members, as well as reducing the need to seek outside help (e.g., from the IMF).

However, in the 1980s there has been a dramatic fall in intra-regional trade in Latin America. Trade within the region (excluding fuel) fell from a peak of 18.8 per cent of total trade in 1979 (rising from 11.6 per cent in 1970) to 9.3 per cent in 1984, the major fall occurring in 1982–3.[9] This huge fall reveals the weakness of the monetary schemes during crisis. In principle, this was a time when there was special advantage to intra-regional trade, which could compensate for declining world trade, and could potentially provide a trade which made minimum use of the increasingly scarce 'hard' currency needed for debt servicing. Two factors explain the decline. The most important was the collapse in incomes and imports that occurred at this time in Latin America. Latin American imports as a whole fell by considerably more than those of any other region – with a drop of 17.7 per cent in 1982 and of 22.3 per cent in 1983, compared with a fall of 0.4 per cent and a rise of 4.6 per cent for all industrialised countries, and a fall of 3.7 per cent in US imports in 1982 and a rise of 13.0 per cent in 1983. This collapse in imports in Latin America, which was due to the stringencies of the debt crisis, meant that countries within the region found the markets of other countries sharply reduced, and this had little to do with monetary arrangements. The monetary arrangements, however, proved inadequate to offset these forces. This was due to the fact that for the most part imbalances in payments in the region were financed with hard currencies, so that countries were as cautious in restricting purchases from each other as from other sources, while some forms of credit that were not on offer in intra-regional trade were available in trade with the North. If regional payment arrangements are to protect intra-regional trade at times of general foreign exchange crisis, then it is essential that the imbalances within the region are not financed by dollars or other hard currency, but by credit with the payments union, or a non-convertible Latin American currency, a 'Peso'. (The Andean Reserve Fund has already issued such an 'Andean Peso', but on a limited scale, and with quite tight restrictions on its use.)

Broadly then, in the 1960s and 1970s the regional monetary arrangements within the South can be regarded as a significant achievement, in contradiction to the widely-propagated myth that unity among the South is all talk and no action. While the experience of the 1980s has revealed problems, countries in Latin America are now beginning to consider some strengthening of arrangements in response to these problems. There is considerable potential for further developments in regional payments arrangements – with respect to country coverage, and the content of the agreements. In particular, clearing house agreements need to put much greater emphasis on credit creation for trade between members, while mutual balance of payments support schemes could be extended in country coverage and in the quality of assistance provided.

Some of the schemes aim eventually at monetary union. While this has major benefits in extending the size of the market, reducing transactions costs, and economising on foreign exchange reserves (especially if trade restrictions are simultaneously abolished within the union), it can also create serious problems for weaker partners, which are not only bad in themselves, but may also prevent the realisation of the union or lead to its break-up. Consequently, monetary union should only be pursued if (1) a system can feasibly be introduced for protecting the weaker partners; and (2) there is full political support for such close relationships, and for the limitations on sovereignty implied. In the absence of these conditions, less ambitious types of cooperation can be extremely fruitful and are likely to have greater long-term viability.

While there has been progress in regional arrangements, almost nothing has been achieved in the monetary area in terms of Third World countries as a whole. Yet all-South monetary arrangements could be of tremendous benefit. In the first place, inter-regional trade is still very small.

The possibilities of developing dynamic export markets among fast-growing countries in different regions are great. An enormous variety of goods is produced within the South, so much so that the less developed countries could get everything they need from other Southern countries. Secondly, developing viable alternative technologies over a wide range of products requires a collective effort across regions. Thirdly, with the debt-led foreign exchange crisis which is so pervasive, South–South trade across regions, making little or no use of Northern currencies, could permit higher growth of output and employment and a higher level of investment. Finally, if the South is to counter the current Northern domination of financial institutions and monetary decisions, effective Southern institutions are needed. The rest of this essay describes some possibilities. Each would not only provide direct benefits to most countries, but would also improve Southern bargaining power on monetary matters.

MONETARY ARRANGEMENTS FOR THE SOUTH AS A WHOLE

Monetary and financial institutions for the South as a whole have been proposed in four areas: the institution of a South Currency or a Payments Union; the development of Commodity Reserves to act as foreign exchange reserves for the South; the institution of a Southern IMF; and a South Bank. There is some potential overlap between the proposals, and any new institution could in principle perform more than one of the proposed functions.

1. *A South currency or payments union*   The proposal for a South

currency is for Third World countries to issue their own currency – Rocnabs – for part payment for goods and services exchanged among themselves.[10] By issuing their own currency, liquidity and purchasing power within the South would be increased. Countries' ability to buy imports from other Third World countries would increase, as would the markets for their products in other countries. The financial restraint on trade would be relaxed. The proposal would be equivalent to a Payments Union or Clearing House which offered mutual credit among members. But unlike existing clearing house arrangements it would cover all the South, or as many countries as wished to join, and would involve less administration than a clearing house, which generally requires all transactions among members to be cleared at the centre. The size of the Rocnab issue could be determined accordingly to the liquidity needs and trade potential of the South. The currency would thus permit Southern levels of liquidity and demand to be partially independent of Northern decisions.

The most frequently raised objection to this scheme is that some countries would accumulate Rocnabs – countries in permanent surplus with other countries in the South – while other countries, in chronic deficit with other Third World countries, would soon run out of Rocnabs. To avoid this, there would need to be incentives and penalties designed to encourage long-run balance. To some extent the scheme itself would automatically generate its own incentives, since those who accumulated Rocnabs would be wasting purchasing power unless they switched their purchases to the South. But in addition, it would be possible to attach special penalties to the accumulation of Rocnabs over a prolonged period (e.g., by charging interest on them). In Keynes's proposals for a world clearing union, which he put forward at Bretton Woods, he devised a set of five penalties for persistent creditors.[11] While something similar would be appropriate here, there is a major difference between a world payments union and one that involves only a sub-set of countries; in the latter case, countries have the option of withdrawing from the Union and trading with other partners, whereas with a world system there is no alternative. However, given the strong mutual advantages to be gained from an operational system, many countries would be likely to opt in.

It must be emphasised that the same advantages would be achieved with a Southern payments union, which offered mutual credit. This credit would be like a Southern currency.

There have been some attempts to link existing clearing arrangements, and a Coordination Committee was established by UNCTAD to help develop such links. Linking existing arrangements could represent a first step towards a Southern payments union. However, the current arrangements cover only about half the countries in the Third World and, in general, credit forms a minor aspect. Establishing a new payments union – to which existing clearing arrangements could be linked – seems likely to be more effective both in terms of creating credit, and in establishing links between current arrangements.

2. *Commodities as foreign exchange reserves*   Non-oil developing countries hold about US$75 billion in reserves, consisting of gold and currencies of developed countries (dollars, chiefly, but also yen, sterling, etc.). They use their own exports (of which a large proportion is commodities) to finance these reserves, thereby strengthening the currencies of the countries whose money is held as foreign exchange reserves, and the economies of gold producers. If they replaced foreign exchange reserves by stocks of commodities, their reserve accumulation would instead strengthen commodity prices and their own economies (see Gulati, where this proposal is advanced).[12] This could be achieved by purchasing and storing commodities produced in the South. There is a variety of ways in which such a store could be financed. The initial build-up could be financed by contributions of commodities, by the use of Southern currencies and/or any Southern credit arrangement (as discussed above), or by using 'hard' currency from existing foreign exchange reserves. The commodity reserves could then be used as existing foreign exchange reserves, selling them when countries needed foreign exchange, or borrowing against the security of the commodity stocks. Countries would need to make contributions to finance the storage costs in proportion to the quantity of reserves held.

Commodities would be more inflation-proof than currency reserves, but they would not earn interest. Therefore, at times of positive real interest rates, there would be a cost to countries of holding such reserves, which would include the cost of handling the stocks of commodities plus the real interest foregone. But at times of rapid inflation and negative real interest rates, countries holding commodities would gain as compared with holding dollars. There could also be cyclical problems. Countries are liable to need to run down reserves when commodity prices are low and accumulate them when prices are high. Consequently, not only would this tendency cause them to buy and sell at the wrong time, from the point of view of commodity prices, but also their actions would accentuate commodity price fluctuations. This represents a serious defect in the proposal. It would suggest that commodities should form only some proportion of total reserves, so that big losses could be avoided by using a combination of foreign exchange and commodity reserves. This cyclical problem could be countered if industrialised countries were also persuaded to hold commodities as reserves.[13] But the latter proposal has not found support among the industrialised countries. While some of the problems noted suggest that commodities should not entirely replace existing reserves, there is a strong case for further exploration of the possibilities of diversifying Third World reserves into commodities and Third World currencies, taking on more of the responsibility for liquidity creation and commodity price stabilisation, and reducing dependence on the North.

3. *A Southern IMF*   This would represent an extension of the mutual balance of payments schemes, currently in use in some regions, to the whole of the South, so that countries in payments difficulties in one part of the Third World could get some financial support (and policy advice) from other parts. It would have considerable advantages compared with regional arrangements, since regional payments problems tend to occur more or less simultaneously in all countries in the region, while there is much greater variation across regions, as for example with the OPEC surplus in the 1970s, and the Asian surpluses in the mid-1980s. A Southern IMF could not replace the present IMF, but could give countries some alternative source of finance and policy advice. The policy-formulation could turn out to be one of the most important aspects of a Southern IMF, as Third World countries would have the opportunity to develop their own conditionality, more in accordance with their objectives and philosophy, which could also prove extremely useful in negotiations with the 'real' IMF.

4. *A South bank*   This was first suggested at a meeting of the Group of 77 in 1982, and UNCTAD produced a feasibility study in 1983.[14] The bank would be financed by subscriptions from member countries. As outlined, the bank would include some of the functions of a Southern IMF, providing balance of payments support to countries in difficulties, using its own conditionality.

Other functions included provision of export credit, or export credit guarantees, finance for commodity price stabilisation and support for regional payments and credit arrangements. As developed, the proposal was probably over-ambitious in covering so many functions, although there is considerable merit in each of the proposals considered separately. No real progress has been made in instituting such a bank.

CONCLUSIONS

Southern monetary arrangements can play a vital role in supporting Third World countries' trade and incomes, and offsetting the balkanisation that followed the previous imperial currency areas. Not only are Southern arrangements valuable for their immediate effects, but they can also strengthen Southern bargaining capacity and power. Their role is particularly important at times of world economic crisis when North–South trade and financial arrangements falter. Over the past thirty years progress has been made in developing and expanding regional payments arrangements in the Third World. But these proved rather ineffective during the crisis in the 1980s, and there have been no arrangements made at the level of the South as a whole. There are very great potential gains from schemes for the South as a whole but also, obviously, many political obstacles to agreement. From a pragmatic point of view, more progress may be made by improving, extending and linking regional agreements than by grand new Southern schemes. But there is no reason why efforts should not be made in both directions. Third World countries could have much more control over economic and financial developments than they are currently exerting. Third World arguments for international monetary reform and a new Bretton Woods arguments have had little response from the North. They could initiate their own South Bretton Woods as a step on the way to realising the international monetary reform which is within the reach of the Third World.

NOTES

1. Williamson (1984).
2. Lipton and Griffith-Jones (1984).

 3. Pratten (1971).
 4. Lewis (1980) pp. 555–64.
 5. Medina (1983).
 6. Robson (1983).
 7. Hulugalle (1990).
 8. Hulugalle (1990).
 9. Ocampo (1985).
10. See Chapter 10 in this volume.
11. Kahn (1976).
12. Gulati (1983).
13. Hatt *et al*. (1964).
14. UNCTAD (1983).

10 A New Currency for Trade Among Developing Countries*
with Michael Stewart

THE NEED FOR NEW MONETARY ARRANGEMENTS

Policies which would encourage the expansion of trade between developing countries include trade preferences and infrastructural and institutional changes, as well as monetary arrangements. This essay concentrates on monetary arrangements, which provide an essential background to other arrangements – a background which may permit or encourage policies leading to an expansion of trade among developing countries, or one which may inhibit such policies. Producing a satisfactory set of monetary arrangements may therefore play an important role in securing the other policy changes needed, as well as having its own effect on trade flows.

Considerable progress has been made, at the regional and sub-regional levels, in developing monetary arrangements which provide for clearing activities, a small amount of mutual credit, and increasingly some joint management of international reserves.[1] But these arrangements, which parallel and support other types of economic cooperation, apply only at the regional and sub-regional levels. There is no special monetary arrangement among different regions in the third world.

The regional and sub-regional trade and monetary arrangements appear to have had considerable success in promoting trade expansion among countries within the groupings. The absence of similar arrangements *between* regions, however, is reflected in the very low level of trade between them. Developing countries' imports of manufactures from developing countries in other regions were only 3.8 per cent of total developing countries' imports of manufactures in 1978, as compared with 7.3 per cent for such trade among countries of the same region. What are needed, therefore, are Third World

* *Trade and Development*, 2 (Autumn 1980).

arrangements to facilitate inter-regional trade, as well as intra-regional trade.[2]

Monetary arrangements form a particularly appropriate instrument for a global approach, as well as being an essential precondition for other arrangements. This is because it is difficult to design infrastructural or institutional changes which would significantly affect trade flows over the Third World as a whole, as compared to such changes designed to encourage trade within a particular region. Moreover, trading preferences at the Third World level have also met with difficulties, as is shown by the few signatories (16) and small scope of the one Protocol designed to encourage Third World trade.[3]

Initiatives to enlarge the 1972 Protocol relating to Trade Negotiations among Developing Countries have not met with success. One reason for the apparent reluctance of many countries to enter trade liberalisation agreements is that they fear possible balance of payments difficulties and a consequent loss of their scarce reserves of convertible currencies. This was one of the main conclusions of the UNCTAD report on payments arrangements,[4] which argued that monetary arrangements could play a critical role in easing such fears by providing a cushion which would make trade liberalisation more acceptable. The arguments in the UNCTAD report related to regional trade liberalisation. They are even more powerful in relation to global measures, where the unknowns and therefore the risks of trade liberalisation are much greater.

Broadly, monetary arrangements may fulfil four functions: (a) to encourage multilateral trade by providing convertibility, via clearing arrangements, between the countries concerned; (b) to encourage the use of local currencies as a means of payment in international trade; (c) to provide for the joint use of reserves of foreign currencies to assist countries in coping with temporary fluctuations; and (d) to create credit.

A global arrangement designed to encourage trade between developing countries should give the fourth function – the mutual creation of credit – the prime emphasis. The first objective would be important if Third World trade were being seriously inhibited by widespread bilateralism or lack of convertibility, but the evidence suggests that this is not the case. The second and third objectives are important in their own right, but are not particularly significant in relation to the encouragement of trade between developing countries. Moreover, at a global level they would be very difficult to negotiate. These, along with other changes, might be the outcome rather than the instrument of successful cooperation. Prime emphasis needs to be placed on the fourth function – credit creation among developing countries – because this would provide fall-back reserves if trade liberalisation did lead to unfavourable balance of payments effects and a consequent loss of reserves, and because the existence of sources of credit which were confined to trade among developing countries would itself encourage the development of such trade.

Two other considerations need to be borne in mind. One is that a successful negotiation covering all or most of the Third World requires the agreement of 100 or so countries differing in their stages of development, economic interests, culture, history and tradition. A very important requirement, for any scheme that is likely to be viable, is thus that it should involve a minimum of negotiation and therefore a minimum of detailed and complex provisions.

Secondly, the big differences between Third World countries in terms of the level of economic development mean that the poorer parts of the Third World may open to the same sort of disadvantages *vis-à-vis* the richer developing countries as the Third World as a whole is *vis-à-vis* the advanced countries. To secure the continuing cooperation of the poorer parts of the Third World, it is essential that any workable scheme should provide adequate protection for the interests of the poorer countries.

PROPOSAL FOR A NEW CURRENCY: Rocnabs

It is proposed that the developing countries should issue a new form of international money.[5] This new currency unit (Rocnab) would be issued to developing countries for use in payment for goods and services from other developing countries. The new currency would be issued by an institution set up for the purpose by the developing countries.

Every developing country which decided to participate in the scheme would agree to accept Rocnabs from other participants in part payment for goods and services rendered, the balance being paid, as before, in convertible currencies. The Rocnabs would thus increase the purchasing power of each developing country over the goods and services of every other developing country. How big the increase in purchasing power would be would depend on the size of the issue and the ratio of payment in Rocnabs to payment in convertible currencies.

The scheme would amount to the provision of credit by each developing country to every other developing country. This would encourage, but not compel, such countries to buy more from each other. Every developing country would be a potential gainer, in that it would acquire purchasing power over the goods of other developing countries and extend its own markets. But no country need lose, since there would be no compulsion on it to sell its goods to other developing countries, if hard currency markets were available. Because of this, and because the scheme would not reduce countries' freedom to impose trade restrictions, it would not endanger the prosperity of the poorer developing countries.

The scheme would thus provide a major incentive for developing countries to redirect their trading activities to other developing countries – as purchasers if they were short of foreign exchange, and as suppliers if they were short of markets. At the same time, it would be relatively simple to operate, and would not require a great deal of preliminary or ongoing negotiation. Nor would it – as many schemes do – endanger the prosperity of the weaker regions.

THE PROPOSAL IN GREATER DETAIL

This section discusses in some detail how the proposed Rocnabs system might work. It is not intended to be an exhaustive or definitive account, but simply to provide a basis for discussion. At various points, alternative solutions to particular problems are suggested.

Eligibility

Basically, all members of the Group of 77 would be eligible to participate in the scheme, though it would be for the Group as a whole to decide on eligibility in marginal cases. It would not be necessary for a very large number of countries to participate initially. Obviously, it would be preferable to start with as wide a participation as possible, in order both to increase the attractiveness of the scheme, which depends on Rocnabs being widely accepted as a means of international payment, and to maximise the scope for the expansion of Third World trade. But the scheme could be started by a relatively small number of countries whose actual or potential trade with each other is large, and others could accede later. One possibility would be to permit additional countries to join only at specified intervals (e.g., three years) so as to increase the incentive to join from the start, and to reduce the administrative complexities which would arise from a continual trickle of new members.

Administration

The countries participating in the scheme would appoint a Board of Management of perhaps 10 or 15 members, serviced by a small permanent secretariat. The Board of Management might at first be required to reach unanimous decisions, but in time this system might be replaced by a system of weighted majority voting.

The Board of Management would be responsible for setting up and operating the Rocnab scheme. In particular, it would be responsible for deciding such questions as the *numéraire* in terms of which the value of the Rocnab is to be fixed; how many Rocnabs should be created; how these Rocnabs should be allocated between the participating countries; what rules would be needed, and how they should be interpreted.

Creation and Allocation of Rocnabs

Rocnabs (like Special Drawing Rights, SDRs) would consist of book entries in ledgers; the ledgers would be kept by the secretariat, under the supervision of the Board of Management. Rocnabs would thus be created by a simple decision of the Board of Management. Similarly, it would be for the Board to decide at what point further units should be created. To avoid the uncertainty that would attend the frequent creation of units, while ensuring that the scheme was flexible enough to evolve in line with changing conditions, the initial creation of Rocnabs might be for a period such as three years, with provision for a review of the scheme after it had been in operation for two years.

Once a decision about the size of the initial creation of Rocnabs had been taken, the Board of Management would choose a formula for allocating them among the countries participating in the scheme. One possibility would be to base the allocation on IMF quotas; such a formula would have a firm basis in existing arrangements, and might be widely acceptable. Other possibilities would be to base the allocation of Rocnabs on the value of a participating country's total imports, or imports of manufactured goods from the rest of the world; or on its imports from developing countries only. Such formulae might be more difficult to compute, and might require relatively frequent reweighting, but they would have the advantage of being based on variables of particular relevance to the scheme.

Method of Operation

The essence of the scheme is that participating countries would agree to accept some agreed proportion of their export receipts from other participating countries in the form of Rocnabs. The proportion in question would need to be carefully chosen by the Board of Management. Initially, at any rate, it would need to be low enough not to involve such an abrupt departure from existing arrangements as to deter countries from participating. At the same time, it would need to be high enough to have a real effect on trading patterns and to make participants feel that the whole operation was worth while. For purposes of illustration, the proportion of export receipts that participating countries would agree to accept in the form of Rocnabs is here assumed to be 25 per cent.

One important question to be decided would be the commodity coverage of the scheme. There are some arguments for confining the scheme to manufactured products. One is that the scheme is primarily designed to promote greater trade in manufactured products between developing countries. Another is that the relatively inelastic demand for primary products, and their relatively homogeneous nature, make it less desirable and less feasible to include them, since in many cases countries can benefit most from selling these commodities on the world markets for hard currencies.

However, there are strong arguments in favour of making the scheme comprehensive in coverage. Many of the less developed among the developing countries might find it difficult to sell manufactures to other developing countries, and would therefore be unable to participate fully in the scheme unless they could earn Rocnabs from primary commodity sales. Similarly, other more developed countries might be in net surplus in manufactures and would find little use for Rocnabs unless they were able to use them to buy primary commodities. There would also be difficulties of classification if the scheme were confined to some particular type of goods. If the scheme included primary commodities, producers of commodities in strong demand in world markets might be unwilling to participate. But if such countries were short of foreign exchange and international liquidity overall, they might none the less be willing to join the scheme for the credit it provided. They could offset the potential loss in convertible currency on their sales of primary commodities either by raising the prices charged when the commodity was sold to developing countries, or by diverting their sales towards advanced countries. A further possibility – if this question proved a major stumbling-block in negotiations – would be to permit countries to exempt one or two specified primary commodities at the start of the scheme. It must be accepted that countries which do not suffer from a shortage of foreign exchange reserves and have plentiful hard currency markets for their goods would not gain from the scheme, and would be unlikely to join except as part of a strategy to support Third World cooperation.

Although some basic rules would need to be laid down by the Board of Management, to a large extent the scheme would be self-operating, and would avoid the need to seek agreement on an extensive set of regulations with which all members would be required to comply. Because it would be in the interests of each participating country to maximise (up to the 25 per cent limit) the Rocnab content of its payments to other participants, each country could be left to work out the method of implementing the scheme within its own borders which best suited its own situation.

For the purpose of illustration, it may be worth considering how the scheme might work in the case of three countries characterised by different degrees of state intervention. In country *A*, where imports are handled by a state trading corporation, the scheme would be activated by instructing officials of the corporation to give a greater degree of preference to imports from other participating countries. In the case of these imports, the Central Bank would arrange for 25 per cent of the payment to be affected by a transfer of Rocnabs.

In country *B*, where there is a fairly comprehensive system of exchange control and import licensing, the government would make it clear to private traders in the granting of import licences and permission to purchase foreign exchange, a certain degree of preference would be accorded to traders importing from other participating countries. In this way, importers would be given an incentive to switch their source of supply from developed to developing countries. The Central Bank's role would be the same as in country *A*.

Country *C* is a country where there is no effective system of import licensing or exchange control. In the case of some such countries – many of the OPEC countries being obvious examples – the reason for the absence of restrictions on trade and payments is that the availability of foreign exchange is not a constraint on development; such countries might not wish to participate in the Rocnab scheme. But in other cases, such countries might feel that they would benefit from joining. If country *C* was of this type, it would probably need to implement the Rocnab scheme by providing private traders with a direct financial incentive to switch imports to other participating countries. One way of doing this would be to make currencies of other developing countries available to traders at a suitable discount. Another method would be for the government to make a grant to the importer which would cover some proportion of the c.i.f. value of his imports from participating countries. Both these solutions, it must be recognised, would create two problems. One is that the government would need to make funds available to finance the discount or grant; the other is that in each case domestically-produced goods would lose some of their preferential treatment in comparison with imports from other participating countries. It would, however, be for the government of the country concerned to weigh these short-term costs of the scheme against its long-term benefits.

These are direct ways in which the scheme would affect trading patterns in the short run. Most countries in fact exhibit characteristics of each of the three models, and would be able to operate the scheme in all three ways. In the longer run, for all types of country, the existence of Rocnabs would encourage the negotiation of trading agreements – tariffs, quotas, trading agreements, and exchange rate manipulation – conducive to greater trade among participating countries – for example, greater concessions under the Agreement on the Global System of Trade Preferences among Developing countries, which was negotiated in the 1980s.

Limits to Changes in Rocnab Balances

In the course of time, as the scheme continued to operate, some countries' balances of Rocnabs would be run down or even eliminated, while those of other countries would increase to levels well above the original allocation. An extreme example of a country which would soon exhaust its holdings of Rocnabs would be one which already imported a lot of its goods from other developing countries, or was induced to do so by the Rocnab scheme, but whose exports went exclusively to developed countries. An extreme example of a country which would soon accumulate large holdings of Rocnabs would be one which imported exclusively from developed countries, and continued to do so despite the Rocnab scheme, and which at the same time exported exclusively to other developing countries. In between these two extreme (and hypothetical) cases would be a large number of countries whose payments and receipts of Rocnabs would not be precisely in balance, and which would therefore either build up or run down their holdings of Rocnabs as time went on.

To some extent, the buildup or rundown of Rocnab balances would be self-adjusting; countries with rising Rocnab balances would have an incentive to switch their imports to other participating countries, and countries with falling Rocnab balances would have an incentive to increase their exports to other participating countries. Nevertheless, there would still be some countries which would build up large Rocnab balances, and others whose balances would run down to little or nothing. The Board of Management would need to decide what action, if any, it should take in order to prevent or minimise this process.

The countries which ran down their Rocnab balances ('Rocnab-deficit countries') would present the lesser problem. By definition, they would be furthering the objectives of the scheme by maintaining or increasing their net imports of goods from other participating countries. The impulse towards these increased imports would cease when their Rocnab balances were exhausted, but would not necessarily be reversed.

A greater problem would be posed by countries which accumulated increasing holdings of Rocnabs ('Rocnab-surplus countries'). If they felt that they were accumulating Rocnabs for which they had no use, instead of the reserves of foreign exchange which would be the alternative, they might leave the scheme – or indeed refuse to join it in the first place – and the viability of the scheme as a whole might be threatened.

There are a number of ways in which these dangers might be reduced. One would be to permit the rediscounting of Rocnabs by Rocnab-surplus countries to Rocnab-deficit countries. This would permit the surplus countries to get rid of their surplus Rocnabs, and deficit countries to replenish their holdings of Rocnabs. There would, however, be two drawbacks to this solution. One is that it would not be attractive to the surplus countries unless the discount was very small, nor attractive to the deficit countries unless it was relatively large. The second and more general drawback is that it might be impossible to establish confidence in the scheme unless it was agreed that Rocnabs were to be regarded as having a standard purchasing power in terms of international currencies, and were not permitted to change hands at a discount.

A second way of trying to deal with the problem would be by

progressively reducing the proportion of Rocnabs which a country with increasing Rocnab balances was required to accept in payment for its exports. Thus, when its Rocnab balances had reached a certain multiple of its original allocation, an Rocnab-surplus country would be required to accept only 20 per cent of its export receipts in the form of Rocnabs; beyond a certain further multiple, only 15 per cent; and so on. This would given Rocnab-surplus countries an assurance that there was some limit to the Rocnab balances they would be required to accumulate, and at the same time would be acceptable to Rocnab-deficit countries whose ability to pay for imports in Rocnabs was in any case being eroded. The point at which the scaling-down of the Rocnab content of export receipts began, and the rate at which it proceeded, would need to be carefully judged by the Board of Management. It should not happen so soon as to prejudice the effectiveness of the scheme, but it should not happen so late as to make the scheme unattractive to potential Rocnab-surplus countries.

It must not be concluded from this discussion that Rocnab-surplus countries would necessarily be net losers from the scheme. They would be gaining markets for their goods – indeed, this is how they would accumulate Rocnabs – and receiving 75 per cent of the pro-ceeds in terms of hard currencies. Moreover, if they believed that they could sell the goods they were selling to participating countries to hard currency markets for 100 per cent hard currency, they would be free to use a combination of controls, direct trading and financial incentives to divert their exports away from participating countries, thus eliminating their surplus position in Rocnabs. They might also, by similar means, increase the price they asked for their goods when sold to participating countries, thus effectively gaining compensation for the Rocnab proportion of payment.

In the longer run, as trade between less developed countries grew, fresh allocations of Rocnabs would be required. The pattern of these fresh allocations would need to take account of the existing pattern of Rocnab holdings.

Interest Payments

One question that would need to be decided is whether interest payments should be made and levied in relation to Rocnab use, and if so what conditions should govern such payments. Interest is earned on most of the assets in which international reserves are held, including SDRs; the only obvious exception is gold. If interest were not paid on holdings of Rocnabs in excess of the initial allocation, this would make them considerably inferior to other reserves, quite apart from their non-convertibility. However, any such interest payments ought not to be too high, since Rocnabs would not be intended as a reserve currency, to be accumulated, but as a trading currency, to be used: the incentive to hold large quantities idle should not be too great. The best way to finance such interest payments would probably be to charge interest to countries which ran down their Rocnab balances. Such countries would have received credit, and would in the normal course of events expect to pay interest on this credit. But again, since the point of Rocnabs would be to spend them, the interest levied should not be excessive. In both cases – interest payments and interest levies – holdings would need to rise above or fall below the par issue by a significant amount – say, 20 per cent – and stay at this level for a period – say, at least 3 months – before interest payments commenced.

Relationship to Regional Payments Arrangements

In recent years a number of regional payments schemes have been established in the Third World, and others are contemplated. The proposed Rocnab scheme would fulfil a different and complementary function from these regional schemes, and would in no way impair their activities. The Rocnab scheme would differ from the regional schemes in two respects. First, it would cover the whole of the Third World, encouraging trade between the regions, as well as within them. Secondly, its prime function would be to create credit between developing countries rather than to ease clearing arrangements. By contrast, the main aim of the regional schemes is to provide clearing arrangements; credit creation is generally very small and of no more than minor significance. The role of regional schemes in easing payments between countries, encouraging the use of national currencies for trade, and providing for joint reserve management on a regional basis would remain as vital as ever. Countries which are members of regional arrangements could hold Rocnabs individually. Alternatively, where a system of joint monetary institutions and reserve management is well advanced, Rocnabs could be held and used by the regional monetary institution. Where joint use is adopted, the Rocnab scheme would strengthen regional institutions. The relationship between the proposed Rocnab scheme and other proposals for developing country monetary cooperation is discussed more fully in the Appendix.

Provisions for Withdrawal From the Scheme

Although it is to be hoped that the dynamic benefits accruing to participating countries in the form of increasing exports and greater specialisation would persuade them to remain in the Rocnab scheme once they had joined it, the possibility remains that some countries might at some point wish to withdraw from it. The Board of Management would need to agree on the conditions upon which withdrawal might be permitted.

The Role of a Reserve Fund

The scheme, as outlined above, would not need any hard currency backing. Its backing would lie in its acceptability. Given the chronic shortage of hard currency reserves among developing countries, this could be a major advantage of the scheme. It might be argued that there could be a role for some degree of hard currency backing were the finance available, either from international institutions (e.g., SDRs allocated for this purpose), or from OPEC countries, or from a general contribution from the participating countries. The use of hard currency backing might be threefold. First, the knowledge of its existence might encourage countries to join the scheme, even if there were no formal role for it. Secondly, the fund could be used to buy back Rocnabs for reallocation from chronic Rocnab-surplus countries, if (a) their surplus had reached a particular level (e.g., more than 200 per cent of their original allocation), (b) they continued to accept Rocnabs in part-payment for exports, and (c) the cause of the chronic surplus were identified and measures taken by the contributory countries to eliminate it. This is an alternative solution to the chronic-surplus country problem to those discussed earlier,[5] assuming the existence of hard currency backing. Thirdly, such a fund could be used to finance the administration of the scheme, and perhaps such outgoings as some of the interest payments on surplus holdings of Rocnabs.

There would, however, be drawbacks in such a fund. First, there are the obvious problems of raising the resources for such a fund. Secondly, the existence and use of a hard currency reserve raises the possibility of its exhaustion, and the severe – quite possibly insuperable – problem that such exhaustion would create. Confidence in Rocnabs would then vary according to the state of the reserve. The scheme would suffer from continually 'looking over its shoulder' at the potential implications for its reserve position of various courses of action, while it would probably be terminated altogether if the reserve ran out. This would be particularly ironic in view of the lack of any real need for reserve backing. Finally, the existence of a reserve fund would give great power to the main actual and potential contributors to the reserve, a power which might not be exercised in the interests of the participating countries as a whole.

ORDERS OF MAGNITUDE

A reference to the size of the initial creation of Rocnabs was made earlier. The appropriate size of the initial creation of Rocnabs is very difficult to determine.[6] It would be influenced by views about the likely growth of world trade and world reserves; by judgements about the extent to which developing countries can satisfy each others' need for manufactured goods, in both the short and the long term; and by the number of countries which decided to participate in the scheme, and the vigour with which they sought to increase their mutual trade.

It is because of these uncertainties that it was suggested above that the initial allocation of Rocnabs should be for only three years, and that the scheme should be reviewed after two years. The fact that after two or three years it would be much easier to create new Rocnabs than to cancel existing ones is an argument for erring on the side of caution in the first allocation. As opposed to this, it can be argued that if participating countries were to make a significant effort to restructure the pattern of their trading relationships, they would have to be confident that Rocnabs would be available on an adequate scale. If it appeared that their allocation of Rocnabs was too small to make much difference, or that it would be quickly exhausted in the event of any significant switch of imports to other participants, it would be difficult ever to get the Rocnab scheme off the ground.

Although the size of the initial creation of Rocnabs would have to be decided by the Board of Management in the light of the detailed consideration of existing and potential trade patterns and of the views of the participating countries, it may be worth making some approximate calculations in order to indicate possible orders of magnitude. Because the main impact of the scheme would be likely to be on trade in manufactures, the calculations are related to this category of trade. They are based on the assumption that the proportion of export receipts that participating countries agreed to accept in the form of

Rocnabs was 25 per cent. It is also assumed, to simplify the exposition, that OPEC countries, whose imports are not on the whole constrained by a shortage of foreign exchange, would not participate in the scheme, but that all other developing countries would; and that Rocnabs are expressed in terms of US dollars, with one Rocnab equalling one US dollar.

In 1988, the latest year for which full figures are readily available, imports of manufactured goods by developing countries from the world as a whole were approximately \$330 billion; of this, around one-quarter came from other developing countries (using 1985 ratios from World Bank, 1987). It does not seem implausible to argue that these imports from other developing countries could have been, say, a third, or \$27 billion, higher had the foreign exchange resources to finance them been available. These extra imports, although large in relation to existing imports from other developing countries, would have raised their total manufactured imports by only 8 per cent, and would have required only a small increase in the manufacturing output of the developing countries as a whole.

Assuming for the sake of simplicity that there was no offsetting fall in developing countries' imports from developed countries, and that this therefore represented a net increase, what availability of Rocnabs might have been expected to bring about this result? If one takes as a guide the fact that for developing countries the ratio of the value of reserves to the value of annual imports in recent years has been about 30 per cent,[7] this might suggest that extra reserves of a total value of \$8 billion might have been associated with \$27 billion of extra imports. However, since Rocnabs would be a very specialised kind of reserve, which could be used in payment only when combined with three times as much foreign exchange, the creation of Rocnabs would need to be \$27 billion. Thus, in 1988, instead of importing \$83 billion worth of manufactured goods from other developing countries at a foreign exchange cost of \$83 billion, participating countries would have imported \$110 billion worth, paying \$83 billion in foreign exchange, and \$27 billion in Rocnabs.[8]

The above calculations relate to 1988. If the scheme is introduced, the initial creation of Rocnabs would need to be higher to take account of inflation. It must again be stressed, however, that these figures are derived from very rough and simplified calculations and are not intended to be at all precise; they are designed solely to give an impression of the order of magnitude that might be involved.

CONCLUSION

It is now widely accepted that if developing countries are to advance and prosper they must rely to a large extent on helping each other. A crucial requirement of such collective self-reliance is an expansion of mutual trade. Although considerable progress has been made in establishing trading arrangements at the regional and sub-regional levels, little or no progress has been made in expanding trade among developing countries as a whole. One reason for this lack of progress is the fear of the balance of payments consequences of trade liberalisation; another is the formidable complexity of the negotiations that would be needed to establish new trading and monetary arrangements for 100 or so countries.

It has been proposed in the present essay that the problem should be approached from a new angle. Developing countries as a whole should take the essentially simple step of creating a new currency and allocating it among themselves. This new currency would be used in part-settlement of transactions between them. Substantial benefits could accrue to developing countries from the adoption of this proposal. In the short run, it would give them an incentive to switch trade away from developed countries and towards each other. Countries with spare capacity, particularly in the manufacturing sector, would find new markets; countries with a shortage of foreign exchange would find a new source of credit. In the longer run, as the incentive to build up new trading links between developing countries bore fruit, there would be increasing scope for mutually beneficial specialisation, for the achievement of economies of scale, and for the employment of appropriate technologies.

In sum, it is argued that a measure which should be relatively easy for developing countries to agree upon and implement could yield very substantial benefits.

Appendix: The Relationship Between the Proposed Rocnab Scheme and Other Proposals for Developing Country Monetary Cooperation

It is worth discussing briefly the relationship of the Rocnab scheme with some other schemes that have been suggested: the proposal for a reserve fund, the proposal for a payments union for all developing countries, the Sanbar proposal for developing country export credits, and the proposal for joint exchange rate management by developing countries.

A RESERVE FUND OR A RESERVE CENTRE

In the report of the Group of Experts on payments arrangements among developing countries for trade expansion,[9] the majority of the experts favoured a reserve fund. Such a fund consists of convertible currencies subscribed by member countries; the managers of the fund then grant credit on an automatic or a discretionary basis. Such credit may be granted according to countries' overall balance of payments, or in relation to countries' payments deficits with other member countries. If credit is granted on the basis of the overall balance of payments position, the scheme does not provide a particular incentive for trade among developing countries, but it does help countries in temporary overall foreign exchange difficulties, and is a first step towards the joint management of international reserves, which could play an important part in developing country monetary cooperation.

If, on the other hand, credit is granted to countries according to their balance of payments position *vis-à-vis* other members, its effects may be similar to those of the proposed Rocnabs, although the reserve fund requires the contribution and therefore the immobilisation of receipts of convertible currencies from members, which the Rocnab would not.

PAYMENTS UNION PROPOSALS

There are many variants of proposals for a developing country Payments Union,[10] just as there are many variants of Regional Payments Unions. Most involve clearing arrangements through the Union between member countries, either on a voluntary or a compulsory basis. Such clearing arrangements have the advantage of encouraging developing country trade where this has been inhibited by the non-convertibility of currencies and bilateral trading arrangements. But generally, given the widespread use of sterling and the dollar as trading currencies, bilateralism and non-convertibility are not major factors inhibiting trade. The provision of clearing arrangements in a Payments Union has the disadvantage that it makes considerable administrative demands on the Union. Payments Unions may also involve the extension of credit, on an automatic or a discretionary basis between members. In so far as the credit provided for is substantial and automatic, the effects would be the same as those of the issue of Rocnabs, and indeed, by describing such credit as Rocnabs, the Rocnab proposal could be incorporated in a general developing country Payments Union. However, the Rocnab proposal, as described, deliberately avoids the full-blown cooperation and administration required of a Payments Union – the requirements for which would probably prevent the Union from ever getting off the ground. Payments Union proposals also sometimes incorporate suggestions for mutual reserve management, which is not provided for in the Rocnab scheme, although it could operate in parallel with it.

THE SANBAR PROPOSAL

The Sanbar proposal for developing country export credit[11] is a proposal for an export credit guarantee facility which would operate through the regional banks, to guarantee long- and medium-term export credit for goods sold by developing countries to other developing countries. The provision of export credit on goods and services sold between developing countries would have the effect of encouraging inter-developing country trade, which, it is argued, is unable to compete normally with the credit terms offered by developed countries. It is intended that such institutions as the World Bank should offer a guarantee of the export credits. This scheme would differ from the Rocnab scheme and the other schemes so far discussed, in that it would have a direct effect on the traders involved, and would not operate through Central Banks and governmental policies. The other similarities or differences between this and other schemes would depend on the orders of magnitude involved, the terms and conditions of use, etc. One obvious difference is that the Sanbar proposal, as it stands, requires outside aid to get the scheme started, but this need not be a feature of the scheme.

JOINT MANAGEMENT OF THE EXCHANGE RATE

It has been suggested that developing countries should jointly devalue their exchange rates against the advanced countries' currencies, while maintaining their exchange rates *vis-à-vis* each other. This would have the effect of encouraging trade between the developing countries, in much the same way as the issue of Rocnabs, since the hard currency price of goods they bought from each other would fall in relation to goods bought from the advanced countries; simultaneously, the hard currency earnings from sales to advanced countries would rise in relation to earnings from sales by developing countries to each other. In both these respects, the scheme resembles the proposed Rocnab scheme. Again, however, the joint devaluation scheme would have a direct effect on incentives for traders, rather than the more indirect effect of the Rocnabs. The chief objection to the joint devaluation proposal is the virtual impossibility of getting it put into effect, given the enormous amount of cooperation it would require, and the complex system of exchange-rate management which would, quite possibly, be countered by the exchange rate management of the advanced countries.

NOTES

1. See 'A survey of monetary co-operation among developing countries', prepared by J. Gonzales del Valle (TD/B/AC.19/R.6). Also see Chapter 8 in this volume.
2. Similar conclusions were reached by the 1975 Group of Experts: 'So far, preferential trading arrangements have proved successful mainly within sub-regional integration schemes, whereas their application at the regional and inter-regional level is still at an incipient stage and of a limited nature', 'Economic co-operation among developing countries', report of the Group of Experts (October–November 1975)(TD/B/AC.19/1).
3. See GATT (1972) for the text of the 1972 Protocol. See also 'Preferences for mutual trade among developing regions' (TD/B/AC.19/R.9) annex I.
4. 'International payments policies among developing countries' (1970) (TD/B/AC.10/4).
5. The Group of Experts (October–November 1975), commenting on an earlier version of this proposal, recommended that 'the proposal to create a special monetary unit issued to, and acceptable by, developing countries should be further explored . . . Such a proposal would be in line with the spirit of collective self-reliance and might avoid some of the difficulties encountered by more complex arrangements' (TD/B/AC.19/1, para. 37).
6. Similar difficulties were encountered in determining the initial creation of SDRs; see Fleming (1971).
7. In 1980 and 1989, the percentages were 34.1 and 27.2, respectively.
8. $26 billion Rocnabs would have been equivalent to approximately 14 per cent of the reserves of developing countries, which at the end of 1989 stood at $186 billion.
9. TD/B/80 (1966).
10. See, for example, Blatt (1969) and 'Financial and Payments Aspects of Trade Expansion, Economic Cooperation and Regional Integration Among Developing Countries', TD/B/AC.10/4 (1970) and the 1966 Group of Experts report (TD/B/80).
11. See Weinberg (1973).

11 The International Debt Situation and North–South Relations*

Chapter 1 argued that little progress has been made on North–South issues because much of the debate and negotiations have been at a general level, ignoring particular interests. In order to make progress in identifying obstacles to reform in North–South relationships and in formulating proposals with more likelihood of success, it is necessary to examine the particular interests involved in each of the major issues, and how they would be affected by various reforms. Matching of interests and vision, which has been lacking in proposals for North–South reforms in recent years, is needed. This essay examines the debt crisis from this perspective.

The debt situation has become of critical importance to the stability of the world economy, as well as to the prospects of particular countries in the 1980s. Like other North–South issues, it has long been a subject of discussion, with a profusion of proposals for change. While quite a number of changes have occurred, the underlying problem has not been solved. This essay will examine the debt issue from the point of view of the particular interests involved, in order to permit a greater understanding of current developments and to identify which reforms incorporate a sufficient element of particular interests to be worth pursuing with a reasonable chance of success.

The second main section of this essay defines the major actors involved in the debt situation, and considers their objectives and likely responses. But before doing so it is helpful to understand the evolution of the debt situation – and, in particular, why what appeared to be a stable situation, with capital flowing from North to South, developed into a crisis situation, in which capital is flowing, in many instances, from South to North.

---

* This is a revised version of a paper that appeared in *World Development*, 13, 2, 1985

BACKGROUND ANALYSIS

A fundamental concept necessary for understanding the evolution of the debt situation, and the reaction of different actors to it, is the 'basic transfer'. The basic transfer of a country is defined as the net foreign exchange inflow (or outflow) associated with its international borrowing. This basic transfer consists of the difference between the net capital inflow and interest payments on existing debt. The net capital inflow is the difference between the gross inflow and amortisation on past debt. The size (and sign) of the basic transfer is very important, because it represents the foreign exchange the country is gaining, in the period considered, from international capital flows.

The net capital inflow, FN, may be expressed as a rate of increase of total foreign debt, so that if total foreign debt accumulated over the past is D, and d is the percentage rate of increase of this debt, then,

$$FN = d.D$$

Interest payments on past debt are equal to the average rate of interest, r, times the outstanding debt, D, so that interest payments consist of $r.D$. The basic transfer is the net capital inflow *less* interest payments, or

$$d.D - r.D = (d - r)D$$

The basic transfer will therefore be positive or negative according as $d >$ or $< r$.[1]

When a country first accumulates foreign debt, the rate of increase, d, may be very high since the base is very small and foreign borrowing forms such a small proportion of total finance. But as foreign finance comes to form a high proportion of total finance, d naturally starts to fall. Ultimately a limit to the rate of increase in foreign-owned capital is set by the rate of increase of the total capital stock, at the point at which foreign finance forms such a high proportion of total finance that either the national government or the foreign lenders do not wish to increase the proportion further. Hence any country where foreign borrowing is a significant source of finance can expect to have a rapid rate of increase in the stock of foreign capital initially, but subsequently some slowdown is inevitable. A slowdown in d can therefore be expected in the normal course of events without any special factors. However, the rate of increase of foreign debt may also slow down sharply (and even become negative) for a variety of special reasons, such as world recession, or a loss of confidence in the country's repayment capacity. Capital flight by local residents for political or other reasons (e.g., because they believe the currency is likely to be devalued) may also create, or magnify, a negative basic transfer.[2] As the passage of time elapses from when substantial borrowing first starts, the rate of amortisation rises, which requires a higher gross inflow (or rollover) to maintain a given net inflow. This in itself does not necessarily cause a slowdown in the net inflow, but it gives rise to the possibility of sharp fluctuations in the net inflow, making confidence factors more important. Whether or not these confidence factors do cause a significant reduction in d depends on many factors. Three are especially relevant to the analysis. First, the debt situation of the country resulting from its own past borrowing and the burden this imposes on the country's foreign exchange position.

Secondly, a country's past development strategy, which determines its potential to earn the necessary foreign exchange to service the debt. Both these factors influence beliefs about its servicing and repayment capacity. Thirdly, the world environment with respect to markets, commodity prices and capital flows may change in such a way as to lead to a change in d. While the last factor is common to all borrowing countries, the first two differ between countries, explaining why some countries have suffered more from withdrawal of confidence than others.

The other element determining the basic transfer is the interest rate payable on past debt. This depends on the type of debt incurred (official or private), since different interest rates are payable on different types of debt; on the course of world interest rates, and the extent to which debt has been incurred on a variable interest basis; and on the margin the country has to pay over and above LIBOR.

As is well known, after being very low in real terms for most of the 1970s, interest rates rose sharply and remained high (with some fluctuations) in the 1980s. The impact of the rise in interest rates was made worse – especially for some countries – by the increase in the proportion of private debt as a percentage of the total, and the increasing proportion of debt subject to variable interest rates, as indicated in Table 11.1.

The proportion of debt subject to floating interest rates varies considerably among countries. Low-income countries – with only a

Table 11.1   All borrowing countries, debt, selected years

Year	Debt with floating interest as % total
1970	27
1980	46
1989	47

Source: World Bank, *World Debt Tables, 1989–90* (Washington, D.C.: World Bank, 1990).

small amount of borrowing from financial markets – have a low proportion, which has not changed much since 1970. Latin American countries have the highest proportion, rising from 45 per cent in 1970 to 74 per cent in 1989. Interest rates, on average, rose from 6.6 per cent in 1973 to 11 per cent in 1982 and from 9.0 per cent to 13.1 per cent on debt from private creditors. There was some fall in rates in the mid–1980s with a further rise at the end of the decade. In real terms (for example, allowing for terms of trade changes) interest rates on developing country debt remained very high throughout the 1980s.

The basic transfer changed from being substantially positive in most cases to a low, or negative, figure because of the coincidence of a number of factors:

1. a natural slowdown in d as foreign borrowing proceeded;
2. a rise in the average value of r because of rising interest rates, an increasing proportion of private debt, and an increasing proportion of debt subject to floating interest rates;
3. a slowdown in private flows because of confidence factors, arising from the world economic situation and the build-up of debt in particular countries;
4. capital flight by residents anticipating crisis measures.

That the basic transfer should become negative after an initial period of sustained borrowing when it was positive is not surprising, nor unreasonable. Borrowing with interest implies that the total to be repaid, if added up, will exceed the sum initially borrowed. However, the emergence of a negative basic transfer can nonetheless create problems, especially in certain circumstances. Very high interest rates may – as they did in the 1980s – bring on a situation of negative balance prematurely. If countries whose basic transfer is negative are still patently under-developed as compared with lending countries, then the world resource flows implied contradict the direction which would appear desirable, involving poorer countries running trade surpluses, producing more than they consume, while richer countries may consume more than they produce. This situation may all the same be acceptable to countries whose past development strategies have made it relatively easy for them to achieve a trade surplus (as, for example, S. Korea today). But countries whose past strategies have been heavily import substituting may find the switch to achieving a trade surplus very difficult, consequently facing acute foreign exchange problems and being forced to undertake deflationary policies to achieve the trade target required by the basic balance. The situation is likely to be more unacceptable if it occurs – as is likely for the reasons given above – at a time when there is an unfavourable international environment, making a turnround in the trade position particularly difficult.

It is important to distinguish those cases where the basic transfer has become zero or negative because of the underlying situation – slowdown in d to below the ruling rate of interest – from those cases where short-run confidence factors have been responsible for a sudden, but quite possibly temporary, fall in d. In the first type of case, the basic transfer is likely to be negative over the medium term, while in the second type a reversal of the adverse confidence factors may again produce a positive basic transfer. Countries in the first category are more likely to take a hard look at adjustment costs and to bargain toughly on adjustment conditions and rescheduling. Since they cannot expect a positive basic transfer even over the medium term, default becomes an option. In contrast, countries whose basic transfer is negative only because of temporary factors will be more anxious to reach a solution which involves a continued flow of finance. In practice, it may be difficult to disentangle these two situations, since a negative medium-term transfer is likely to produce adverse confidence factors.

The expression above describing the determinants of the basic transfer facilitates an analysis of the various ways in which the debt situation may be transformed. Any improvement, from the point of view of debtor countries, requires a change in the basic transfer. This may be achieved by increasing the net flow (raising d) or reducing interest payments (r). The net inflow may be expressed as the difference between the gross inflow and amortisation. Suppose g expresses the gross inflow as a proportion of existing debt and a, amortisations as a proportion of existing debt. Then the basic transfer may be rewritten:

$$(g.D - a.D) - r.D$$

or

$$(g - a - r)D \tag{11.2}$$

Historically, when the debt burden became too great, the burden was reduced in two ways: (1) bankruptcies and defaults which had the effect of reducing both amortisation and interest payments; (2) inflation (with fixed interest rates) reduced the value of r in terms of d (since r was fixed in money terms and d rose with inflation).[3]

Today, both these methods of reducing the debt burden have been largely eliminated. Sovereign lending has made bankruptcies and defaults much rarer, and short-term borrowing and floating interest rates and longer-term loans have reduced the significance of inflation in lowering the burden of debt.

By ruling out both these possibilities, countries today have been put in a straitjacket which may not be acceptable when the basic transfer becomes negative over a prolonged period and the costs of adjustment are high. The IMF provides short-term assistance which is relevant to countries where the negative basic transfer is of a short-term nature, but does not help solve the problem of countries where it is long-term. It is the latter countries for which some 'solution' to the debt problem is essential, if they are not to take radical action unilaterally.

The next section of this essay will consider the objectives and interests of the various actors involved in the debt situation and in potential solutions.

MAJOR ACTORS IN THE DEBT SITUATION

There are five main categories of actor:

(a) the international banks;
(b) governments of borrowing countries;

Table 11.2   Debt exposure of major banks, selected years

Bank	(1) Latin American debt as % equity (1983)	(2) % excluding Mexico (end 1983)	(3) Provisions as a % of exposure (1989)
Citicorp	195	124	29[a]
J. P. Morgan	136	96	100[a]
Bank of America	164	87	42[a]
Chase Manhattan		147	46
Midland	189	213	50
Lloyds	164	228	70

Note:
a Expressed as % of medium- and long-term debt.
Sources:
Cols (1) and (3) ICBA, *Banking Analysis*
Col. (2) De Zoete and Bevan, quoted in *Financial Times* (31 May 1984).

(c) governments of countries where the major banks have their
    headquarters;
(d) international institutions;
(e) individuals from debt countries who have placed their funds
    overseas.[4]

International Banks

These are the banks which have been responsible for much of the
lending to the Third World. They need to be subdivided into two
groups:

(1) banks whose loans to LDCs form a large proportion of their total
    loans, in many cases exceeding their capital;
(2) banks whose loans to LDCs are of subsidiary importance to their
    activities.

Table 11.2 illustrates the major significance of loans to the Third
World for some major banks for 1983. Since then most banks have
made provisions for losses on these loans as indicated in column (3),
thereby reducing their vulnerability to default. As the *International
Herald Tribune* noted in September 1988, 'For Latin lenders, the
crisis is over'.

(1) The major interest of this category of banks is twofold: first to avoid any major default or appearance of default – hence the anxiety to avoid a situation in which loans become non-performing while delayed amortisation, which does not get classified as default in the same way, is more readily accepted. In general, these banks would prefer to extend new credit and maintain interest payments, rather than having interest unpaid. The second objective of these banks is to maximise profitability, but this is less important than the avoidance of default.

This group of banks will: (1) pressurise others to take action to help avoid defaults (including their own governments, international institutions and government of LDCs); (2) extend loans themselves, even if not justified on 'economic' grounds, to avoid default; (3) be prepared to sacrifice the profitability objective, as indicated by the 'softening' of terms on margins and rescheduling and sale of debt on the secondary market, if this is judged necessary to avoid default; (4) treat countries differently according to the size of the stake involved in each country, but still be unwilling to see any default because of its possible significance as a precedent; (5) have an interest in ensuring *joint* action so that their own finance is not threatened by the action of other banks. They therefore have an interest in using international institutions to secure this.

(2) The second category of banks has rather different interests. Being less involved, their survival does not depend on avoiding default. Consequently, their concerns are (1) to maximise yields; and (2) to withdraw their loans wherever they consider them unsafe. Their interests, therefore, may come into conflict with those of the first category of banks, since in the desire to maximise returns and withdraw from insecure situations, the second category could precipitate a crisis which would threaten the major banks. This category of banks may thus be pressured by the major banks or international institutions to stay in the LDCs, despite their wishes (as with the 7 per cent solution).[5]

Borrowing Country Governments

There are important differences between countries which lead to differences in response to the debt situation. These differences include the following.

1. *Differences in the balance of debt borrowed from official and private institutions* While it is the private debt situation which is primarily relevant to countries' attitudes towards this type of debt, their attitudes may also be influenced by possible implications for official flows of finance, where countries rely heavily on these. A tough stance towards private debt might trigger off retaliatory action on official finance. This possibility may be ignored where official finance is insignificant, either in total or in terms of current net flows.

2. *Prospects for the basic transfer, as defined above* Where the basic transfer is large and positive, countries are unlikely to take action which might threaten it. But where the transfer is small or negative, a tougher negotiating position is likely, especially if the situation is expected to persist over a period of years.

3. *The foreign exchange and trade position* If the foreign exchange position is strong and has been achieved by expansion of export earnings rathen than by drastic cuts in imports and deflation then, irrespective of the basic transfer, a country is not likely to bargain toughly on debt. A debt crisis involves a foreign exchange crisis. An adverse balance on debt, however, often causes a foreign exchange crisis. But a country which expects that it will be able to achieve the required turnround on the trade balance without excessive deflation is less likely to negotiate strongly on debt than one where the required trade surplus appears to be achievable only by sustained reductions in expenditure (contrast, for example, S. Korea and Mexico).

4. *The potential for others to retaliate on non-debt issues in reaction to action on debt* Countries which are heavily dependent for exports and/or imports, or other factors, on countries most seriously affected by their actions on debt will tend to be more cautious than countries which are more independent. For example, because of oil exports and food self-sufficiency, Venezuela and Mexico are less likely to worry about trade retaliation than Brazil whose exports (of steel and orange juice) are particularly vulnerable to possible US action.

5. *Attitudes towards Fund programmes* These may be influenced by the potential size of Fund finance as compared with the finance a country would gain by postponing payments on debt servicing. Where the latter greatly exceed the former, the country has little to gain in the way of import finance from reaching a speedy

agreement with the Fund, especially if a Fund programme is unlikely to produce a substantial net inflow of finance from other sources. Countries in this position will thus tend to weigh the costs of Fund programmes more heavily than those where they gain substantial finance for imports by concluding a programme.

6. *Internal politics* Even where the 'objective' circumstances are identical, internal politics may differ, leading to different reactions. Internal politics may differ with respect to the attention paid to local public opinion, demonstrations, etc. and also with respect to the dependence of the regime on foreign support. The political bases of the various regimes, and how they would be affected by different strategies, are of major importance in determining country reactions. Internal politics are themselves affected by past strategies, including past policies, but it would be too complex and lengthy to discuss the taxonomy here.

7. *Because of the regionalisation effect* In other words, that lack of confidence in one country can lead to a general lack of confidence in countries in the same area – neighbouring countries, especially if heavily indebted themselves, have an interest in how a country treats its debt situation. Consequently, they may take action (as in the Argentinean situation in the first half of 1984, when loans were advanced to Argentina by major Latin American countries to prevent non-payment of interest). Regional cooperation may also be sought to coordinate action, to present a wider front to creditors. This could be of significance to the outcome because a major influence on bank reaction is the extent of their involvement; while loans to any one country may be insignificant, added together they may become of major importance. This factor is obviously of greater relevance to smaller countries, such as Costa Rica, Ecuador or Bolivia, which have shown greater eagerness for coordinated action, than to some of the major debtors.

Governments of Countries Where the Banks Have Their Headquarters

An overriding objective of these governments is to prevent the collapse of a major bank, which could threaten the stability of their financial systems. But they also wish, as a subordinate objective, to maintain interest payments from borrowing countries. In order to achieve the overriding objective, such governments are prepared to put pressure on borrowing governments and international institutions, and to extend finance themselves. This has been illustrated by the US administration's activities in recent years – e.g., in the series of debt initiatives, in the treatment of major debtors, and in supporting increases in the IMF quotas and a widening of the General Agreement to Borrow. Perhaps surprisingly, in view of the heavy involvement of UK banks, the UK government has adopted a much more passive role. However, as Japanese banks become more involved in Third World lending, the Japanese government has begun to take a more active interest in supporting changes which would avoid a debt crunch.

These governments, of course, represent trading nations as well as financial headquarters. Their trading strategy does not always seem to support their financial objectives – by giving way to protectionist pressures, for example, they make it more difficult for borrowing countries to meet their interest obligations, while world recessions (by depressing export markets generally) have been a major cause of the debt servicing problem. However, protectionist sentiment has not been fully translated into policy, whilst the USA has greatly increased its imports from developing countries in the 1980s. Nonetheless, monetary policy, involving very high interest rates, has been a major factor threatening the stability of the debt servicing and has thus contradicted leading countries' objectives of maintaining financial stability.

Developed country governments, like those of borrowing countries, are subject to many internal political pressures (often of a contradictory nature), which help to explain the contradictions in policy stance.

International Institutions

These institutions – notably the IMF, the Bank for International Settlements (BIS) and the World Bank – are the creatures of the governments which control them, and do not have a genuine independent existence. However, their officials take their own line, trying to push member governments to follow, while in the short run they have some independence of action. But if their policies conflict in a major way with those that the powerful governments want, then they will be pushed to one side and alternative mechanisms devised.

The BIS is more obviously a creature of governments than the IMF and played an interesting role in the early 1980s, permitting governments to bypass the slow and stringent Fund procedures when they seem to be getting in the way, without actually abolishing them. If default is threatened because the borrowing countries have run out of cash, and they are unable to come to speedy accomodation with the Fund, the BIS can provide short-run bridging finance, and can help maintain pressure on the banks to extend credit and deadlines.

The IMF is concerned with short- and medium-term adjustment policies so as to produce a stable financial system: its interest in financial flows is (1) to secure the necessary finance while adjustment takes place, but (2) only if the country is following the adjustment prescribed by the Fund.

The Fund's concern with securing adjustment (which reflects the objectives of the controlling countries over the medium term) means that it cannot act as 'lender-of-last-resort', providing near-automatic short-term finance, because if it did so its ability to enforce conditionality would be lessened. Emergency finance has thus to be sought elsewhere (from governments themselves, and from the BIS). The existence of more than one international institution is necessary to achieve the twin objectives of the major lending countries – to prevent short-term financial collapse, while securing the adjustment policies which will ensure repayment over the medium term.

The international institutions have the role of countering the Prisoner's Dilemma aspect of international debt. Some coordination among banks is necessary, and to the extent that private cartels are prohibited, public institutions have to play that role. The Fund 'seal of approval' does this, but there is no mechanism for ensuring that individual banks respect it to the point of extending credit to countries they consider a bad risk. It is thus only a partially satisfactory solution. There is a need either for more public finance (e.g., through the Fund) or for some better way of enforcing cooperation from the private banks.

Debtor Nationals With Money Overseas

Although precise estimates are not possible, it is known that very large sums have been remitted overseas by nationals of debtor countries (see Table 11.3).

Repatriation of these sums could thus make a major contribution to the debt situation in a number of countries (and continued remittance overseas could worsen it). Repatriation would occur if the investors thought it made sense from the perspective of risk and rate of return. Their actions are likely to be influenced by macro-

Table 11.3   Capital flight, 1988

	Estimated total 'flight capital' ($ billion)	As % of total foreign debt
Mexico	83.8	78
Venezuela	58.1	166
Argentina	45.9	77
Brazil	31.2	26
Colombia	7.1	41
Ecuador	7.0	64
Bolivia	4.4	77
Uruguay	4.0	89
Peru	2.1	11
Chile	2.1	10

Source: Intridos Group, quoted in *Sunday Telegraph* (9 July 1989).

economic policy changes (exchange rate, inflation rate, interest rate) at home and abroad, by the prospects for sustained growth, and by how far a sustainable solution to the debt crisis has been realised, as well as by political conditions. Return capital flight cannot be relied upon as a major solution to the debt crisis, since it will occur only *after* the elements of a lasting solution have been arrived at, but given that these elements were in place it could lead to a greater and more rapid improvement in the situation.

POLICY RESPONSES AND REFORM

It was argued above that powerful particular interests are the main determinants of policy in both North and South. Our first section described the evolution of the debt situation which has led to a position in which many countries have a negative basic transfer over the medium term. Combining these arguments with the analysis of major interests presented in the last section, will make it easier to predict policy responses and assess the feasibility and desirability of various reforms.

In the early 1980s, two types of policy response were often discussed: *default* and *rescheduling*, the first being unilateral action by debtor countries, the second being agreed between debtors, banks and governments. More recently, a third approach has been widely advocated: *debt reduction*. Each of these concepts needs further clarification since they cover a variety of measures, with different implications.

1. *Default* may involve: (a) 100 per cent default with complete and apparently permanent termination of all payments of interest and amortisation; (b) moratorium on payments of amortisation, for varying lengths of time; (c) moratorium on payments of interest, for varying lengths of time; (d) moratorium on payments of interest and amortisation; (e) write-down of total service payments to some proportion of exports, GNP or some other level – which may or may not be temporary, and may or may not be compensated for later by higher payments.
2. *Rescheduling*, involving banks and borrowing countries, leads to a rearrangement of the timing of payments (amortisation and sometimes interest); so far, it has always involved *higher* total payments with less payable immediately and more in the future.
3. *Debt reduction* consists of write-down of the outstanding debt, *agreed* between the various parties. It thus involves some features of partial default, but it is not expected to be unilaterally imposed but like rescheduling to be a negotiated solution.

It is helpful to consider each of these possibilities in terms of the way in which they affect the net present value of the debt (NPVD). Any given debt may be expressed as a stream of payments of interest and amortisation which, when discounted at the ruling interest rate, gives an NPVD.

From the point of view of the debt burden of countries, there is a crucial distinction between those measures which reduce the NPVD and those which increase it, or leave it unchanged. In addition, there is the question whether the solution will eliminate the negative basic transfer, and thus debtor countries' interest in taking unilateral action. In general, solutions which reduce the NPVD also improve the basic transfer, but it is possible for a scheme to reduce the NPVD while leaving the basic transfer negative, or to increase the NPVD while producing a short-term improvement in the basic transfer.

All the varieties of default involve a reduction of NPVD, in the extreme case (100 per cent default) reducing it to zero, while in the other cases (moratorium, write-down) reducing it by varying amounts. In contrast, rescheduling (as practised) involves increasing the NPVD by varying amounts, depending on the precise conditions, while relieving the immediate liquidity problem. It may thus reverse a negative transfer in the immediate future, while leading to a greater negative transfer in the medium term, by which time the country might be in a better position to pay. Debt reduction in principle, like default, involves a reduction in the NPVD, and an improvement in the basic transfer.

Countries with prospects of a negative basic transfer over the medium term have a strong motive to reduce the NPVD of their debt obligations, if necessary by unilateral action, until such time as the basic transfer becomes positive. But this does not imply 100 per cent default. In many cases, a quite modest write-down or reduction in service payments will achieve the required turnround in the basic transfer. This will represent a much more attractive option for most countries than 100 per cent default since the implications for other aspects of North–South relations (e.g., trade; aid) would be less serious. Moreover, 100 per cent default would also prevent a positive basic transfer (by reducing capital inflow to zero) for an indefinite period, and could lead to very strong reactions including the possibility of military action. Write-down of some sort may be a temporary device until such a point as international interest rates fall and the basic transfer becomes positive.

The major banks (and headquarters governments) have a strong motive to avoid creating a situation in which major unilateral write-off occurs. Hence their adoption of rescheduling, and support for IMF programmes throughout the 1980s. But these policies, since they do not reduce the NPVD, often leave the countries with a negative basic transfer, reduced in the short term but increased in the longer term. They do not, therefore, represent a permanent solution in most cases, as is becoming apparent with the experience of those countries which have had to undergo a series of rescheduling operations and IMF programmes. So long as the negative basic transfer remains, the possibility of unilateral action to reduce the NPVD also remains. A satisfactory medium-term solution must (a) alter the terms of the debt so that the basic transfer becomes positive; (b) reduce the NPVD; and (c) improve the foreign exchange earning capacity of the country so as to meet the required debt servicing (albeit at reduced rates). Debt reduction is an attempt to meet these requirements. The extent to which it does so depends on the precise terms.

Possible solutions may be analysed in terms of expression (11.2) above, describing the determinants of the basic balance, $(g - a - r)$. D, where g, a and r are defined as a stream of payments over time.

A large number of proposals for reform have been put forward.[6] These may be briefly categorised as follows:

1. *Insurance for commercial banks' portfolios* This scheme[7] would be financed by both governments and the banks. The main objective would be to stabilise financial flows, possibly encouraging additional lending as a result of the reduction in risk. The reform would make little contribution to reducing the NPVD.
2. *Lender-of-last-resort facilities*[8] This is a contingency plan whereby some central institution (IMF, BIS, or some other body) would provide finance for banks in difficulties due to LDC inability to repay. The main burden of the scheme would be borne by supporting governments. The scheme, like the insurance scheme in 1 above, would help secure financial stability.
3. *Central bank discounting of commercial bank loans with LDCs* The scheme (put forward by Lever)[9] would help stabilise bank lending, by reducing banks' liquidity problems. It would not, it appears, reduce LDC obligations.
4. *Exchange of LDC debt for ownership of assets in LDCs* Such a scheme would provide a temporary relief from payment obligations, but at the cost of alienating assets at a low price. In the longer run, the new debt burden would probably be at least as great as the old.
5. *Provision of finance by the Fund to compensate for high interest rates* This gives countries temporary relief, but does not alter either NPVD or the basic transfer.
6. *Proposals to 'cap' interest rates* This would limit LDC debt servicing obligations to payment capacity (e.g., some fixed proportion of export earnings).[10] The precise implications for LDC debt burden would depend on whether the net effect was to stretch out the total, while leaving the NPVD unchanged, or to reduce the NPVD.
7. *Debt restructuring and debt reduction proposals* There are a great variety of schemes with different terms and institutional forms.[11] All involve the transformation of existing debt into longer-term maturity, of lower total value and with reduced interest.

The schemes just described are intended to fulfil different types of objective. The first three are primarily designed to secure greater financial stability. New capital flows (and reduced withdrawal) are likely to be encouraged, and some reduction of risk premia might result. The negative basic transfer might be temporarily reduced, as *g* rises, but the NPVD is likely to increase as a result, so that the long-run problem might become worse. Schemes 4–7 assist the current payments position by reducing the short-run servicing costs (reducing interest and amortisation payments in the short run.) In so doing, they will also contribute to increased confidence and reduced instability. Whether they will lead to a reduction in the NPVD depends on whether long-run service payments rise to compensate for short-term reductions (as with rescheduling exercises). The gross inflow of funds may be reduced by such schemes, where they involve substantial reductions in the NPVD and the commercial banks bear a high proportion of these losses. But the increased confidence – in particular the reduced likelihood of unilateral and substantial defaults – will work to increase the inflow.

Table 11.4 summarises some of these effects. For countries with a negative basic transfer over the medium term, only schemes that reduce the NPVD and lead to positive net transfer are likely to be sufficient to avoid unilateral action. Hence while Schemes 1–3 in Table 11.4 could be attractive from the point of view of the Northern interest in financial stability, they are not likely to be sufficient to avoid more radical action by some Southern governments. The next set of solutions (4–6) – 'cap' proposals, debt for equity and high interest compensation schemes – offer relief in the short term, but at the possible expense of greater payments in the future. The final set of schemes (7) offers a permanent reduction of amortisation and interest. These schemes should therefore be more attractive to borrowers than unilateral action. When considered on their own, they involve losses for the banks and the headquarters governments, but in terms of the opportunity cost (unilateral action by borrowers) they offer gains. This type of scheme therefore potentially provides for a genuine identity of interest in reform between powerful groups among lenders and borrowers; it is on this category that attention is increasingly being focussed.

The Brady plan is designed to achieve 'orderly' debt reduction of this type, with finance from the international financial institutions and the Japanese government. Schemes were agreed for Mexico (1989) and the Philippines (1990) and are underway in Costa Rica. Despite large financial support from the international institutions, the debt reduction is small in relation to the outstanding debt in both the Mexico and Philippine case: for example, in Mexico, it is estimated that the debt stock will be reduced by $0.5 billion out of a total

Table 11.4 Schemes for reducing improving debt situation

Scheme/Source	Variable affected	Effect on new flows	Effect on NPVD	Effect on stability	Burden sharing	Comment
1. Insurance (Wallich, 1984)	Raise g	Positive in short run	Small	Positive	Little burden; Northern governments	Inadequate – does not reduce NPVD, unlikely to raise g much.
2. Lender of last resort (Lipton and Griffith–Jones, 1984)	Raise g	Positive in short run	Small	Positive	Northern governments	Inadequate – deals with financial instability
3. Discount banks loans by Central Banks (Lever, 1983)	Raise g	Positive in short run	Small	Positive	Little; mainly Northern governments	Inadequate
4. Exchange debt for equity	Mainly timing	Little	Could increase NPVD	Probably positive	Banks could lose now; gain later	LDC hostility likely
5. High interest compensatory fund at IMF?	Reduce r, temporarily	None	Little; depends on terms	Small, positive	Govts. temporarily	Temporary solution
6. 'Cap': reducing current interest to be compensated later (Solomon, 1977)	Affects timing, may not affect total of any variable	Could be negative	None, unless later compensation is small	Probably positive	Banks, temporarily and possibly headquarters governments	Helps current situation, may worsen future
7. Debt reduction by exchanging debt at discount	Reduces r, and a	Probably negative	Some reduction	Small, positive	Shared between Banks and Northern governments	Helps, but only if carried out on massive scale will it be 'solution',

debt of $120 billion; in the Philippines, outstanding debt is little changed when account is taken of new loans as well as debt reduction.[12] Thus while the principle of debt reduction is the right one, in practice the magnitudes associated with the Brady plan are far too small to produce a lasting solution, and debtor countries will continue to have to reduce their investment and/or consumption so as to transfer resources overseas.

The Brady plan has followed the practice of the 1980s in requiring a country-by-country approach. A more generalised solution would be preferable from many points of view:

1. It would prevent the lurch from crisis to crisis, which has negative effects on world trade, financial confidence and capital flows, and especially on the ability of particular developing countries to undertake long term development plans.
2. Compared with unilateral default the process of negotiations would offer the chance of combining some conditionality and adjustment with a solution to the debt problem.
3. Unilateral negotiations secure a solution only for countries in a strong bargaining position – those with negative basic transfers and which have borrowed enough to have a significant effect on major banks. Other countries which have major problems but are in a weaker position to enforce a solution by threatening unilateral action are excluded. A generalised solution is needed to extend the benefits to countries in a weak position to bargain individually.

The next section of this essay will provide a tentative classification of countries' debts and bargaining positions.

COUNTRY CLASSIFICATION

The earlier analysis suggests that there are big differences in countries' policy responses and negotiating strengths, according to their particular circumstances. One critical factor is whether the basic transfer – over the medium term – is expected to be positive or negative. Another factor is the relative significance of official and private capital. A country's importance to the banking community – in terms of the magnitude of outstanding debt – is the major determinant of negotiating strength. (There are many other relevant differences – some noted above – for example, with respect to past

Table 11.5   Major debtors with negative transfers from commercial banks, 1988

	Transfer commercial banks $billion (1988)	Overall transfer	Overall transfer as % imports (1988)	Debt as % total[a]	GNP per capita growth, (1980–7) % p.a.
Algeria	−0.73	−0.42	−4.4	2.7	+0.6
Argentina	−1.06	−2.31	−17.6	6.7	−1.8
Brazil	−5.12	−9.62	−30.0	12.5	+1.0
Chile	−0.6	−0.06	−0.7	2.1	−1.1
Egypt	−0.03	+0.14		5.5	+2.9
Indonesia	−1.2	−1.1	−4.8	5.7	+1.7
S. Korea	−1.26	−4.3	−7.4	4.1	+7.3
Malaysia	−0.85	−3.1	−13.7	2.2	+1.1
Mexico	−2.98	−8.0	−122.2	11.1	−1.6
Morocco	−0.26	−0.34	−5.2	2.2	+0.3
Nigeria	−0.60	−1.21	−13.8	3.4	−4.7
Philippines	−1.5	−1.59	−13.4	3.2	−3.3
Poland	−0.64	−1.09	−5.9	4.6	+1.4
Thailand	−0.12	−0.96	−5.4	2.2	+3.4
Turkey	−0.13	−0.05	−0.3	4.3	+3.0
Venezuela	−1.97	−3.32	−19.1	3.8	−3.1
Yugoslavia	−0.28	−1.35	−8.5	2.4	0

Note:
   a   % of total debt 1988 among all countries listed in World Debt Tables.
Source: World Bank, *World Debt Tables 1989–90, Vol. II* (Washington, D.C.: World Bank, 1990).

development strategy and trading potential – but these will not be explored here.)

There is a substantial statistical problem in classifying countries: in many countries, the quantities of debt are unknown. The Argentinian case provided an example: the Minister of Finance stated in April 1984: 'We still don't know the debt; there were no registers in the central bank . . . with most loans we could not identify the purpose, the amount, the interest or the grace period'. According to a report in the *International Herald Tribune*, more than 100 officials were searching through stacks of paper piled six feet high.[13]

Table 11.5 lists 16 major debtors (defined as having 2 per cent or more of outstanding debt) which have a *negative* transfer with the commercial banks. Of those 16, two – Algeria and Egypt – have a positive overall balance, allowing for official flows. The remaining 14 can be presumed to have a potential interest in unilateral action to reduce debt servicing. Within this group, countries that are managing to increase *per capita* incomes are more likely to want to avoid the disruption of international relations associated with unilateral action than those whose incomes are stagnating or deteriorating. Taking GNP *per capita* growth (1980–7) of 1 per cent or less as an indicator, it appears that countries with the strongest interest in unilateral action on debt, among the large debtors, were Algeria, Argentina*, Brazil*, Chile, Mexico*, Nigeria*, the Philippines*, Venezuela*, and Yugoslavia (countries with an asterisk* are those whose overall negative transfer in 1988 exceeded 10 per cent of the value of their imports). Because of their sizeable debt, these are the countries where the banks and international financial institutions would be most concerned to prevent unilateral action and to secure 'orderly' arrangements. The Brady plan, which is primarily directed at these countries, is a response to the underlying bargaining situation identified in this analysis.

The banks and international financial institutions can be less concerned with small debtors; by the same token, such countries may take unilateral action with more impunity than large debtors.

39 countries with relatively small debts (i.e., less than 2 per cent of world debt) had negative transfers with the commercial banks. Of these 15 countries had negative overall transfers (Table 11.6) and at least eight of this group of countries had low or negative growth *per capita* incomes. These eight countries have a strong incentive to stop or reduce debt servicing so as to eliminate the negative transfer. Together the eight countries account for less than 5 per cent of outstanding debt of all debtors listed in the *World Debt Tables*. Sizeable negative transfers (over 10 per cent of imports) in this group of countries were experienced by Jamaica, Paraguay, Romania, Uruguay and Zimbabwe.

This classification of countries' bargaining position has been done on the basis of just one year's figures, and the classification could change radically with economic changes that may occur. 'Bargaining position' does not derive from the current position alone, but also from what is expected in the short and medium term, for which the current position is not always a good proxy. Consequently, detailed country-by-country knowledge is necessary for an accurate identification of country prospects. Nonetheless, the variables identified do permit a broadly accurate indication of country position and potential action.

Table 11.6   Small debtor countries with negative overall transfer

	1988 Overall transfer as % imports	Debt as % total	Growth of per capita income (1980–7)
Bahamas	–2.6	0.02	n.a.
Columbia	–7.2	1.9	+0.9
Costa Rica	–9.7	0.5	–0.5
Cyprus	–5.3	0.22	n.a.
Fiji	–0.3	0.05	n.a.
Hungary	–6.0	1.92	+1.8
Jamaica	–10.2	0.47	–2.5
Jordan	–1.7	0.60	–0.7
Maldives	–2.3	.01	n.a.
Papua New Guinea	–9.4	0.25	+0.1
Paraguay	–11.7	0.27	–2.1
Rumania	–30.3	0.30	n.a.
Tunisia	n.a.	n.a.	+3.0
Uruguay	–15.4	0.42	–2.3
Zimbabwe	–11.9	0.29	–1.3

Source: World Bank, *World Debt Tables, 1989–90, Vol. II:* (Washington D.C.: World Bank, 1990); tables from *Human Development Report* (New York: United Nations, 1990).

CONCLUSIONS

The accumulation of debt, by some countries, together with high interest rates, has led to a position of negative basic transfer not only on flows to the commercial banks, but overall, including official flows. Where countries are facing foreign exchange problems, and are having to sacrifice output growth in order to meet debt obligations, such countries are likely to negotiate toughly on debt and consider taking unilateral action if these negotiations do not succeed. At the same time, the big borrowers form such an important element of total bank finance that neither the banks nor the headquarters governments can afford to face any major defaults with equanimity, though the banks were much less vulnerable to developing country default at the end of the 1980s than at the beginning of the decade.

This is a situation where there is an identity of interests – in an *operational* sense – among the major actors in achieving reforms which will make the burden of debt tolerable to the debtors, while avoiding large-scale defaults.

In principle, debt reduction schemes are of this type. In so far as they reduce the NPVD and permit positive basic transfer, they are preferable to default among borrowing countries and consequently reduce the risks lenders face. However, to achieve this they must be on a sufficient scale to eliminate the negative transfer over the medium as well as the short term, and they must extend to all indebted countries. So far, while the principle of debt reduction has been accepted, the scale has been inadequate, so that the debt problem remains an albatross for both borrowing and lending countries.

NOTES

1. This approach to analysing financial transfers was developed by Domar (1957) in his analysis of the burden of domestic debt. It was applied to foreign direct investment in developing countries by Paul Streeten (1972).
2. There is evidence that this has been of major magnitude in some countries. The BIS estimated that Latin Americans 'had spirited away $55 billion in the six years to 1983 – almost a third of the region's increase in borrowing during the period' (*Guardian*, 19 June 1984).
3. See Dommen (1989), Felix (1987) and Eichengreen and Portes (1988) for an analysis of how past debt crises were handled.
4. It should be noted that when individuals in developed countries place funds overseas, it is regarded as 'overseas investment', with a legitimate, indeed laudable, role to play in world capitalism. But when individuals from debtor countries do the same, it is termed 'capital flight', and is regarded as morally deplorable.
5. This was the exercise conducted by the IMF and the major banks at the end of 1982, when the Fund coordinated the activities of all lenders to Mexico, securing an agreement that they would increase their lending by 7 per cent.
6. A detailed summary of many of the schemes, together with references, is contained in Commonwealth Secretariat (1984) Appendix 2.2. *AMEX Bank Review* 11 (5) (19 June 1984) and Griffith-Jones (1986) also provide a useful survey of proposals.
7. See Wallich (1984).
8. See Lipton and Griffith-Jones (1984).
9. *The Economist* (July 1983).

10. R. Solomon, Senate Banking Committee Hearings (May 1984); M. Baily, *Business Week* (10 January 1983); limitation of debt services to a predetermined proportion of export earnings was one of the demands in the Consensus of Cartegna, signed by 11 Ministers of countries in Latin America (June 1984).
11. F. Rohatyn, *Business Week* (28 February 1983); P. Kenen, *New York Times* (6 March 1983); Mahbub ul Haq, paper for North–South Round-table on Money and Finance (September 1984); Robinson (1988); see *Financial Times* 25 August 1989 for an outline of the Brady plan.
12. Percy Mistry's analysis: seminar, Queen Elizabeth House, Oxford (January 1990).
13. Quoted in *International Herald Tribune* (10 April 1984).

12 Back to Keynesianism: Reforming the IMF*

The 1944 Bretton Woods conference may be seen as an attempt to institutionalise at an international level the revolution in economic ideas brought about by John Maynard Keynes. Keynes believed that the prosperity of nations – in particular, their levels of production and employment – did not need to be the unplanned outcome of an uncoordinated and erratic system, but could be controlled by government. At a national level, this revolution in theory did not require new mechanisms and institutions, but rather new approaches to existing ones: adjustments had to be made in government spending and taxation and in central banks' money creation and interest rate determination. But no mechanisms existed at the international level to perform these functions; there were no international counterparts to central banks or national budgets. In 1941, then, Keynes developed the idea of an International Clearing Union – a sort of world-level central bank. His plan provided the main basis for the Bretton Woods discussions.

The 44 nations represented there had set out to create international institutions that would prevent the recurrence of a 1930s-style depression, with its massive unemployment, escalating tariffs, and collapsing commodity prices. After considerable negotiation, the International Monetary Fund (IMF) and World Bank were established. Although in structure and functioning the IMF differs quite radically from Keynes's own plan,[1] its fundamental objective was decidedly Keynesian. According to the first of its Articles of Agreement, one of the IMF's basic purposes was

> to facilitate the expansion of balanced growth in international trade, and to contribute thereby to the promotion and maintenance of high levels of employment and real income and to the development of the productive resources of all members as primary objectives of economic policy.

The Bretton Woods Agreement charged the IMF with prime

* *World Policy Journal* (Summer 1987).

responsibility for short-term macroeconomic developments – specifically, with maintaining stable exchange rates, except in situations of fundamental disequilibrium, and with providing finance to assist countries whose balance of payments were in short-term disequilibrium. The World Bank was oriented more toward development. As indicated by its official name – the Bank for International Reconstruction and Development – it initially had two main functions. The first was temporary: to help finance the reconstruction of the war-devastated economies of Europe. The second primary duty, as described by Keynes, was 'to develop the resources and productive capacity of the world with special attention to the less developed countries, to raise the standard of life and the conditions of labour everywhere, and so to promote and maintain equilibrium in the international balance of payments of all member countries'.[2]

During the 50 years that have elapsed since Bretton Woods, there have been many changes in the international economy. New centres of economic power, notably Japan, have developed; and the positions of old centres such as Great Britain have sharply eroded. International capital markets have grown enormously, and have changed in nature. Of major significance, both politically and economically, has been the displacement of colonialism and the subsequent emergence of 100 or so independent Third World governments.

Such shifts have contributed to changes in the Bretton Woods institutions. The World Bank has become a major development institution – a significant source of finance and advice for projects, sectoral development, and development policy – but it contributes little to the making of world macroeconomic policy. This has been the responsibility of the IMF. At regular intervals, the Fund makes assessments of the world economy. Although it has made some moves toward generalised interventions, it has for the most part – especially in recent years – focused most closely and vigorously on influencing the policies and finance of deficit countries seeking access to its resources. Accordingly, any attempt to analyse the IMF's effects on Third World countries and on the world economy as a whole must concentrate on IMF country programmes.

The IMF's influence on the policies of individual countries has grown over the decades. The 1950s saw the development of the practice of 'conditionality', which makes access to IMF finance conditional on a country's adopting certain macroeconomic policies. Initially, conditionality requirements were imposed only on a minority of countries receiving loans (about one out of four in the 1970s, for example); but by the 1980s conditionality had become more pervasive, applying to over three-quarters of IMF loans. At the same time, as more countries experienced economic difficulties, more turned to the Fund for finance. In the 1970s, an average of 10 countries initiated programmes each year. In the 1980s, this number never fell below 20, and throughout the first half of the decade over 40 countries had IMF programmes in effect for at least one month each year.

The Fund itself generally only provides a small proportion of most countries' financial needs. Yet its influence extends well beyond its strictly financial significance, since other institutions have come to demand that countries have IMF agreements before they will agree to supply additional finance. The private banking sector almost universally makes such a requirement before rescheduling Third World countries' loans, as does the Paris Club, which deals with official loans from bilateral borrowers. This type of 'cross-conditionality', whereby conditions imposed by one institution (the IMF) serve as requirements of other institutions as well, has also extended to the World Bank's structural adjustment loans. Consequently, for countries in financial difficulty, obtaining finance from nearly any source – the private banking sector, bilateral donors, the World Bank – has become contingent on the country's agreeing to IMF conditionality.

While the Fund's influence has grown over the decades, the condition of the world economy has declined. Unemployment in developed nations has risen in every decade since the 1940s. Output growth has slowed. The 1980s proved the worst decade for all countries – especially the poorer ones – since the Great Depression. Indeed, in many respects they seemed to be a repeat of that time: as in the 1930s, the markets of the developed countries were stagnant and protectionism rose, while the terms of trade of primary producers worsened and commodity prices fell lower than for 50 years. To make matters worse, voluntary private lending to developing countries through the banking system, which became a dominant source of finance in the 1970s, more or less stopped.

This widespread economic deterioration caused acute problems for many developing countries. The stagnancy of world markets, the growth of protectionism, and the fall in commodity prices made it increasingly difficult for them to earn their way out of their economic troubles. In 1985, their export earnings were 15 per cent below the

1980 level. At the same time, trade deficits have become less and less easy to finance. The bank lending that flowed freely in the 1970s dried up in the 1980s, yet debt service obligations continued to mount, pushed upward by high interest rates. Some countries had to set aside more than half of their export earnings for debt servicing, which left only a small portion of a declining total available to pay for imports. From this situation emerged an acute foreign exchange crisis, which led more and more Third World countries to turn to the IMF.

Indeed, the first half of the decade could be described as years of IMF conditionality in Africa and Latin America. Two-thirds of the countries in those regions undertook IMF programmes; the overall shift in economic climate caused many others to adopt policies similar to IMF programmes in order to satisfy their hungry creditors. In effect, the IMF thus became the major policy-maker in most African and Latin American countries. These years therefore provide an opportunity to assess the impact the Fund's advice had on individual countries. Moreover, because of the IMF's central role in the world financial system, and because its advice has been taken by so many countries, its impact has extended well beyond developments in individual countries to the world economy as a whole.

There is a paradox in the events of the first half of the 1980s. These were years when Keynesian policies were most needed, and when the IMF had more influence than at any time in its history. Yet they were also years when the world economy, and particularly developing countries, veered away from the path envisioned by the IMF's founders – that of high income and employment and development of productive resources. Faced with this seeming contradiction, one has to ask what effect IMF conditionality programmes have had on the world economy.

CONDITIONALITY PROGRAMMES IN THE 1980s

It would be impossible to provide a thorough and fair assessment of IMF programmes in the 1980s. Not all the facts are in; moreover, because the international economic environment was deteriorating so sharply, it is difficult to determine how countries would have fared if Fund programmes had *not* been in place. Nevertheless, a general examination of the IMF's impact during this period does lead to some broad conclusions, and suggests that all concerned parties would most likely benefit from a search for improved alternatives to IMF conditionality.

The Fund programmes applied to different countries have a great many characteristics in common. They are usually negotiated in secret on a bilateral basis – in other words, independent parties, other countries, and international institutions besides the IMF are not involved. Instead, the details of the conditionality agreement are typically worked out between IMF representatives and officials from the country's finance ministry and central bank. It is partly because of these individuals' orientation that IMF programmes rely heavily on macroeconomic policy instruments and tend to neglect the social and political aspects of a country's situation.

Fund programmes are usually introduced when a country's economy is in severe imbalance – externally with large current account deficits in the balance of payments; internally, with high rates of inflation and deficits in the domestic budget. In order to correct these imbalances, IMF programmes use three types of policy. One is to restrain demand, through cuts in government spending, limits on credit creation, increases in taxation, and restraints on wages and public sector employment. Another is to encourage the channelling of resources into tradable goods, through devaluations in the country's currency and through price reforms. The third is to implement such measures as financial reform and import liberalisation intended to raise the medium- and long-term efficiency of the economy.

In actuality, the second and third types of policy, which are supply-oriented, tend to receive less emphasis than the first. This heavy reliance on demand restraint is due partly to the short time horizon of most programmes – typically 12 to 18 months. Such a period is long enough to make short-term improvements in the balance of trade by curtailing incomes, expenditure, and demand and thereby almost immediately reducing imports. Measures to expand supply, on the other hand, nearly always take much longer. For example, Brazil's highly successful import substitution strategy in the 1980s was based on massive investments it had made during the 1970s in energy and machinery production. Sri Lanka's tremendous surge in rice production after 1977, which allowed it to eliminate rice imports, was the result of a decade-long investment in irrigation. Without such substantial, long-term investment, it is extremely difficult to significantly increase output of products that can be exported or can serve as substitutes for imports. Accordingly, any programme requiring short-term improvements in the balance of trade will inevitably stress reduction of demand. (It should be noted that in the IMF's 1952 decision to endorse conditionality, the adjustment period was defined as 3 to 5 years – far longer than today's normal standby.[3] The IMF's Extended Fund Facility, introduced during the late 1970s, is usually for three-year periods; but it was used relatively infrequently in the 1980s.)

Perhaps more than any other factor, it is the IMF's philosophy – its beliefs about political economy and economic causality – that most influences the specific content of Fund programmes. In general, this philosophy, largely shared by the World Bank, is monetarist and laissez-faire, with emphasis on prices rather than controls, the private rather than the public sector, and free trade rather than protectionism. Because of its strong and pervasive philosophy, the IMF is not only concerned with policy objectives but also takes a firm view about which policy instruments are preferable. Thus even though the intentions of the Bretton Woods fathers were Keynesian, the institutions they created have turned out to be anti-Keynesian.

It is not surprising, then, that the original Keynesian objectives have not been achieved. The record of the 1980s shows just how far short of achieving those objectives IMF programmes have fallen. Many countries with Fund programmes experienced severe economic difficulties:

1. *Per capita* incomes tended to contract. This was true of more than 70 per cent of IMF-assisted countries in Africa and Latin America; by contrast, 83 per cent of Asian countries had rising *per capita* incomes.

2. Unemployment rose. In most Latin American countries, urban unemployment increased dramatically: in Chile, from 10.4 per cent in 1981 to 15.9 per cent in 1984; in Bolivia, from 7.5 per cent in 1980 to 13.3 per cent in 1984; in Mexico, from 11.7 per cent in 1980 to 18.5 per cent in 1984.

3. Urban poverty increased, as both employment and real incomes decreased. For example, between 1981 and 1984 real wages fell by 28 per cent in Brazil, 13 per cent in Peru, and 30 per cent in Mexico. In Ghana, the real urban wage in 1985 was less than one-quarter of what it had been in 1974; in Zambia, real wages were cut by half. In general, there was less change in the situation of the rural poor.

4. *Per capita* government spending, including expenditure on social services and food subsidies, was reduced. As a result, between

1980 and 1984 real government current expenditure per head fell in over 50 per cent of African countries and in 70 per cent of Latin American countries.

5. There was a rise in malnutrition among children in a large number of African countries, many of which also suffered from acute drought, and in several Latin American countries – Bolivia, Jamaica, Brazil, Chile, Guyana, and Uruguay, all of which had Fund programmes at some time in the 1980s.

6. Between 1980 and 1983, levels of real investment were stagnant or falling in 60 per cent of African countries with IMF programmes and in 58 per cent of Latin American countries.

7. Between 1980 and 1984, there was no improvement in the current account of the balance of payments in 40 per cent of African IMF-assisted countries and in 52 per cent of Latin American countries. In some cases, the payments balance actually deteriorated.

Current levels of output and income fell; and the combination of stagnant real investment, rising malnutrition, and falling health and educational standards adversely affected physical and human capital. As a result, the prospects for medium- and long-term economic growth were undermined. After undergoing tough IMF programmes, many countries found themselves with reduced real incomes, increased poverty, deteriorating social conditions, reduced growth potential – and, often, no significant improvement in their external accounts balance. In this last respect, the IMF programmes failed even to meet their most narrowly defined goal – to improve the imbalance on the external account.

It must be emphasised that these negative developments were not confined to countries with Fund programmes and therefore cannot be wholly attributed to Fund conditionality as such, especially because the external economic environment worsened significantly over this period. The facts do not prove that the situation would have been better without IMF conditionality: indeed, it might have been worse. But the facts do show – unambiguously – that the developments associated with Fund programmes in the 1980s were highly unsatisfactory.

This is particularly evident in the experience of sub-Saharan Africa.[4] At one time or another, most countries in this region had IMF programmes. Many had a succession of them, often broken off as performance criteria were violated. From 1980 to 1985, the Fund's cumulative lending to sub-Saharan Africa was approximately $4.6 billion followed by repayment of $1.5 billion, 1986–1989. Despite this substantial inflow of funds, and despite the fact that over this period African countries made a 15 per cent cut in imports, the region's current account deficit did not improve: it was − $7 billion both in 1980 and in 1989, and worse during the intervening years. And further repayment is due.

This repayment will be made more difficult by the deterioration in the domestic economies of most sub-Saharan countries in the 1980s. *Per capita* incomes fell. Progress toward improving health, education, and nutrition was brought to an abrupt halt, and in many countries was reversed. Newly established clinics could not operate effectively because of lack of medicine. Schools had no money for books or paper; low salaries led to high teacher absenteeism; and children dropped out in increasing numbers, since household survival depended on their working. Malnutrition rates of 50 per cent and over among children under five were recorded in many countries in addition to those affected by drought. Even those countries that fared better than average in economic terms – such as Zimbabwe, Kenya, and Ghana – remain in precarious positions, with large deficits and foreign exchange shortages that threaten to undermine their growth potential.

AGGREGATE EFFECTS OF IMF ACTIVITIES

The inadequacy of Fund programmes at a world level becomes clearer if one examines the impact they have had not only on individual countries but on the world economy as a whole. In general, the IMF's approach to correcting payments imbalances has created a worldwide tendency toward deflation. Adjustment programmes require deficit countries to attempt to eliminate their deficits by cutting expenditure and employment so that their imports fall. Such a strategy might, under the right conditions, help reduce deficits in Third World countries' current account balances. But when applied to many of these countries simultaneously, it also causes a significant drop in Third World demand for both Third World and Western products. A significant part of the US trade deficit, for example, can be traced to decreased demand in the Third World; 70 per cent of the $23 billion drop in US exports in the early 1980s resulted from lower demand for US products in Latin America alone.

IMF-mandated cutbacks in Third World spending and employment have thus caused worldwide decreases in demand, and therefore output.

Deflation is not the only way to correct imbalances in external accounts. The alternative would be to correct surpluses through reflation: surplus countries would try to eliminate their surpluses by increasing their spending so that their imports rose. The net effect on external accounts would be the same – because exports, output, and incomes of deficit countries would be raised, their deficits would be lowered. The IMF's original charter did include a 'scarce currency' clause designed to encourage symmetry of adjustment by placing pressure on chronically surplus countries to bring their surpluses down. But that clause has never been invoked, and the Fund's approach has remained highly asymmetrical: the major burden of policy change and adjustment is imposed on deficit countries.

Other aspects of IMF conditionality have had similarly negative effects when the same programme is imposed on many countries at once. At the same time that the Fund's overall impact has been deflationary, so that basic demand for developing country products has not been sustained, Fund programmes have also tended to increase the supply of these products. IMF country programmes have been tailored to expand production of primary commodities – in some cases, the same product in more than one country. For example, both Ghana and the Ivory Coast have had programmes to increase cocoa production. This upward shift in cocoa output, because it did not result from, or cause, an upward shift in demand, had the result that could have been predicted by anyone with a rudimentary knowledge of the laws of supply and demand: prices were driven down. In fact, for commodities with low demand elasticities – commodities for which a price cut does not induce a substantial rise in demand, since consumption is not much affected by price – an increase in production may lower prices so much that a country's total earnings from those commodities actually fall. Past experience has shown that this is the case for many commodities, especially those in which some very poor countries specialise, such as cocoa, tea, and coffee.[5]

Thus when the IMF encourages production increases from a number of major producers of particular commodities without simultaneously taking action to increase demand for those commodities, the net result may be to decrease deficit countries' foreign exchange earnings from commodity production while increasing the resources they devote to that production. Fund programmes have thereby contributed to primary producers' worsening terms of trade, which were in turn partly responsible for the limited improvements many Third World countries were able to make in their current account balances. Once again, IMF policy worked at cross-purposes to its stated goals.

Currency devaluations have often had a similarly damaging effect on the terms of trade of exporters of manufactured goods, since such devaluations lower the relative price that producers receive for their manufactured exports. But in this case, as opposed to that of primary commodities, there is more potential for the Third World as a whole to increase its share of the world market. As a result, reduced prices may be more than offset by an increase in the quantity sold – provided, of course, that developed countries do not impose trade restrictions.

When assessing the aggregate effect of Fund financing in the 1980s, one must consider the economic environment in which deficit countries operated. This environment was one of sharp decline, not only in world output and trade, but also in financial flows to the Third World. In 1977–8, there was a positive net transfer of $8.6 billion to Africa; by 1984–5, that had become a negative flow of $5.4 billion. The change was even more dramatic for Latin America, where a positive balance of $4.9 billion had become a negative transfer of $39 billion by 1984–5. To make matters worse , in 1986 real commodity prices, measured in dollars, were 24 per cent below their 1980 level. Measured against this background of great need, the IMF's own contribution to developing countries was small. From 1980 to 1985, the cumulative net transfer of Fund credit to capital-importing countries was $31.5 billion; their cumulative current account deficit was $464.3 billion. By 1985, the net transfer from the IMF had actually become negative, as money borrowed earlier came due for repayment. This negative transfer persisted for the rest of the decade, so that the IMF made no net financing contribution in the difficult years 1985–9, but repayments exceeded new flows by $16 billion. In fact, the real net transfer that was effected through the Fund is even smaller than the above figures suggest, since deficit countries have often been required to channel IMF finance toward repayment of arrears to other debtors.

Another way in which the Fund has had an impact on deficit countries is through its role in the debt crisis. Because debt servicing accounts for such a large proportion of countries' external payments

– \$24 billion among capital-importing countries in 1985 – the IMF's approach to the debt situation greatly influences countries' financial situations. As the crisis unfolded after 1982, the commercial banks turned to the IMF to provide coordination and leadership. The IMF's general approach has been to deal with each country in turn, 'case by case'. First, the country must accept an IMF programme. At that point, the debt is rescheduled. This delays the immediate burden of amortisation, but it increases the amount ultimately owed, since interest accumulates on the unpaid debt and since banks charge a servicing fee for the rescheduling exercise. Throughout this process, the debtor country is required to maintain interest payments.

This approach has placed heavy financial demands on debtor countries – so much so that that the IMF can almost be viewed as the major commercial banks' debt collector. Recently, a few countries have rebelled, arguing that the payments demanded are too large for them to stick to the IMF agreements while also trying to maintain investment, economic growth, and basic social services. For example, in 1986 Peru announced that it would lower debt service payments to 10 per cent of export earnings. But subsequent difficulties forced Peru to go back to the Fund. Similarly, Zambia found Fund requirements too harsh, and has tried go-it-alone programmes.

That countries are taking such measures is an indication of how hostile the world economic climate has become. According to its originally stated goals, the IMF should be responsible for ensuring that the international environment be compatible with increasing world output, employment, and development. Yet the IMF has not made its own programmes – much less the world economy – consistent with these goals. The basic hopes and intentions of the Bretton Woods founders have not been realised, as the IMF has not evolved in such a way as to discharge its original responsibilities. The problem is not technical but political: the dominant governments, which set the major limits on Fund functioning, have imposed their own vision on the IMF.

There are two different ways to interpret the role of international financial institutions. As originally stated at Bretton Woods, the IMF's and World Bank's objectives were to promote world employment, incomes, and growth, and to work to eliminate world poverty. But these institutions have also been seen as having the primary function of preserving world financial stability and an open trading environment – one in which MNCs can invest freely and with confidence. Put more crudely, this means ensuring that debtors do not renege but rather repay the commercial banks, and that developing countries maintain open markets for Western products, imposing no troublesome restrictions on multinational investment. In this view, international financial institutions are meant primarily to support the interests of Western banks and companies.

The history of the IMF and World Bank, especially the policies they have followed in the 1980s, suggests that the second function has been given absolute supremacy and that the first has been sacrificed to it. Some observers would argue that there is no real conflict between the two, and that achieving the second – making the world economy safe for Western banks and companies – is a prerequisite to achieving the first. It is true that there are some positive inter-relationships, which work both ways, and that a certain amount of stability in finance and trade is necessary for international economic prosperity, including that of the Third World. But financial stability maintained at the *expense* of Third World prosperity actually threatens the long-term profitability of Western interests. Third World markets for Western producers will not grow if Third World incomes do not grow, or if all available resources are preempted for debt servicing. Moreover, countries that are forced to pursue defla-tionary policies in order to service their debts may eventually refuse to continue playing the bankers' game – much to the banking com-munity's loss. By giving so much priority to international financial interests and so little to Third World well-being, the international financial institutions have secured a financial stability that is tempor-ary and fragile. Rather than forcing deficit countries to bear the entire burden of adjustment, the IMF would be better advised to work toward Third World prosperity, which would provide a much more secure basis for world economic growth and vitality.

ALTERNATIVES

Changes in the world's economic and financial arrangements are needed at two levels – the international and the country-specific. At present, it seems more feasible to take action on the second level, that of individual countries' policy-making, in order to prevent the further impoverishment of those who are most deprived. But unless alterations are also made at the international level, other changes can be only a kind of mopping-up operation. It is thus important to work toward a consensus on the long-term adjustments that need to be made in the international economy, especially as it affects the Third World.

Particularly crucial is the need to expand world demand and trade. If countries are to continue to grow at the same time that they work to improve their trade imbalances, they must be able to expand their export earnings rather than simply cutting their imports, which results in decreased output and investment. Export expansion, however, does not automatically occur when countries increase their supplies – there must also be increased demand, so that those exports can be absorbed. So if the Third World as a whole is to pursue a path of growth-oriented adjustment by increasing its exports, there must be a sustained rise in world demand.

Such growth in demand for Third World products depends largely on the major industrialised countries' domestic policies – specifically, those regarding growth in their domestic demand and access to their markets by developing nations. Such growth in demand and free market access do not come about simply through the operations of an unregulated world economy; international intervention is needed. Of the institutions currently in existence, the IMF is the most appropriate one to undertake such intervention. In addition to monitoring world economic developments, which to some extent it already does, the Fund should be empowered to take actions that would ensure a world environment conducive to balanced growth.

Two sorts of actions are appropriate. First, pressure should be put on countries that chronically run surpluses. This pressure could be backed by sanctions, such as trade and exchange rate discrimination to force surplus countries to expand their domestic demand, thereby increasing their imports and reducing their surpluses. In the past, the Fund has not taken this kind of symmetrical approach to adjustment – requiring policy changes in surplus countries as well as deficit countries. But today there may be more support for adjustment steps aimed at surplus countries, given that the USA has become the world's largest debtor. Indeed, Washington has already moved in that direction, initiating sanctions against surplus countries both multilaterally, through the Group of Five, and bilaterally, by restricting imports. These efforts are bearing some fruit because of America's strong position in the world. What is needed is to systematise and institutionalise sanctions so that all deficit countries benefit, as was intended at Bretton Woods. The object would not be to prevent any and all sustained surpluses, but rather to ensure that at a minimum they are balanced by long-term capital outflows on reasonable terms, so as to prevent major deflationary impact on other countries.

Second, if adequate adjustment does not occur among surplus countries, the IMF should be empowered to issue additional Special Drawing Rights (SDRs) to deficit countries in order to grant them the liquidity needed to finance their deficits. Under Keynes's original plan prepared for Bretton Woods, an international central bank would have been in a position – indeed, would have had the duty – to sustain world output by issuing new money (bancors, to use Keynes's term) if the policies of national governments seemed likely to lead to world depression. The IMF has never had that authority as such. But the creation in 1969 of the SDR, which was designed to cope with a shortage of liquidity, has given the Fund potentially the same power – if, that is, member governments authorise an SDR issue. Currently, however, the IMF must seek explicit approval from donor governments before issuing SDRs, a requirement that has prevented it from playing a more substantial role in maintaining world growth and output. The IMF charter should be altered to give the Fund itself discretionary power to make special SDR issues.

Beyond these two adjustment mechanisms, consideration must also be given to stabilising the prices of commodities, upon which many developing countries remain dependent, and to ensuring adequate long-term development financing. Expanded world output and trade would help sustain commodity prices and could make commodity price agreements unnecessary. But given the presently uncertain prospects for world commodity demand – compounded by IMF and World Bank policies that mandate increased commodity production – commodity prices are likely to continue their slide unless commodity price agreements are reached. Such agreements should stipulate floor prices, limitations on supply, and the creation of buffer stocks. Again, additional SDRs could be issued to support commodity prices when they fell below a certain level. This would help stabilise both prices and world demand.

By boosting the prices of Third World products and improving the markets for them, the changes described above would reduce the extent of adjustment that deficit countries needed to make. But it would be necessary not just to reduce deficits in the short term, but also to improve the prospects for long-term growth and development. This means that developing countries must have access to adequate development financing. Expansionary and growth-oriented adjustment typically requires a significant amount of foreign exchange to finance the investment and imports that are needed for constructing a productive base. Currently, growth prospects in many countries are being undermined by a lack of finance, which forces cuts in investment, maintenance, and spending on education and health – the crucial element of 'human capital'. In Zambia, for instance, copper exports are falling because of the scarcity of foreign exchange for essential equipment and parts; in Tanzania, shortage of import finance has led to the deterioration of the transport system and extreme shortages of incentive consumer goods, with the result of continued stagnation in the production of export crops. A downward spiral of disequilibrium can occur in cases like these: a shortage of foreign exchange causes a drop in export production, which in turn exacerbates the foreign exchange crisis.

Substantially more finance – particularly more medium-term finance – is essential for growth-oriented adjustment. What is needed is a large additional net transfer of funds – inflows of new money beyond what flows out for amortisation and interest. In this sense, much existing finance is not additional, as it simply finances repayment of old debts. Moreover, banks today are making virtually no additional voluntary loans; since other funding is also relatively scarce, perhaps the most effective way to gain additional net transfer is to slow down or limit outflows for debt servicing. In general, the smaller the new inflows from aid or commercial sources, the more likely it is that additional net transfer will have to come about as a result either of renegotiation of payments on existing debt or of unilateral moratoria on debt servicing. What is required is across-the-board reductions in debt servicing, instead of the current case-by-case approach.

If these proposed changes in the international environment – increased finance for development, support for commodity prices, expansion of world demand and trade – are to have the necessary beneficial impact, they must be considered in relation to each other. In other words, they must be considered as a whole, not one by one. On the one hand, the extent of change needed in one area depends on what happens elsewhere; for example, less finance would be necessary if countries could earn more through commodity sales. On the other hand, changes in one area can actually be quite ineffective unless changes are made elsewhere – more aid can simply mean more debt servicing. Such a 'holistic' approach would be quite alien to the international financial institutions; they treat each issue separately, discussing different ones in different arenas and dealing with countries' problems on an individual basis. These procedures need to be substantially revised.

If these revisions were made, and major changes were effected in the world economy, there would be less need for adjustment by individual developing countries (although some adjustments would still be necessary to permit countries to take full advantage of the improved external conditions). But since, in the near future, radical changes in the international economy are unlikely, substantial country adjustment will continue to be necessary.

At present, the IMF affects the Third World primarily through country conditionality programmes. These programmes have been accompanied in recent years by negative effects on output and social welfare, as described earlier. For long-term development to occur, present trends must be reversed: imbalances in external and domestic accounts need to be reduced, yet at the same time there should be efforts to maintain the incomes of the poorest, protect social welfare, and promote the conditions for medium-term growth. What is needed is adjustment with a human face.[6]

To begin with, the IMF and Third World countries need to reach agreement about the legitimate boundaries of conditionality.[7] Some conditionality is legitimate and may be necessary. Lenders, including the IMF (which is not an aid institution but has to revolve the funds at its disposal), do require some assurance that they will be repaid. When there is no suitable collateral, policy conditionality provides some assurance of repayment for international loans intended to support balance of payments adjustments.

At the same time, conditionality has, in practice, far exceeded admissible and legitimate limits. Conditionality has been applied to nearly any country seeking IMF finance, regardless of the country's repayment record or prospects. Furthermore, the policies prescribed go well beyond those strictly related to repayment.

In attempting to reformulate conditionality along more appropriate lines, one should keep in mind that it must be country-specific, geared toward each individual country's economic, social, and political situation and prospects. One cannot, therefore, lay out a detailed conditionality programme that could be universally applied. But it is possible to point to the kinds of changes that in most cases are needed:

1. The IMF and World Bank need to take a more open and less dogmatic view both of the underlying workings of the world

economy and of the desirability of particular policy instruments and institutions. The prevalent philosophy in the international financial institutions – broadly neoclassical and monetarist, laissez-faire and anti-state – is not proven theoretically or empirically. Certainly, as we have seen, its recent achievements have not been spectacular. Unless a more open, flexible, and empirical view is adopted by all parties, the search for a better alternative will be impeded; and progress toward programmes that are jointly initiated and developed, rather than imposed, will be limited.

2. Conditionality programmes need to take fuller account of social and political realities. Economists' 'first-best' solutions, such as large currency devaluations or eliminations of consumer subsidies, may need to be discarded in order to avoid political unrest and disruption of the programme. In Zambia and the Sudan, for instance, tough 'first-best' programmes led to civil unrest, political upheaval, and the abandonment of a series of IMF agreements.

3. Macroeconomic policies need to be more expansionary (or less deflationary). How far this is possible depends partly on the availability of external finance. But even within financial constraints, more expansion can be achieved if greater stress is placed on import substitution and sectors with low imports.

4. Short-term policy changes should be designed to be consistent with the requirements of medium-term development. In sub-Saharan Africa, for instance, the present conditionality is focused mostly on agriculture and is having deindustrialising effects. Yet for the medium to long term, a country's industrial sector must play an important role in providing simple consumption and investment goods for the domestic economy, for export to the region, and eventually for world markets.

5. Within any given macroeconomic policy framework, *mesopolicies* must be used to channel resources toward economic growth and to meet the needs of the vulnerable. Mesopolicies are those that take into account the impact of all policy instruments – including taxation, government expenditure, tariffs, foreign exchange allocations, and credit policies – on the distribution of resources and income. Priorities need to be established for the way goods and services will be distributed to different income groups, and all mesopolicies should be used consistently to ensure that economic growth and alleviation of poverty are given

precedence. Current conditionality programmes often do not allow for this setting of priorities for resources and spending.

6. Sectoral policies should be introduced that would restructure the productive sector in order to strengthen employment and income generation and to raise productivity in low-income activities. Particular attention should be paid to small farmers and informal sector producers in industries and services.

7. Policies should also aim to restructure the social sector, in order to increase its equity and efficiency, and to redirect public spending toward low-cost basic services and growth promotion.

8. There should be compensatory policies to protect basic health and nutrition during adjustment, until resumption of growth permits low-income households to meet their basic needs independently. Such programmes would include employment creation schemes and nutrition support for the most deprived.

9. IMF monitoring should be broadened, so that it covers not just monetary targets but also indications of growth performance, such as output growth and investment levels, and of social development, such as nutrition levels and the incomes of the poorest 40 per cent.

10. There need to be changes in the system by which IMF agreements are negotiated. At both national and international levels, discussions should be broadened to include those parties concerned with economic growth and the social sectors, as well as those responsible for financial matters. Developing countries need technical support to help them fashion and negotiate workable alternatives.

These changes are not just theoretical possibilities: each has been successfully adopted in some country or countries in recent years. For example, S. Korea, Botswana, and Zimbabwe have all achieved significant adjustments, while restoring growth and protecting the vulnerable in society, at times of considerable economic or climatic adversity. In each case, many of the policies suggested above were used.[8]

A RETURN TO BRETTON WOODS?

Beyond doubt, the present international institutions are not fulfilling the objectives laid down for them at Bretton Woods. Apart from recent moves to coordinate policies on, for example, exchange rates among the major industrialised countries, these institutions have more or less abandoned any attempts to exert broad influence on the international economic system in such a way as to maintain balanced growth throughout the world. Their impact has been mainly at the level of individual countries, through IMF conditionality programmes. As we have seen, the results of these programmes have often been cutbacks in expenditure and employment, which have weakened growth prospects and threatened the living standards of many who are already just barely subsisting.

It is sometimes suggested that the world needs to hold a new Bretton Woods, but the agenda is rarely defined with any precision. The analysis outlined here suggests a very clear agenda: restructuring the institutions so they do fulfil their original aim of maintaining output, employment, and development. The necessary policies might cause short-term losses among particular interests, such as bankers and industrialists in developed countries, who may therefore oppose such changes. But in the long run, these parties would gain by a return to high growth throughout the world. The challenge is to generate political alliances that respond to long-term creative vision – the type that was displayed at the original Bretton Woods and in America's Marshall Plan – rather than to the currently predominant short-term considerations of financial interests.

NOTES

1. Kahn (1976).
2. Keynes's opening remarks at the first meeting of the Second commission on the Bank for Reconstruction and Development, in Moggeridge (1980).
3. Horsefield (1969).
4. See, for example, Green (1986) and Helleiner (1983).
5. Godfrey (1985).
6. See Cornia *et al.* (1987).
7. See the more detailed discussion in Chapter 13.
8. For detail and further examples, see Cornia *et al.* (1987).

Part IV
Technology Transfer

13 Technology Transfer for Development*

INTRODUCTION

In some respects developing countries today have fantastic opportunities that were not open to the now-developed countries: there is a vast and growing array of technological knowledge, to which developing countries have potential access, that, with proper use, may transform them from a preindustrial state to a high-income, fast-growing sophisticated economy, in just a few decades. Yet this opportunity is also a threat. The highly advanced state of knowledge possessed by a few economies can lead to domination over less developed countries, with a high price levied for the technology they acquire, their main industries owned and controlled elsewhere, the characteristics of the technology transferred leading to imbalanced forms of development and environmental degradation, and attempts to avoid this situation by developing their own technology thwarted by competition from the highly efficient technology of the more advanced countries.

A few countries – for example S. Korea – have avoided most of the downside and succeeded in incorporating the technology transferred into their economic system, effectively adapting it to their own conditions, with a rapid and fairly balanced pattern of development resulting. But elsewhere experience has been less good: the technology transfer (TT) has created a dualistic society; productivity of the technology transferred has fallen much below what it was in the initiating country; growth has been slow; the technologies have been viable only under stringent protection; local technological efforts have been vapid; and the majority of the population has been left out of the growth process, experiencing only the negative and not the positive effects of TT. Sub-Saharan African countries present the most obvious example (see Lall, 1987b). But there are also examples in parts of Asia and Latin America, and many countries have experienced some negative effects of TT along with some positive effects. Even the most positive case – S. Korea – has experienced social,

* From Evenson and Ranis (eds.), 1990.

311

cultural and environmental dislocations as a result of the rapid transfer of technology.

The critical issues to be considered in this essay arise from these contrasting experiences. The question is what policies will help governments maximise the benefits and minimise the costs from TT. What form of TT should be encouraged? How much should be transferred, in which industries, at what price? What should government policy be towards R and D and other technological infrastructure? How do general economic policies influence the benefits and costs from TT? These are very difficult questions, and a short discussion cannot provide the answers. Experience also suggests that there may not be a single answer (i.e., alternative patterns of development are possible, depending on initial conditions and country objectives), while the answers change as development proceeds and countries' technological competence and negotiating ability improves.

Objectives

It is necessary to begin this discussion by defining the objectives governments may have in their policy towards TT. We assume that a prime objective is economic growth that is equitable, in which most of the population participate, and that protection of the environment is also desired. Increased domestic technological capability is an important aim, both in itself and as necessary to achieve sustained and balanced growth. Economic growth that is totally reliant on foreign resources of technology and management and skilled personnel on a continuing basis would not be acceptable to most countries; moreover, it would not be efficient, as local technological capability is essential for attaining efficient levels of productivity and increasing productivity over time. The weight given to different objectives may alter the relevant strategy. While growth maximisation is a commonly agreed objective, whether or how much most governments are concerned about equity or the environment is less clear.

The Market and TT

Recently market philosophy has come to dominate both much development writing and the major financial institutions. It has been suggested that the market is preferable to government intervention in most economic decisions.[1] Whatever the rights and wrongs of the general case for exclusive reliance on the market, the argument is clearly inapplicable with respect to decisions about technology. This is because technology shares many of the characteristics of a public good. While it is expensive to develop, once developed it costs relatively little to communicate.[2] This means that if allocation of technology-creating activity were left to a perfect market, very little technology would be developed (although, once developed, it would be almost freely available). This is clearly not a 'first-best' solution, since the total social benefits of technological developments would greatly exceed social costs. Two approaches have been developed to circumvent this problem in the developed countries: one is to provide public funds for R and D, usually requiring institutions so funded to provide the results to anyone who wants them free of charge. The other is to permit the private sector to keep secret or sell the results of their research, by allowing short-term monopoly practices and providing a legal system of protection in the form of patents. For the most part, the first solution has been adopted for basic research and also for much applied research for agriculture, while the second solution has applied to most industrial technologies.[3]

The system means developing countries can get free access to much basic research[4] and also to a good deal of agricultural research. But for industrial technology they must buy the knowledge from the companies who have developed it. The price they have to pay is dependent on the nature of the legal system protecting technology in the originating countries, the monopoly or oligopoly position of the technology sellers, and the bargaining position of the technology buyers.

While this system may be justified pragmatically by reference to the fact that it has been effective in producing considerable techno-logical advances, it cannot be claimed that it necessarily produces the 'right' amount of research and development, with the 'right' charac-teristics, or at the 'right' price, from a theoretical point of view. This is even true for the developed countries – in whose environment and interests the system has evolved. The developing countries have been mainly peripheral to the system – both with respect to its institutional features and to the resultant technologies. Being more remote to the evolution and purpose of the system, there is more reason to suppose that a laissez-faire approach will not get the best results, and that an active strategy is necessary.

The developing countries are thus faced with an intrinsically imper-fect market as far as TT is concerned, and with the need to develop

their own system of government interventions to promote and protect technology-creating activities if they are to develop their own
technology. They have to decide how far to intervene, and where, in
the light of their own objectives.

Further to complicate the decision-making process, an essential
characteristic of most efforts to develop or buy technology is uncertainty. When technology is being developed there is uncertainty with
respect to what results the research will produce, as well as all the
other uncertainties associated with any economic activity (e.g., about
prices and markets). When buying technology, the uncertainty is
caused by the fact that the buyers do not know what they are getting –
if they did they would not need to buy it (Arrow, 1962). Against this
background of basic uncertainty, the usual technique of decision-
making, cost–benefit analysis, is inapplicable because too little is
known about costs or benefits. Consequently, with neither the market nor cost–benefit analysis as a guide, countries are unavoidably
making decisions on an inadequate basis. The best guide to decisions
is to look and see what has happened elsewhere, but even here there
are no infallible guides because it is normally not possible to discern
which conditions were essential to success or failure, and which were
just coincidental with them.

This essay aims briefly to review some of this experience to provide
some policy guidance in this area. The next section discusses some
basic facts about technological development and TT. The third
section provides a quick overview of how the 'new' technologies bear
on the issues being considered here. Policies towards TT in the light
of the earlier discussion are then considered, and conclusions are
presented.

SOME BASIC CHARACTERISTICS OF
TECHNOLOGY TRANSFER

A high proportion of world R and D takes place in developed
countries, and much of that in large companies, often multinationals
MNCs[5]. A 1978 survey of world R and D showed that only 2.9 per
cent of expenditure (although a significantly higher proportion of
scientists and technologists) was located in developing countries
(Annerstadt, 1979). In 1975, 94 per cent of world patent rights were
owned by entities located in developed countries, and of the 6 per
cent registered in developing countries, 85 per cent were owned by

MNCs. Only 1 per cent of world patents were owned by LDC firms (UNCTAD, 1976).

In the early 1970s, the advanced countries had a near-monopoly on the world technology market, indicated, for example, by the fact that only 3 per cent of world production of engineering and electrical goods was located in developing countries, and just twelve developing countries accounted for over 90 per cent of this 3 per cent (United Nations, 1974). But this has been modified by some significant technology developments in a few developing countries – especially India, China, Brazil and S. Korea. Much of the R and D in developing countries has been concerned with adapting advanced country technology to LDC conditions, and – in contrast to advanced countries – a smaller proportion is spent primarily on product innovation, as compared with process innovation.[6] Technology-creation among some developing countries has widened the potential market for developing countries, but the advanced countries still largely dominate the nature and direction of technical change.

The value of TT – as indicated by royalties, fees and technical services – has grown greatly. For the five major industrialised countries it was $27 billion in 1973 and had grown to $222 billion by the mid-1980s. Receipts from developing countries represented around 20 per cent of total receipts for the USA and UK and a much higher proportion for Japan (nearly 60 per cent). By the mid-1980s, the approximate value of developing country payments to the major industrialised countries for technology was $6–7 billion (data from United Nations Centre on Transnational Corporations, 1987). This understates the true cost of TT since over-invoicing of imports and/or under-invoicing of exports is known to add substantially to the cost, while the price of imported capital goods includes some element of payment for TT (see the estimates of Vaitsos, 1974; Murray, 1981).

The choice of form of TT involves a varying degree of packaging of TT. At one end of the range is multinational investment, in which ownership and control remains with the technology seller. This was the dominant mode until the 1960s. However, new forms then emerged as countries pressed for more control; the development of international capital markets made it possible for finance and technology to be separated; and specialist engineering firms and smaller firms emerged, mainly in the developed countries, prepared to sell and service technologies on an arm's-length basis. Consequently, less packaged forms of TT developed, including joint ventures (shared ownership and control); licensing (ownership and management responsibilities lie with the host country, but the detailed conditions associated with the technology licence often introduce constraints on decision-making); franchising (sale of the use of a brand name and technical and managerial support); management contracts (supplying management and routine technical assistance); marketing and technical service contracts; turnkey contracts (supplying a 'finished' factory which is then handed over to the buyer); and sub-contracting (where the sub-contractor provides technical information to the sub-contractee).

Each of these arrangements involves specific payment for TT. In addition, TT takes place through trade – by importing machinery or by exporting when buyers often provide some TT. The range of options depends on the industry: the more monopolistic industries often prefer to keep control and will not agree to licensing (this has been the policy, for example, of IBM and Coca Cola, but competitive technologies have reduced this monopoly power). In general, more complex and more recent technologies are more difficult to acquire except through direct foreign investment (DFI). For example, a Japanese MNC refused to pass onto a Malaysian licensee the latest information on synthetic fibre, believing: 'it is not in the company's interest to pass all the technological information, which it had developed at great expense, to the host country' (Fong, 1987). A Korean firm was unable to secure technology for manufacturing polyester film (Lee, 1987).

Despite the emergence of 'new' forms, TT through direct foreign investment remains the dominant model. For the USA, four-fifths of receipts for technology are intra-firm; for West Germany over 90 per cent. The ratios are less for the UK and significantly less for Japan. The proportion of 'arm's-length' TT is higher for those countries that have aimed to avoid DFI and secure technology by other means. For example, India and S. Korea both made heavy use of licensing in the 1970s and for both DFI accounted for only a fraction of total TT.[7] Nonetheless there is heavy concentration as to source (a few industrialised countries), while those supplying technology under the new forms very largely consist of the 'same multinationals which dominate direct foreign investment . . . [who] also account for large proportions of production, trade and "new forms" of TT' (Lall, 1987c). According to Lall 'the supply side of technology still remains very oligopolistic in several industries'.

The origins of a technology strongly influence its characteristics, since most technologies are developed initially for production and

consumption in the home market. Moreover, when there are major
innovations (new 'technology paradigms'), a 'technological trajectory' follows, which clusters new innovations around the early developments, and locks further innovation into a particular direction (see
Nelson and Winter, 1977). The continued domination of technology
creation by the developed countries has thus meant that the developing countries are locked into the technological trajectories determined by the developed countries. The major characteristics of the
technology have been determined by the environment in the developed countries with respect both to production conditions and consumption patterns. While growing technological efforts in developing
countries have led to some adaptation, outside primary production
these are all within broadly the same technological paradigm and
trajectory. Consequently, technologies have tended to have characteristics corresponding to conditions in developed countries – being
capital- and skill-intensive, and relatively large scale, producing
products with characteristics suited to high-income markets – relative
to the conditions and needs of developing countries. For the most
part, these tendencies have increased over time, as real incomes have
risen in the advanced countries, accompanied by rising capital per
head and expanding education and skills, with the generation of
demands for an ever-changing variety of increasingly sophisticated
products. The technology emanating from the advanced countries
has thus tended to become inappropriate over time, in relation to the
needs of developing countries, especially low-income or slow-
growing countries, both with respect to product characteristics and to
techniques. (The one major exception to this trend comes from the
microelectronics revolution – see below – which has reduced the
minimum efficient size of production in some areas.)

Figure 13.1 shows changes in technology in the developed
countries in recent years, indicating that in all industries capital–
labour ratios and labour productivity have risen; in most industries
this has been associated with rising capital–output ratios, but in the
three industries most closely associated with the microelectronics
revolution – electronics, instruments and data processing equipment
– capital productivity as well as labour productivity has risen.
Countries that adopt the more capital-intensive of the technologies
produced by developed countries, without modifications, face a
dualistic pattern of development with a small high-income sector
absorbing almost all the countries' investible resources, its infrastructure and skills, generating demand among a small elite for the

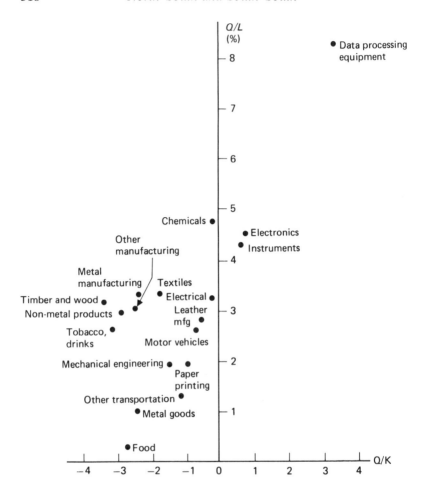

Q: net output; L: employees in employment; K: official SCO capital stock estimates. All figures are average annual growth rates.

Source: Soete (1986)
Figure 13.1   Post-war change in labour (*Q/L*) and capital productivity (*Q/K*) in the UK manufacturing sectors, 1948–84 by SIC sector

modern products produced in the sector, while the remainder of the economy, encompassing the majority of the population, remains deprived of investment resources, modern technology or appropriate products, in conditions of extreme poverty (see Stewart, 1977). Yet there remains considerable choice of technique: countries can choose to focus more on labour-intensive products, to direct more of their resources of credit and infrastructure to the rural areas and small-scale industry, to select older technologies and to modify imported technologies to suit local conditions, thereby avoiding the dualistic pattern associated with excessive and unselective use of advanced-country technology. Taiwan's development path presents an example: labour-intensive industries, many small scale and located in the rural areas, were the spearhead of the industrialisation efforts so long as the labour surplus remained (see Fei, Ranis and Kuo, 1979). Only as the labour surplus has been exhausted has the economy started to move towards more capital-using and sophisticated technologies.

Technology does not come gift-wrapped and ready to work at 100 per cent efficiency. Its development consists in a rather unstructured process of large discoveries associated with major changes in processes and products, followed by small improvements that, when added together, often amount to as great a change in resource use and productivity as the radical innovations.[8] Its efficient use requires considerable technological capability in the recipient for installation, adaption to local conditions, operation and maintenance. The way technology develops has considerable implications for the process of TT. As Rosenberg and Frischtak (1985) state:

In so far as technology is conceived as firm-specific information concerning the characteristics and performance properties of production processes and product designs, and to the extent that it is tacit and cumulative in nature, the transfer of technology is not as easy as the purchase of a capital good or a blueprint. It involves positive and sufficient costs, reflecting the difficult tasks of replicating knowledge across the boundaries of firms and nations; recipients would normally be obliged to devote substantial resources to assimilate, adapt, and improve upon the original technology.

For developing countries the process is usually even more difficult than for transfer among developed countries because more often the availability and quality of inputs, of experienced labour and of necessary infrastructure cannot be assumed to be the same as in the initiating country. Consequently, a considerable local technological effort is necessary to absorb the technology efficiently. Very often, the productivity of the technology falls considerably below levels

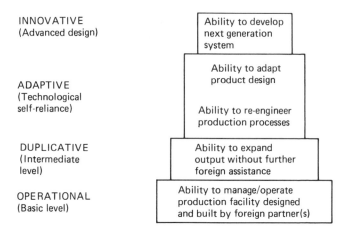

Source: Lall (1987c)
Figure 13.2   Levels of technological capability

experienced in the developed country.[9] The need for such a local technological effort for efficient TT has been the theme of much writing – for example, Katz (1982), Lall (1987c), Enos (1989), Westphal, Kim and Dahlman (1985).

Moreover, it has become apparent that TT is not itself an on–off phenomenon; either it has happened or it has not. There are stages of assimilation, ranging from the machinery being dumped in the host country where it is operated at low capacity and high cost, to full technological capability being transferred, when the host country becomes able not only to operate the technology efficiently, maintain and repair it and innovate to raise productivity over time, but ultimately to design the next stage of the technology itself. The various stages of TT are shown on Figure 13.2. How far up the figure a country wants to go (or can reasonably be expected to go) depends on the particular technology in question, on the stage of development of the country concerned, especially the technological capability, and on the nature of the TT transmission – i.e., whether the form of technology transfer permits the higher-stage developments. Both DFI and licensing may prohibit major (and sometimes minor) local innovations. But in the process of development most countries are striving to mount the ladder of full assimilation for a variety of reasons: partly because higher stages permit more efficient operation of the technology; partly because the ability to operate at higher stages indicates increased local technological capability and, therefore, increased ability to assimilate other technologies efficiently and to acquire and bargain over new transfers; and partly because, in the higher stages, countries can take control over the direction of technological change.

NEW TECHNOLOGIES

In recent years, there has been very rapid advance in two areas – biotechnology and microelectronics – with major implications for developing countries' strategy towards TT and indigenous technological efforts. This section briefly reviews developments in these industries, partly to assess developments in these important areas, but also because the industry studies illuminate the general process of TT.

Biotechnology[10]

Biotechnology consists of the use of biological organisms for commercial activities. The history of biotechnology goes back centuries in such activities as fermentation and brewing of alcohol, bread and cheese making, but new developments in genetic engineering and other ways of transforming biological organisms in the 1970s revolutionised commercial possibilities, giving rise to a large number of applications with the development of new products and new techniques.[11] Potential applications lie in agriculture (seeds, livestock development); medicine (diagnostic kits, vaccines and drugs); food production and processing (with substitutes for natural products such as sugar, meat, soy beans); mining and pollution control. The first biotechnology firm was established in the USA in 1976. By 1981, there were over 80 new firms in the USA and several large established firms branching out into this area. In the UK, too, a sizeable number of small and medium-sized firms emerged. In Europe and Japan, developments have been mainly confined to established firms.

In contrast to the earlier seed revolution, biotechnology has been heavily privatised, with even developments in basic science being patented (see Buttel, Kenney and Kloppenburg, 1985). Stanford University patented the recombinant DNA processes and products in 1980. In that year, the Supreme Court ruled that microorganisms could be patented. The US Patent and Trademark Office first agreed to patent seeds in 1985.

From very preliminary evidence it is possible to sketch out some implications of the new technology for developing countries:

1. There will be some negative effects for primary producers, as new products substitute for their exports. An obvious example is starch-based sweeteners which substitute for sugar. In 1980, Coca Cola switched half its purchases of sugar to high fructose corn syrup. Another example is the development of 'artificial' livestock feed. These changes will reduce demand for the products currently produced by LDCs.

2. The new technology may greatly increase agricultural productivity, while economising on most inputs, including herbicides and fertilisers. Countries will have to adopt the new seeds if they are to compete, and as levels of output rise, prices will fall. For many primary products, with elasticities of demand less than 1, net revenues for producers will fall. It seems likely that the new technology will shift the terms of trade against primary producers, while, because of the heavy privatisation, the cost of importing the technology will be high.

3. Both production and consumption characteristics of the new technologies are likely to be mainly in line with developed country demands and conditions. Production scale of bioprocesses is large and growing,[12] and capital intensity is high relative to traditional methods of food processing. The very small producers in the informal sector will find it difficult if not impossible to get access to the processes, yet demand for competing products they produce is likely to be reduced. Thus the adverse developed country – developing country terms of trade effect will probably be reproduced between formal and informal sectors within countries. For the USA it has been predicted that the technology will further accentuate the trend towards large-scale farming and increase the degree of vertical coordination and control (US Congress Office of Technology Assessment, 1986). These effects are likely to be greater in developing countries, where the typical farm size is much smaller and the degree of vertical integration less. It is likely, unless major modifications are made, that the technology will tend to worsen income distribution in countries adopting new technology. For example, a study of the production of a single cell protein for animal feed in Nigeria suggested that if there were gains, the major beneficiaries would be poultry farmers and feed millers and consumers of poultry and eggs, all of whom are in the

upper-income groups; the losers would be the current producers of poultry feed (i.e., small farmers producing vegetable protein).[13]

4. There will be major consumer benefits – in terms, especially, of more and better food, and improved medicines. But to realise these benefits fully it will be necessary for the research to be adapted to the needs of the country.

5. The biotechnology story presents a strong argument for developing countries to 'get in on the act' and to do some R and D of their own. Independent R and D will help to hold down excessive costs of TT and to ensure that the research responds to their own needs and conditions. But evidence from developments in the advanced countries suggests that it may be difficult for many countries do effective research in this area. Developments in the USA and UK have shown very strong links between basic research at the universities and applied work within companies (see Table 13.1). Such links are much less well developed in most developing countries. Moreover, the cost of the research has been high, relative to the budgets of many developing countries. Monsanto's budget for research on the life sciences in 1985 was $270 million. The smaller companies have spent less, but still employ large numbers of Ph.Ds. A synergistic relationship has been identified between specialisation on new biodevelopments, microprocessing and marketing and distribution (Fransman, 1986a). Competitive success requires all three, which can be achieved by joint ventures or close collaboration or by uniting the three specialisations in a single firm. Many developing countries have too 'thin' an industrial structure to operate effectively over such a large area.

6. It seems likely, therefore, that countries that are mainly primary producers, that lack flexibility in terms of diversification potential, and that do not have the capacity to enter the field themselves may suffer some major losses as a result of the technology and will have to pay heavily for its use. The net gains are likely to be small. In contrast, countries able to diversify out of primary products, and to establish some local R and D capacity will be able to use the technologies to raise productivity and employment.

Microelectronics[14]

The microelectronics revolution was based on scientific and technological breakthroughs in transistors and semiconductors. It represents a technology revolution because it has not only created a new

Table 13.1 Agricultural biotechnology venture capital firms: selected University-based researchers, financial linkages, and areas of research

Company	Principal university-based researcher affiliation	Financial linkages	Areas of research
Agrigenetics	Timothy Hall, U. of Wis. John Kemp, U. of Wis./USDA Vernon Gracen, Cornell	Hoffman–La Roche Kellogg Co. Rothschild Bank	Seed-related biotechnologies
Advanced Genetics Science	Lawrence Bogorad, Harvard Milton Schroth, U. of Calif. Berkeley	Rohm & Haas Hilleshog	Cloning of disease-resistant potatoes
International Plant Research Institute	Oluf Gamborg, Prairie Regional Laboratory, Canada (Formerly) Martin Apple, U. of Calif., San Francisco	Davy–McKee Corp. General Foods Bio-rad Laboratories	High-yielding potatoes, saline-resistant wheat, virus-free cassava
Zeocon Corp.		Sandoz (formerly Occidental Petroleum)	Soybean and cotton breeding
Calgene Genetic Engineering Co.	Raymond Valentine, U. of Calif; Davis Edwin Adair, U. of Colo. Thomas Wagner, Ohio U.	Allied Chemical (20%) Johnson & Johnson	Plant genetics Animal reproduction
DNA Plant Technology Co.	Norman Boriaug, Texas A&M Philip Ammirato, Columbia Melvin Calvin, U. of Calif.	Campbell Soup (40%) Koopers Co. General Foods	Tomatoes, tobacco, forestry products
Molecular Genetics	Anthony Faras, U. of Minn. Charles Green, U. of Minn. Lynn Enquist, NIH	American Cyanamid Moorman Manufacturing US Dept. of Defense	Corn, scours prevention, and non-agricultural applications

Sources: Buttel, Kenney, and Kloppenburg (1985).

cluster of industries to produce the new producer goods and a further cluster of industries to produce the consumer goods that microelectronics makes possible, but its applications potentially extend throughout production and affect much of consumption. The potential effects are thus more far ranging than those of biotechnology. The full effects on developing countries have not yet been felt, and, as pointed out in James's survey, many of them are unresearched. This brief overview is therefore necessarily incomplete.

Like biotechnology, the microelectronics technology is a proprietary technology: 'whether final goods or components, vital technical information regarding design engineering specification, process know-how, testing procedures etc. is proprietary in nature, covered by patents or copyrights, or closely held within various electronics firms from developed countries' (O'Connor, 1985a).

The first direct effects of the revolution on LDCs was the location of production for export in the Third World. While production of mainframe computers was mainly located in the advanced countries, production of smaller computers, more subject to price competition, was shifted to low-wage locations 'as a short-term survival strategy' (O'Connor, 1985b). Countries were selected on the basis of low wage costs, political stability, labour docility, and government incentives, including the availability of low-priced infrastructure (Nayyar, 1978; Ernst, 1985). These factors led to the initial choices of Singapore, Taiwan, and S. Korea. Subsequently, there was some relocation, as wages rose in S. Korea and Taiwan, to Malaysia, the Philippines and Thailand.

Location of production for local and regional consumption followed. The countries concerned were mainly middle-income. Three-quarters of US investment overseas in the industry in the Third World was concentrated in 12 countries.[15]

The export-oriented investments were more associated with direct foreign investment than firms producing for the local market (ESCAP, 1979). Evidence from Brazil is that DFI was associated with larger firms in developed countries, licensing with smaller firms (Tigre, 1985). Both these findings echo findings for TT in general (See Reuber, 1973; Lall, 1987c). It also appears that in this industry, as elsewhere, firms were reluctant to license the more recent and advanced technologies:

Japanese firms prefer to transfer know-how only for small portables, using older technology in tubes and semiconductors. Japanese producers have been unwilling to provide Korean firms with technical know-how for new products such as VCRs and video discs (Clarke and Cable, 1982).

Sub-contracting by MNCs was used for the transfer of more standardised and unsophisticated products, especially where there was a strong risk of fluctuations in demand which could be offloaded to the LDC firm (Plesch, 1979).

Microelectronics has been an area where proprietary rights have been discarded by some firms in the more technically advanced LDCs (Brazil, Taiwan and S. Korea), with reproduction of goods produced by the MNCs by unlicensed firms. This was made possible by outside sourcing which disclosed technical information to supplying firms (see O'Connor, 1985a; 1985b). The longer-term implication of this form of TT has not been investigated. It has a parallel in some pharmaceutical industries which do not respect proprietary rights and is one of the major factors underlying the recent demand to extend the GATT to cover intellectual property.

The use of microelectronics in production saves on one or another or all inputs, including skilled and unskilled labour, energy, materials and capital, while it also can make possible new products and better product quality of existing products. Where all inputs are saved, the new technology dominates and is efficient at any wage level, and consequently early adopters will be able to outcompete non-adopters. In these industries, LDCs will lose any competitive advantage unless they also introduce the new technology. But for some industries – as is the case with textiles and garments – the new technologies save on labour and materials, but use capital, so that whether they are economically efficient depends on relative prices. Studies of computer-controlled machine tools show that there is a significant saving in skilled labour (James, 1986). As noted above, microelectronics also permits smaller-scale production in some sectors. Product quality is generally improved. Consumer products generally have high-income characteristics.

In some respects, then, the production characteristics associated with microelectronics are more appropriate than previous technologies – especially with respect to scale and savings of skilled labour, energy and materials – while the product characteristics are typically inappropriate. Moreover, adaptations can make the technology more appropriate. In Taiwan, product innovations have led to reduced performance of numerically controlled machine tools which was more than compensated for by reduction in price (Fransman, 1986b). Efforts to apply microelectronics to improve traditional technologies – in what has been termed 'technology blending' (Bhalla and James, 1986) – have produced some major improvements in productivity, including, for example, the use of electronic load controllers in microhydro projects.

However, the introduction of the technologies requires certain new skills (of design, maintenance and management, Hoffman, 1985) and complementary infrastructural facilities, including telephone systems and reliable power supplies. Deficiencies in these factors in the less developed countries prevents the widespread adoption of the technologies (Munasinghe, Dow and Fritz, 1985).

Taking these considerations together, it appears that the more advanced developing countries, with a good basis of skills and infrastructure and a flexible labour force, may be in at least as good a position to adopt the new technologies as the developed countries; the production characteristics of the technologies are not inappropriate, and the consumption characteristics can potentially be adapted to the country's needs. For these countries, the technologies will increase their productivity and their international competitiveness. But the less developed Third World countries, with inadequate skills and infrastructure, low labour productivity and lack of capital resources, will find it difficult to adopt the new technology. They are likely to suffer a deterioration in international competitiveness *vis-à-vis* both developed countries and the more advanced developing countries.

POLICIES TOWARDS TT

The previous two sections have indicated the broad dimensions of TT transfer relevant to LDCs in determining their policies. In summary, developing countries face a technology market that is typically oligopolistic, especially for the more recently developed technologies. While some technologies are available at low cost, many, again especially the latest, are subject to tight control, and a high cost is exacted. The characteristics of the technology are often inappropriate for the production and consumption needs of poorer countries, but this inappropriateness can be substantially lessened by making appropriate choices and adaptations of the technologies available. To operate the technologies efficiently and to adapt them to their own needs, it is essential for LDCs to build up technological capacity. Despite the problems associated with TT, much modern technology is highly efficient and offers poor countries huge potential for improving their productivity. As seen in the previous section, these broad dimensions characterise the 'new' technologies as well as mainstream TT.

Given the objectives of equitable growth and the development of technological capability, developing countries' policies towards TT should therefore be designed to improve the terms of TT, enhance the efficiency of the transfer, and increase the appropriateness of the technology in use. There may be some trade-off between these aims, and countries will then have to decide where their priorities lie. Three types of policies are relevant: direct regulation of the form and terms of TT policies to build up local technological resources; and general policies towards the economic environment. These will be discussed in turn.

Direct Regulation

An important issue is whether countries should intervene on the form of technology transfer, either by providing special incentives for DFI or by limiting the areas in which it may operate, requiring MNCs to participate in joint ventures or permitting only arm's-length TT. Different countries have adopted each of these approaches: for example, many countries provide generous tax incentives to encourage DFI, while others only permit minority ownership in some or all industries. Singapore is a successful example of the first approach; Japan, historically, and S. Korea until recently, have mainly encouraged arm's-length TT, again successfully. Less successful examples can also be found of both approaches.

The most appropriate approach partly depends on the stage of development. In the early stages countries may lack the capacity to put the package together themselves, and therefore may need to rely on DFI. But at intermediate stages of development, there is considerable evidence that arm's-length transfer is associated with considerably greater technological learning than DFI.

In a survey of six Asian country studies, Enos (1989) repeatedly found that there was greater local technological effort associated with non-equity transfers. For example, in Indonesia it was found that 'the degree of technological mastery is greater in the national companies' (Thee, 1987); in S. Korea, Lee (1987) found that local effort was greater in local firms; in Malaysia, where there was heavy reliance on DFI, it was found that the technology was not transferred to non-Malaysians; in Thailand, Santikarn (1987) showed that the technology was transferred more effectively where foreign equity was absent. However, Pack (1987) found that in a Kenya–Philippines comparison of the textile sector, total factor productivity was higher in Kenya, and he attributed this to the presence of international managers of high quality, associated with DFI.

The development of technological capability is shorthand for a complex set of events, including training, experience, local R and D and diffusion of the technology throughout the economy. While the record is mixed, the MNCs appear to perform adequately on training (UNCTC, 1987), but are relatively weak on R and D and on generating sufficient local experience in management, technology choice and innovation. There is evidence for US MNCs only for 1982. This showed that they did very little R and D outside the USA (9 per cent of a total of $41 billion), and of this a tiny fraction (0.6 per cent) was spent in developing countries (UNCTC, 1987). Country comparisons of R and D and innovation among foreign and local firms generally show somewhat more innovative activity among local companies, though there are cases where MNCs have undertaken significant amounts of R and D in developing countries.[16]

The nature of the industry is also relevant. On the one hand, in the more sophisticated industries it may be impossible to secure the technology without DFI, as noted earlier. On the other, the ability to put the package together without DFI will be less – for any stage of development – the more sophisticated the technology. Also where the technology is changing rapidly, it may be difficult for local firms to get access to the latest developments. Consequently, S. Korea encouraged DFI for the more sophisticated industries and for export industries, where market access can provide another reason for having DFI.

The extent of diffusion of the technologies – including knowledge about the hardware and operating skills – varies with the type of industry. Export industries established in export-processing zones have low diffusion due to the nature of the zones with limited linkages to the rest of the economy and also the rather standard low-skill technologies involved; the more technologically sophisticated activities are concentrated in the advanced countries. However, a comparative study of diffusion of innovations in S. Korea exhibited that both subsidiaries of MNCs and local firms showed a

Table 13.2   Frequency of selected restrictive clauses in contracts in four Southeast Asian developing countries, %

Restrictive clauses relating to	Republic of Korea	Malaysia	Sri Lanka	Thailand
Export	24.0	30.4	41.4	27.2
Purchase of inputs	16.5	14.6	22.1	8.3
Confidentiality	80.5	54.0	37.1	45.6
Rights granted to recipients	49.0	44.8	–	50.3
Manufacture of competing or similar product	11.5	10.3	–	–
Cease-use clauses	33.5	20.2	21.4	19.3

Source: ESCAP/UNTC (1984)

high rate of diffusion (Westphal, Rhee, and Pursell, 1981).

A second consideration is the price of the technology transferred in different ways. Research in the 1970s showed that DFI can be associated with very high costs, especially if over-invoicing is allowed for, and particularly in the more oligopolistic industries (Vaitsos, 1974; Helleiner, 1981a; Murray, 1981). The use of joint ventures may not alter the costs significantly compared with DFI. However, technology licensing can also be costly, involving not only explicit payments but also various clauses restricting the freedom of technology recipients. Table 13.2 shows the restrictive clauses found in a 1977 survey. Some of the restrictions inhibit effective TT and technology diffusion. For example, in Indonesia it was found that restrictions were imposed on major product innovations (Enos, 1989). 8 per cent of technology contracts to Thai firms were found to forbid the duplication of know-how or reverse engineering (Santikarn, 1987). Such restrictions may, of course, also be present (but with no need for any explicit clause) in DFI or joint ventures. But the evidence suggests following a strategy of licensing alone is not enough to ensure that monopolistic rents are not being levied.

The costs of TT vary inversely with stage of development according to a UN study of eight Asian countries (quoted in Enos, 1989). They are also greater the more complex the technology. The highest fees are to be found in petroleum, chemicals, metals, machinery, electrical equipment and electronics.

A third consideration is the appropriateness of the technology and products transferred. Research into the relative capital intensity of technology adopted by MNCs and local companies on balance shows little difference (and in some cases a difference favouring the MNC) if one compares production of the same product, at similar scale (see Pack, 1976; ILO, 1972; Wells, 1973; 1979; Reuber, 1973). However, more significant differences arise from differences in choice of product and of scale, with the MNC on average being associated with more 'high-standard' and capital-intensive products, and producing on a larger scale than local companies (see examples in Stewart, 1987).

Over the past twenty years, Third World MNCs have developed on a quite substantial scale, generally concentrated on mature technologies in well-established industries (see Lall, 1983; Green, 1988). On balance they have a better record on cost of technology transfer and on appropriateness of products and techniques than advanced country MNCs.[17]

In conclusion, there seem to be strong reasons for preferring arm's-length 'unpackaged' TT, from most points of view, especially in relation to building up local technological capability. But this may not be a realistic possibility for the more sophisticated technologies, nor an efficient alternative for countries at an early stage of development, with weak domestic technological capability. For the latter, Third World MNCs may have more to offer at less cost than advanced country MNCs.

Joint ventures represent an intermediate option between DFI and licensing. Whether, in practice, the joint venture approximates more nearly DFI or arm's-length TT depends on the specific conditions of the joint venture and the capabilities and bargaining power of the two partners. In the less-developed countries, joint ventures appear to be very similar to DFI.

In the 1970s a number of countries developed regulatory policies designed to control the price of TT, reduce restrictive clauses and encourage local technological development.[18] These policies generally require draft technology contracts to be submitted for government approval. Regulations may be imposed on the import of technology where there is a local alternative, on the extent of royalty payments and of restrictive clauses, and on the duration of the contract. Evidence may also be required that the licensee has made an adequate search for alternatives and that the contract will be associated with training and local R and D.

The evidence suggests that these regulations had a substantial effect on the formal terms of TT, without affecting the level of transfer, and that some countries made 'substantial savings of foreign exchange'.[19] There was a reduction in rates charged and of restrictive clauses, while the number of contracts was maintained or increased in all regulating countries, except for Argentina. However, it is not known how far the regulations were circumvented informally. Collusion between licensee and licensor can make regulation ineffective.

Regulations of this sort have the effect of increasing the bargaining power of the recipient firm. In conditions where markets are imperfect and oligopolistic rents are being earned, such regulations ought to be effective in reducing costs without adversely affecting quantity. Taxation is another mechanism which can be used to reduce excessive payments for TT (see Stewart, 1981).

Regulations have also been used to protect local technological efforts, by restricting imports. India followed a very restrictive policy, which led to a significant build-up in local technological capability. Some of the technologies that resulted were internationally competitive, as indicated by significant technology exports. According to Lall: 'low reliance on imports of technology in the process of industrialization . . . contributes to buildup of a diverse and deep technological capability' (Lall, 1985). However, India fell behind the international technological frontier in many areas, and this had adverse effects on the competitiveness of India's industries (Lall, 1985). Japan and S. Korea also regulated technology imports, but much less comprehensively than India, importing the initial technology, learning to reproduce it locally, and subsequently restricting imports when local technological alternatives became available. R and D and other technological efforts were thus complementary to technology imports in the policies of Korea and Japan, in contrast to the competitive policies in India. While the Indian policies were effective in boosting technological capability, they had a much higher economic cost than the policies of Korea and Japan.

Policies to Build Up Local Technological Capacity

Much research suggests that active local efforts are needed to ensure efficient TT, with consequent learning effects. Thus, according to Santikarn (1987):

> Ownership and control by nationals is not, however, sufficient to ensure success in absorbing technology . . . The degree of

success . . . depends upon the ability, awareness and management skills possessed by recipient enterprises, its investment in human resources through training and upgrading of skills.

Following a detailed survey of TT and learning, Bell (1986) emphasised that learning does not take place automatically, but requires a conscious local effort.

High levels of human capital are essential for this process. Government policy to build up education in general and scientific and technical education in particular has been a vital element in the success of technological development in Japan, S. Korea and Taiwan, and its absence one of the major missing factors in many African countries. Comparing Korea, Argentina, Brazil, India and Mexico, Westphal, Kim, and Dahlman (1985) conclude:

What stands out about the educational pattern are the high proportion of postsecondary students abroad, the high secondary enrollment rate and the high percentage of engineering students among postsecondary students . . . by the late 1970s South Korea had by far the highest percentage of scientists and engineers.

In addition to support for general education, government support is needed for R and D institutions. As noted above, the public goods aspects of R and D make this essential. Local R and D is needed to adapt products and techniques to local conditions, especially to generate appropriate technologies. The biotechnology and microelectronics cases illustrated how important local efforts are if the revolutions are to be harnessed to local needs.

However, it is not a matter of supporting any old R and D. Much developing country R and D has produced 'white elephants' (Beranek and Ranis, 1978), duplicating the research efforts of advanced countries rather than aiding industry to adapt imported technologies, or upgrade local technologies. Too little is known about the inner workings of R and D institutions, the motivations of scientific personnel and how best they can be channelled to useful activities. It appears that close ties with users, a clear, defined mandate and high-class personnel are essential. There are successful 'models' – including notably the Korean Institute of Technology, the Madras Leather Institute and the Electronics Institute in Taiwan. More research is needed to learn from these and other successes.

General Government Policies

The general policy environment is of major significance to the effectiveness of TT. It can affect the cost of the transfer, the efficiency of its use, learning effects and the appropriateness of TT.

The cost of the transfer in an oligopolistic market is in part a function of how much consumers are prepared to pay. Consequently, if the market is highly protected against internal and/or external competition, high rents can be levied by the producer, and part of these rents may not be retained in the country, but transmitted to the technology supplier. This certainly occurs in the pharmaceutical industry, and it is likely to be a phenomenon associated with bio-processes. A competitive environment would thus be associated with lower costs of technology imports. This can be achieved through internal competition policy or through trade policy, where competition from imports or from other countries' goods in export markets may reduce rents.

However, in some industries with large economies of scale and learning economies, an excessively competitive environment may prevent what would ultimately be desirable production activities from taking place (this is elucidated in Pack and Westphal, 1986). Moreover, the desire to promote local technological activity may justify monopolistic or oligopolistic production, given the strong externalities. On the other hand, competitive pressures may be needed to provide an incentive to increase technological efforts and raise productivity. There can be conflicts, therefore, but these may be moderated by policies reducing the rent potential of such monopolistic activities. This appears to have been achieved in Korea by strong regulatory pressures (see Pack and Westphal, 1986; Enos and Park, 1987). Without such regulatory pressures, local technological activity can be misdirected – as in the case of India, according to Lall – where considerable local technological efforts has resulted in some rather inefficient technologies, compared with international standards.

General government policies are extremely important in influencing choice of technology and the direction of local technological change (see Stewart, 1987; Stewart and Ranis, 1990). Policies towards factor prices (e.g., tax incentives for investment, wages policies), credit markets, international trade, income distribution and product standards help determine the choice of products and techniques made by individual enterprises, and also the composition of units (i.e., the proportion of total investable resources controlled by different types of decision-makers). In many countries, macropolicies systematically favour inappropriate technologies.[20] Policies that support appropriate products and labour-intensive techniques will lead to a greater use of older more standardised technologies; these technologies are thus likely to be more accessible to arm's-length transfer, to be available from a wider range of technology sources, including developing country sources, and to be transferred at lower prices than the technologies associated with more capital-intensive strategies.

Policies Toward the Environment and TT

It is now generally agreed that excessive environmental degradation can occur if investment decisions are motivated only by profit or output maximisation, without consideration of environmental effects. Developing countries can use policies regulating the import of technologies, in addition to policies applicable to all productive activities in the economy, to moderate environmental destruction. However, problems arise in devising appropriate standards (as well, of course, as in enforcing them). Being poorer, countries may be prepared to accept lower standards than in the rich countries, especially if this permits more rapid elimination of poverty, which is itself a major cause of environmental problems. However, although there is a strong case to be made for different standards in developing countries than in advanced countries, this does not mean there should be no standards – the very rapid rates of industrialisation in some countries, technological developments and the potential export of 'dirty' technology from developed countries, make a strong case for the imposition of environmental standards.

A further problem is caused by the fact that some of the environmental costs associated with developing country growth are imposed on the world at large and not solely on the country concerned. An obvious example is the 'greenhouse' effect resulting from use of carbon fuels. Here global action is needed with the advanced countries supporting action by developing countries with research, subsidised technologies in 'clean' fuels, and finance. For world environmental problems, the technology-exporting countries can contribute by imposing export controls on dirty technologies.

SOME CONCLUSIONS

TT is an interactive process between technology suppliers and technology users. Developing countries have a difficult balance to strike in choosing which technologies to import and how to import them. On the one hand, they need the productivity increases modern technologies confer. On the other hand, they do not want to pay an excessive price, which the oligopoly position of suppliers permits; they want to avoid the more inappropriate characteristics of imported technology; and they want to build up their own technological capacity, which can be inhibited by excessive dependence on imports.

Appropriate technological strategies depend on the stage of development. The least developed countries have no choice but to import technology, often in a packaged form. But they can avoid paying too high a price by sticking to older technologies and searching for Third World suppliers, while developing their own human capacities by education and training. These older technologies often have more appropriate characteristics. However, the highly efficient 'new' technologies create problems for these countries because they add very greatly to productivity, but require skills and infrastructure that the countries lack.

For countries with more industrial experience, importing technology in unbundled form has considerable advantages from the point of view of learning effects and the creation of technological capacity. It may not be possible for very recent technologies as suppliers may refuse to sell the technologies in this form, and in some cases the management and scientific requirements may be too great. But as countries acquire experience with the more mature technologies, they also acquire the expertise to manage later technologies. The example of biotechnology underlines the need for local R and D capacity to adapt technological advances to local conditions.

Middle-stage developing countries with high levels of education and skills and a significant R and D capacity are in a very good position to exploit the new technologies effectively. Indeed, given their adaptable workforce and lack of cultural rigidities, they may be able to use the technologies more effectively than the advanced countries. In so doing, they present a competitive threat both to the advanced countries and to the least developed countries. For the former, their lower wages and more disciplined workforce may mean that their unit costs are potentially considerably lower than in the advanced countries in many industries; the inability of the least developed countries to apply some of the new technologies effectively (e.g., computer-aided design in textiles, or biotechnology in primary products) may mean that they become relatively high-cost producers who can compete only with very adverse movement in the terms of trade.

Recent advances are creating a new technological division in the world economy; the late latecomers will find it increasingly difficult to take off industrially because of these technological advances and the success of the NICs and near NICs in making use of them.

NOTES

1. See, eg., Little (1982), Lal (1983), and World Bank *World Development Reports*, but see also comments by Stewart (1985b) and Toye (1985).
2. For an estimate of the costs of communication in some industries see Teece (1976).
3. An intermediate solution is sometimes adopted in which companies are encouraged to collaborate on R and D (or even to amalgamate) so as to internalise major externalities. This appears to have been the policy promoted by MITI in Japan, and also in some sectors (e.g., planes, electronics) in the USA and Western Europe.
4. The precise distinction between what is basic and what is applied, which has always been unclear, is getting more blurred; recently patents have been granted in what would appear to be basic areas, with respect, for example, to biotechnology and superconductivity.
5. In the UK, for example, firms with less than 1000 employees account for only 3 per cent of R and D expenditures, but a very much larger proportion (more than 30 per cent) of 'significant innovations commercialised in the UK'. Firms with more than 10,000 employees account for over 80 per cent of R and D and 47 per cent of significant innovations. In the USA the top 100 firms account for 90 per cent of R and D expenditure, and 60 per cent of a measure of technological activity (Pavitt and Patel, 1988).
6. Surveys of firms' R and D efforts in developed countries typically find that about three-quarters is spent on efforts intended to bring about product innovation, with one-quarter devoted primarily to process innovation (see, e.g., Gustafson, 1962). In developing countries most research suggests that a smaller proportion of efforts is mainly devoted to product innovation. Of course, the distinction is not hard and fast since some firms' products are in fact other firms' processes, while much innovation in processes results in product modification and vice-versa.
7. Enos (1989) estimates that DFI and joint ventures accounted for only 14.7 per cent of India's technology acquisitions between 1969 and 1979

and 48.3 per cent of the Philippines'. For S. Korea they accounted for 27.4 per cent of the number of approvals of technology imports between 1962 and 1981. (These figures exclude purchases of capital goods as a source of technology.)

8. Powerful empirical support for this view is provided by Hollander (1965) and the ECLA/IDB/UNDP/IDRC studies in Latin America.

9. See, e.g., Teitel (1984), who shows major divergences in productivity between the USA and Latin American countries.

10. This section draws heavily on the work of Fransman (1986a) and others in the New Technologies Centre Feasibility Study.

11. Two basic scientific discoveries lie at the heart of the revolution: recombinant DNA technology, which allows new genetic combinations (applications include pharmaceuticals, chemicals, food processing, improved mining techniques and pollution control), and cell fusion technology, which permits the desirable properties of different cells to be combined into a single cell (applications include improved diagnostic techniques). Improvements in bioprocess technology have also resulted in the large scale use of biological processes.

12. See evidence from Cellnet quoted in Fransman (1986b).

13. See Okereke (1988). In fact it is questionable whether there would be net gains, as on present estimates the feed is expected to cost 10 per cent more than traditional feed, but supplies might be of higher quality.

14. This section draws heavily on James's (1986) and on Soete's (1986) papers for the New Technologies Centre Feasibility Study.

15. India, Brazil, Mexico, Colombia, Malaysia, Hong Kong, the Philippines, Singapore, Taiwan, S. Korea and Thailand.

16. Two examples of major local innovations by MNCs in Argentina are reported in UNTC (1987). In the Brazil computer industry, high learning effects from DFI were reported in James (1986).

17. In a study of Thailand, for example, Lecraw (1977) found that Third World MNCs were significantly less capital intensive than those from advanced countries.

18. See United Nations, TD/B/C.6.48; United Nations, TD/B/C.6/55; Correa (1981).

19. UNCTC (1987) p. 63. Policies to regulate TT to Japan also had negligible effects on the inflow of technology. According to Ozawa (1981): 'Foreign licensors did complain about the government's intervention, but kept supplying technology – a clear sign that the prices they received were acceptable to them.

20. See Stewart (1987) and Stewart and Ranis (1990) for evidence of this in a large number of countries.

14 Technical Change in the North: Some Complications for Southern Options*

INTRODUCTION

The debate about choice of technique in developing countries has been about choice at a particular point in time.[1] Yet perhaps the most obvious fact about technology in modern economies is that it is continuously changing, both with respect to products and processes. Conclusions based on the static picture (given technology set and product) are likely to become obsolete. The nature and direction of technical change determines the set of technologies available to a developing country at a point of time, and how that set is changing: hence the nature of technical change has considerable implications for development patterns. This essay discusses aspects of this question.

Technical change has long been dominated by the advanced countries – described here as 'the North'. Evidence on significant innovations– inventions, patents issued, technology balance of payments, distribution of research and development expenditure, and scientific manpower,[2] all support this conclusion. In the years since 1975 there has been a certain amount of innovative activity in the South; the development of scientific infrastructure, many minor and a few major innovations, and evidence of growing technology exports by the South (Lall, 1982a). Despite this, technology change in the North still dominates, being responsible for the major directions of change, even though Southern efforts may modify the results in some respects.

Why distinguish between North and South in this way? As has often been pointed out, there is considerable heterogeneity within both groups, but especially within the South. Because of this hetero- geneity it is not possible to come to conclusions which are univer- sally applicable to all economies in the South. However, there are

---

* First published in Pasinetti and Lloyd (1987).

differences between the 'typical' Southern economy and that of the North which are of relevance to the question being considered here. These differences include the following:

1. the South has substantially lower *per capita* incomes;
2. the South has lower *per capita* savings;
3. the South generally has lower *per capita* levels of education–skill;
4. the South has lower levels of social and economic infrastructure per person;
5. the South has higher rates of population growth;
6. the South has smaller markets in aggregate and for most products expressed in terms of monetary demand;
7. the average size of productive unit (firm and plant) tends to be substantially smaller in the South;
8. the South has a markedly different distribution of its output between different types of goods (e.g., more agriculture, less manufacturing) and an even more marked difference in the distribution of its workforce.

Most of the differences (2)–(8) arise from, or are reflections of, the first difference – in *per capita* incomes: this in turn reflects differences in average labour productivity for the economy as a whole (although not necessarily for particular industries).

Because of these differences (and others not specified), the South's requirements of its technology differ in some major respects from those of the North.

Both North and South share the requirement that technologies should maximise the productivity of their resources in aggregate, which is equivalent to maximising the productivity of the total population. But technologies also affect the level and distribution of employment, the distribution of incomes, patterns of consumption, organisation and nature of work. Technologies which fulfil the output-maximising criterion may involve adverse effects on the other variables: for brevity, we shall describe these as 'distorting' effects. New technologies designed in and for the North may be assumed not to have distorting effects in the North (although many would challenge this assumption – see Norman, 1981). But even where they maximise output, they may have distorting effects in the South, given the difference in conditions (e.g., they may be associated with much under-employment). Hence new technologies from the North may:

1. raise output in the South, without 'distorting' effects;

2. raise output in the South, with 'distorting' effects;
3. not raise output in the South, and not be selected;
4. not raise output in the South, and be selected.

Obviously, the welfare effects of the new technologies will depend critically upon which category technical change (*tc*) generally falls into, as will the policy implications.

Techniques in mainstream economics, both with respect to technical choice and technical change, are usually categorised in two dimensions: these are the capital and labour requirements for the production of a given product. There are three respects in which this categorisation is inadequate. First, there are the well-known problems of measuring capital such that two techniques may turn out to be more or less capital-intensive than each other, according to the interest rate assumed. Secondly, the approach cannot deal with changes in products. Yet changes in product characteristics (minor and major) are an intrinsic aspect of technical change being the dominating motive of R and D,[3] constituting a main element in the success of new technologies, and forming a major part of increased income. Thirdly, the two dimensions selected form only one small aspect of a true description of a technology. How one describes a technology depends on the point of view of the observer. For example, an artist's description would differ from that of a transport firm whose task was to carry a machine to the factory; a worker would describe it in terms of the requirement it imposes upon the worker (e.g., monotony of operations, physical effort, etc.), while a cleaner would have a different point of view. What is the relevant point of view? In one way all these (and many others) are relevant, since all affect welfare when a technology is installed.

The major focus here is on characteristics relevant to the decision as to whether to introduce the technique, to the efficiency of the technique and to the social consequences of its introduction. (This last aspect, of course, could be interpreted to include more or less all aspects.) Major relevant characteristics, then, include the resources the technology uses, including unskilled labour and labour of various skills; the machinery involved (cost, durability, likely maintenance expenditure); the scale of production and managerial requirements; raw materials and semi-processed materials. We then have a vector, T_a, consisting of the set of characteristics of a technique a: t_i, t_{ii}, t_{iii}, . . . etc. (Stewart, 1977, p. 2) which describe the technique a as a process of production. It is necessary to add a description of the product P_a, which in turn is a vector whose components, p_i, p_{ii},

p_{iii} . . . describe various aspects of the product: for example, its broad function (e.g., to provide nutrition) and its specific aspects (e.g., calories, protein, process requirements). A full description of a technique, then, will include details of both product and process characteristics. For simplicity, we may include P_a as a member of T_a, so T_a consists of t_i, t_{ii}, t_{iii} . . . P_a. Technical change then consists in the development of a new technology vector, say T_a', whose characteristics differ in some respects from the previous one; the new technique might thus use less energy, or be of a larger scale, or involve some major or minor improvement in product. It might also involve a change in the conventional dimensions (value of machinery, quantity of labour). But it is necessary to look at the many dimensions suggested here – first, because many technical changes may not affect the conventional dimensions at all but could still be of major significance; secondly, because many changes which do in fact fit into the usual category, changing the ratio of value of machinery to labour employed, may also be associated with other changes (in scale, material use, product characteristics) which determine the effects of the technology on patterns of development.

In practice, it is not possible to disentangle processes and products, since each process produces a (more or less) specific product, while the process itself embodies, in the form of machines, transport equipment, etc., the products of other industries. A very large proportion of changes in techniques, then, are at the same time changes in process and changes in product. Often if a process becomes obsolete, the product associated with it will too, while if a product is no longer demanded then the process of production associated with it is also discarded (e.g., the technology of horse-upkeep has become obsolete with the replacement of horses by mechanised horse-power). This interactive process is a major source of obsolescence, reducing the number of 'vintage' technologies which remain economic. Despite the close connection between processes and products, these are discussed separately. The next section considers technical change in processes.

PROCESS TECHNOLOGY

The Neoclassical Approach

As stated, most economic analysis has been concerned with a rather narrow sub-set of this type of change – i.e. the way in which capital/labour (K/L) requirements and capital/output requirements (K/O) change over time. The first attempt to incorporate *tc* into economic models did so very crudely, simply assuming that technology change occurred at some independent rate (not as an outcome of the economic system) in the form of 'increase in knowledge', with uniform effects on each of the potential techniques (Solow, 1957). Thus the whole traditional production function, embodying different combinations of capital and labour, was shifted out uniformly. Hence productivity of techniques most relevant to the South (more labour-using) was raised proportionately[4] with more capital-intensive techniques (used by the North). If this were a good description of technical change, then it would raise productivity in the South, with no adverse effects. However, the most casual of empirical evidence suggests that this is an incorrect description; technical change has been uneven. Very labour-intensive technologies – the traditional technologies of the masses in the South – have been untouched by technical change, while the major new technologies have been concentrated in new industries (e.g., chemicals, and now biotechnology), generally of high capital-intensity, and often also of high skill-intensity and of increasing scale of production.

There is no question, then, that the simple 'uniform' technical change neoclassical model is incorrect as a description of reality. It is also subject to severe theoretical defects. Two different types of criticism have been made; both are illuminating with respect to the nature of technical change. One accepts the basic framework of capital and labour being the main dimensions of technology but tries to locate innovatory activity in an economic setting rather than as 'manna from heaven'; it consequently sees *tc* as the outcome of particular economic pressures and incentives, with consequences for the rate and direction of *tc*.[5] The other is premised on a more radical critique of the concept of capital, thereby rejecting the use of the conventional framework, even as a starting point.

Technical Change as the Outcome of Economic Activity

Once it is accepted that the process of producing technical change, with respect to research, development and the introduction of new technologies, is an economic activity, mainly carried out by profit-making firms in order to generate (or preserve) their profits, then it can readily be shown that the actual technologies developed will be formed in the light of the economic conditions when and where they are developed. Given the big differences noted between the economic conditions in the North and South, it follows that the characteristics of the new technologies will often be unsuitable for the South. This is the broad conclusion to be derived from all the theories of technical innovation as an economic activity.

The simplest of these is that of Salter (1966), who argued that while in some sense the 'state of knowledge' may increase at a rate which is independent of actual economic developments, any actual technique is developed and produced in a particular context. The traditional production functions cannot thus be a description of actual techniques in use but, at the most generous interpretation, hypothetical techniques that might be developed were there to be a favourable economic environment.

Techniques that are actually developed will be those which are profitable in the prevailing economic environment. As real wages rise, it can easily be shown that the low K/L ratio and, low labour productivity techniques will not generate enough output per man to pay the wage bill. Hence, over time, with rising real wages, the techniques that are developed in the North will be increasingly capital-intensive.

A major weakness of this approach is to assume the existence of a set of hypothetical production functions, representing potential techniques which may be developed according to prevailing economic conditions. While there are general scientific advances over time, which make it likely that new techniques will be more productive than old, those carrying out innovatory activity do not know what the potential set of techniques are.

In this view, the direction of tc (in terms of the K/L ratio) is indeterminate, but a greater proportion of new technologies will tend to raise the K/L ratio, the higher the real price of labour in relation to capital. The concept of an 'innovation possibility curve' (IPC) of Ahmad and others suggests that relative factor prices influence the direction of tc, with more capital-intensive (higher K/L) techniques being developed the more expensive labour is in relation to capital. Innovations in industrialised countries would tend to generate increasingly capital-intensive techniques over time.

This approach to innovation has been rightly criticised for hypothesising a curve (the IPC curve) which has no empirical foundation, and is simply a convenient theoretical device (see especially Nelson and Winters, 1982). A fundamental fact about R and D and technical development is that when decisions are made, entrepreneurs do not know what they are going to find, whereas the IPC assumes that they

do. Nelson and Winters start from a much less presumptuous position, simply assuming that entrepreneurs search in a somewhat
random fashion for new techniques subject to two restrictions: first,
they start the search wherever they are at the moment, and the
innovations tend to be clustered around that point. Secondly, they
pursue only innovations which are cost-reducing. These rather modest assumptions are sufficient to lead to the conclusion that Northern
innovations will tend to be biased against the needs of LDCs, as
compared with own-generated innovations. A random search produces a range of research results, while the ones worth pursuing are
those which reduce costs. North innovation will produce more
capital-intensive results than South innovation, first because of differences in prices which lead to differences in costs associated with each
technique, and secondly because of differences in starting point, with
the North generally exploring new ideas in the context of a more
capital-intensive environment. Over time, Northern innovation will
become increasingly inappropriate for the South, with changes in
factor prices and in the point of departure.

To summarise, adopting a neoclassical approach to production
possibilities and innovation, there is strong theoretical support for
the view that economic conditions in the North will influence the
nature of *tc*. It seems that new technologies are likely to use more
capital and less labour than would be best from the point of view of
the South. However, while the new technologies are likely to be
associated with higher capital intensity, in the sense of K/L, there is
no reason why they should be associated with *higher capital requirements per unit of final output*. In so far as new techniques are
associated with the same (or lower) K/L than previous techniques,
they will raise productivity in the South as well as the North, as
compared with old techiques. In terms of the earlier classification,
then, they will tend to fit into the first two categories, being output-
raising. But the higher K/L may mean that they are also 'distorting',
in the sense that – given limited savings – the countries can afford to
equip only a minority of the labour force with them. It follows that
there will be under-employment in the rest of the workforce, while
inequality of income distribution is also often associated with such
uneven availability of capital equipment.

Extending the discussion to include changes in skill requirements,
scale and infrastructure produces similar results: new techniques will
follow the supply availabilities and organisational structure of the
North. Over time, this means a tendency to use more skills and more

sophisticated infrastructure to produce techniques designed for a larger scale of production. This does not mean that every innovation from the North will have these characteristics: science and technology can produce innovations of many kinds and some may be economic in the North, while having Southern-type characteristics. But taken together there will be broad tendency in this direction.

Capital Measurement, Technical Choice and Technical Change

The previous discussion sidestepped the issue of capital measurement. But according to Pasinetti (1981), very different conclusions follow once it is accepted that capital is not a distinct entity, but simply labour of a different kind (i.e., indirect or embodied labour).

The basic point is that capital consists of *produced* goods; these goods are produced by labour together with machines, which were themselves produced at an earlier period. Ignoring, for the moment, the vintage machines which help make machines, capital goods consist solely of embodied or indirect labour. A rise in the wage rate, then, will affect the cost of machines (the indirect labour) as well as the labour directly employed. A rise in the real wage does not affect the cost of techniques of differing capital intensities (defined as techniques with differing ratios of indirect to direct labour) since it raises the costs of indirect labour just as much as the costs of direct labour. A change in the profit rate will affect the choice in so far as different techniques are associated with different ratios of embodied to direct labour, but 'the influence of changes in the rate of profit on the choice of technique is basically inconclusive as to the direction. In any case, whatever the direction, it is very likely in practice to be of secondary importance' (Pasinetti, 1981, p. 194).[6]

As far as choice of technique in industrialised countries and LDCs are concerned, these propositions lead to very strong conclusions. For convenience we may assume that the profit rate is roughly the same in North and South, but the real wage is very different, being much lower in the South. According to Pasinetti (1981, p. 196):

> A different wage rate – when the rate of profit is the same and the technical possibilities are exactly the same – does not make the slightest difference to the choice of techniques!

A simple arithmetical example bears out the Pasinetti conclusion:

	'Capital' = 'indirect labour'		Direct labour		Total cost
	Quantity	Cost	Quantity	Cost	
Automated loom	10	10w	1	1w	11w
Hand loom	2	2w	10	10w	12w

In the example, the total cost of the hand loom is greater than that of the automated loom, irrespective of the wage rate. An example illustrating the reverse situation could have been chosen, but the basic conclusion would have been the same: that the *same technique turns out to be the most profitable or least cost, irrespective of the wage rate*. However, the conclusion depends on each technique being manufactured in the same country in which the technology is introduced.

Suppose initially that every technique is manufactured in the North. Then the costs of embodied labour will reflect Northern labour costs, while the costs of direct labour will reflect Southern labour costs, as follows:

	'Capital' = 'indirect labour'		Direct labour		Costs in North	Costs in South
	Quantity	Cost	Quantity	Cost		
			N	S		
Automated loom	10	10Wn	1	1Wn 1Ws	11Wn	10Wn + 1Ws
Hand loom	2	2Wn	10	10Wn 10Ws	12Wn	2Wn + 10Ws

In this case, Southern choice of technique will differ from Northern (in the predicted direction of lesser capital intensity) so long as

$$(2Wn + 10Ws) < (10Wn + 1Ws) \text{ or } Ws < \frac{8}{9}Wn$$

In this example it has been assumed that the cost to the South of importing a machine can be expressed as the labour cost of producing that machine in the North. In fact, the South has to expend labour resources on producing some exportable goods (which has its own costs) which it exports, and buys the imported machine with the proceeds. Hence a more complex procedure is required for calculating relative costs. In what follows we shall stick to the simplification of ignoring this procedure. This could well alter the results in any particular case, but would not be likely to affect the general conclusions. If one technique is produced only in the North (automated loom) and one only in the South (hand loom), the costs will be as follows:

	Capital costs		*Direct labour*		*Total costs*	
Automated loom	$10Wn$	$10Wn$	$1Wn$	$1Ws$	$11Wn$	$10Wn + 1Ws$
Hand loom	$2Ws$	$2Ws$	$10Wn$	$10Ws$	$2Ws + 1Wn$	$12Ws$

Hence where $Wn > 2Ws$ the North will choose the automated technique, and the South will choose the hand loom.

Only if both techniques are produced in both North and South, under the same technical conditions, will the same technique *necessarily* be best (i.e., of least cost) for both. But this is almost never the case, because of the general technological backwardness of the South relative to the North. This relative backwardness means that many Southern countries have virtually no capital goods capacity; those that do have capital goods capacity specialise in older technologies;[7] and those that attempt to produce the latest technologies tend to do so relatively inefficiently (i.e., the technical conditions are not the same). Hence we can assume that the typical case is one where the North produces the most recent technology, while older technologies are produced in the North and South, or in only one of the two. It follows that the least-cost technique in the South is not always the same as that in the North, although it may be. Where there is a difference, the least-cost technique for the South will tend to be less capital-intensive (i.e., involve a lower ratio of indirect to direct labour) than the least-cost technique in the North. This, of course, accords with the predictions of conventional theory (although for different reasons) and of empirical findings.

Technical change will take the form of reducing the total cost (i.e. the combined quantity of indirect and direct labour). It will appear to raise capital intensity defined as K/L, because the capital requirements (K) are normally measured as a cost (e.g., the cost of producing the machinery) and therefore rise over time with a rise in the real wage (which in turn is the consequence of technical change), while labour (L) is a physical quantity. The rise in K/L, for which there is plentiful evidence, tells us nothing, however, about what happens to capital intensity defined as the ratio of indirect to direct labour, nor capital intensity defined as capital requirements per unit of output. There is no reason, if the real wage rate is the same in each sector (ignoring any influence of the profit rate) why *tc* should be systematically biased towards increasing or reducing the ratio of indirect to direct labour, nor why it should be capital-using or saving in terms of the K/O ratio.

As far as the South is concerned, whether or not there is such a bias is not particularly important. What is significant is that:

1. *tc* is labour-saving, normally in terms of indirect and direct labour requirements per unit of output; so for any given additional output fewer jobs are created;
2. the price of equipment imported from the North rises over time, with the rising real wage. This means the capital–labour ratio, or the cost of providing equipment for each worker rises; so for any given expenditure on capital fewer jobs are created;
3. there is no particular reason why the capital requirements per unit of output should rise or fall.

It follows that *tc* in the North may well contribute to the output-maximising object of the South – although there can be cases, as discussed above, where the output maximisation criterion suggests a different and more labour-intensive technological choice than that in the North – but it may also make it more difficult for the South to create enough extra jobs, and also to meet other objectives. The precise effects depends not only on the characteristics of the new technologies, as compared with older ones, but also where they are made – and hence the implications for relative costs and for the creation of indirect as well as direct employment opportunities. If new technologies reduce direct labour requirements while increasing indirect requirements, they may increase employment in the North, which specialises in capital goods, while decreasing it in the South, which uses these goods.

In most cases, new technologies *from* the North displace old technologies *in* the South, after a time-lag. This displacement occurs (a) because the new technology is cost-reducing and output-raising for the South; (b) because the products of the new technologies differ from those of the old, and these products displace old products because they are preferred and because they are linked to the rest of technology in use (e.g., as inputs); (c) because production of the old technology stops; (d) because of biased selection mechanisms favouring these technologies (these include capital and labour prices, exchange rate policies, the influence of MNCs on choice of technology, the influence of elites on choice of products).

If the first reason applies, the displacement will contribute to raising output in the South; with the other reasons, it may not do so. But whatever the reason, the displacement affects the pattern of development as well as output levels, because of the many characteristics of technologies noted at the beginning of this essay.

The most obvious effect is on employment. As stated, for any given capital expenditure fewer jobs are created. Since more output is normally made possible, a classic conflict between output and employment maximisation emerges.[8] In theory governments should be able to tax part of the additional output and redistribute income to the unemployed or underemployed (for example, by 'creating' jobs in public works). But in practice administrative and political restraints often prevent this. The new high-productivity technologies then contribute to a worsening of income distribution and an accentuation of employment problems.

In addition, as noted earlier, significant changes occur in scale, the use of materials, skill and managerial requirements, infrastructural requirements (transport, legal structure, financial services, energy) which make heavy demands on Southern economies, requiring them to devote considerable resources to meet the demands, leading to heavy reliance on imports to supplement local efforts, and notwithstanding these efforts, often involving relatively inefficient production.

Technological change from the North often creates problems for the South, not because it fails to raise output there, but because it does raise output in the South as well as the North, but the changing requirements that go along with the change are ill-suited to conditions in the South. Both types of theory considered above suggested that *tc* from the North would often, but not always, be output-raising for the South: it is precisely in these cases that the tendency towards 'distorting' impact becomes relevant.

PRODUCTS[9]

Any empirical investigation into *tc* at once notes the dominating feature is change in *products*. Yet theory has concentrated on change in inputs, mainly because it is difficult to deal with changing products in a conventional framework. However, the Lancaster (1966) way of dealing with products as bundles of characteristics makes it possible to treat change in products as (partly) endogenous, rather in the same way as changes in techniques. Assume any product consists of a vector of characteristics, $P_a = p_i, p_{ii}, p_{iii}, \ldots$, where p_i, p_{ii} represent different characteristics, such as energy-giving, protein-providing, or colour. A change in product consists in a change in this vector. Let us assume, for simplicity, that the new product involves the same cost of production (however defined); a new product will be introduced if it produces more of the previous characteristics, or a different (and by some preferred) ratio of characteristics, or, perhaps, some entirely new characteristics. The new product may in practice do all of these things.

It may be assumed that an increase in quantity of characteristics always raises welfare (since we are assuming same cost); a change in the ratio of characteristics will please some (those who prefer the new ratio) and displease others.

Some significant conclusions follow: some new products improve the welfare of everyone; if tastes differ, some new products may incrase the welfare of some people but not others; people lose by new products only if the availability of the old products changes (i.e., their cost increases or they are withdrawn). (The conclusions are complicated by imperfect information, the presence of advertising, and 'demonstration' effects and the interdependence of consumers' welfare.)[10]

The analysis is relevant to the North–South question because a major determinant of 'tastes' is incomes. Engels noted this in relation to the broad categories of products people spend their incomes on, and the way this changes with income. It is also true with respect to a narrower definition of product (e.g., the way people meet their transport needs changes from walking to cycling–riding, to buses, to private cars, to airplanes as income rises). Hence there is a tendency for a systematic difference in tastes between North and South, with the tastes for South being for goods with more 'low-income' characteristics.

New products, designed in the North, will therefore tend to be suited to high-income consumers embodying increasingly high-income type characteristics over time. While they may raise the welfare of rich consumers in the South, they will often not increase the welfare of poorer consumers, who form the majority of the population in Southern countries. Whether their welfare actually decreases absolutely will then depend on whether the old products continue to be available. In practice, they are often withdrawn, because of economies of scale, which makes it economic to produce only a limited number of products. Since the bulk of monetary demand lies with higher-income Northern consumers plus elites in the South, there will be a tendency for Northern-style products to displace low-income products. Moreover, since new processes tend to displace old ones and new processes often produce new products, new products will tend to displace old ones. However, in this situation the 'constant cost' assumption has to be relaxed, since the new technologies are often of lower cost than the old.

There is a parallel here with the development of techniques of production. There is a systematic tendency for the new products to involve more high-income and less low-income characteristics. But the tendency to lower costs as a result of technical progress means that the total available low-income characteristics may nonetheless rise. The new products will tend to be inegalitarian, in the sense that they will benefit the higher-income consumers most, while low-income consumers may not benefit at all, or may even be adversely affected.

The introduction of product change modifies some of the conclusions about change in technique. It was assumed earlier that each new technique involved the 'same' product. But in practice, almost invariably, the new technologies also produce new products. In some cases the new products will be preferred in the South as well as the North, so that the superiority of new technology will be enhanced by considering product characteristics. But in others, the new product may involve an 'excess' of some characteristics for low-income consumers and a deficiency of others; hence while the new technology may be output-raising in the North, it may not be in the South, since valuation of output should include valuation of the product characteristics. For example, a new technology for block-making which produces stronger and more uniform blocks may be output-raising in the North, where the new blocks save labour in sorting and testing the blocks; but not in the South, where the blocks are intended to be used for single-storey accommodation so that the additional strength is not needed.

CONCLUSIONS

Technical change in the North inevitably affects the South – changing, often dramatically, the technology available. Some of the changes – in both methods of production and products – undoubtedly contribute to meeting development objectives, making it possible to produce more, for a given outlay of resources. But there are other effects – intrinsically and inseparably connected – which may be undesirable. Notable among these are inegalitarian effects, resulting from the low employment potential of the new technologies and the high-income characteristics of the new products. New technologies have also often been of an excessive scale for many Third World economies; and they require increasing levels of skills, and rising levels of infrastructural facilities. In order to provide the environment and services necessary for the new technologies to operate efficiently, many economies have become excessively dependent on industrial economies, while devoting most of their investment (public and private) to serving the advanced country technologies, neglecting the traditional sector where, often, a majority of the people find a living. The output creating aspects of modern technology make it difficult to resist. But the 'distorting' effects make it desirable to consider policy options.

Policy Options

1. To reject modern technology. This is the Kampuchea option: it generally involves loss in output, but an increase in equality.
2. To be selective, accepting only the output-raising techniques, and products which increase the availability of low-income characteristics. This (perhaps) is exemplified by China. It is difficult politically and administratively and may also involve some loss in output. A major problem is the many links between technologies, so that it is difficult to operate part efficiently without accepting the whole. India, for example, seems to have followed an inefficient selective policy. One form of selectivity occurs automatically via the price system; a highly protected economy will tend to be less selective from this point of view than one which is open and competitive (contrast, for example, Mexico and Taiwan).
3. Generation of indigenous *tc* in both techniques and products. From one point of view, this appears the most attractive option, since it should enable the South to make use of the latest scientific

and technical developments, but direct them to its own needs and thus avoid the distorting effects of Northern technology. But it can be very expensive, since the South lacks many of the resources necessary to generate *tc*. Secondly, Southern *tc* often produces technologies similar to Northern ones, because of the organisation of R and D and the structure of incentives. Since the very poor lack purchasing power and access to credit, there is little incentive to produce technologies which they need (either machines or products).

4. Adaptation of Northern technologies to Southern conditions. This is less ambitious than (3) above. There is more possibility of some success, but it implies that the Southern economies would continue to accept the broad sweep of Northern *tc*, providing minor modifications. It seems, empirically, that there has been more success in modifying methods of production than in modifying product characteristics.

5. Individual Southern economies also have the option, increasingly being exercised, of getting their technology from other Southern economies. Collectively, because of the larger markets and greater resources, the South is likely to make more headway in creating alternative technologies, but many Southern economies are too closely linked with the North to wish to do so.

The discussion in this essay suggests that it is not possible to come to any *general* conclusion about whether *tc* in the North benefits or disadvantages the South. While this might not seem a strong conclusion, it contradicts both those who have argued that modern technology is always the best, and those who argue the opposite, that it is always disadvantageous.[11] Each technology has to be judged on its own merits, paying especial attention to the source and terms of acquisition of capital goods and the nature of product characteristics. Innovation in and for the South potentially offers *tc* with more desirable characteristics, but it has a cost in terms of resource use and levels of output, at least in the short run.

NOTES

1. See, for example, Sen (1968); Dobb (1956–7); Kahn (1951); Galenson and Leibenstein (1955).

2. See, for example, Annerstadt (1979).
3. According to a McGraw-Hill survey, 83 per cent of R and D among manufacturing firms was devoted to product innovations. See Link in Sahal (1982) p. 48.
4. The precise meaning of 'proportionately' in this context depends on the precise assumptions made about the process of technical change. It is not necessary to specify these here.
5. See Binswanger *et al.* (1978) for a survey of work adopting this approach and some applications to developing countries.
6. This conclusion follows where the stream of costs and benefits of a project are even. However, with very simple assumptions about the timing (where, for example, the two projects consist of different ratios of labour at time t to labour at time t-1, and the output is identical and occurs at time t) it seems that a higher rate of interest would increase the cost of the capital-intensive techniques, that is the one with the higher ratio of labour at time t-1. However, the essay follows the Pasinetti conclusion.
7. In general there is a much greater time-lag between transfer of technology from the North to developing countries and transfer to other developed countries. See Mansfield in Sahal (1982) p. 16. It seems probable that the lag is greater in capital goods production.
8. This is discussed at length in Stewart and Streeten (1971).
9. See James and Stewart (1981), which elaborates on some of the discussion here.
10. Some of these are discussed in more detail in James and Stewart (1981).
11. Each view has strong advocates. Emmanuel (1982) is an adherent of the 'latest is best' school. Some of those promoting intermediate technology come near to arguing the opposite – see Schumacher (1973).

Bibliography

Agarwala, P. N. (1984) 'Trade Goes Over the Counter', *Far Eastern Economic Review* (23 August).

Agarwala, P. N. (1986) *Countertrade Policies and Practices of Selected Asian Countries and their State Trading Organizations*, UNCTAD/ECDC/176/Corr. 1.

Ahmad, S. (1966) 'On the Theory of Induced Invention', *Economic Journal*, 76.

Alston, P. (1987a) 'Out of the Abyss: The Challenges Confronting the New U.N. Committee on Economic, Social and Cultural Rights', *Human Rights Quarterly* (August).

Alston, P. (1987b) 'The Nature of International Human Rights Discourse: the Case of the "New" Human Rights', paper presented to conference on 'An Interdisciplinary Inquiry into the Value of the So-called "New Human Rights"', University of Oxford (29–31 May).

Alston, P. and G. Quinn (1987) 'The Nature and Scope of States' Parties Obligations Under the International Covenant on Economic, Social and Cultural Rights', *Human Rights Quarterly* (May).

Altschuler, A. *et al.* (1984) *The Future of the Automobile* (Cambridge, Mass.: MIT Press).

Amsalem, M. (1983) *Technology Choice in Developing Countries: The Impact of Differences in Factor Costs* (Cambridge, Mass.: MIT Press).

Amsden, A. (1977) 'The Division of Labour is Limited by the Type of Market: The Case of the Taiwanese Machine Tool Industry', *World Development*, 5 (3): 217–34.

Anjaria, S. J. (1987) 'Balance of Payments and Related Issues in the Uruguay Round of Trade Negotiations', *The World Bank Economic Review*, 1 (4): 669–88.

Annerstadt, J. (1979) 'A Survey of World Research and Development Efforts' (Anselm: UNESCO).

Arrow, K. J. (1962) 'Economic Welfare and the Allocation of Reserves for Invention' in NBER *The Rate and Direction of Inventive Activity* (Princeton: Princeton Univ. Press).

Avramovic, D. (1985) 'Commodity Problem: What Next?' (October) (Washington, D.C.: Bank of Credit and Commerce) (mimeo).

Bagachwa, M. D. (1988) 'Choice of Technology in Grain Milling Industry in Tanzania' Ph.D. thesis, University of Dar es Salaam, Tanzania.

Balassa, B. (1970) 'Growth Strategies in Semi-industrial Countries', *Quarterly Journal of Economics*, 84: 24–47.

Balassa, B. (1975) 'Reforming the System of Incentives in Developing Countries', *World Development*, 3: 365–82.

Balassa, B. (1982) 'Disequilibrium Analysis in Developing Countries: an Overview', *World Development*, 10: 12.

Balassa, B. *et al.* (1971) *The Structure of Protection in Developing Countries* (Baltimore: Johns Hopkins University Press).

Baldwin, R. E. (1969) 'The Case Against Infant Industry Protection', *Journal of Political Economy*, 77: 295–305.

Baldwin, R. (1988) 'High Technology and Strategic Trade Policy in Developing Countries: The Case of Brazilian Aircraft', paper prepared for WIDER Conference on 'New Trade Theories and Industrialisation in Developing Countries', Helsinki (2–5 August).

Baloff, N. (1966) 'The Learning Curve – Some Controversial Issues', *Journal of Industrial Economics*: 275–82.

Balogh, T. and P. P. Streeten (1963) 'The Coefficient of Ignorance', *Oxford Bulletin of Economics and Statistics*, 25 (2).

Banks, G. (1983) 'The Economics and Politics of Countertrade', *The World Economy*, 6 (2).

Banks, G. (1985) 'Constrained Markets, "Surplus" Commodities and International Barter', *Kyklos*, 38 (2).

Bardhan, P. (1978) 'External Economies, Economic Development and the Theory of Protection' in S. P. Singh (ed.), *Underdevelopment to Developing Economies* (Oxford: Oxford University Press).

Barker T. S. (1977) 'International Trade and Economic Growth: an Alternative to the Neoclassical Approach', *Cambridge Journal of Economics*, 1: 153–72.

Barovick, R. L. (1986) 'Study Confirms Growth of Counter-Trade', *Journal of Commerce*, 6 (January).

Bates, R. H. (1983) *Essays on the Political Economy of Rural Africa* (New York: Cambridge University Press).

Bautista, R. M., H. Hughes, D. Lim, D. Morawetz and F. E. Thoumi (1981) *Capital, Utilisation in Manufacturing* (New York: Oxford University Press).

Bell, M. (1986) 'Technical Change in Infant Industries: a Review of Empirical Evidence' Development Research Dept (Washington, D.C.: World Bank) (mimeo).

Bell, M. and D. Scott-Kemmis (1987) 'Transfers of Technology and the Accumulation of Technological Capability in Thailand' (Washington D.C.: World Bank) (mimeo).

Beranek W. and G. Ranis (eds) (1978) *Science and Technology and Economic Development* (New York: Praeger).

Berg, A. (1981) *Malnourished People, a Policy View* (Washington, D.C.: World Bank).

Beveridge, W. and M. Kelly (1980) 'Fiscal Content of Financial Programmes Supported by Stand-by Arrangements in the Upper-Credit Tranches 1969–78', *IMF Staff Papers*, 27.

Bhaduri, A. (1973) 'On the Formation of Usurious Interest Rates in Backward Agriculture', *Cambridge Journal of Economics* (December).

Bhagwati, J. (1965) 'On the Equivalence of Tariffs and Quotas', in R. Baldwin *et al.* (eds), *Trade, Growth and the Balance of Payments* (Chicago: Rand-McNally).

Bhagwati, J. (1978) *Foreign Trade Regimes and Economic Development: Anatomy and Consequences of Exchange Control Regimes* (Cambridge, Mass.: Ballinger).

Bhagwati, J. and Y. Onitsuka (1974) 'Export–Import Responses to Devaluation: Experience in the Non-industrial Countries in the 1960s', *IMF Staff Papers*, 21.

Bhalla, A. and D. James (eds) (1986) *New Technology Applications in Traditional Sectors* (Geneva: ILO).

Bhatt, V. V. (1969) 'A Payments Union for Developing Countries', *Economic and Political Weekly* (Annual Number) (January).

Binswanger, H. P., V. W. Ruttan and others (1978) *Induced Innovation* (Baltimore: Johns Hopkins University Press).

Bird, G. (1988) *Managing Global Money* (London: Macmillan).

Blackhurst, R. (1981) 'Are Trade Restrictions an Alternative to Devaluation?', *Wirtschaftspolitische Blätter*, 1: 52–61.

Blackhurst, R. and J. Tumlir (1980) *Trade Relations Under Flexible Exchange Rates*, GATT Studies in International Trade, 8 (Geneva).

Blejer, M. and A. Hillman (1982) 'On the Dynamic Non-equivalence of Tariffs and Quotas in Monetary Models of the Balance of Payments', *Journal of International Economics*, 13: 163–9.

Borrus, M., L. d'Andrea Tyson and J. Zysman (1987) 'Creating Advantage: How Government Policies Shape International Trade in the Semiconductor Industry', in P. R. Krugman (ed.), *Strategic Trade Policy and the New International Economics* (Cambridge, Mass.: MIT Press).

Brander, J. A. and B. J. Spencer (1985) 'Export Subsidies and International Market Share Rivalry', *Journal of International Economics*, 18.

Branson, W. H. and A. K. Klevorick (1986) 'Strategic Behaviour and Trade Policy' in P. Krugman, *Strategic Trade Policy and the New International Economics* (Cambridge, Mass.: MIT Press).

Brodsky, D., G.K. Helleiner and G. Sampson (1981) 'The Impact of the Current Exchange Rate System on the Developing Countries', *Trade and Development* 3: 31–52.

Bruntland Report (1987) *Our Common Future* (Oxford: Oxford University Press).

Buttel, F. H., M. Kenney and J. Kloppenburg (1985 'From Green Revolution to Biorevolution: Some Observations on the Changing Technology Bases of Economic Transformation in the Third World', *Economic Development and Cultural Change*, 34: 31–55.

Cambridge Economic Policy Review (CEPR) (1975) (February) (Cambridge: Cambridge University Press).

Castana, A., J. Katz and F. Navajas (1981) *Etapas Historicas y Conductas Technologicas en una Planta Argentina de Maquinas Herraminenta*, IDB/ECLA/UNDP/IDRC Research Programme on Scientific and Technological Dependence in Latin America, working paper, 38 (Buenos Aires: ECLA).

Caves, R. E. (1974) 'The Economics of Reciprocity: Theory and Evidence on Bilateral Trading Arrangements', in W. Sellekaerts (ed.) *International Trade and Finance Essays in Honour of Jan Tinbergen* (Basingstoke: Macmillan).

Central Policy Review Staff (CPRS) (1975) *The Future of the British Car Industry* (London: HMSO).

Chadha, G. K. (1986a) 'The Off-Farm Economic Structure of Agriculturally Growing Regions: A Case Study of Indian Punjab', in R. T. Shand (ed.), *Off-Farm Employment in the Development of Rural Asia*, Vol. 2 (Canberra: Australian National University).

Chadha, G. K. (1986b) *The State and Rural Economic Transformation: The Case of Punjab 1950–85* (New Delhi: Sage Publications).

Chaudhri, D. P. (1979) *Education, Innovations and Agricultural Development* (New Delhi: Vikas Publishing House).

Chenery *et al.* (1974) *Redistribution with Growth* (Oxford: Oxford University Press).

Child, F. C. and H. Kaneda (1975) 'Links to the Green Revolution: A Study of Small Scale, Agriculturally Related Industry in the Pakistan Punjab', *Economic Development and Cultural Change*, 23 (2) 249–75.

Chowdury, N. and K. Bhuiyan (1985) 'Wages in Bangladesh Industries, 1972/3–1981/2: Levels and Structure', *Bangladesh Development Studies*, 13 (2).

Chung, I.-Y. (1988) 'Infant Industry Protection and Industrialisation: the Case of Korea', M.Sc. essay, Oxford University (mimeo).

Clarke, J. and V. Cable (1982) 'The Asian Electronics Industry Looks to the Future', *Institute of Development Studies Bulletin*, 3 (2).

Cline, W. and S. Weintraub (1981) *Economic Stabilisation in Developing Countries* ((Washington D.C.: Brookings).

Cline, W. R., N. Kawanabke, T. O. M. Kronsjo and T. Williams (1978) *Trade Negotiations in the Tokyo Round, A Quantitative Assessment* (Washington, D.C.: Brookings).

Coase, R. H. (1960) 'The Problem of Social Cost', *Journal of Law and Economics*, 3: 1–44.

Commonwealth Secretariat (1984) 'The Debt Crisis and the World Economy' , Report by a Commonwealth Group of Experts.

Cooper, R. (1971) 'An Assessment of Currency Devaluation in Developing Countries', in G. Ranis (ed.), *Government and Economic Development* (New Haven: Yale University Press).

Cooper, R. N. (1984) 'Why Counter-Trade?', *Across the Board* (March).

Cooper, C. and F. Sercovich (1970) 'The Channels and Mechanisms for the Transfer of Technology from Developed to Developing Countries' (UNCTAD TD/D/AC, 11/5, 1970).

Corden, W. M. (1974) *Trade Policy and Economic Welfare* (Oxford: Clarendon Press).

Cornia, G. A., R. Jolly and F. Stewart (1987) *Adjustment with a Human Face* (Oxford: Oxford University Press)

Correa, M. (1981) 'Transfer of Technology to Latin America: a Decade of Control', *Journal of World Trade Law*.

Cortez, M. (1978) 'Argentina: Technical Development and Technology Exports to LDCs', (Washington D.C.: Economics of Industry Division, World Bank).

Council of Economic Advisors (1984) *Economic Report to the President* (Washington D.C.: GPO).

Crawford, J. G. (1969) 'India' in R. T. Shand (ed.), *Agricultural Development in Asia* (Canberra: Australian National University).

Da Cruz, H. N. (1980) *Mudanca Tecnologia no Seta Metal Mecanico: Um Estudo de Caso de Maquinas para Processar Gerais*, IDB/ECLA/UNDP/

360   *Bibliography*

IDRC Research Programme on Scientific and Technological Dependence in Latin America (Buenos Aires: ECLA) (mimeo).

Da Cruz, H. N. and M. E. da Silva (1981) *Mudanca Tecnologia Setor Metal Mecanico: Relatocio Parcia, Parte II*, IDB/ECLA/UNDP/IDRC Research Programme on Scientific and Technological Dependence in Latin America (Sao Paulo: Fundação Instituto de Perquisa Economicas) (mimeo).

Dahlman, C. J. and L. Westphal (1982) 'Technological Effort in Industrial Development: A Survey', in F. Stewart and J. James (eds), *The Economics of New Technology in Developing Countries* (London: Frances Pinter).

Dasgupta, P. and J. Stiglitz (1988) 'Learning by Doing: Market Structure and Industrial and Trade Policies', *Oxford Economic Papers*, 40 (2): 246–68.

Dell, S. (1981) 'On Being Grandmotherly: the Evolution of Conditionality', *Essays in International Finance*, 144 (Princeton: Princeton University).

Dell, S. (1988) *Policies for Development* (London: Macmillan).

Dell, S. and R. Lawrence (1980) *The Balance of Payments Adjustment Process in Developing Countries* (Oxford: Pergamon).

Denison, E. (1967) *Why Growth Rates Differ* (Washington, D.C.: Brookings).

Department of Trade and Industry (1985) *Countertrade, Some Guidance for Exporters* (London: HMSO).

Dhagamwar, V. (1987) 'The Disadvantaged and the Law', paper presented at Workshop on 'Poverty in India: Research and Policy', Queen Elizabeth House, University of Oxford (October).

Dhawan, B. D. (1982) *Development of the Tubewell Irrigation* (New Delhi: Agricole).

Diebold, J. (1986) 'The Information Technology Industries: A Case Study of High Technology Trade', in W. R. Cline (ed.), *Trade Policy in the 1980s* (Washington, D.C.: Institute for International Economics).

Dixit, A. (1984) 'International Trade Policies for Oligopolistic Industries', *Economic Journal*, 94 (Supplement).

Dixit, A. K. and G. M. Grossman (1986) 'Targeted Export Promotion with Several Oligopolistic Industries', *Journal of International Economics*, 21.

Dobb, M. (1956–7) 'Second Thoughts on Capital-intensive of Investment', *Review of Economic Studies*, 24: 33–42.

Dodwell, D. (1986) 'Expertise in Short Supply', *Financial Times* (11 February 1986).

Domar, E. (1957) *Essays in the Theory of Economic Growth* (Oxford: Oxford University Press).

Dommen, E. (1989) 'Lightening the Debt Burden – Some Sidelights from History', *Unctad Review*, 1.

Drèze, J. (1960) 'Quelques Réflections Sérènes sur l'Adaptation de l'Industrie Belge au Marché Commun', *Comptes Rendus des Travaux de la Société Royale d'Economie Politique de Belgique*: 275.

Driscoll, N. and J. Ford (1983) 'Protection and Optimum Trade-restricting Policies under Uncertainty', *Manchester School of Economics and Social Studies*, 51 (1): 21–32.

Eaton, J. and G. M. Grossman (1986) 'Optimal Trade and Industrial Policy under Industrialisation', *Quarterly Journal of Economics.*

Eckaus, R. S. (1955) 'The Factor Proportions Problem in Underdeveloped Areas', *American Economic Review*, 45.

Economic Survey (1986) (New Delhi: Government of India).

Edirisinghe, N. (1986) *The Food Stamp Programme in Sri Lanka: Costs, Benefits and Policy Options*, Research Report (Washington D.C.: International Food Research Institute).

Eglin, R. (1987) 'Surveillance of Balance-of-Payments Measures in the GATT', *The World Economy* (March): 1–26.

Eichengreen, B. and R. Portes (1988) *Settling Defaults in the Era of Foreign Bound Finance* (London: Centre for Economic Policy Research).

Eisenbrand, L. (1985) 'Why is Counter-trade Thriving?', *Industry and Development*, 15.

Emmanuel, A. (1972) *Unequal Exchange, A Study of the Imperialism of Trade* (London: Monthly Review Press).

Emmanuel, A. (1982) *Appropriate or Underdeveloped Technology* (Chichester: John Wiley).

Enos, J. (1989) 'The Transfer of Technology', *Journal of Asian–Pacific Economic Literature* (March).

Enos, J. L. and W. H. Park (1988) *The Adoption and Diffusion of Imported Technology: The Case of Korea* (New York: Croom Helm).

Ericson, H. (1985) 'Firms Soften Handicaps with Counter-trade Deals', *Journal of Commerce*, 28.

Ernst, D. (1985) 'Automation and the Worldwide Restructuring of the Electronics Industry; Strategic Implications for Developing Countries', *World Development*, 13 (3).

ESCAP (1979) 'Transnational Corporations in the Consumer Electronics Industry of Developing ESCAP Countries', UN working paper, 5 (Bangkok).

ESCAP/UNTC (1984) *Costs and Conditions of Technology Transfer through Transnational Corporations*, Series B, 3, April (Bangkok: ESCAP/UNTC).

Ethier, W. (1979) 'Internationally Decreasing Costs and World Trade', *Journal of International Economics*, 9: 1–24.

Evans, D. (1990) 'Outward Orientation: an Assessment', in C. Milner (ed.), *Export Promotion Strategies: Theory and Evidence from Developing Countries* (Hemel Hempstead: Harvester–Wheatsheaf).

Evenson, R. and G. Ranis (1990) *Science and Technology: Lessons for Development Policy* (Boulder: Westview).

External Affairs Canada (1985) *Countertrade Primer for Canadian Exports* (Government of Canada: Ottawa).

Fei, J., G. Ranis and S. Kuo (1979) *Growth with Equity: the Taiwan Case* (New York: Oxford University Press).

Felix, D. (1987) 'Alternative Outcomes of the Latin American Debt Crisis: Lessons from the Past', *Latin American Research Review*, 22 (2).

Ffrench-Davies, R. (1983) 'The Monetarist Experiment in Chile: a Critical Survey', *World Development*, 11.

Finan, W. F. and A. M. Lamond (1985) 'Sustaining U.S. Competitiveness in Microelectronics: The Challenge to U.S. Policy', in B. R. Scott and G. C. Lodge (eds), *U.S. Competitiveness in the World Economy* (Boston, Mass.: Harvard Business School).

Fishelson, G. and F. Flatters (1975) 'The (Non)-equivalence of Optimal Tariffs and Quotas under Uncertainty', *Journal of International Economics*, 5: 385–93.

Fleming, J. M. (1971) 'The SDR: Some Problems and Possibilities', *International Monetary Fund Staff Papers*, 18.

Fong, C. O. (1987) 'Technology Acquisition under Alternative Arrangements with Transnational Corporations: Selected Industrial Case Studies in Malaysia', ESCAP/UNCTC, *Technology Transfer under Alternative Arrangements with Transnational Corporations* (Bangkok: United Nations ESCAP/UNCTC Joint Unit on Transnational Corporations).

Forsyth, D. (1977) 'Appropriate Technology in Sugar Manufacturing', *World Development*, 5: 189–202.

Fransman, M. (1986a) 'Biotechnology and the Third World: an Interpretative Survey', The United Nations University, New Technologies Centre Feasibility Study, Rijksuniversiteit Limburg (Maastricht).

Fransman, M. (1986b) 'International Competitiveness, International Diffusion of Technology and the State: a Case Study from Taiwan and Japan', *World Development*, 14: 12.

Fransman, M. and K. King (eds) (1984) *Technological Capability in the Third World* (London: Macmillan).

Galenson, S. and H. Leibenstein (1955) 'Investment Criteria, Productivity and Economic Development', *Quarterly Journal of Economics*, 69.

GATT (1972) *Basic Instruments and Selected Documents, Eighteenth Supplement* (Geneva: GATT).

GATT (1983) *International Trade 1982–3* (Geneva: GATT).

GATT (1988) *International Trade 1987–88* (Geneva: GATT).

Godfrey, M. (1985) 'Trade and Exchange Rate Policy: a Further Contribution to the Debate', in T. Rose (ed.), *Crisis and Recovery in Sub-Saharan Africa* (Paris: OECD).

Gopolan, C. (1983) 'Undernutrition: Measurement and Implications', paper presented at WIDER conference on 'Poverty, Undernutrition and Living Standards', Helsinki (August).

Green, R. H. (1986) 'The IMF and Stabilisation in Sub-Saharan Africa: A Critical Review', IDS discussion paper, 216 (Falmer: Sussex: IDS).

Green, R. H. (1988) 'Operational Relevance of Third World Multinationals to Collective Self-reliance: Some Problems, Provocations and Possibilities', in H. Singer, N. Hatti and R. Tandon (eds), *Technology Transfer by Multinationals* (New Delhi: Ashish Publishing House).

Greenwald, B. C. and J. E. Stiglitz (1986) 'Externalities in Economies with Imperfect Information and Incomplete Markets', *Quarterly Journal of Economics*, 101: 229–64.

Grieves, R. T. (1984) 'Modern Barter', *Time* (11 June).

Griffith-Jones S. (1986) 'Ways Forward From the Debt Crisis' *Oxford Economic Review*, 2 (1).

Grilli, E. and M. Chang Yeng (1988) 'Primary Commodity Prices, Manufactured Goods Prices and the Terms of Trade of Developing Countries:

What the Long Run Shows', *The World Bank Economic Review*, 2 (1).

Grossman, G. M. (1986) 'Strategic Export Promotion: a Critique', in Krugman (ed.), *Strategic Trade Policy and the New International Economics* (Cambridge, Mass.: MIT Press).

Grubel, H. G. and Lloyd, P. J. (1975) *Intra-Industry Trade* (London: Macmillan).

Guitan, M. (1981) 'Fund Conditionality, Evolution of Principles and Practices', International Monetary Fund, *Pamphlet Series*, 38.

Gulati, I. (1983) 'Cooperative Monetary Action: a Few Suggestions for the Developing Countries', in B. Paulic, R. Uranga, B. Cizelj and M. Svetlicic (eds), *The Challenges of South–South Cooperation* (Boulder, Colorado: Westview).

Gulhati, R. (1988) 'Impasse in Zambia: The Economics and Politics of Reform', EDI Development Policy Case Series, 2 (Washington, D.C.: World Bank).

Gustafson, W. E. (1962) 'Research and Development, New Products and Productivity Change', *American Economic Review*, Papers and Proceedings, 52.

Hall, P. and A. Markusen (eds) (1985) *Silicon Landscapes* (London: Allen & Unwin).

Hall, P., A. Markusen, R. Osborn and B. Wachsman (1985) 'The American Computer Software Industry: Economic Development Prospects', in P. Hall and A. Markusen (eds), *Silicon Landscapes* (London: Allen & Unwin).

Harriss, D. (1984) *The European Social Charter* (University of Virginia Press).

Hart, A. G., N. Kaldor and J. Tinbergen (1964) *The Case for an International Reserve Currency*, UNCTAD (Geneva: United Nations).

Heckscher, E. (1919) 'The Effect of Foreign Trade on the Distribution of Income' *Ekonomisch Tidskrift*, 21, reprinted in H. S. Ellis and L. A. Metzler (eds) *Readings in the Theory of International Trade* (Blackiston, 1949).

Helleiner, G. K. (1973) 'Manufactured Exports from Less-developed Countries and Multinational Firms', *Economic Journal*, 83: 21–47.

Helleiner, G. K. (1981a) *Intra-firm Trade and the Developing Countries* (London: Macmillan).

Helleiner, G. K. (1981b) 'The Impact of the Exchange Rate System on the Developing Countries: a Report to the Group of 24' (Canada: University of Toronto) (mimeo).

Helleiner, G. K. (1983) 'The IMF and Africa in the 1980s', Essays in International Finance, Princeton, 152 (Princeton, New Jersey: Princeton University).

Helleiner, G. K. (1989) 'Structural Adjustment and Long-term Development in Sub-saharan Africa', paper for Workshop on Alternative Strategies in Africa (11–13 June).

Helpman, E. and Krugman, P. (1985) *Market Structure and Foreign Trade* (Cambridge, Mass.: MIT Press).

Henderson, P. D. (1977) 'Two British Errors: Their Probable Size and Some Possible Lessons', Oxford Economic Papers, 29.

Hendrix, W. E. (1981) 'Availability of Capital and Production Innovations on Low-Income Farms', *Journal of Farm Economics* (February).

Hicks, N. (1979) 'Growth vs Basic Needs: Is there a Trade-Off?', *World Development*, 7.

Hicks, N. (1982) 'Sector Priorities in Meeting Basic Needs: Some Statistical Evidence', *World Development*, 10.

Hirschman, A. O. (1958) *The Strategy of Economic Development* (New Haven: Yale University Press).

Hoffman, K. (1985) 'Clothing, Chips and Comparative Advantage: the Impact of Electronics on Trade and Production in the Garment Industry', *World Development*, 13 (3).

Hollander, S. (1965) *The Sources of Increased Efficiency: a Study of Du Pont Rayon Plants* (Cambridge, Mass.: MIT Press).

Horsefield, J. K. (ed.) (1969) *The International Monetary Fund 1945–1965* (Washington D.C.: International Monetary Fund).

Horstmann, I. and J. R. Markusen (1986) 'Up the Average Cost Curve: Inefficient Entry and the New Protectionism', *Journal of International Economics*, 20.

Hufbauer, G. C. (1966) *Synthetic Materials and the Theory of International Trade* (London: Duckworth).

Hufbauer, G. C. (1970) 'The Impact of National Characteristics and Technology on Commodity Composition of Trade in Manufactured Goods', in R. Vernon (ed.)' *The Technology Factor in International Trade* (New York: Columbia University Press).

Hulugalle, L. (1990) 'South–South Trade: Developments in the 1980s and Policies for the 1990s', *IDS Bulletin*, 21 (1).

Hussain, M. N. and A. P. Thirlwall (1984) 'The IMF Supply-side Approach to Devaluation: an Assessment with Reference to the Sudan', *Oxford Bulletin of Economics and Statistics*, 46 (2) 145–67.

ILO (1972) *Employment, Incomes and Equality, A Strategy for Increasing Productive Employment in Kenya* (Geneva: ILO).

ILO (1976) *Employment, Growth and Basic Needs, A One World Problem* (Geneva: ILO).

ILO/JASPA (1982) *Basic Needs in Danger: a Basic Needs Oriented Development Strategy for Tanzania* (Addis Ababa: ILO/JASPA).

Isenman, P. (1980) 'Basic Needs: the Case of Sri Lanka', *World Development*, 8.

James, J. (1981) 'Growth, Technology and the Environment in Less Developed Countries: A Survey' in P. Streeten and R. Jolly (eds), *Recent Issues in World Development* (Oxford: Pergamon).

James, J. (1986) 'Microelectronics and the Third World: an Integrative Survey of Literature', The United Nations University, New Technologies Centre Feasibility Study, Rijksuniversiteit Limburg (Maastricht).

James, J. and F. Stewart (1981) 'New Products: A Discussion of the Welfare Effects of the Introduction of New Products in Developing Countries', *Oxford Economic Papers*, 33 (1).

Jhabvala, F. (1984) 'On Human Rights and the Socio-Economic Context', *Netherlands International Law Review*, 31.

Johnson, H. G. (1970) 'The State of Theory in Relation to the Empirical Analysis', in R. Vernon (ed.), *The Technology Factor in International Trade* (New York: Columbia University Press).

Jones, S. F. (1984) *North/South Counter-trade Barter and Reciprocal Trade with Developing Countries* (London: The Economist Intelligence Unit).

Kahn, A. E. (1951) 'Investment Criteria in Development Programs', *Quarterly Journal of Economics*, 65.

Kahn, R. F. (1976) 'Historical Origins of the International Monetary Fund', in A. P. Thirlwall (ed.), *Keynes and International Monetary Arrangements* (London: Macmillan).

Kaldor, N. (1957) 'A Model of Economic Growth', *Economic Journal* (December).

Kaldor, N. (1978) 'The Effects of Devaluations on Trade in Manufactures', in *Further Essays on Applied Economics* (London: Duckworth).

Kaplinsky, R. (1984a) 'Trade in Technology – Who, What, Where and When?', in M. Fransman and K. King (eds), *Technological Capability in the Third World* (London: Macmillan).

Kaplinsky, R. (1984b) *Sugar Processing: the Development of a Third World Technology* (London: Intermediate Technology Development Group).

Katz, J. (1978) 'Technological Change, Economic Development and Intra and Extra Regional Relations in Latin America', IDB/ECLA/UNDP/IDRC Research Programme on Scientific and Technological Dependence in Latin America, working paper, 30 (Buenos Aires: ECLA).

Katz, J. (1980) 'Domestic Technology Generation in LDCs: a Review of Research Findings', IDB/ECLA/UNDP/IDRC Research Programme on Scientific and Technological Dependence in Latin America, working paper, 35 (Buenos Aires: ECLA).

Katz, J. (1982) 'A List of "Main" Issues from Recent Research on Science and Technology in the Framework of the IDB/ECLA/UNDP/IDRC program' (Buenos Aires) (mimeo).

Katz, J. (1984) 'Dynamic Technological Innovation and Dynamic Comparative Advantage: Further Reflections on a Comparative Case Study Program', *Journal of Development Economics*, 16: 13–38.

Katzman, M. (1974) 'The von Thünen Paradigm, the Industrial–Urban Hypothesis and the Spatial Structure of Agriculture', *American Journal of Agricultural Economics* 56: 683–96.

Keesing, D. B. (1966) 'Labor Skills and Comparative Advantage', *American Economic Review*, 56: 249–58.

Kenen, P. B. (1965) 'Nature, Capital and Trade', *Journal of Political Economy*, 73: 437–60.

Kierskowski, H. (ed.) (1984) *Monopolistic Competition and International Trade* (Oxford: Oxford University Press).

Killick, T. (1982) 'The Impact of IMF Stabilisation Programmes in Developing Countries', Overseas Development Institute, working paper, 7.

Killick, T. and M. Sutton (1982) 'An Overview', in T. Killick (ed.), *Adjustment and Financing in the Developing World: The Role of the International Monetary Fund* (Washington, D.C.: IMF in association with ODI).

Killick, T. *et al.* (1984)   *The Quest for Economic Stabilisation, the IMF and the Third World* (London: Heinemann).

Kim, L. (1981)   'Technological Innovation in Korea's Capital Goods Sector: A Micro Analysis' (mimeo).

Kopinski, T. C. (1985)   'Global Perspectives on Economic Motivations, Opportunities and Risks for State Trading Organisations of Developing Countries Engaged in Counter-trade', paper for International Workshop on Counter-trade, Belgrade (25–28 June).

Krueger, A. (1974)   'The Political Economy of the Rent Seeking Society', *American Economic Review*, 64: 291–303.

Krueger, A. O. (1978)   *Foreign Trade Regimes and Economic Development: Liberalisation Attempts and Consequences* (Cambridge, Mass.: Ballinger).

Krueger, A. O. (1984)   'Trade Policies in Developing Countries', in P. Kenen (ed.), *Handbook of International Economics* (Amsterdam, North-Holland).

Krugman, P. (1979a)   'Increasing Returns, Monopolistic Competition and International Trade', *Journal of International Economics*, 9: 469–79.

Krugman, P. (1979b)   'A Model of Innovation, Technology Transfer, and the World Distribution of Income', *Journal of Political Economy*, 87: 253–63.

Krugman, P. (1980)   'Scale Economies, Product Differentiation and the Pattern of Trade', *American Economic Review*, 70: 950–9.

Krugman, P. (1983)   'Targeted Industrial Policies; Theory and Evidence', in *Industrial Change and Public Policy*, Symposium Sponsored by Federal Reserve Bank of Kansas City (Wyoming: Federal Reserve Bank of Kansas City).

Krugman, P. (1984)   'Import Protection as Export Promotion: International Competition in the Presence of Oligopoly and Economies of Scale', in H. Kierskowski (ed.), *Monopolistic Competition and International Trade* (Oxford: Oxford University Press).

Krugman, P. (ed.) (1986)   *Strategic Trade Policy and the New International Economics* (Cambridge, Mass.: MIT Press).

Krugman, P. (1989)   'New Trade Theory and the Less Developed Countries', in G. Calvo, R. Findlay, P. Kopuri and J. B. de Macedo (eds), *Debt, Stabilisation and Development* (Oxford: Blackwell for WIDER).

Kuznets, S. (1955)   'Economic Growth and Income Inequality', *American Economic Review*, 45, 1.

Lal, D. (1983)   *The Poverty of Development Economics*, Hobart Paperback, 16 (London: Institute of Economic Affairs).

Lall, S. (1973)   'Transfer Pricing by Multinational Firms', *Oxford Bulletin of Economics and Statistics*, 35: 173–95.

Lall, S. (1980)   'Vertical Inter-Firm Linkages in LDCs: an Empirical Study', *Oxford Bulletin of Economics and Statistics*, 42 (3): 203–26.

Lall, S. (1982a)   *Developing Countries as Exporters of Technology* (London: Macmillan).

Lall, S. (1982b)   'The Emergence of Third World Multinationals', *World Development*, 10: 127–46.

Lall, S. (1985)   'Trade in Technology by a Slowly Industrialising Country:

India' in N. Rosenberg and C. Frischtak (eds), *International Technology Transfer: Concepts, Measures and Comparisons* (New York: Praeger).

Lall, S. (1987a) 'Long-term Perspectives on Sub-Saharan Africa' (Washington, D.C.: World Bank).

Lall, S. (1987b) 'Technology Transfer, Foreign Investment and Indigenous Capabilities' (mimeo) Institute of Economics and Statistics, Oxford University.

Lall, S. (1987c) *Learning to Industrialise* (London: Macmillan).

Lall, S. *et al.* (1983) *The New Multinationals: The Spread of Third World Enterprises* (London: Wiley).

Lall, S. and F. Stewart (eds) (1986) *Theory and Reality in Development* (London: Macmillan).

Lancaster, C. and J. Williamson (eds) (1986) *African Debt and Financing* (Washington: Institute for International Economics).

Lancaster, K. (1966) 'Change and Innovation in the Technology of Consumption', *American Economic Review*, 56.

Lancaster, K. J. (1971) *Consumer Demand: A New Approach* (New York: Columbia University Press).

Lancaster, K. (1979) *Variety, Equity and Efficiency* (Oxford: Blackwell).

Lancaster, K. J. (1980) 'Intra-Industry Trade Under Perfect Monopolistic Competition', *Journal of International Economics*, 10: 151–76.

Lancaster, K. (1984) 'Protection and Product Differentiation', in H. Kierskowski (ed.), *Monopolistic Competition and International Trade* (Oxford: Oxford University Press).

Landes, D. S. (1969) *The Unbound Prometheus* (Cambridge: Cambridge University Press).

Lecraw, D. J. (1977) 'Direct Investment by Firms from Less Developed Countries', *Oxford Economic Papers*, 29: 442–57.

Lee, J. (1987) 'Technology Acquisition under Alternative Arrangements with Transnational Corporations: Selected Industrial Case Studies in the Republic of Korea', ESCAP/UNCTC, *Technology Transfer under Alternative Arrangements with Transnational Corporations* (Bangkok: United Nations ESCAP/UNCTC Joint Unit on Transnational Corporations).

Leontief, W. W. (1953) 'Domestic Production and Foreign Trade: the American Capital Position Re-examined', *Proceedings of the American Philosophical Society*, 97: 332–49.

Levin, R. C. (1982) 'The Semi-conductor Industry', in R. R. Nelson (ed.), *Government and Technical Progress: A Cross-Industry Analysis* (New York, Pergamon Press).

Lever, H. (1983) 'The International Debt Threat: A Concerted Way Out' *The Economist*, 9 June.

Lewis, W. A. (1980) 'The Slowing Down of the Engine of Growth', *American Economic Review*, 70 (3).

Limburg Principles (1987) 'The Limburg Principles on the Implementation of the International Covenant on Economic, Social and Cultural Rights', *Human Rights Quarterly*, 9.

Linder, S. B. (1961) *An Essay on Trade and Transformation* (Stockholm: Almqvist Wiksell).

Lipton, M. and S. Griffith-Jones (1984) 'International Lenders of the Last

Resort: Are Changes Required?', *Midland Bank Occasional Paper*, 1.

Little, I. M. D. (1982) *Economic Development: Theory, Policy and International Relations* (New York: Basic Books).

Little, I. M. D., T. Scitovsky and M. Scott (1970) *Industry and Trade in Some Developing Countries* (London: Oxford University Press).

Little, I. M. D. and J. A. Mirrlees (1969) *Manual of Industrial Project Analysis* (Paris: OECD).

Little, I. M. D. and J. A. Mirrlees (1974) *Project Appraisal and Planning for the Developing Countries* (London: Heinemann).

Madeuf, B. (1977) *La Notion de Dépendence Technologique en Economie Internationale*.

Mahmood, S. A. (1989) 'The Performance of Selected Public Sector Industries in Bangladesh, 1972–1985', D. Phil. thesis, Oxford University.

Malerba, F. (1985) *The Semiconductor Business* (London: Frances Pinter).

Markusen, J. R. and A. J. Venables (1988) 'Trade Policy with Increasing Returns and Imperfect Competition', *Journal of International Economics*, 24.

Markusen, A., P. Hall and A. Glasmeier (1986) *High Tech America* (London: Allen & Unwin).

Marshall, A. (1920) *Principles of Economics* (London: Macmillan).

Maxcy, G. (1981) *The Multinational Motor Industry* (London: Croom Helm).

Meade, J. E. (1952) 'External Economies and Diseconomies in a Competitive Situation', *Economic Journal*, 62: 54–67.

Medina, T. A. (1983) 'Monetary and Payments Agreements among Developing Countries', in B. Paulic, R. Uranga, B. Cizelj and M. Svetlicic (eds), *The Challenges of South–South Cooperation* (Boulder, Colorado: Westview).

Miles, M. (1979) 'The Effects of Devaluation on the Trade Balance and the Balance of Payments: Some New Results', *Journal of Political Economy*, 87 (3).

Mishan, E. J. (1971) 'The Postwar Literature on Externalities', *Journal of Economic Literature*, 9: 1–28.

Moggeridge, D. (ed.) (1980) *The Collected Writings of John Maynard Keynes*, Vol. XXVI (Cambridge: Cambridge University Press).

Morawetz, D. (1974) 'Employment Implications of Industrialisation in Developing Countries', *Economic Journal*, 84: 491–542.

Munasinghe, M., M. Dow and J. Fritz (eds) (1985) *Micro-computers for Development: Issues and Policy* (Cintec-Nas Publication).

Murray, R. (ed.) (1981) *Multinationals Beyond the Market* (Brighton: Harvester Press).

Myrdal, G. (1957) *Economic Theory and Underdeveloped Regions* (London: Duckworth).

Nayyar, D. (1978) 'Transnational Corporations and Manufactured Exports from Poor Countries', *Economic Journal*, 88.

Ncube, P. D., M. Sakala and M. Ndulu (1987) 'The International Monetary Fund and the Zambian Economy – a Case', in K. Havenik (ed.), *The IMF and the World Bank in Africa* (Uppsala: Scandinavian Institute of African Studies).

Nelson, R. and S. Winter (1974) 'Neo-classical Versus Evolutionary Theories of Economic Growth: Critique and Prospects', *Economic Journal*, 84.

Nelson, R. and S. Winter (1977) 'In Search of a Useful Theory of Innovation', *Research Policy*, 6: 36–37.

Nelson, R. and S. Winter (1982) *An Evolutionary Theory of Economic Change* (Cambridge, Mass.: Harvard University Press).

Newbery, D. M. G. (1980) 'Externalities: The Theory of Environmental Policy', in G. A. Hughes and G. M. Heal (eds), *Public Policy and the Tax System* (London: Allen & Unwin).

Newson, M. and D. Wall (1985) 'Policy and Institutional Obstacles to South–South Trade in Manufactures' UNIDO/IS, 584 (Vienna: UNIDO).

Nicholls, W. (1969) 'Industrial-Urban Development as a Dynamic Force in Transforming Brazilian Agriculture', in E. Thorbecke (ed.), *The Role of Agriculture in Economic Development* (New York: National Bureau of Economic Research).

Norman, C. (1981) *The God That Limps* (New York: Norton).

Oakey, R. (1985) 'High Technology Industry and Agglomeration Economies', in Hall, P. and A. Markusen (eds), *Silicon Landscapes* (Allen & Unwin).

Ocampo, J. A. (1985) 'Financial Aspects of Intra-regional Trade in Latin America', in A. Gauhar (ed.) *Regional Integration: The Latin American Experience* (London: Third World Foundation).

Ocampo, J. A. (1987) 'The Macro-economic Effect of Import Controls: a Keynesian Analysis', *Journal of Development Economics*, 27: 285–305.

Ocampo, J. A. (1988) 'The Effects of Liberalisation and Direct Import Controls on Colombian Manufacturing, 1976–1986', paper for WIDER conference on 'New Trade Theories and Industrialisation in Developing Countries', Helsinki (2–5 August).

O'Connor, D. (1985a) 'Global Trends in Electronics: Implications for Developing Countries' (Washington D.C.: World Bank).

O'Connor, D. (1985b) 'The Computer Industry in the Third World: Some Policy Options and Constraints', *World Development*, 13 (3).

OECD (1981) *East–West Grade: Recent Developments in Counter-trade* (Paris: OECD).

OECD (1985a) *Counter-trade: Developing Country Practices* (Paris: OECD).

OECD (1985b) *The Semiconductor Industry: Trade Related Issues* (Paris: OECD).

Ohlin, B. (1933) *Interregional and International Trade* (Harvard University Press).

Okereke, G. U. (1988) 'Biotechnology to Combat Malnutrition in Nigeria', World Employment Programme Research, working paper WEP 2–22/WP 190 (Geneva: ILO).

Outters-Jaeger, I. (1979) *The Development Impact of Barter in Developing Countries, Synthesis Report* (Paris: OECD).

Ozawa, T. (1981) 'Technology Transfer and Control Systems: Japanese Experience', in T. Sagafi-Nejad, R. W. Moxon and H. Perlmutter (eds), *Controlling International Technology Transfer: Issues, Perspectives and Policy Implications* (New York: Pergamon).

370 *Bibliography*

Pack, H. (1976) 'The Substitution of Labour for Capital in Kenyan Manufacturing', *Economic Journal* 86: 45–58.

Pack, H. (1987) *Productivity, Technology and Industrial Development, A Case Study in Textiles* (New York: Oxford University Press).

Pack H. (1988) 'Industrialisation and Trade', in H. B. Chenery and T. N. Srinivasan (eds), *Handbook of Development Economics* (Amsterdam: North-Holland).

Pack, H. and L. Westphal (1986) 'Industrial Strategy and Technological Change: Theory vs Reality', *Journal of Development Economics*, 22: 87–128.

Page, S. (1987) 'The Rise in Protection Since 1974', *Oxford Review of Economic Policy*, 3 (1): 37–51.

Paine, S. (1971) 'Lessons for LDCs from Japan's Experience with Labour Commitment and Subcontracting in the Manufacturing Sector', *Oxford Bulletin of Economics and Statistics*, 33: 115–34.

Pasinetti, L. (1981) *Structural Change and Economic Growth* (Cambridge: Cambridge University Press).

Pasinetti, L. and Lloyd, P. (eds) (1987) *Structural Change, Economic Interdependence and World Development* (London: Macmillan).

Pavitt, K. and P. Patel (1988) 'The International Distribution and Determinants of Technological Activities', *Oxford Review of Economic Policy*, 4 (4): 35–55.

Pelcovitz, M. (1976) 'Quotas versus tariffs', *Journal of International Economics*, 6.

Phan-Thuy, N., R. R. Betancourt, G. C. Winston and M. Kabaj (1981) *Industrial Capacity and Employment Promotion* (Westmead: Gower).

Pigou, A. C. (1938) *Economics of Welfare* (London: Macmillan).

Plesch, P. (1979) 'Developing Countries' Exports of Electronics and Engineering Products' (Washington, D.C.: World Bank).

Posner, M. V. (1961) 'International Trade and Technical Change', *Oxford Economic Papers*, 13: 323–41.

Pratten, C. F. (1971) *Economies of Scale in Manufacturing Industry* (Cambridge: Cambridge University Press).

Rahman, A. (1973) 'Exports of Manufactures from Developing Countries', *Erasmus*, 1–11.

Ranis, G. (1973) 'Industrial Sector Labor Absorption', *Economic Development and Cultural Change*, 21.

Ranis, G. (1978) 'Growth with Equity: the Taiwan Case', *World Development*, 6.

Ranis, G. and G. Saxonhouse (1987) 'Determination of Technology Choice: The Indian and Japanese Cotton Industries' in K. Ohkawa and G. Ranis (eds), *Japan and the Developing Countries* (Oxford: Blackwell).

Ranis, G., F. Stewart and E. Angeles-Reyes (1990) *Linkages in Development: A Philippine Case Study* (San Francisco: International Center for Economic Growth).

Ranis, G. and J. Fei (1988) 'Development Economics: What Next?', in G. Ranis and T. P. Schultz (eds), *The State of Development Economics* (Oxford: Blackwell).

Rawls, J. (1971) *A Theory of Justice* (Oxford: Clarendon Press).

Reichman, T. (1978) 'The Fund's Conditional Assistance and the Problem of Adjustment, 1973–75', *Finance and Development* 15.

Reuber, G. L. (1973) *Private Foreign Investment in Development* (Oxford: Clarendon Press).

Rhee, Y. W., B. Ross-Larson and G. Pursell (1984) *Korea's Competitive Edge: Managing the Entry into World Markets* (Baltimore: Johns Hopkins University Press).

Richter, S. (1982) 'Hungary's Foreign Trade with CMEA Partners in Convertible Currency', *Soviet and Eastern European Foreign Trade*, 8(2).

Robinson, J. D. (1988) 'A Comprehensive Agenda for LDC Debt and World Trade Growth', *The AMEX Bank Review*, special papers, 13.

Robson, P. (1983) *Integration, Development and Equity: Economic Integration in West Africa* (London: Allen & Unwin).

Rodrik, D. (1988) 'Closing the Technology Gap: Does Trade Liberalization Really Help?', paper for WIDER conference on New Trade Theories and Industrialisation in the Developing Countries, Helsinki (2–5 August) (Helsinki: WIDER).

Rodriguez, C. (1974) 'The Non-equivalence of Tariffs and Quotas Under Retaliation', *Journal of International Economics*, 4: 295–8.

Roessler, F. (1987) 'The Relationship Between the World Trade Order and the International Monetary System' (GATT) (mimeo).

Rosenberg, N. (1976) *Perspectives on Technology* (Cambridge: Cambridge University Press).

Rosenberg, N. (1982) *Inside the Black Box: Technology and Economics* (Cambridge: Cambridge University Press).

Rosenberg, N. and C. Frischtak (eds) (1985) *International Technology Transfer: Concepts, Measures and Comparisons* (New York: Praeger).

Rosenstein-Rodan, P. N. (1943) 'Problems of Industrialisation of Eastern and South-Eastern Europe', *Economic Journal* (June–September).

Roskamp, K. W. and G. C. McMeekin (1968) 'Factor Proportions, Human Capital, and Foreign Trade: the Case of West Germany Reconsidered', *Quarterly Journal of Economics*, 82:152–60.

Sahal, D. (ed.) (1982) *The Transfer and Utilisation of Technical Knowledge* (Lexington, Mass.: Lexington Books).

Salter, W. E. G. (1966) *Productivity and Technical Change* (Cambridge: Cambridge University Press).

Santikarn, M. (1987) 'Technology Acquisition under Attentive Arrangements with Transitional Corporations: Selected Industrial Case Studies in Thailand' in ESCAP/UNCTC *Technology Transfer Under Attentive Arrangements with Transitional Corporations* (Bangkok: United Nations ESCAP/UNCTC).

Saxenian, A. (1985) 'The Genesis of Silicon Valley', in P. Hall and A. Markusen (eds), *Silicon Landscapes* (Allen & Unwin).

Saxonhouse, G. R. (1971) 'Productivity Change in the Japanese Cotton Spinning Industry 1891–1935', D.Phil, Yale University.

Shaked, A. and J. Sutton (1984) 'Natural Oligopolies and International Trade' in H. Kierskowski (ed.), *Monopolistic Competition and International Trade* (Oxford: Oxford University Press).

Schnapp, J. *et al.* (1979)   *Corporate Strategies of the Automotive Manufacturers* (Lexington, Mass.: Lexington Books).

Schultz, T. W. (1964)   *Transforming Traditional Agriculture* (New Haven: Yale University Press).

Schultz, C. (1983)   'Industrial Policy: A Dissent', *Brookings Review* (Fall).

Schultz, T. Paul (1989)   'Women and Development Objectives, Frameworks and Policy Interventions', Policy, Planning and Research Working Paper, WPS 200 (Washington, DC: World Bank).

Schumacher, E. F. (1973)   *Small is Beautiful* (Blond and Briggs).

Scitovsky, T. (1954)   'Two Concepts of External Economies', *Journal of Political Economy* (April).

Scitovsky, T. (1976)   *The Joyless Economy: An Enquiry into Human Satisfaction and Consumer Dissatisfaction* (Oxford: Oxford University Press).

Scott, M. F. (1986)   'Explaining Economic Growth', Keynes Lecture in Economics (London: The British Academy).

Scott, M. F., W. M. Corden and I. M. Little (1980) 'The Case Against General Import Restrictions', Thames Essay, 20 (London: Trade Policy Research Centre).

Seers, D. (1983)   *The Political Economy of Nationalism* (Oxford: Oxford University Press).

Sen, A. K. (1968)   *Choice of Techniques* (Oxford: Blackwell).

Sen, A. K. (1981)   'Public Action and the Quality of Life in Developing Countries', *Oxford Bulletin of Economics and Statistics*, 43: 287–319.

Sen, A. K. (1985)   *Commodities and Capabilities* (Amsterdam: Elsevier Science Publishing).

Shand, R. T. (ed.) (1986)   *Off-Farm Employment in the Development of Rural Asia*, Vol. 2 (Canberra: Australian National University).

Sheehan, G. and M. Hopkins (1979)   *Basic Needs Performance: An Analysis of Some International Data* (Geneva: ILO).

Sherwell, C. (1985)   'South-east Asia: Of Growing Importance in Obtaining Business', *Financial Times* (7 February).

Singer, H. and P. Gray (1988)   'Trade Policy and Growth of Developing Countries: Some New Data', *World Development*, 16 (3): 395–403.

Singh, H. V. (1981)   'Appropriate Technology', M. Phil. thesis Oxford University.

Soete, L. (1986)   'The Social and Economic Implications of Microelectronics on the Economies of Industrialised Countries: a Survey', The United Nations University, New Technologies Centre Feasibility Study, Rijksuniversiteit Limburg (Maastricht).

Solomon, R. (1977)   'A Perspective on the Debt of Developing Countries', *Brookings Papers on Economic Activity* 2, 479–501.

Solow, R. (1957)   'Technical Change and the Aggregate Production Function', *Review of Economics and Statistics* 39 (3): 312–320.

Solow, R. (1970)   *Growth Theory* (Oxford: Clarendon Press).

Spencer, B. J. and J. A. Brander (1983)   'International R and D Rivalry and Industrial Strategy', *Review of Economic Studies*, 50.

Spraos, J. (1986)   'IMF Conditionality: Ineffectual, Inefficient, Mistargetted', *Essays in International Finance*, Princeton 166 (Princeton: New Jersey: Princeton University).

SRI International (1980) 'Technology Choices in Developing Countries', Final Report, SRI Project, 7295.

Srinivasan, T. N. (1989) 'Recent Theories of Imperfect Competition and International Trade: Any Implications for Development Strategy?', *Indian Economic Review*, 23 (1): 1–24.

Stern, R. M., J. Francis and B. Schumacher (1976) *Price Elasticities in International Trade: An Annotated Bibliography* (London: Trade Policy Research Centre).

Stewart, F. (1977) *Technology and Underdevelopment* (London: Macmillan).

Stewart, F. (1981) 'Taxation and Technology Transfer', in T. Segafi-Nejad *et al.* (eds), *Controlling Technology Transfer*, (New York: Pergamon).

Stewart, F. (1982) 'Industrialization, Technical Change and the International Division of Labour', in G. K. Helleiner (ed.), *For Good or Evil: Economic Theory and North–South Negotiations* (London: Croom Helm).

Stewart, F. (1983) 'Macro-policies for Appropriate Technology: an Introductory Classification', *International Labour Review*, 122: 279–93.

Stewart, F. (1984) 'Recent Theories of International Trade: Some Implications for the South', in H. Kierskowski (ed.), *Monopolistic Competition and International Trade* (Oxford: Oxford University Press) (Chapter 4 in this volume).

Stewart, F. (1985a) *Planning to Meet Basic Needs* (London: Macmillan).

Stewart, F. (1985b) 'The Fragile Foundations of the Neo-classical Approach to Development Economics', *Journal of Development Studies*, 23 (2).

Stewart, F. (1986) *Economic Policies and Agricultural Performance: the Case of Tanzania* (Paris: OECD)

Stewart F. (1987) 'Should Conditionality Change?' in K. J. Havenik (ed.), *The IMF and the World Bank in Africa* (Uppsala: Scandinavian Institute of African Studies).

Stewart, F. (ed.) (1987) *Macro-Policies for Appropriate Technology* (Boulder, Colorado: Westview).

Stewart, F. and Ranis, G. (1990) 'Macro-Policies for Appropriate Technology: A Synthesis of Findings' in F. Stewart, H. Thomas and T. de Wilde (eds) *The Other Policy* (London: Intermediate Technology Publications).

Stewart, F. and M. J. Stewart (1980) 'A New Currency for Trade among Developing Countries', *Trade and Development*, 2: 69–82 (Chapter 10 in this volume).

Stewart, F. and P. Streeten (1971) 'Conflicts Between Output and Employment Objectives in Developing Countries', *Oxford Economic Papers*, 23.

Stiglitz, J. E. and Weiss (1981) 'Credit Rationing in Markets With Imperfect Information', *American Economic Review* LXXI.

Stiglitz, J. E. (1987) 'Some Theoretical Aspects of Agricultural Policies', in *Research Observer*, 2 (1) (January): 43–60, (Washington, D.C.: World Bank).

Streeten, P. (1972) *The Frontiers of Development Studies* (London: Macmillan).

Streeten, P. (1976) 'The Dynamics of New Poor Power', *Resources Policy* 2.

Streeten, P. *et al.* (1981) *First Things First: Meeting Basic Needs in Developing Countries* (New York: Oxford University Press for World Bank).

Suhatme, P. V. (1982) 'One Measurement of Undernutrition', *Economic and Political Weekly* (11 December).

Tang, A. (1974) *Economic Development in the Southern Piedmont* (University of North Carolina: Chapel Hill).

Taylor, C. T. and Z. A. Silberston (1973) *The Economic Impact of the Patent System* (Cambridge: Cambridge University Press).

Teece, J. (1976) *The Multinational Corporation and the Resource Costs of Technology Transfer* (Cambridge, Mass.: Ballinger).

Teitel, S. (1984) 'Technology Creation in Semi-industrial Countries', *Journal of Development Economics*, 16 (1–2).

Thee, T. (1987) 'Technology Acquisition under Attentive Arrangements with Transnational Corporations: The Case of Indonesia' in ESCAP/ UNCTC *Technology Transfer Under Alternative Arrangements with Transnational Corporations* (Bangkok: United Nations ESCAP/UNCTC).

Thirlwall, A. P. (1983) *Growth and Development* (London: Macmillan).

Tigre, P. (1985) 'The Mexican Professional Electronics Industry and Technology' (Vienna: UNIDO/IS).

Tower, A. (1975) 'The Optimum Quota and Retaliation', *Review of Economic Studies*, 42: 623–30.

Toye, J. (1985) 'Dirigisme and Development Economics', *Cambridge Journal of Economics* 9: 1–14.

Tribe, M. A. (1979) 'The Choice of Technique in the Sugar Industry in Some Developing Countries', David Livingstone Institute, Strathclyde (mimeo).

Trubeck, D. (1984) 'Economic, Social and Cultural Rights in the Third World: Human Rights Law and Human Needs Programmes', in T. Meron (ed.), *Human Rights in International Law* (Oxford: Clarendon Press).

Tschoegl, A. E. (1985) 'Modern Barter', *Lloyds Bank Review*, 158.

UNCTAD (1976) 'Technological Dependence: the Nature, Consequences and Policy Implications', in *Proceedings of the United Nations Conference on Trade and Development*, Fourth Session, Vol. III, *Basic documents*, TD/190, 1976.

UNCTAD (1983) 'The Study of the Feasibility of a Bank for Developing Countries', UNCTAD (May) (Geneva: United Nations).

UNICEF (1984) *The State of the World's Children 1984* (Oxford: Oxford University Press).

United Nations (1974) 'The Role and Place of Engineering and Electrical Industries in National Economies in the World Economy' (New York: United Nations).

United Nations Centre on Transnational Corporations (UNCTC) (1987) 'Transnational Corporations and Technology Transfer: Effects and Policy Issues', ST/CTC/86.

US Congress Office of Technology Assessment (1986) *Technology, Public Policy and the Changing Structure of American Agriculture* (Washington, D.C.: US Government Printing Press).

Vaitsos, C. V. (1974) *Intercountry Income Distribution and Transnational Corporations* (Oxford: Oxford University Press).

Van de Hoeven, R. (1987) *Planning for Basic Needs: a Basic Needs Simulation Model Applied to Kenya* (Amsterdam: Free University Press).

Van Ginneken, W. and C. Baron (eds) (1984) *Appropriate Products, Employment and Technology* (London: Macmillan).

Venables, A. J. (1985) 'Trade and Trade Policy with Imperfect Competition', *Journal of International Economics*, 19.

Vernon, R. (1966) 'International Investment and International Trade in the Product Cycle', *Quarterly Journal of Economics*, 53: 190–207.

Vernon, R. (ed.) (1970) *The Technology Factor in International Trade* (New York: Columbia University Press).

Verzariu, P. (1984) *International Counter-trade: A Guide for Managers and Executives* (Washington, D.C.: US Department of Commerce, International Trade Administration).

Vincke, C. (1972) 'Trade Restrictions for Balance of Payments Reasons and the GATT: Quotas Versus Surcharges', *Harvard International Law Journal*, 13: 289–315.

Viner, J. (1931) 'Cost Curves and Supply Curves', *Zeitschrift für Nationalokonomie*, 3: 23–46, reprinted in American Economic Association (1953) *Readings in Price Theory* (London: Allen & Unwin).

Wade, R. (1988) 'The Rise of East Asian Trading States – How They Managed Their Trade' (Washington, D.C.: World Bank) (mimeo).

Waldmeir, P. (1985) 'Lagos Keeps the I.M.F. at Bay', *Financial Times* (5 June 1985).

Wallich, H. (1984) 'Insurance of Bank Lending to Developing Countries' (New York: Group of Thirty).

Watanabe, S. (1978) *International Subcontracting: a Tool of Technology Transfer* (Tokyo: Asian Productivity Organisation).

Weinberg, C. (1973) 'Sanbar Proposal: Plan for Increasing Trade Between Developing Countries', *KIDMA*, 2.

Wells, J. (1977) 'The Diffusion of Durables in Brazil and its Implications for Recent Controversies Concerning Brazilian Development', *Cambridge Journal of Economics*, 1.

Wells, L. T. (1973) 'Economics Man and Engineering Man: Choice and Technology in a Low-wage Country', *Public Policy* 21.

Wells, L. T. (1979) 'Developing Country Investors in Indonesia', *Bulletin of Indonesian Economic Studies*.

Wells, L. T. (1983) *Third World Multinationals* (Cambridge, Mass.: MIT Press).

Westerveen, G. (1984) 'Towards a System for Supervising States' Compliance with the Right to Food', in P. Alston and K. Tomasevski (eds), *The Right to Food* (Dordrecht: Netherlands Institute of Human Rights).

Westphal, L. (1981) 'Empirical Justification for Infant Industry Protection', World Bank Staff working paper, 469 (Washington D.C.: World Bank).

Westphal, L. (1982) in M. Syrquin and S. Teitel (eds), *Trade, Stability, and Equity in Latin America* (London: Academic Press).

Westphal, L., Y. Rhee and G. Pursell (1981) 'Korean Industrial Competence: Where It Came From', World Bank Staff working paper, 469 (Washington, D.C.: World Bank).

Westphal, L., L. Kim and C. Dahlman (1985) 'Reflections on the Republic of Korea's Acquisition of Technological Capability', in N. Rosenberg and

C. Frischtak (eds), *International Technology Transfer: Concepts, Measures and Comparisons* (New York: Praeger).

Williamson, J. (1984) *A New SDR Allocation?* (Washington D.C.: Institute for International Finance).

Williamson, J. (1990) *The Progress of Policy Reform in Latin America* (Washington D.C.: Institute of International Economics).

Willmore, L. N. (1972) 'Free Trade in Manufactures Among Developing Countries: The Central American Experience', *Economic Development and Cultural Change*, 20: 659–70.

Wolf, M. (1986) 'Timing and Sequence of Trade Liberalisation in Developing Countries', *Asian Development Review*, 4 (2).

World Bank (1978) *World Development Report* (Washington D.C.: World Bank).

World Bank (1986) *Financing Adjustment with Growth in Sub-Saharan Africa 1986–1990* (Washington, D.C.: World Bank).

World Bank (1987a) *The Social Effects of Adjustment: A Review of Issues and Implications for the Bank* (Washington D.C.: World Bank).

World Bank (1987b) *World Development Report 1987* (Washington, D.C.: World Bank).

World Bank (1988) *World Development Report 1988* (Washington, D.C.: World Bank).

World Bank (1989) *World Development Report 1989* (Washington, D.C.: World Bank).

World Bank (1990) *World Development Report 1990* (Washington, D.C.: World Bank).

Yoon, C. H. (1988) 'International Competition and Market Penetration: a Model of the Growth of the Korean Semiconductor Industry', paper for WIDER conference on 'New Trade Theories and Industrialisation in Developing Countries', Helsinki (August).

Index

377

Index